D0087118

Principles of Instructional Design

FIFTH EDITION

ROBERT M. GAGNÉ
Florida State University, Emeritus (deceased)

WALTER W. WAGER
Florida State University

KATHARINE C. GOLAS
Southwest Research Institute

JOHN M. KELLER
Florida State University

THOMSON
WADSWORTH

Australia · Canada · Mexico · Singapore · Spain
United Kingdom · United States

THOMSON
WADSWORTH

Education Editor: *Dan Alpert*
Development Editor: *Tangelique Williams*
Assistant Editor: *Jennifer Wilkinson*
Editorial Assistant: *TK*
Technology Project Manager: *Barry Connolly*
Marketing Manager: *Doug Schaeffer*
Marketing Assistant: *Andrew Keay*
Advertising Project Manager: *Tami Strang*
Project Manager, Editorial Production: *Jennifer Klos*
Print/Media Buyer: *Lisa Claudeanos*
Permissions Editor: *Sommy Ko*

Production Service: *Stratford Publishing Services, Inc.*
Copy Editor: *Stratford Publishing Services, Inc.*
Illustrator: *Stratford Publishing Services, Inc.*
Cover Designer: *TK*
Cover Image: *TK*
Cover Printer: *TK*
Compositor: *Stratford Publishing Services, Inc.*
Printer: *Phoenix BTP*

COPYRIGHT © 2005 Wadsworth, a division of Thomson Learning, Inc. Thomson Learning™ is a trademark used herein under license.

ALL RIGHTS RESERVED. No part of this work covered by the copyright hereon may be reproduced or used in any form or by any means—graphic, electronic, or mechanical, including but not limited to photocopying, recording, taping, Web distribution, information networks, or information storage and retrieval systems—without the written permission of the publisher.

Printed in the United States of America
1   2   3   4   5   6   7   08   07   06   05   04

For more information about our products, contact us at:

Thomson Learning Academic Resource Center
1-800-423-0563

For permission to use material from this text or product, submit a request online at:
http://www.thomsonrights.com
Any additional questions about permissions can be submitted by e-mail to:
thomsonrights@thomson.com

Library of Congress Control Number: 2004104325

ISBN 0-534-58284-2

Wadsworth/Thomson Learning
10 Davis Drive
Belmont, CA 94002-3098
USA

Asia
Thomson Learning
5 Shenton Way #01-01
UIC Building
Singapore 068808

Australia/New Zealand
Thomson Learning
102 Dodds Street
Southbank, Victoria 3006
Australia

Canada
Nelson
1120 Birchmount Road
Toronto, Ontario M1K 5G4
Canada

Europe/Middle East/Africa
Thomson Learning
High Holborn House
50/51 Bedford Row
London WC1R 4LR
United Kingdom

Latin America
Thomson Learning
Seneca, 53
Colonia Polanco
11560 Mexico D.F.
Mexico

Spain/Portugal
Paraninfo
Calle/Magallanes, 25
28015 Madrid, Spain

This edition of *Principles of Instructional Design* is dedicated to the memory of Robert M. Gagné and Leslie J. Briggs, for their many contributions to educational psychology and instructional systems design.

—WW, KG, JK

Contents

Chapter 16

Evaluating Instruction   346

Index   377

Preface

Dr. Robert Gagné (1916–2002) was truly a giant in the field of instructional systems design. His theories about conditions of learning and principles derived from information processing theory are still employed in numerous design models today. Many educators have classified Gagné as a behaviorist, because his early training in animal psychology and his work with Skinner is mentioned in many of his early writings. However, Gagné was one of the early cognitive psychologists. He recognized the shortcomings of behavioral psychology when explaining human behavior, and he broke away strict behaviorist principles to consider what was going on inside the brain. At that time, information processing theories of learning were popular topics of research. From this early research a large number of concepts like short-term memory, working memory, cognitive-load capacity, encoding, retrieval, and schemata became common jargon terms in the field. Gagné was very interested in K–12 school learning, especially reading, and he participated in many curriculum development projects. He was also in high demand by the military for his knowledge and experience with simulations design. It would not be an overstatement say that Robert M. Gagné, and his colleague Leslie Briggs, initiated the direction of contemporary instructional systems design with the first edition of this book.

Subsequent editions expanded on how the information-processing model and conditions-of-learning model formed the foundation for understanding learning environments and designing learning materials. The popular Dick and Carey model of instructional design was derived from the early work of Gagné and Briggs, for example. Wager developed the technique of instructional curriculum mapping to integrate intellectual skills with supporting objectives from different domains, and Briggs expanded on prescriptions for media based on desired instructional functions.

This edition takes another step forward in looking at principles associated with instructional design. Two new authors, Katharine Golas, and John M. Keller, add their knowledge, experiences, and perspectives. Golas, Vice President of the Training, Simulation & Performance Improvement Division at Southwest Research Institute (SwRI), was a student of Gagné. She received her Ph.D. from Florida State University in 1982 and has worked in the instructional systems field since 1977. Her work at SwRI included the development of a new instructional design model for the U.S. Air Force. She has experience with emerging technologies, including multisensory virtual reality, and distributed mission simulations. She has worked with many contemporary instructors of instructional design including David Merrill, Robert Tennyson, and Michael Spector. Dr. Golas's experience with technology and military training adds a new dimension to the text.

John M. Keller developed the Attention, Relevance, Confidence, and Satisfaction (ARCS) model of motivational design. In Chapter 6, he adds his perspectives on the nature of the learner, and how it affects instructional design decisions. Dr. Keller is a professor of instructional systems and educational psychology at Florida State University and is a well-known consultant on large-scale instructional design and electronic-performance design projects. Two recent clients include Citibank and the Federal Aviation Association. He is an expert on design models and assessment models. He has completely rewritten two chapters of this book, and his expertise in motivational design will give new insights into how to make instruction more effective.

Walter Wager was one of the early coauthors of this text, and was a colleague of Leslie Briggs and Robert Gagné. He is now coordinator of instructional development services for Florida State University. Wager works extensively with faculty to integrate technology into instruction, promote active learning, and develop effective courses. He commonly employs principles from this text in helping faculty to define course outcomes, and assessments.

NEW TO THIS EDITION

The authors have rewritten much of the text to make the writing style less formal and more approachable. We have also included new examples from the military and training venues, and addressed issues associated with constructivist philosophy and practices. All of the chapters have been updated and most contain minor to moderate revisions; four of them have been completely revised. Chapter 2, Designing Learning Environments, addresses the differences between systems design and instructional design models. Chapter 6 includes a discussion of the APA learner-centered principles and how they relate to instructional design. Chapter 11 has been completely rewritten to reflect emerging technologies and their impact on learning. Chapter 15, Online Learning, is a new chapter, replacing a chapter on individualized instruction. However, the conditions of learning and information processing model, as they relate to instructional design, are still the foundations of the text.

ACKNOWLEDGMENTS

We wish to acknowledge Drs. John Dempsey, James Applefield and Rodney Earle for their contributions to the *Learner's Guide for the Principles of Instructional Design*. The *Learner's Guide* is no longer in print, but readers of this book will be able to access an online learner's guide developed by Dr. Dempsey and his students at the University of South Alabama. The link to this site is *http://www.southalabama.edu/coe/idbook*. We also wish to acknowledge the many publishers and authors who have given us permission to use graphic images from their publications and Web sites.

We also wish to thank the following reviewers of the fifth edition revision plan for their thoughtful guidance and constructive criticism:

Frederick B. King, University of Hartford
Steven Crooks, Texas Tech University
Temba C. Bassoppo-Moyo, Illinois State University
Robert C. M. Branch, University of Georgia

INTRODUCTION TO INSTRUCTIONAL DESIGN

The purpose of instruction is to help people learn. Can learning occur without instruction? Certainly. We are continuously encountering and interpreting our environment and the events in it. Learning is a natural process that leads to changes in what we know, what we can do, and how we behave. However, one function of an educational system is to *facilitate intentional learning,* in order to accomplish many goals that would take much longer without instruction. Schools teach knowledge and skills that the community feel are desirable, even if they are not of immediate personal interest to the student, and even if they would not be encountered naturally in nonschool environments. The federal government and commercial industries provide both initial skills training and continuing refresher training to help employees acquire the skills and learning needed to succeed in a changing workplace. Training is the vehicle through which the military is transforming itself to better prepare U.S. forces from all services to engage in joint operations. The purpose of this book is to describe how principles of learning inform the design of effective instruction for intentional learning.

We define instruction as a set of events embedded in purposeful activities that facilitate learning. Normally, we think of these events as being external to the learner, for example, events embodied in the display of printed pages, an instructor's lecture, or the activities of a group of students. However, there are also internal mental events, such as directing attention, rehearsing, reflecting, and monitoring progress. Educational psychologists hypothesize about the nature of these internal events, and from that research derive principles about the learning process. Instructional designers apply these principles to the design of the external events we call instruction. For example, it is a generally accepted principle that short-term memory has limited capacity. With this principle in mind, organizing information into clusters or categories has been found to facilitate learning.

Why talk about instruction rather than teaching? Because teaching is only one part of instruction. The word *teach* infers that a person is lecturing or demonstrating something to the learner. However, the teacher or trainer's role includes many different tasks, such as selecting materials, gauging student readiness to learn, managing class time, monitoring instructional activities, and finally serving as a content resource and a learning facilitator. So the broader term, *instruction,* puts the emphasis on a whole range of activities the teacher uses to engage the students. An instructor who has knowledge of the principles of instructional design has a broader vision of what it takes to help students learn: when it would benefit students to be put into groups, when practice and feedback will be most effective, and the prerequisites for problem-solving and higher-order learning skills, for example.

Who else would benefit from applying principles of instructional design? We believe that anyone in the business of producing instructional materials, such as textbook writers, curriculum materials developers, Web-based course designers and even knowledge-management system designers will benefit from these principles.

In summary, instruction is much more likely to be effective if it is planned to engage students in those events and activities that facilitate learning. Using principles of instructional design, the teacher or trainer can select, or plan and develop activities to best help students learn.

BASIC ASSUMPTIONS ABOUT INSTRUCTIONAL DESIGN

It would be a mistake to think that there is a single best model of instructional design. In actuality, there are as many models as there are designers and design situations. Each designer brings to the process his or her understanding of the principles and events that affect learning, and how to best structure instruction. There are, however, basic common assumptions that we bring to the process of design.

First, we adopt the assumption that instructional design must be aimed at aiding the process of learning rather than the process of teaching. Instructional design is also aimed at "intentional" learning as opposed to "incidental" learning. This implies that the target goals and desired learning outcomes guide the design and selection of learning activities. Meaningful learning outcomes are a starting and ending point for most design processes, because it is against the accomplishment of the objectives that the effectiveness of the design is assessed. We believe this is true whether the desired outcomes are information learning or problem-solving skills, because the learning activities that are chosen depend upon the type of outcome desired.

Second, we recognize that learning is a complex process affected by many variables. John Carroll (1963) in his Model of School Learning defined at least five major variables that affect the degree of learning attained by a student: (1) learner perseverance, (2) time allowed, (3) quality of instruction, (4) aptitude, and (5) student's ability to learn. These variables are not unrelated, however, and an effective model of instructional design cannot focus on just one of these variables. For instance, high-quality instruction is not likely to be effective if it does not take into account learner motivation and learner aptitude for the task.

Third, instructional design models can be applied at many levels. Principles of instructional design can be of immediate value to a teacher or trainer who is planning a lesson for a day's activity, a trainer preparing a three-day workshop, or a curriculum developer designing a course of study. Instructional design can be an individual effort, or at another level, can involve a team of designers, subject-matter experts, evaluation experts, and production personnel on a large-scale project. Although the specific design models would be different, the underlying principles of instructional design remain pretty much the same.

Our fourth assumption is that design is an iterative process. Given our current understanding of how people learn, we can't design instruction without involving learners in the process. Instructional materials and activities must be tested with learners to determine what works and what doesn't. One way of thinking about this is that designers don't design perfect instruction; they perfect instructional designs. Design and development may be carefully planned ahead of time, or they may evolve as a continuous process, as in rapid prototyping (the process of rapidly developing an instructional treatment with the idea that use will inform changes). However, both processes use feedback from the learning population to revise instruction and make it more effective.

The fifth assumption is that instructional design itself is a process consisting of a number of identifiable and related subprocesses. At the simplest level, instructional design is aligning desired outcomes, instructional methods, and student assessments. More elaborate process models include processes for determining desired outcomes, developing learning activities that involve students in authentic tasks, and designing alternative forms of practice, assessment, and feedback.

Our sixth and final point, to be expanded in Part 2 and throughout the book, is that different types of learning outcomes call for different types of instruction. There is no best way to teach everything, and the conditions for learning that are appropriate to the type of outcomes we desire will affect our thinking about the design of learning activities and materials. For example, problem-solving skills cannot be developed without having learners engaged in solving problems. Learning materials like Jasper (Cognition and Technology Group at Vanderbilt, 1993), provide the external events needed, including collaborative learning group activities, to enable students to engage in these activities.

SOME LEARNING PRINCIPLES

We all have personal beliefs about how we learn. These come from personal experience, self-reflection, observation of others, and through the experience of trying to teach or persuade someone else to our way of thinking. There is also a considerable body of theory and knowledge about learning gathered from research on both animal and human learning. From these beliefs and research come principles or rules we can apply to the design of instructional materials and learning activities.

Learning, as defined by Robert Gagné (1985), is a process that leads to a change in a learner's disposition and capabilities that can be reflected in behavior. As human beings we perceive and process information every waking minute. Some of this information is filtered out and some is incorporated into what we know and remember. These changes in capabilities are the result of what we call learning situations.

A learning situation has two parts: one external to the learner and the other internal. The internal part of the learning situation, it appears, derives from the stored memories and intentions of the learner. A person may encounter the statement that presidential elections in the United States are held on the first Tuesday after the first Monday in November. If that fact is to be learned, however, it is evident that certain internal conditions, provided by memory from previous learning, must also be present. The learner must recall (1) the meanings of Monday, Tuesday, and November as designations of times; (2) the meaning of presidential election as the identification of an event, and (3) the basic skills involved in comprehending an English sentence. A person with these "internal" capabilities (and certain others we will mention later), presented with the statement about presidential elections in oral or printed form, is in a learning situation and potentially could learn from it. However, without the internal conditions, including a desire to learn, the external message is not likely to be meaningful, and that person is not likely to learn from it.

The process of learning has been investigated by the methods of science for many years. As scientists, learning investigators are basically interested in explaining how learning takes place. In other words, they want to relate both the external and internal parts of a learning situation to the process of behavior change called learning. The relationships they have found, and continue to find, between the learning situation and the behavior change may be appropriately called the "conditions of learning" (Gagné, 1985). These are the conditions, both external and internal to the learner, that enable learning to occur. If one has the intention of making learning occur, as in designing instruction, one must deliberately arrange these external and internal conditions of learning. Increasingly important is an understanding of the roles culture and activities play in the learning process. Learning is affected by sociocultural expectations, values, and declared or public knowledge. The learner is not an isolated being, and the context in which learning takes place interacts with what is being learned, and the processes of learning.

In the course of pursuing knowledge about how learning takes place, theories are constructed about structures and events (generally conceived as occurring in the central nervous system) that could operate to affect learning. The effects of particular events on learning may be, and usually are, checked again and again under a variety of conditions. In this way, a body of knowledge about learning is collected along with a body of principles that hold true in a broad range of situations. The aspects of learning theory that are important for instruction are those that relate to controlled events and conditions. If we are concerned with designing instruction so that learning will occur efficiently, we must look for those elements of learning theory that pertain to the events about which an instructor can do something.

Some Examples of Learning Principles

What are some of the principles derived from learning theory and learning research that may be relevant to instructional design? First, we mention some principles that have been with us for many years, and serve us well when applied to the design of instruction.

Contiguity   The principle of contiguity states that the stimulus situation must be presented simultaneously with the desired response. Suppose, for example, that the goal for a soldier is to reassemble his or her weapon without aids. The inexperienced teacher might start by giving the soldiers an exploded diagram of a weapon, and then asking them to practice reassembling the weapon using the diagram. However, the objective requires that this should be done without aids, so the stimulus is, "reassemble your weapons," and the response would be to reassemble the weapon, not consult the diagram. Although the diagram might serve as a learning aid, it would have to be removed before there is contiguity between the stimulus and the response. A second school example of contiguity would be giving a student the task of classifying an example of a concept. For instance, faced with a page of animals and the instruction to touch the duck, the student touches the duck, and receives affirmative feedback. The objective of instruction in this case would be the student identifies a picture of a duck.

Repetition   The principle of repetition states that the stimulus situation and its response need to be repeated, or practiced, for learning to be improved and for retention to be more assured. There are some situations where the need for repetition is very apparent. For example, if one is learning to pronounce a new French word, such as *varieté,* repeated trials certainly lead one closer and closer to an acceptable pronunciation. Modern learning theory, however, casts much doubt on the idea that repetition works by strengthening learned connections. Furthermore, there are many situations in which repetition of newly learned ideas does not improve either learning or retention (see Ausubel, Novak, & Hanesian, 1978; Gagné, 1985). It is perhaps best to think of repetition not as a fundamental condition of learning, but merely as a practical procedure (practice), which may be necessary to make sure that other conditions for learning are present.

Reinforcement   Historically, the principle of reinforcement has been stated as follows: Learning of a new act is strengthened when the occurrence of that act is followed by a satisfying state of affairs (Thorndike, 1913). Such a view of reinforcement is still a lively theoretical issue, and there is a good deal of evidence for it. For instructional purposes, however, one is inclined to depend on another conception of reinforcement. Reinforcement may be internal as well as external. For example, a student might report feeling good that he completed his homework. A social-cultural view of reinforcement might relate this feeling to societal expectations and the student's desire to meet these expectations. Because achievement is generally recognized by others in the culture, reinforcement becomes internalized. We might call learners who have internalized these reinforcements "self-motivated."

Social-Cultural Principles of Learning   Most early educational psychologists studied how individuals learned from instruction without consideration of the student's social-cultural environment. Variables like the rate of instruction, the use of illustrations, and the mode of presentation, among others, were isolated in attempts to determine the variance they contributed to differences in learning situations. However, more recent research has suggested that the social-cultural context of learning may be as important a factor as other more discrete components attended to by instructional designers. Again, reflecting on the Carroll (1963) model, we can imagine that student persistence is one of the internal conditions that must be present for intentional learning to occur. In trying to isolate effects of individual variables such as content sequencing on student learning, we are likely to overlook other related factors, such as the student's perception of the relevance of the content, that make our instruction less effective than it could be. A few examples of principles that might be derived from social-cultural models include the following.

NEGOTIATED MEANING   Learning is a social process of constructing meaning. This principle, when applied, would call for a context in which the student would work with other students and knowledgeable others in determining the meaning of information. The implications are that collaborative learning environments can facilitate this process. Many of the other principles of practice, feedback, and reinforcement can be seen at work within this learning environment, but there is more going on than simply the use of effective learning materials. What is present is a social-cultural influence on the importance of the information, and how it fits into a broader context of group-supported learning.

SITUATED COGNITION   Learned capabilities are acquired in a particular context, and the perceived utility of that context has implications for later retrieval and use. A related concept is "inert knowledge" (Whitehead, 1929). To Whitehead, inert knowledge is represented by ideas that are learned as disconnected bits and pieces, without reference to a context of use. Whitehead writes, "[T]heoretical ideas should always find important applications within the pupil's curriculum. This is not an easy doctrine to apply, but a very hard one. It contains within itself the problem of keeping knowledge alive, of preventing it from becoming inert, which is the central problem of all education" (p. 17). The guiding principle to be derived is that learning that occurs in authentic contexts where it can be meaningfully applied is more likely to be remembered and recalled when needed.

We see the inclusion of social-cultural principles in instructional design as a perfectly logical step in the development of a design model that attends to the multidimensional nature of learning, and definitely in line with the conditions of learning. These conditions might be more general in nature than those for specific kinds of learning. For example, a group discussion of current events might add relevance to subject matter knowledge and skills that can be related to these events. These principles, then, might inform practice for a large number of learning situations.

ACTIVITY THEORY   Principles of activity theory include the notion that learning occurs as a result of activity. All activity is purposeful, and by participating in activities, learning occurs. One hypothesis proposed by Brown, Collins, and Duguid (1989) is that learning occurs best during authentic activity—an activity that is part of a culture's work. Learning is a process that transmits the knowledge and practices of a culture. While this is a vast oversimplification of a complex set of propositions and the activity theory framework, the principle of active learning is important for instructional designers, especially in the selection of learning outcomes, and the design of learning activities.

THE CONDITIONS OF LEARNING

So, it appears that instruction must take into account a whole set of factors both external and internal to the learner that collectively may be called the conditions of learning (Gagné, 1985). External factors, like the learning environment, the resources in that environment, and the management of learning activities interact with internal conditions, such as states of mind that the learner brings to the learning task, previously learned capabilities, and personal goals of the individual learner. These internal capabilities appear to be a highly important set of factors that affect learning.

The Processes of Learning

In order to take into account the conditions of learning, both external and internal, we must begin with a *framework,* or model, of the processes involved in an act of learning. A model widely accepted by modern investigators that incorporates the principal ideas of contemporary learning theories is shown in Figure 1–1. This stage theory model developed originally by Atkinson and Shiffrin (1968), conceives of learning as information processing that consists of a number of stages between perception and memory. Although there are other models of information processing, such as the parallel-distributed processing model, and connectionists models (McClelland & Rumelhart, 1986), they are basically extensions of rather than replacements for the stage model. Brain research, such as that being done by LeDoux (1996) and others might provide insight in the future about how emotions affect cognition. It is safe to say that we don't really know exactly how the brain works, but the stage theory model has given us a number of insights about how to design instruction that facilitates learning, and many principles in this book are built on that framework.

In the staged information processing model, sensory receptors transmit information from the environment to the central nervous system. The information attains a brief registration in one of the sensory registers and is then transformed into recognizable patterns that enter short-term memory The transformation that occurs at this point is called selective perception or feature perception. The visually presented marks on a page of print become the letters a, b, and so on, when they are stored in short-term memory A set of particular angles, corners, and horizontal and vertical lines becomes a rectangle.

Storage of information in the short-term memory has a relatively brief duration, less than 20 seconds, unless it is rehearsed. The familiar example is remembering a seven-digit telephone number long enough to punch it in. Once the number is entered, it disappears from short-term memory; but if it must be remembered longer, it can be done by internal rehearsal. Another aspect of the short-term memory of considerable importance for learning is its limited capacity. Only a few separate items, perhaps as few as four to seven, can be "held in mind" at one time. Since short-term storage is one stage of the process of learning, its capacity limits can

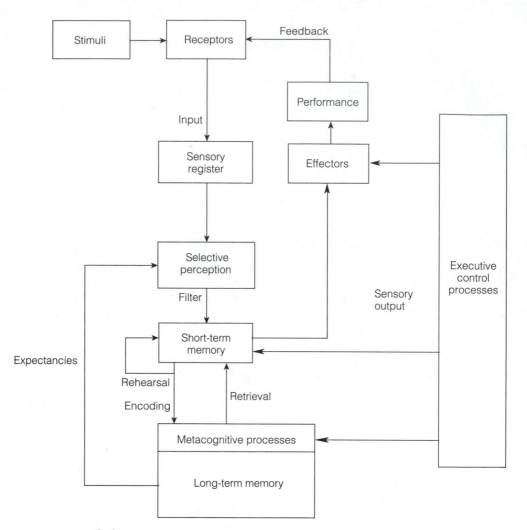

FIGURE **1–1**
**AN ELABORATED MODEL OF LEARNING AND MEMORY UNDERLYING MODERN
COGNITIVE (INFORMATION PROCESSING) THEORIES OF LEARNING**

Source: Adapted with permission from R. M. Gagné and M. P. Driscoll. *Essentials of Learning
for Instruction*, 2nd Ed. Copyright © 1988 Pearson Education.

strongly affect the difficulty of learning tasks. For instance, the process of mentally
multiplying 29×3 requires that two intermediate operations (30×3 and $90 - 3$) be
held in short-term memory. This makes the learning of such a task considerably
more difficult than, say, 40×3, which requires only one operation.

Information to be remembered is again transformed by a process called
semantic encoding to a form that enters long-term memory. When encoded information in long-term memory is meaningful, much of it has the form of propositions; that is, entities of language possessing sentence components of subjects and

predicates. In this form, information may be stored for long periods of time. It may be returned to short-term memory by the process of retrieval, and it appears that such retrieved items may combine with others to bring about new kinds of learning. When functioning in this manner, the short-term memory is often referred to as a working memory.

Information from either the working memory or the long-term memory, when retrieved, passes to a response generator and is transformed into action. The message activates the effectors (muscles), producing a performance that can be observed to occur in the learner's environment. This action is what enables an external observer to tell that the initial stimulation has had its expected effect. The information has been "processed" in all of these ways, and the learner has, indeed, learned.

Control Processes   Two important structures shown in Figure 1–1 are executive control and expectancies. These are processes that activate and modulate the flow of information during learning. For example, learners have an expectancy of what they will be able to do once they have learned, and this in turn may affect how an external situation is perceived, how it is encoded in memory, and how it is transformed into performance. The executive control structure governs the use of cognitive strategies, which may determine how information is encoded when it enters long-term memory, or how the process of retrieval is carried out, among other things (see Chapter 4 for a fuller description).

The model in Figure 1–1 introduces the structures underlying contemporary learning theory and implies a number of processes made possible thereby. All of these processes comprise the events that occur in an act of learning. In summary, the internal processes are as follows:

1. Reception of stimuli by receptors
2. Registration of information by sensory registers
3. Selective perception for storage in short-term memory (STM)
4. Rehearsal to maintain information in STM
5. Semantic encoding for storage in long-term memory (LTM)
6. Retrieval from LTM to working memory (STM)
7. Response generation to effectors
8. Performance in the learner's environment
9. Control of processes through executive strategies

The learning environment can be arranged to influence the processes of learning, particularly those numbered 3 through 6. For example, the selective perception of the features of a plant can be aided by emphasizing them in a diagram. The semantic encoding of a prose passage can be done more readily if the passage opens with a topic heading.

Instruction and Learning Processes

Instruction will facilitate learning when it supports the internal events of information processing. The external events we are calling instruction, then, must align with the internal events to support different stages in the process. Instruction, then, may be conceived as a deliberately arranged set of external events designed to support internal learning processes. We shall have occasion throughout this book to refer to the *events of instruction* (Gagné, 1985). Their purpose is to bring about the kinds of internal processing that will lead to efficient learning.

The events of instruction involve the following kinds of activities in roughly this order and are related to the learning processes previously listed:

1. Stimulation to gain attention to ensure the reception of stimuli
2. Informing learners of the learning goals to establish appropriate expectancies
3. Reminding learners of previously learned content for retrieval from LTM
4. Clear and distinctive presentation of material to ensure selective perception
5. Guidance of learning by suitable semantic encoding
6. Eliciting performance, involving response generation
7. Providing feedback about performance
8. Assessing the performances involving additional response feedback occasions
9. Arranging variety of practice to aid future retrieval and transfer

These events will be more fully and precisely described in Chapter 10. They are presented here in this form to give a general impression of their relation to the processes of learning.

The Contributions of Memory Besides the external events of instruction, the conditions of learning include the presence in working memory of certain memory contents. As previously noted, these are retrieved from long-term memory during the learning episode. Instruction can aid this recall by reminding (or asking the learner to recall) the contents learned on previous occasions. For example, learners who are acquiring new knowledge about the presidential election of 2000 might be asked to recall prior general knowledge about elections when they are held, what events they include, and so on. Learners who are acquiring the skills for writing effective sentences might be asked to recall the skills they learned previously for spelling, word sequence, and punctuation.

Kinds of Learning The contents of long-term memory, when retrieved to working memory, become essential parts of the internal conditions of learning for the new material. Learned capabilities can be classified into one of five domains of capabilities. Briefly, the five kinds of learned capabilities with which this book deals are as follows:

1. *Intellectual skills:* Which permit the learner to carry out symbolically controlled procedures using discriminations, concepts, rules, and problem-solving skills
2. *Cognitive strategies:* The means by which learners exercise control over their own learning processes
3. *Verbal information:* The facts and organized "knowledge of the world" stored in the learner's memory

4. *Attitudes:* The internal states that influence the personal action choices a learner makes
5. *Motor skills:* The movements of skeletal muscles organized to accomplish purposeful actions

What is interesting is how different types of learned capabilities facilitate other types of learning. Obviously, the capabilities that were previously learned fall into the same categories as those that are to be newly learned. Chapters 3, 4, and 5 describe in detail the five categories of learned capabilities and the conditions of learning that relate to them.

Concentrating instruction on any one type of these capabilities alone, or any two in combination, is insufficient. Verbal information, in and of itself, represents a highly inadequate instructional goal. Learning intellectual skills leads to practical competence, yet instruction of these skills, depends upon verbal information during the learning process. Furthermore, the learning of intellectual skills does not by itself equip learners with the cognitive strategies they need to become independent self-learners. Cognitive strategies themselves cannot be learned or progressively improved without the involvement of verbal information and skills—they must, in other words, have "something to work on." Attitudes are generally supported by a substrate of information and intellectual skills, as are motor skills. So, multiple aims for instruction must be recognized. Learners need to attain several varieties of learned capabilities.

Intellectual Skills as Building Blocks for Instruction

Intellectual skills are import building blocks for most curricula. They include concept learning, principles and rules, and problem-solving behaviors. They are what most would call higher-order learning skills, because they involve more than memorization. An intellectual skill cannot be learned simply by hearing someone describe it. It must be practiced and applied. However, intellectual skills can be learned relatively quickly if the learner has the appropriate prerequisite knowledge. The content of most disciplines is characterized by intellectual skills in the form of concepts, principles, and processes. Problem solving is a higher-order intellectual skill. In order to be considered competent in a subject area, a student has to master many intellectual skills. As an example, consider the intellectual skill of multiplying two multidigit whole numbers. When learners possess this skill, they are able to perform multiplication rapidly, without having to look up the rules each time. Their performance shows that they are able to recall such rules and put them immediately into effect. At the same time, learning to multiply can be accomplished in a relatively short time. There are other advantages to intellectual skills as a major framework for instruction and instructional design. Such skills are highly interrelated and build elaborate internal intellectual structures of a cumulative sort (Gagné, 1985). The learning of one skill aids the learning of other higher-order skills. Suppose an individual has learned the skill of substituting specific numerical values for letters in a symbolic expression such as the following:

$$A^2 + B^2 = C^2$$

Such a skill will aid the learning of many kinds of advanced skills, not simply in mathematics, but in many areas of science and social studies. Intellectual skills are rich in transfer potential, which allows the building of increasingly complex structures of intellectual competence.

Another advantage of intellectual skills as a primary component in instruction is the relative ease with which they can be reliably observed. When a learner has attained an intellectual skill as, for example, "representing data values graphically," it is relatively easy to show that the skill has indeed been learned. One would provide numerical data and ask the person to construct a graph to display the values. An intellectual skill can always be defined in operational terms; that is, it can always be related to something the successful learner is able to do.

The choice of intellectual skills as a primary point of reference in the design of instruction, then, is based mainly upon practical considerations. In contrast to verbal information, skills cannot be simply looked up or made available by "telling," but must be learned. In contrast to cognitive strategies, intellectual skills are typically learned over relatively short time periods and do not have to be refined and sharpened by months or years of practice. Intellectual skills build upon each other in a cumulative fashion to form increasingly elaborate intellectual structures. Through the mechanism of transfer of learning, they make possible an ever-broadening intellectual competence in each individual. And finally, such skills can be readily observed so that it is easy to tell that they have been learned.

THE RATIONALE FOR INSTRUCTIONAL DESIGN

We propose the design of instruction with suitable attention to the conditions under which learning occurs, conditions which are both external and internal to the learner. These conditions are in turn dependent upon what type of learning outcome is desired.

The planning of instruction in a systematic manner, with attention to the consistency and compatibility of technical knowledge at each stage of design, is usually termed the "systems approach." This kind of design uses various forms of information, data, and theoretical principles as input at each planning stage. Furthermore, the prospective outcomes of each stage are checked against whatever goals may have been adopted by those who manage the system as a whole. It is within this framework that we seek to apply what is known about the conditions of human learning to instructional design. The systematic planning of instruction to achieve learning is characterized by a process of stating goals, selecting or developing instructional interventions, and using feedback from learners to improve the instruction.

The Derivation of an Instructional System

From our assumptions about instruction and the desire to use the conditions of learning as a framework for designing instruction, we can develop a model for instructional design. As mentioned previously, however, models serve a purpose

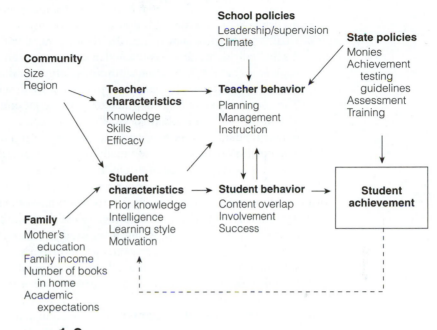

FIGURE **1–2**

HUITT'S MODEL OF THE TEACHING LEARNING PROCESS

Source: Huitt, (2003); http://chiron.valdosta.edu/whuitt/materials/tchlrnmd.html. Used with permission of the author.

within the context they are going to be used. For example the systems model shown in Figure 1–2, by Huitt (2003), diagrams the many components of an educational system and their relationships. Instruction is only one component of this system, and design must consider other parts of the system and how they affect variables related to student performance.

A teacher or trainer using instructional design principles to design a lesson may need only a simple model for lesson planning. If the desired objectives have already been specified, and curriculum materials developed, the teacher might have only to (1) manage the students' use of the materials, (2) guide their activities, and (3) assess learning and provide corrective feedback. However, a larger curriculum project, like developing a 40-hour course to teach air-traffic control procedures will require a more thorough model. The rational steps of a thorough model, which we will describe more completely in the next chapter, may be outlined briefly as follows:

1. Determine the purposes for the instruction. The needs for instruction are investigated as a first step. These are then carefully considered by a responsible group to arrive at consensus on the goals of instruction. The resources available to meet these goals must also be carefully weighed, along

with those circumstances that impose constraints on instructional planning. An example of a constraint is time allowed for instruction.

2. Goals of instruction may be translated into a framework for a curriculum and for the individual courses contained in it. Likewise the goals of individual courses reflect the instructional purposes determined in step 1. The outcomes of this step are the course goals and course description.

3. The course objectives are then analyzed and major units of instruction are identified. The unit goals are derived from the course goals, with attention to how they support the types of outcomes represented at the course level.

4. The determination of types of capabilities to be learned, and the inference of necessary learning conditions for them, makes it possible to plan the sequences of lessons. These sequences facilitate cumulative learning.

5. Lessons are further broken down into events and/or learning activities. Attention centers on the arrangement of external conditions that will be most effective in bringing about the desired outcomes. Consideration must also be given to the characteristics of the learners, because these will determine many of the internal conditions involved in the teaming. Planning the conditions for instruction also involves integrating technology in a meaningful way.

6. The additional element required for completion of instructional design is a set of procedures for assessment of what students have learned. In conception, this component follows naturally from the instructional objectives. The objectives describe domains from which items are selected. Assessment procedures and instruments are designed to provide criterion-referenced measurement of learning outcomes (Popham, 1981).

7. The design of lessons and courses, with their accompanying techniques of assessing learning outcomes, makes possible the planning of entire systems. Instructional systems aim to achieve comprehensive goals in schools and educational programs at all levels. A means must be found to fit the various components together in a management system, sometimes called an *instructional delivery system.* Naturally, teachers or instructors play key roles in the operation of such a system. A particular class of instructional systems is concerned with learning in settings apart from the school or classroom, as in distance or e-learning. However, the conditions of learning for these audiences must also be taken into consideration.

8. Finally, attention must be paid to evaluation of the instructional effort. Procedures for evaluation are first applied to the design effort itself. Evidence is sought for revisions that would improve and refine the instruction (formative evaluation). At a later stage, summative evaluation is undertaken to seek evidence of the learning effectiveness of what has been designed.

WHAT THIS BOOK IS ABOUT

The design of instruction, the background of knowledge from which its procedures are derived, and the various ways in which these procedures are carried out are described in each of the 16 chapters of this book, arranged as follows:

Part 1: Introduction to Instructional Systems

Chapter 1, the introduction, outlines our general approach to instruction, and includes an account of some principles of human learning that form the bases of instructional design.

Chapter 2 introduces the reader to instructional systems and the systems approach to the design of instruction. The stages of instructional system design described here are developed further in subsequent chapters. Also addressed are issues associated with designing for open systems, based on social-cultural models of learning and closed systems with predefined outcomes. Because most educational systems are social institutions, we will briefly discuss the effects of politics in design decisions. Finally, the role of instructional design in the broader context of performance improvement will be addressed.

Part 2: Basic Processes in Learning and Instruction

Chapter 3 introduces the reader to the five major categories of instructional outcomes—the human capabilities that are learned with the aid of instruction. The varieties of human performance that these capabilities make possible are described and distinguished.

Chapter 4 describes the characteristics and conditions of learning for two of these categories of learning outcomes: intellectual skills and cognitive strategies.

Chapter 5 extends this description of learned capabilities to the three additional categories, with definitions and examples of information, attitudes, and motor skills. The importance of attitudes and information are discussed within the context of higher-order learning.

Chapter 6 gives an account of the principles associated with the human learner, and how these principles affect design decisions. Keller's (1987) model of motivational design is presented with its implications for the design of learning activities.

Part 3: Designing Instruction

Chapter 7 deals with the derivation and description of specific instructional objectives (performance objectives). These are related, on the one hand, to the categories of objectives previously defined, and on the other, to the particular learned capabilities that are the focus of interest for instruction.

Chapter 8 describes procedures for learning-task analysis, beginning with a consideration of purposes and goals of instruction. The aim of analysis is the classification of objectives for use in instructional planning. Prerequisites are identified for various kinds of learning outcomes.

Chapter 9 describes procedures for constructing sequences of lessons in making up larger units of instruction, such as topics, modules, and courses.

Chapter 10 shows how the "Events of Instruction" can be arranged to support learning.

Chapter 11 discusses the role of technology and its potential for providing new ways for thinking about instruction.

Chapter 12 gives an account of the design of learning activities and lessons, including the placement of parts of lessons in sequence, the arrangement of effective conditions of learning, and the selection of methods and/or technology.

Chapter 13 deals with methods of assessing student performances as outcomes of instruction, describing appropriate uses of criterion-referenced and norm-referenced tests.

Part 4: Delivery Systems for Instruction

Chapter 14 discusses individual and group learning environments and the implications for instructional "scaffolding" and learning activities.

Chapter 15 discusses online learning and the implications for instructional design.

Chapter 16 describes the basic logic for evaluating designed products and procedures, from lessons to systems and issues associated with the overall evaluation of the instructional design effort.

SUMMARY

Instruction is planned for the purpose of supporting the processes of learning. In this book, we describe methods involved in the design of instruction aimed at the human learner. We assume that planned instruction has both short-range and long-range purposes in its effects on human development.

Instructional design is based upon principles of human learning, specifically, the conditions under which learning occurs. Principles derived from educational research indicate some of the conditions external to the learner that can be incorporated into instruction. A model of information processing that identifies a number of internal processes underlies contemporary theories of learning. These processes bring about several successive stages in the transformation of information on its way to storage in the long-term memory. The purpose of instruction is to arrange external events that support these internal learning processes. In addition, a designer must consider principles associated with the social-cultural aspects of learning and how they affect the selection of educational outcomes, and the design of learning activities.

An act of learning is greatly influenced by previously learned material retrieved from the learner's memory. The effects of prior learning on new learning are seen in the acquiring of verbal information, intellectual skills, cognitive strategies, attitudes, and motor skills. These varieties of learned capabilities and the conditions for their learning constitute the basis for instructional planning. Derived from these principles is the rationale for a set of practical procedures for the design of instruction.

Students who use this book will find it possible to follow up the ideas derived from research on human learning with further exploration and study of the references at the end of each chapter.

REFERENCES

Atkinson, R., & Shiffrin, R. (1968). Human memory: A proposed system and its control processes. In K. Spence & J. Spence (Eds.), *The psychology of learning and motivation: Advances in research and theory* (Vol. 2). New York: Academic Press.

Ausubel, D. P., Novak, J. D., & Hanesian, H. (1978). *Educational psychology: A cognitive view* (2nd ed.). New York: Holt, Rinehart and Winston.

Brown, J. S., Collins, A., & Duguid, P. (1989). Situated cognition and the culture of learning. *Educational Researcher, 18,* 32–42.

Carroll, J. (1963). A model of school learning. *Teachers College Record, 64,* 723–733.

Cognition and Technology Group at Vanderbilt (1993). Anchored instruction and situated cognition revisited. *Educational Technology, 3,* 52–70.

Gagné, R. M. (1985). *The conditions of learning* (4th ed.). New York: Holt, Rinehart and Winston.

Huitt, W. (2003). Model of the teaching learning process. Retrieved on 10/1/2002 from: http://chiron.valdosta.edu/whuitt/materials/tchlrnmd.html.

Keller, J. M., (1987). The systematic process of motivational design. *Performance and Instruction, 26*(9), 1-8.

LeDoux, J. E. (1996) *The emotional brain.* New York: Simon and Schuster.

McClelland, J., & Rumelhart, D. (1986). *Parallel distributed processing.* Cambridge, MA: MIT Press.

Popham, W. J. (1981). *Modern educational measurement.* Englewood Cliffs, NJ: Educational Technology Publications.

Thorndike, E. L. (1913). *The psychology of learning. Educational psychology* (Vol. 2). New York: Teachers College Press.

Whitehead, A. N. (1929). *The aims of education and other essays.* New York: Free Press.

CHAPTER 2

DESIGNING INSTRUCTIONAL SYSTEMS

An *instructional system* may be defined as an arrangement of resources and procedures used to facilitate learning. Instructional systems have a variety of forms, ranging from narrowly focused technical training courses to loosely structured student-focused learning environments, and exist in virtually any institution with the express purpose of developing human capacities. These include public schools, universities, military organizations, business and industry, public service, and non-profit organizations. In all of these settings, the instructional systems are sometimes referred to as *training systems* when their goals are primarily on skill development, and *educational systems* when they focus more on generalized intellectual development and personal competence. Another characteristic of instructional systems is that they can reside within many types or combinations of delivery systems, such as face-to-face classrooms, Web-based virtual classrooms, and self-directed learning environments, ranging from print-based to technology-based. Furthermore, instructional systems can function in coordination with other human performance improvement systems, such as knowledge management systems, incentive systems, organizational development systems, and personnel selection systems.

Instructional systems design (ISD) is the process for creating instructional systems. It is both *systematic* and *scientific* in that it is documentable, replicable in its general application, and leads to predictable outcomes. Yet, it also requires *creativity* in identifying and solving instructional problems. ISD includes several phases, including analysis, design, development, implementation, and evaluation, and is characterized by the overarching concept of design. Note that the word *design* appears at two levels. At the more general level it is the central concept in the overall process of ISD, and at the more specific level it refers to a phase within the process; but this seems to be unavoidable and is generally not a problem because the contexts of usage differ. ISD includes systems theory and problem-solving methodology, which constitute its basic paradigm for describing and producing learning environments for training and education. ISD also incorporates knowledge of the principles of learning and instruction from learning science and instructional psychology that will optimize learning environments and learner achievements to achieve the goals of the system.

ISD can occur at many different levels of application and in virtually all cultures. In school settings, micro-level usage includes the preparation of individual achievement plans for students with special needs. At a macro level, ISD is used to plan major educational systems for entire countries—for example, in Indonesia where the Ministries of Education used it for the systematic planning of educational curricula for their open junior high schools and Open University. Major organizations such as IBM, NASA, the Federal Aviation Administration, and Samsung also use ISD at a macro level for their training and education systems. College and university programs that train people to do instructional design have grown exponentially since the first edition of this book was published.

The common thread in all these applications is design, which by definition implies a systematic process, as opposed to trial and error or random assemblage. This systematic approach is used in many disciplines including medicine, architecture, landscape design, and psychotherapy. It is essentially a process of identifying a goal that may be based on a gap between the way things are and the way you want them to be, or on a desire to reach out and accomplish something new. As expressed by Koberg and Bagnall (1981), "Design is a process of making dreams come true."

The systematic design process begins with a goal and proceeds through an interconnected set of stages that build upon each other by means of a series of inputs, processes, and outputs. The outputs of one stage become, together with other relevant information and products, inputs to other stages. The stages normally include, in varying degrees of detail, analysis, design, development, implementation, and evaluation. Generally the stages are performed in this sequence: One identifies a particular problem or goal, analyzes the requirements to solve the problem, creates a design for a solution, and then develops, implements, and evaluates the solution. However, the starting point of a design process can be within any of the phases as, for example, when one is revising a curriculum. Here, a designer might start with the student assessment instruments to see if they suggest that there are specific problems with the learning activities and if changes are recommended. But note that, even though the designer began with modifications to the design, all stages of the ISD process will eventually be revisited to ensure that the changes are consistent with the objectives and are matched to identified needs.

Even though ISD is used at so many different levels, instructional designers don't always have a chance to work on large-scale comprehensive projects or even all phases of the process. They generally design smaller instructional systems such as courses, units within courses, or individual lessons. Despite the differences in size and scope, the process of designing an instructional system has features in common at all levels of the curriculum. Instructional systems design of the smaller components is simply referred to as instructional design, because the focus is the piece of instruction itself rather than the total instructional system.

There are many specific representations, or models, of the instructional design process, but virtually all of them share certain elemental characteristics. The majority of this chapter describes a general model and the primary components of each stage. The chapter concludes with a description of two models that illustrate specific kinds of variations on the general model. But first, there are three important assumptions to be considered.

ASSUMPTIONS

An *instructional system* can also be called a *learning environment* because both phrases refer to a set of elements that interact in the process of promoting and supporting learning activities. Some might argue that instructional systems are more *instructivist*; that is, that they focus more on telling the learners what they need to know, but that learning environments focus more on learners by providing opportunities for them to explore and develop their own potentials as in a *constructivist* or humanistic pedagogical frame of reference. However, the position taken in this book is that both instructivist and constructivist learning environments are also instructional systems, because both are organized to stimulate and support learning, regardless of whether the focus is on learner acquisition of prespecified objectives or more toward learner self-discovery and intellectual development.

Another assumption in this book is that ISD does not imply a particular pedagogy or learning theory. Some of the critics of instructional system design (Gordon & Zemke, 2000) have equated ISD with a behavioral psychology approach to instruction, but there is no basis for this in the conceptual foundation or history of practices of ISD. Some applications of ISD, as in the "heyday" of programmed instruction, were in the context of using behavioral psychology principles of stimulus, response, and reward (Markle, 1969; Skinner, 1968), and this seems in recent years to be viewed by some as the defining history of ISD. But, this perspective omits much if not the majority of historical development (Saettler, 1968) and current practices of ISD. The development of a focus on behavioral objectives, which are an important element in ISD and are often associated with a behaviorist approach, and indeed were a central component of this empirical approach to defining outcomes and arranging stimuli and consequences to achieve those outcomes. Gagné, for example, built hierarchies of instruction to support behavioral objectives (1977). However, the development of the concept of operationalized learner outcomes in the form of observable behavior occurred prior to and independently of their development in the context of task analysis. Ralph Tyler (Smith & Tyler, 1942; Tyler, 1950) was one of the first people to emphasize the importance of defining student outcomes operationally, in terms of observable behavior and content. Bloom (1956), Krathwohl (Krathwohl, Bloom, & Masia, 1964), and others developed taxonomies of educational objectives in the cognitive and affective domains, a development spurred primarily by developments in psychometrics and testing. Our point is that any number of learning theories and educational philosophies can be incorporated into an instructional system. These include a focus on categories of learning (Gagné, 1985; Merrill, 1994), expository learning strategies (Ausubel, 1963), discovery learning methods (Bruner, 1967), and constructivist principles (Duffy, Lowyck, & Jonassen, 1993). An instructional system provides the framework for the processes of developing these environments.

A third assumption is that ISD is a special case of a larger process called human performance technology (HPT). The two processes are almost identical, structurally, in their overall stages of analysis, design, development, implementation, and evaluation. In the analysis stage of both processes, one attempts to identify gaps in performance relative to desired outcomes, the causes of the gaps, and the types of solutions that might close the gaps. In this process, several causes and kinds of solutions relative to the human performance problems may be discovered. For example, the performance gaps could be due to a lack of knowledge and skill, lack of motivation, unavailability of resources required to do the task, ineffective working conditions, or an excessive work load, to name a few. ISD is employed when the gap is due to lack of knowledge or skill, whereas HPT attempts to address all of the problems with an integrated set of solutions (Stolovitch & Keeps, 1999). However, the focus of this book is on instruction, so we will stay within the confines of instructional design.

THE BASIC PROCESS: THE ADDIE MODEL

Most systematic models of design have similar components, but can vary greatly in the specific number of phases and their graphic representations. The most basic model of the ISD process is one that contains five phases, or components (Figure 2–1). In this particular representation, the model takes the initial letter from each of the five components portrayed in Figure 2–1 and is referred to as the ADDIE ("add-ee") model of instructional design. Each of the five stages has substeps that receive more or less emphasis in other models of the ISD process. For example, some models have more than five stages by specifying more than one type of design or evaluation stage, or by including separate stages for such things as "getting started," "course maintenance," and/or revision. In the model we will develop throughout this book, we will use the ADDIE model as an organizing framework, although we recognize different interpretations of each of the components.

Figure 2–1 illustrates how each major component is linked to the others. The solid lines indicate that the process flows from analysis to evaluation and the dotted lines indicate feedback pathways. Evaluation activities can reveal where revisions are required in each of the other four components. The overall process is based on

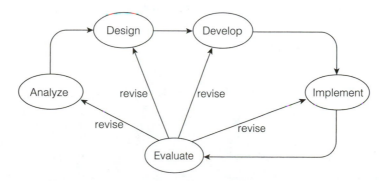

FIGURE **2–1**
THE **ADDIE** MODEL OF INSTRUCTIONAL DESIGN

systematic problem-solving models, but it is also important to understand that problem-solving activities occur within each component and that the overall process is not always followed in a strictly linear manner. Figure 2–1 illustrates logical connections and not necessarily procedural ones. This is because many activities occur within each of the major components (see Table 2.1), and the instructional design process does not always begin at the "beginning" with a "blank tablet of paper." For example, the process might begin with a request to redesign an existing course or curriculum. The instructional designer might begin within the design component by using evaluation data to determine which parts of the existing design and content are satisfactory and which require revision. Based on

---

TABLE 2.1   SUMMARY OF ADDIE MODEL COMPONENTS AND SUBCOMPONENTS

I. Analysis
    a. First determine the needs for which instruction is the solution.
    b. Conduct an *instructional analysis* to determine the target cognitive, affective, and motor skill goals for the course.
    c. Determine what skills the entering students are expected to have, and which will impact learning in the course.
    d. Analyze the time available and how much might be accomplished in that period of time. Some authors also recommend a context or resources analysis.

II. Design
    a. Translate course goals into performance outcomes, and major course objectives (unit objectives).
    b. Determine the instructional topics or units to be covered, and how much time will be spent on each.
    c. Sequence the units with regard to the course objectives.
    d. Flesh out the units of instruction, identifying the major objectives to be achieved during each unit.
    e. Define lessons and learning activities for each unit.
    f. Develop specifications for assessment of what students have learned.

III. Development
    a. Make decisions regarding the types of learning activities and materials.
    b. Prepare draft materials and/or activities.
    c. Try out materials and activities with target audience members.
    d. Revise, refine, and produce materials and activities.
    e. Produce teacher training or adjunct materials.

IV. Implementation
    a. Market materials for adoption by teachers or students.
    b. Provide help or support as needed.

V. Evaluation
    a. Implement plans for student evaluation.
    b. Implement plans for program evaluation.
    c. Implement plans for course maintenance and revision.

these gaps, the instructional designer would move back into the analysis component to reexamine previously collected data to determine if changes had occurred in learner characteristics or job requirements. Then, the designer would move back into the design component to prepare a list of revisions to the objectives, content, and learning activities. Thus, the instructional designer must engage in problem-solving activities within a given component of the process in addition to fulfilling the requirements of the overall process.

The steps, or subcomponents, within each of the major components will vary depending on the context in which the model is used. In Table 2.1, the steps within each component illustrate a somewhat procedural flow from the determination of instructional requirements through the various steps involved in creating objectives, tests, and materials to the tryout and evaluation of the materials. This illustration portrays an instructional design application of the model in that it focuses on instructional materials. The development of a large-scale instructional system would require many additional steps pertaining to curriculum development, course sequencing, and delivery-system options.

Analysis

In instructional design it is important to ask, "For what problem is instruction the solution?" This question is often overlooked or taken for granted. For example, in a particular college curriculum in speech pathology, the students are required to take a course in anatomy. This same course is required of premed students and sports-psychology students. Why? Because students in each of these majors has to understand something about various components of the human body. The questions that should be asked are, "What components of the human body do each of these different career paths need to know?" and "How can an anatomy course be constructed so that each of the students leaves the course knowing and remembering what they will need to know to engage in their chosen occupation?"

In instructional systems, this type of analysis is associated with the general concept of needs assessment. Kaufman (1996), Rossett (1988), and others define need as a discrepancy between a desired and current state of affairs, or more formally as a gap in results (Kaufman, 1996). To continue the preceding example, if it is important for students in speech pathology to be able to name and identify each of the muscles contributing to the production of speech and they can't, then there is a performance deficiency. One possible solution to this deficiency is learning facilitated by instruction. During the analysis process, the designer should ask about *ends*; for example, "Why is it important for the speech pathologist to learn the muscles and other components associated with speech?" The answer might be that the therapist would have to describe the treatment in technical detail in patient records, be able to read technical articles dealing with speech mechanisms, and to communicate accurately to other speech pathologists about problems. Obviously, the speech pathologist has little need to know the names of the bones in the feet, the nerves in the intestines, or the veins in the hand, all of which might be important to the premed student.

It is important to note that not all performance deficiencies or needs are instructional problems. For example, a recent review of school safety data collected from a particular state's school systems showed disturbing inconsistencies. The data did not appear reliable, and it was decided to develop instruction to train the data-entry operators. However, an analysis of the situation turned up the following information: (1) school systems that turned in few safety violation reports were considered safe schools and were rewarded with extra funds; (2) school systems that turned in more reports were considered unsafe, were reprimanded, were told to rectify the situation, and were denied additional funds; (3) as there was no common definition of safety infractions, each school district had its own definitions and learned that it was better to report low volumes of infractions. The analysis showed that there were many factors affecting the reporting and reliability of data, and that simply training the operators to input data would not solve the problem, because school systems were being rewarded for inaccurate reporting. It would require the full application of the HPT process, not just instructional design, to solve all of these problems. Thus, the purpose of analysis is to accurately describe the actual and desired states of affairs, and to examine elements of the context of the situation that might influence achieving that desired state. In instructional situations, the context includes such things as the availability of resources, administrative requirements, and the incoming skills of the learners.

Analysis in support of instructional design can take place at a number of different levels.

1. First determine the needs for which instruction is the solution. Determining these needs involves answering questions like:
   - What purpose does this course serve in the students' education? Is this a general education course or a professional skills course? What does this mean in terms of the types of learning activities and assessments?
   - How important is this course to the student's success in a career field (or, What are the occupational performance requirements that require the knowledge and skill from this course?)? Part of this question has to do with relevance, or perceived relevance, of the course. Relevance is one component of motivation (Keller, 1987a; 1999) and how hard a student will work in a course.
   - What are the social needs for this course? Is it important to address social issues like multiculturalism, diversity, honesty, sexual harassment, moral turpitude, and so on? Some of the most complex and important issues today might be called affective or social issues, and course developers should address them.
   - How does this course add to the student's personal development? Does this course make this student a better person? How?
   - What other courses does this course build on? Is it expected that the skills learned in other course will be needed in this course? What will you have to do to explain these prerequisites to students?
   - What other courses depend upon skills learned in this course? What will the students use from your course in other courses? Are your goals articulated with the next level course? Are the connections clear to the students?

- How much time do you have to develop this course? Course development takes time and energy. Are there existing materials available that you can use?
- Where does student-directed learning fit in? What types of learning activities can maximize authenticity by connecting your course to realistic contexts of application?

2. After identifying the needs to be served by the course and some of the situational factors, then conduct an *instructional analysis* to determine the target cognitive, affective, and motor skill goals for the course.
   - What knowledge, skills, and attitudes (KSAs) should a student leave this course with? It is important to define these in terms of what the student will be able to do (as apart from what content they should study). For instance, a student in leisure studies might be expected to list key principles in park planning (knowledge) and generate solutions to novel problems, such as making a plan for a park to serve the needs of the local community (skill). This is quite different from saying the student will "understand" park planning, which accomplishes little more than specifying the content area to be included in the course.
   - Are there any standards or expectations for this course (from other sources) that must be met? Is the student expected to pass a standardized test at the end of the course? Are there professional standards that will be tested? What entry skills or knowledge from this course will the next course require?
   - An important outcome of instructional analysis is *task classification*. Task classification is the categorization of the learning outcomes into domains or subdomains of types of learning (for example, Bloom, 1956; Gagné, 1985; Merrill, 1994). Task classification can assist instructional design in several ways. Classifying the target objectives makes it possible to check whether any intended purpose of an instructional unit is being overlooked. Briggs and Wager (1981) have presented examples of how target objectives may be classified and then grouped into course units in the form of instructional curriculum maps. The resulting maps can then be reviewed to check whether necessary verbal information, attitudes, and intellectual skills are included in the instructional unit. Learning outcome classification also provides the conditions most effective for different types of learning outcomes.

3. Next, determine what the entry skills and motivational characteristics of the students are.
   - What related skills do you expect the students to come in with? The most predictive variable about what students will learn in a class is their success in mastering prerequisite and related knowledge and skills in the given subject area. Many students don't succeed in a course, or get a slow start, because they don't possess the necessary prerequisite competencies needed to support the new learning.
   - What motivates these students? Are they self-starters, responsible learners, beginning undergraduates? What are their needs? Keller's ARCS model

(1987b) contains a process for identifying the specific motivational characteristics and requirements of learners with regard to their desire to learn in specific situations.

4. Finally, a fourth area of concern is conditions and constraints. Analyze the time available, how much can be reasonably accomplished, and the context (resources and constraints)?

   • What resources do you need for this course? Do your course outcomes require special equipment or learning experiences? For example, if your course is filmmaking the student will probably have to shoot and edit film. Do you have the resources you need? Will students have to share resources? How will this affect what you can expect them to learn? Are these distance-learning students? If so, what support will they need? Film is expensive; could the same skills be learned using the less expensive video camera? If so, what transfer problems might occur, and how might they be prevented?

   • What can you reasonably expect the student to learn in 16 weeks (or however long the course is)? Learning takes time, and the average student is splitting time among a number of other courses or activities. What is the best use of that time with regard to your goals?

In summary, the analysis stage provides important information to support decisions during the subsequent design stage. If we were designing a residence, we would have considered the purpose of the residence, the nature of the occupants and their needs, and the budget, timeline, and resources we have to work with. This is essentially the same thing we are doing in instructional design.

Design

The design component of the instructional systems design process results in a plan or blueprint for guiding the development of instruction. Just as an architect produces a blueprint for constructing a building after learning what the goals and needs are, the designer constructs a plan for the instruction based on the learning requirements. Depending upon the scope of the problem, the design may be created by a single individual or a design team. During the process of design, the instructional designer will ordinarily work with a subject-matter expert to determine the skills to be taught and a strategy for teaching them. However, sometimes designers are also subject-matter experts, for example teachers or professors who are designing their own courses. The important thing to realize is that instructional design expertise and subject-matter competence are two different things, and even though it is possible for a person to play both roles, it is not necessary for an instructional designer to be a content expert in order to work effectively with the content expert. By the same token, it follows that knowledge of content does not imply knowledge of effective instructional design.

The product of design is a set of specifications or plans for the developers to follow in producing the instructional support materials. The guidelines they follow to do this, or the amount of detail they specify in their design, depends a great deal upon the situation and the scope of the project. Again, using the construction analogy, if I need to construct a building to house an old tractor it is going to take a lot less planning and thought than building a public library. Designing a single lesson or instructional activity on a technical subject is a lot less complex than designing a whole course that incorporates higher-order learning outcomes like problem solving and self-regulated learning.

If the designers are working quickly and the developers are a part of the design team all along, the developers might begin developing prototypes of materials quite early in the process. This process of *rapid prototyping* provides an early opportunity for client feedback concerning the functionality, feasibility, and appearance of the instruction. If the same person or team will do both design and development, the same technique of rapid prototyping can be employed. This is a highly useful approach because early approval of a prototype reduces the risk of the complete product, being "off target," not meeting the instructional goals, at the formative evaluation stage. In relatively small projects, it is usually better to prepare a complete draft, because a small portion of the whole might not give an adequate representation. The final decision on approach depends partly on risk analysis. The less likely that one can be "off target," the less benefit there is from interrupting the process to develop an early prototype.

In either case, the design process is dynamic and creative, and no two designers will ever come to exactly the same resolution of a problem. The particular design procedure we describe in this book uses a "top-down" approach of translating course goals into course level performance objectives (What the learner should be able to do after completing the course.) This is accomplished by determining the subordinate skills and knowledge that support the attainment of these course objectives.

The steps in the design stage of the ISD process are summarized below:

1. *Translate course goals into major course objectives.* The question to be answered is, What will students be expected to do to at the completion of this course that they couldn't do when they came in?

   The goal of step one is to define the highest-level learning outcomes of the course. These will generally fall into one of four categories: intellectual skills, cognitive (learning) strategies, attitudes, and/or motor skills.

2. *Determine the major units or topics of instruction, the major outcomes for each unit, and how much time will be spent on each unit.* These unit objectives should all lead to accomplishing the broader course objectives. If, for example, one of the course objectives of a leisure studies course is, "The student will plan a park to meet the needs of local residents," one of the course units might be, "determining recreational desires." An associated learning objective from this unit might then be, "The student will be able to generate and administer a survey instrument to determine local recreational desires." Another unit in the course might be "constructing inexpensive playground equipment," and the associated learning objective might be, "The student will be able to construct swings and climbing pyramids with chains and used tires."

In almost all cases, the time for instruction or learning in this course will be limited, and so decisions must be made about what will be included and what won't. This is a good time to develop a weekly course calendar to specify how much time will be allotted to each course unit. A common mistake is to put too much breadth and not enough depth into a course. Generally too much breadth means the course focuses on "covering" information rather than developing skills. This is a decision that has to be made by the subject-matter expert, but most often instructors expect their students to achieve new skills. Depth means that enough time must be allowed for activities and feedback that lead to higher-order skills.

3. *Flesh out the unit objectives by specifying the learning outcomes for each unit.* This may consist of a list of important concepts, principles and rules, or it may involve defining types of problems students will be expected to solve. However, it leads to a list of learning outcomes or objectives that are then related to each other in the form of a diagram or instructional curriculum map (ICM). The ICM is the designer's rough sketch of the course, much as a 3-D rendering is an architect's sketch of a building.

Determining types of capabilities to be learned, combined with the instructional designer's *inferences* about the learning conditions necessary for students to learn these capabilities, make it possible to plan *sequences of instruction*. This is because the mastery of a new learning objective requires the recall and use of previously learned information and skills. An instructional sequence is therefore implied, because different types of learning outcomes require the recall of different types of information. For example, problem-solving skills and rule-using skills require concept learning as prerequisites, so instruction would be sequenced so that students possessed these concepts before they were needed for higher-level outcomes. The process of diagramming these relationships using ICM helps to reveal the necessary links in instruction, see where the gaps are, and determine what other skills might be necessary.

4. *Break the units down into lessons and learning activities.* The concept of lesson implies a starting point and an ending point for instruction. A lesson plan is a set of specifications about what learning activities will happen during the instructional period, including out-of-class activities, what the instructor will do, and what the student will do. As you will see later in this book, we suggest that lessons be built from specific events of instruction that will facilitate achievement of the objectives.

A *learning activity* is an element of a lesson plan and consists of a specific event or processes in which a learner engages in active responding or construction during learning. A lesson may consist of one or more learning activities. For example, writing a summary of a reading assignment is a type of learning activity. The goal of the activity might be to have the learner become a more critical reader. However, the activity itself does not constitute a lesson unless it also includes other elements, such as an introduction, some direct instruction, examples, and an assessment.

The achievement of unit objectives often requires many lessons with their embedded learning activities.

The design of units of instruction, consisting of lessons and learning activities that are smaller in scope and thus more detailed in character than an entire course, requires grouping related unit objectives into unit and lesson maps. This again employs the process of curriculum mapping to visualize the relationships among learning outcomes and their prerequisite skills.

5. *Develop specifications for lessons and learning activities.* Design of the lessons and learning activities centers on the development of external events that will be most effective in bringing about the desired conditions of learning. Consideration must also be given to the characteristics of the learners, because these will determine many of the internal conditions involved in the learning. Planning the conditions for learning also involves consideration of the media and delivery systems that will be used.

Gagné and Briggs (Briggs, 1977) defined nine external events of instruction, as summarized in Table 2.2. These events are correlated with a learner's internal processes that take place during information processing. They proposed that instruction built around these external events could facilitate the internal events that constitute learning. We see these external events as a framework for the development of lessons or learning activities. It is not always necessary for the instructional designer to provide all of these events, because good learners provide many of them for themselves in the form of learning strategies. However, one way or another, these events, or combinations of them, have been shown to support the learning process for all learners. In fact, we define instruction as "the purposeful arrangement of external events to facilitate the process of learning." To that end, they serve a very important function in the design of lessons.

6. *Design specifications for assessment of what students have learned.* This is called *assessment planning*. In conception, this component follows logically from the contents of the instructional objectives. These assessments are expected to be valid and reliable measures of what students have learned as a result of instruction on specific objectives. This kind of assessment, or testing, is sometimes called *objectives-referenced assessment*.

We define assessment in this context as the collection and processing of data for the purpose of making decisions. There are two types of learner assessment: *criterion referenced* and *normative*, and both can claim to be objectives-referenced. The difference between the two is how the standard for performance is set. In normative referenced measurement, a comparative standard is set based on the norm or average performance of the group, and is often referred to as "grading on the curve." Normative standards are set after the performance of the group and the standard for success is defined in reference to group performance. For example, the top 10 percent might get the highest grade, and so forth. In this system, a test score that equates to an "A" in one class could equate to a "C" in the same class the following semester if there were a larger number of even higher scores on the test. In contrast,

TABLE 2.2   EXTERNAL EVENTS OF INSTRUCTION

Event	Purpose
1. Provide for attention and motivation	Establishes a learning set, directs learner's attention toward the relevance or purpose for the instruction.
2. Present the learning objective(s)	Establishes an expectation of the performance desired.
3. Recall prerequisites or related knowledge	Provides an anchor for new learning, relating what is to come to what the learner already knows.
4. Present the new content	Presents the new information, procedure, process, or problem-solving task to be learned. This is often the focus of the lecture or printed text. Tying this to previous learned knowledge facilitates encoding into long-term memory.
5. Provide for learner guidance	Elaborates the content presented in event 4. It may take the form of examples, stories, descriptions, discussion, or anything else to help make the content more memorable. This step facilitates encoding and building a rich knowledge structure.
6. Provide for practice	Elicit responses from learners. This has to do with retrieving what has been learned in the context of cues. The purpose is not as much for assessment as it is for detecting uncertainty or misunderstandings.
7. Provide feedback	Provides information to the learners regarding the accuracy of their understanding.
8. Assess performance	Tests the delayed retention of learned knowledge or skills.
9. Provide for retention and "transfer"	Strengthens what is learned with spaced practice. "Transfer" means being able to apply what was learned in different contexts or situations.

criterion referenced evaluation sets a predetermined standard against which personal performance is gauged. This standard is set prior to the performance of the group, usually as a function of the perceived importance of the performance objective. Every student who then achieves at the same predefined level will get the same grade. It is important to note that the two types of evaluation serve different types of decisions. The first asks how well the student performed in comparison to the other students, and the second indicates the degree to which the student mastered the learning objective.

Most instructional design models focus on criterion referenced measurement, because the objective of design is to improve instruction so that a majority of students reach the course goals. It is true that there are elements of normative decision making even in criterion referenced testing because the pre-defined standards are set with regard to some feasible range of performance for the target population of learners in the given subject matter area. However, once established, the standards are in reference to levels of accomplishment instead of "floating" in reference to other learners. Setting standards, always a controversial and difficult issue, will be discussed in more detail later.

Development

Development refers to the preparation of materials to be used in the learning environment. It is a challenging stage in instructional design, because it can be approached from several directions, depending on the relationships among the instructional objectives, degree of detail in the design documents that provide input to development, the characteristics and appropriateness of existing materials, and the delivery system. In many settings, a course or curriculum already exists and can, or must, be used to the fullest extent possible because of curriculum approval processes or the need to be as cost-efficient as possible. In other settings, there are no existing materials that relate directly to the objectives, which means that new materials must be prepared. In still other settings, there are existing materials or parts of existing materials to be incorporated along with new materials and perhaps adapted to a different delivery system.

Generally speaking, there are four categories of development situations:

1. *Working within an existing curriculum (augmenting existing material)*
   This is a typical situation in schools where teachers work with the curriculum, textbooks, and supplementary materials that have been adopted and purchased by the school system. Typically, teachers will build lesson plans within the context of the objectives and content that are provided in curriculum materials. This is different from the practices of ISD, which stresses the importance of defining goals and objectives before designing and developing instruction. However, provided curriculums may be the result of development processes that resulted in meaningful and appropriate goals and content for the given school setting. In this case, teachers will develop lesson plans that incorporate their own styles of teaching, and may even create units of work with locally developed objectives to supplement the curriculum. In any case, the amount of development of original material in this setting is relatively small, even though it might be critically important to meet the needs of the students.

2. *"Repurposing" existing material (modifying some of the goals or content and/or moving to a new delivery system)*

This situation exists frequently in the development of employee education and can also occur in schools. One example would be adapting an existing program to a specific setting, as in modifying or supplementing generic seminars to meet the requirements of a specific organization. A good example is supervisor training. There are many commercially available training materials, workshops, and training consultants who offer programs for the training of newly appointed supervisors. These training materials can be useful, because it is expensive, especially for smaller organizations, to develop such a program. However, these programs are usually quite generic and might not be sufficiently matched to an organization's requirements. Sometimes an organization can modify one of these programs to better match its needs without having to undergo major training development. Vendors recognize this and will often assist in the modification process. The task for the instructional designer is to conduct analysis and define needs and objectives within the organization, and then to study the existing materials to determine what modifications and supplements will be necessary to meet their requirements.

Another type of repurposing occurs when one attempts to change a course from one delivery system to another. It has become quite common to shift courses from the classroom to a Web-based environment. To be done properly, it is necessary to go through a detailed design process to examine the existing features and content of the course and the specific characteristics and features of the new delivery system, and then to create a design document that provides developers with the specifications for the modification. Too often, Web courses are little more than a set of materials that have been scanned from the original print-based or videotaped setting and then programmed into the Web setting. It requires an expert instructional designer to prepare specifications for the organization of content, incorporation of interactive instructional activities, and testing that will guide development in this context.

3. *Incorporating elements of existing material into a new course*

In this case, a major amount of new development will be required, but it may be possible to incorporate various amounts of existing material to reduce development time and costs. This situation can occur in a school, especially when developing an innovative course that is not part of the "traditional" curriculum in math, language arts, or science. One of the authors facilitated the development of a seventh-period course in a middle school, which was to be an interdisciplinary course and for which the teachers wanted to have a set of complex cognitive learning objectives. After working through the analysis and goal-setting processes, the course design called for considerable development of new materials, but allowed for the incorporation and adaptation of some existing materials. This situation also occurs frequently in employee learning settings when a course has to be redesigned for a new system but can incorporate elements of existing courses.

4. *Building a new course*

    This is the primary situation for which most instructional designers are trained. In most courses of study and workshops, instructional designers will work through the entire ISD process and will develop an original lesson or module. This comprehensive level of instructional design can occur in a school setting, but it occurs more often in employee education settings.

In the development stage of ISD, there are several principles related to the above contexts:

1. *Well-established objectives:* The more well-established the objectives are and hence the more precisely determined the content of the materials, the more likely it is that suitable materials will already be on the market. It is possible that available materials will be able to provide some of the needed instruction. In this case, a module could be designed to take advantage of the existing materials and could be supplemented with other materials to provide for the missing objectives. Materials production is a costly process, and it is desirable to take advantage of existing materials when possible.

2. *Innovative objectives:* The more innovative the objectives, the more likely it is that a greater portion of the materials must be developed, because they are not likely to be available commercially. In the early stages of an ISD process, it is natural to want and envision a highly innovative, new approach to a subject. When doing so, it is important to keep in mind that the time and financial resources for development of such an innovative program might not be available. However, this should not necessarily be a deterrent. If one creates a set of goals and a design for an "ideal" situation, it might be possible to come closer to the ideal than one expected, which certainly won't happen if no attempt is made to envision the ideal.

3. *Team approach:* Generally, it is best to use a team approach in development, with the instructional designer in the lead facilitating role. Many talents are required to produce an appealing and effective set of instructional materials. An instructional designer might have excellent analysis and design skills, but not have excellent writing or media production skills. It requires a special talent to write effectively for specific audiences, and media design and production also requires many specialized skills. Additionally, a subject-matter expert will be able to assist in having up-to-date, technically accurate content.

4. *Instructional design versus media production:* Instructional design criteria should take precedence over media production priorities. Don't let media production criteria override design criteria. There are many examples of technology delivered courses that have wonderful production qualities and innovative, interactive navigation, but lack essential instructional and motivational qualities.

5. *Make or buy:* Always examine the "make" or "buy" issue before undertaking the development of entirely new materials. It may be possible to save development expenses by selecting available materials and integrating them into a module that provides coverage of all the desired objectives of instruction. Similarly,

when using existing materials, leave them in their original delivery format unless there are sound logistical or instructional reasons for changing them. Developing materials for a particular delivery system is almost always more expensive than making a selection from those available.

Implementation

Implementation as a stage in the ADDIE model can be of two types, and it can be confusing to determine what actually happens here. The first refers primarily to implementation activities that occur while the course is still being created and evaluated, and is usually called *pilot testing* or *field-testing*. The second refers more to "launching" the course after development is complete. Adding to the confusion is the placement of implementation prior to the evaluation stage that also consists, broadly speaking, of two types: evaluation that occurs *while* the course is still being created, and evaluation activities that occur *after* the course is fully launched. In this book, we discuss implementation planning requirements of the instructional designer in preparing for a successful launching of the course. Implementation activities that occur during the ISD process are incorporated below in the evaluation stage.

Five principles that apply to implementation planning are in the areas of learning management systems, student guidance, change management, delivery environment conditions, and course maintenance plans.

1. *Develop a learning management system that is adequate for the requirements of the situation.* These systems can be as simple as a teacher grade book or as complex as an information system that contains individual records of each student's learning requirements, specific competencies acquired in each completed learning event, time and date of completed learning events, and a schedule for future events.

2. *Provide for student guidance and support.* In all too many situations, students do not have a clear idea of what will be expected of them, the schedule of events that will occur, or how to prepare for success on the learning requirements. In individualized systems of instruction, including distance education, it is equally important to provide student guidance for learning management. Materials developed at the British Open University include student study guides (including time-management information) and assessment guides, in addition to the instructional readings and activities. They have found that this type of student support lowers dropout rates and improves the quality of the student learning.

3. *Plan for change.* Change management, also referred to as "diffusion and adoption," is one traditionally important element of implementation. This includes ways to train the instructors and provide them with the support they need to be effective facilitators. The adjunct materials help teachers use instructional materials more effectively by showing how to include events of instruction in classroom activities. Textbook publishers typically provide materials to support instructors, but the instructional designer might have to

modify them or develop original implementation manuals that support the learning objectives more closely than the provided materials. In employee education, it is typical for instructional designers to develop instructor guides to support the facilitators in the delivery of a course.

4. *Plan for delivery environment.* Instructional designers should examine and prepare for aspects of the delivery environment that will affect course implementation, including technology requirements, local support for distributed learning, acceptable schedules for classes, availability of instructors, and potentially conflicting demands in learner schedules. For example, school administrators and education managers may express positive attitudes toward distributed learning systems, such as Web-based courses, in contrast to face-to-face environments. They see this as an opportunity to reach greater numbers of learners without the cost of live instructors and residential facilities. However, they might not give adequate consideration to the environmental requirements for distributed learning to be successful. In a large banking organization in the northeastern part of the United States, branch managers supported the development of training modules to be distributed in the workplace. This would allow employees to study at convenient times during the workday instead of having to miss work to go to a training center. However, implementation became difficult. There was never enough "spare" time for employees to study on site, there were not enough quiet, unobtrusive places for them to study, and some managers were uncomfortable when they actually saw an employee sitting and reading instead of "being productive." Thus, instructional designers must take all aspects of the delivery environment into consideration when planning implementation.

5. *Plan for maintenance of the system.* Instructional designers may be called upon to include a *course maintenance plan*. This consists of schedules for various types of course evaluations that might be conducted, collection and utilization of evaluation results, monitoring course content for accuracy and timeliness, continued linkages to other components of a curriculum, and relevance of the course to the organization's goals and learning requirements.

Evaluation

Evaluation is the final stage in the ADDIE model. This placement reflects its logical function as the point at which you determine whether your proposed solution to a problem has succeeded. However, in the ISD process, evaluation actually occurs at several points and may even be included in all of the stages of the process, including the postdevelopment phases after the product has been implemented. When conducting evaluations, it is useful to distinguish between the *type of evaluation* and the *type of decision* to be made. There are, generally speaking, five types of evaluations and in each case there are two possible types of decisions.

1. *Materials evaluation:* The first type of evaluation is the one that is most familiar to all instructional designers. It consists of the reviews that take place while instructional products are being created and validated. Materials evaluation

usually begins with reviews by subject-matter experts of the design documents, including the learning objectives and the initial drafts of instructional materials. Next, a small number of learners who are characteristic of the target audience, even if they are not actual members of the target audience, are asked to read the materials and respond to all learning activities, including self-checks and tests. Normally, this evaluation activity is conducted with one learner at a time and the instructional designer takes note of how well the learner understands the materials, how interesting the learner finds the materials, and how well the learner performs on the test. This is called "developmental tryout" or "one-on-one evaluation" (Dick & Carey, 1996). After a final draft of the materials is completed, the instructional designer conducts a pilot test, or small-group tryout. Again, the participants might be characteristic of the target audience rather then being actual members of it. This is because one might not want to use target audience members until the final version of the materials are ready for field testing, which is the final type of evaluation in this category. A field test is conducted with actual members of the target audience under actual classroom conditions, or whatever learning environment is specified for the instruction. The difference between pilot and field tests is one of degree. In the pilot test, the materials are still in more of a developmental phase and more observations and evaluative measurements are taken than in the field test. In other words, the pilot test is conducted in more of a "laboratory" environment whereas the field test should appear to the learners to be an "ordinary" learning environment. In practice, because of the expense of conducting all these evaluations, pilot and field tests are often combined, and the pilot-test evaluations become part of the first actual offering of a class to the target audience.

2. *Process evaluation:* This type of evaluation is focused on the instructional system design process itself. It consists of quality reviews of how well each phase of the ISD process has been conducted. At the end of each phase, members of the project team, or an outside evaluator, can review documents and answer questions about how effectively and efficiently that phase of work was conducted and whether there are things that could be done to make it better. This type of evaluation is in keeping with the concepts of total quality management and continuous improvement. It is an acknowledgement that there is no one best way to do instructional systems design. Any given model of the process has to be adapted in terms of tasks, roles, and procedures to meet the instructional design requirements and personnel structures in any given organization. Thus, it is beneficial to examine one's application of the process and how it can be improved. Even if an organization's use of the process has been highly effective, changes in personnel, technology, clients, or budgets can require modification of the process in order for it to continue to be efficient and effective.

3. *Learner reactions:* This is the first of four types of outcomes evaluation described by Kirkpatrick (1959) that can be conducted after a course has been implemented. There are many formats and designs (Keller, 1996) for this and the other three types, which are learner achievement, instructional

consequences (transfer of learning), and organizational benefit (or, results). Learner reactions evaluation is by far the most commonly used one, and it generally consists of a self-report survey conducted at the end of a course module. It asks learners about the clarity of instruction, the logical connectedness of all the parts, the quality of the instructional strategies, the effectiveness of the instructor— if it is a facilitated course— and the comfort of the environment. A typical learner reaction item is, "I felt the objectives of the instruction were clear." To which the student would respond by checking, ( ) strongly agree; ( ) agree; ( ) neutral; ( ) disagree; ( ) strongly disagree.

4. *Learner achievement:* This is the second level of outcomes evaluation and utilizes the tests that were developed and validated during design and development. These tests are used to determine how well learners are achieving the course objectives and can be used to obtain feedback about the effectiveness of the course as well as to determine whether individual learners are passing or failing. The tests can also be used to provide performance feedback to learners even if the learners are not being graded.

5. *Instructional consequences:* These are outcome evaluations of (a) transfer of training to a job or other application environment, and (b) whether there is a measurable organizational benefit from the course of instruction. There are two levels from Kirkpatrick's model (1959) in this category. We have combined them because they have more to do with the implementation of an instruction system than the design of one. The third level, transfer of instruction, refers to how well people are applying what they have learned. Their ability to do this depends in part on how well they were prepared for transfer by such things as authentic learning experiences with levels of complex cognitive skill development that matches the requirements of the job environment; but transfer also depends upon environmental conditions. For example, transfer can be limited or even prohibited by such things as lack of resources, management philosophies and practices that contradict the training, ineffective incentives, and inappropriate job requirements. A challenge in the design of transfer evaluation studies is to be able to identify, measure, and estimate the influence of all of these elements.

In organization benefit evaluations, one attempts to determine whether there is a measurable improvement in an organizational performance indicator, such as higher output, reduced error rate, increased profitability, increase in school district standardized test scores, increased college admissions of high school graduates, and so forth. This type of study can be based on perceptual data such as interviews, measures of increased performance, or cost-benefit ratios based on financial data. In the latter case, one has to estimate the total cost of designing, developing, and implementing the educational program and then measure the financial benefit resulting from its implementation. For example, if there is a measurable reduction in defective products, then a financial estimate of savings or cost avoidance can be determined. By dividing the costs into the benefits, one can determine whether there was a positive result.

Regardless of the *type* of evaluation, there are two types of *decisions*, called *formative* and *summative*, that one can make based on the results and one's purpose for doing the evaluation. Formative decisions are those in which the results of the evaluation provide guidance on how to improve instructional materials or the procedures by which they are designed and developed. Summative evaluation leads to decisions about the worth and value of a product or activity. Formative evaluation occurs most frequently during materials and process evaluation, while summative evaluation is more common during outcomes evaluation. However, either type of decision can made with respect to any of the types of evaluation. For example, measures of learners' reactions can identify areas where the implementation of a course can be improved, or they can be used to determine whether an instructor should be retained, promoted, or released. This is certainly true in private-sector training, but is also happening with greater frequency in higher education.

OTHER TYPES OF MODELS

The ADDIE model has become a frequently referenced generic model of the ISD process. Its stages represent the major steps in systematic problem-solving models, which begin with identification of the problem and its causes (analysis), proposing a solution (design) preparing the solution (development), trying it out (implementation), and determining whether the solution was successful (evaluation). This model is useful for conveying the general characteristics of ISD, but it is not always useful as a concrete model that meets the needs of specific ISD theories or environments. Thus, there are scores if not hundreds of models that have been published in the instructional design literature and developed within organizations in the United States and abroad. Two broad categories of models are generalized and situated.

Generalized Models

These models tend to represent an author's concept about how ISD should be conducted, or an approach that can apply broadly across a variety of contexts, delivery systems, or ISD environments. Gustafson and Branch (1997) provide a collection of such models that they categorize into a three-part taxonomy based on the orientation of the model. The three orientations are classroom, product, and system. Classroom models include those that provide guidance for ISD in school settings, which tend to have intact curricula and limited resources for innovation. Product models such as Bergman and Moore's (1990) guidelines for the production and management of interactive video/multimedia projects apply to specific delivery systems. System models range from comprehensive approaches to large-system development (Branson, 1977) to more detailed and precise approaches, such as Dick and Carey's (1996), which focuses primarily on the design of lessons, with an emphasis on rigorously defined and measured objectives.

Probably the best known of all instructional design models is Dick and Carey's (1996). On the surface (Figure 2–2) it appears to be dramatically different from the ADDIE model. However, it incorporates to differing degrees all aspects of the ADDIE model. There are three elements on the left that encompass analysis.

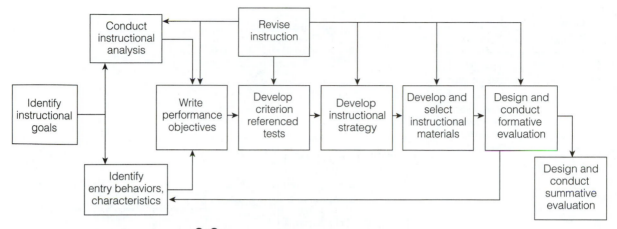

FIGURE 2–2
THE DICK AND CAREY (2001) MODEL OF INSTRUCTIONAL DESIGN

Source: From W. Dick, L.. Carey, and J. Carey, *The Systematic Design of Instruction,* 5th Ed., copyright © 2001. Reprinted by permission of Allyn & Bacon and the authors.

Design is included in the next three elements dealing with performance objectives, criterion referenced tests, and instructional strategies. The actual development or selection of materials occurs in the next step and is followed by the various evaluation steps. Implementation is not included as a separate step. The aspects of implementation that occur during the design and development of the course are incorporated within the evaluation steps. They include pilot and field tests.

Situated Models

These are models that are developed by an organization specifically to guide and control its ISD process. Usually, they are not published, because they are proprietary or are specific to the requirements of an organization and are not as adaptable as the published models. These models not only portray the ISD process as it is followed in the specific setting, they also provide a basis for project planning, assignments of responsibilities, documentation of work, and accountability. Figure 2–3 illustrates a model utilized by a division within a large multinational banking organization.

In comparison to the ADDIE model, this one includes clearly articulated phases for analysis, design, and development. In the implementation stage, a distinction is made between pilot testing, which occurs during the development process, and the formal phase of implementation, which refers to the actual launching of the course. There is no phase called "evaluation" because evaluation activities are incorporated throughout the process. There is a getting-started phase, in which one collects all of the inputs pertaining to the situation and prepares a business case to predict whether the benefits of the project are likely to be substantial enough to justify the project. It is also of interest to note that there are two phases of design. The first, high-level design incorporates an ideal from a similar project for IBM.

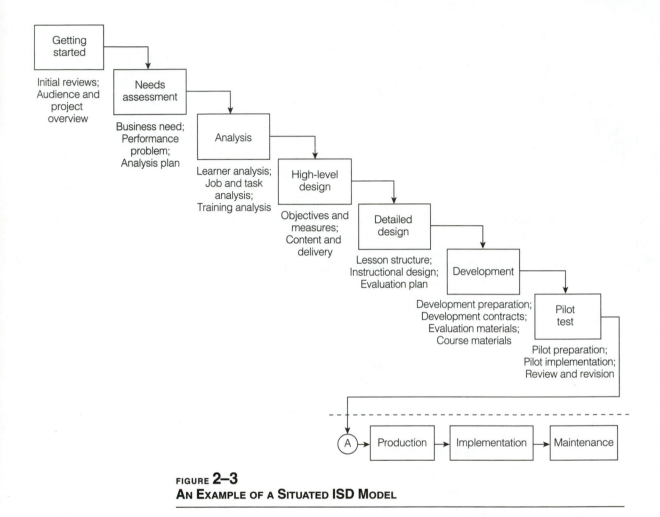

FIGURE **2–3**
AN EXAMPLE OF A SITUATED ISD MODEL

This phase consists of the preparation of learning objectives, test specifications, availability of content, and selection of an appropriate delivery system or combination of systems. After determining the delivery system, one proceeds to detailed design and follows an approach that is appropriate for that delivery system.

THE ISD PROCESS VERSUS REPRESENTATIONS OF THE PROCESS

There is a problem in instructional design, as in other fields that follow complex cognitive processes, in trying to distinguish between the process itself and representations of the process. The process of ISD is defined by logical connections between inputs, such as needs, job performance requirements, or deficiencies in the current quality of performance, and the remaining phases of design, development, implementation, and evaluation. Most "models" of the process tend to portray these logical connections of parts in sequential representations such as those in Figures 2–1, 2–2, and 2–3. However, these representations do not adequately illustrate the dynamics of the ISD process, which, as we have pointed out previously in this chapter, is not necessarily linear, can begin in virtually any phase of the process, and includes iterative and parallel activities throughout the process.

There are alternate representations of the process, such as spiral and curvilinear models (Gustafson & Branch, 1997), that have been proposed in the past by theorists (for example, Kemp, Morrison, & Ross, 1994) and by organizations such as Control Data Corporation in the 1980s and Samsung in the 1990s. These representations attempt to illustrate more of the dynamics of the ISD process. One such approach is that of the Southwest Research Institute (Figure 2–4). This representation depicts how each phase of the process depends on the other phases. The spiral ISD model represents a continuous process where the instructional developer or design team can enter or reenter the various phases of the process, depending on the nature and scope of the development or revision activity.

Unlike the model shown in Figure 2–3, which has the appearance of a "waterfall" moving forward in a linear manner, the spiral model has the benefit of emphasizing the iterative components of instructional design and development, in which tasks from each of the five main phases represent ongoing activities that continue throughout the life of the training program. Once the training program is implemented, the other phases don't simply end; they are continually repeated on a regular basis to see if further improvements can be made.

As shown in Figure 2–4, as the spiral increases, the resulting ISD products mature. This figure illustrates how the ISD process can be tailored to any kind of instructional product that is developed. It also illustrates how experts can use the ISD process with maximum efficiency by entering it at any phase or maturity level. In industry and government, entry points are commonly determined by the sponsor of the program and depend on previous work efforts and constraints, such as time and money. Regardless of the ISD task or a given entry point into the process, the job of the instructional designer or training developer is to pursue the task with the goal of producing a total training solution.

In conclusion, it is important to realize that the ISD process is highly complex and cannot likely be reduced to a single structural, logical, or dynamic representation. Most all descriptions of the ISD process comment on the fact that it combines linear, parallel, and iterative aspects. Furthermore, each type of representation has benefits in terms of assisting in communicating the overall process. However, there is no doubt that some representations are more effective than others. Each representation, to be fully effective, must be tied to the nomenclature, roles, and tasks performed by ISD experts in a given organization. In some settings, ISD is a linear, procedural process, because that is what best meets the needs of the ISD requirements. In other settings, the ISD process is highly complex, as in the 4C/ID approach (van Merriënboer, 1997), which incorporates complex cognitive skill instruction together with constructivist learning goals. Part of the challenge of an

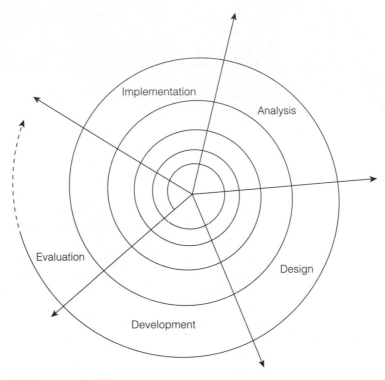

FIGURE **2–4**

ISD Represented as a Spiral Model Figure

Source: Adapted from Southwest Research Institute proposal no. 07-37413. Reprinted with permission of SWRI, San Antonio, TX, copyright © 2003.

instructional designer is to know how to build and apply the process in a given setting; another challenge is how to communicate the process by means of graphic representations. However, the representations of the process should not be viewed as adequate "models" of all the complexities of the process itself.

Summary

ISD models are representations of the concept of a systematic approach to instructional design. There is not one best model, a right model, or a wrong model in any theoretical or abstract meaning of the concept. The ISD process can be represented in any number of ways when one creates models that are operational and effective in specific contexts. Yet, all of these models must contain certain elements, regardless of how they are labeled or dissected, if they are to achieve the purposes of an ISD process. That is why the ADDIE model has become the somewhat prototypical representation of the process. It illustrates the essential components for models that have a higher level of theory-based guidance for any of the phases. These would include principles of instructional psychology, which are used in the instructional strategy design phase, or a greater level of procedural guidance for specific situations in which different people have responsibility for specific tasks.

REFERENCES

Ausubel, D. P. (1963). *The psychology of meaningful verbal learning*. New York: Grune & Stratton.

Bloom, B. S. (Ed.) (1956). *Taxonomy of educational objectives: The classification of educational goals. Handbook 1: Cognitive domain*. New York: McKay.

Bergman, R., & Moore, T. (1990). *Managing interactive video/multimedia projects*. Englewood Cliffs, NJ: Educational Technology Publications.

Branson, R. K. (1977). Military and industrial training. In L. J. Briggs (Ed.), *Instructional design: Principles and applications*. Englewood Cliffs, NJ: Educational Technology Publications.

Briggs, L. J. (Ed.) (1977). *Instructional design: Principles and applications*. Englewood Cliffs, NJ: Educational Technology Publications.

Briggs. L. J., & Wager, W. W. (1981). *Handbook of procedures for the design of instruction*. Englewood Cliffs, NJ: Educational Technology Publications.

Bruner, J., Goodnow, J. J., & Austin, G. A. (1967). *A study of thinking*. New York: Science Editions.

Dick, W., & Carey, L. (1996). *The systematic design of instruction* (4th ed.). New York: Harper Collins College Publishers.

Duffy, T. M., Lowyck, J., & Jonassen, D. H., (1993). *Designing environments for constructive learning*. New York: Springer-Verlag.

Gagné, R. M. (1977). Analysis of objectives. In L. J. Briggs (Ed.). *Instructional design: Principles and applications*. Englewood Cliffs, NJ: Educational Technology Publications.

Gagné, R. M. (1985). *The conditions of learning* (4th ed.). New York: Holt, Rinehart and Winston.

Gordon, J., & Zemke, R. (2000, April). The attack on ISD. *Training*, 43–53.

Gustafson, K. L., & Branch, R. M. (1997). *Survey of instructional development models* (3rd ed.). Syracuse, NY: ERIC Clearinghouse on Information & Technology.

Kaufman, R. A. (1996). *Strategic thinking: A guide to identifying and solving problems*. Alexandria, VA: American Society of Training and Development.

Keller, J. M. (1987a). Development and use of the ARCS model of motivational design. *Journal of Instructional Development, 10*(3), 2–10.

Keller, J. M. (1987b). The systematic process of motivational design. *Performance & Instruction*, 26(9), 1–8.

Keller, J. M., in collaboration with Young, A., & Riley, M. (1996). *Evaluating diversity training: 17 ready-to-use tools*. San Diego: Pfeiffer.

Keller, J. M. (1999). Motivation in cyber learning environments. *International Journal of Educational Technology, 1*(1), 7–30.

Kemp, J. E., Morrison, G. R., & Ross, S. M. (1994). *Designing effective instruction.* New York: Merrill.

Kirkpatrick, D. L. (1959). Techniques for evaluating training programs. *Journal of the American Society of Training Directors, 13,* 3–9, 21–26.

Koberg, D., & Bagnall, J. (1981). *The All New Universal Traveler.* Los Altos, CA: William Kaufmann.

Krathwohl, D. R., Bloom, B. S., & Masia, B. B. (1964). *Taxonomy of educational objectives: The classification of educational goals. Handbook 2: Affective domain.* New York: McKay.

Markle, S. (1969). *Good frames and bad: A grammar of frame writing* (2nd ed.). New York: John Wiley.

Merrill, M. D. (1994). *Research support for component display theory.* In M. D. Merrill (Ed.). *Instructional design theory.* Englewood Cliffs, NJ: Educational Technology Publications.

Rossett, A. (1988). *Training needs assessment.* Englewood Cliffs, NJ: Educational Technology Publications.

Saettler, P. (1968). *A history of instructional technology.* New York: McGraw-Hill.

Skinner, B. F. (1968). *The technology of teaching.* New York: Appleton-Century-Crofts.

Smith, E. R., & Tyler, R. W. (1942). *Appraising and recording student progress.* (Adventure in American Education Ser., Vol. 3). New York: Harper.

Stolovitch, H. D., & Keeps, E. J. (Eds.) (1999). *Handbook of human performance technology* (2nd ed.). San Francisco: Jossey-Bass; Englewood Cliffs, NJ: Educational Technology Publications.

Tyler. R. W. (1950). *Basic principles of curriculum and instruction.* Chicago: University of Chicago Press.

van Merriënboer, J. J. G. (1997). *Training complex cognitive skills: A four-component instructional design model for technical training.* Englewood Cliffs, NJ: Educational Technology Publications.

THE OUTCOMES OF INSTRUCTION

Instruction is a purposeful activity, that is, it is a means to an end. The ends are often described as the goals or objectives of instruction. These terms have different meanings in different contexts, but goals are generally understood to be broad statements of desirable outcomes, and objectives are more specific. The instructional outcomes introduced and defined here in terms of five broad categories run throughout the book as the framework on which the design of instruction is built.

GOALS, OBJECTIVES, AND INSTRUCTION

The basic reason for designing instruction is to make possible the attainment of a set of educational or training goals. The society in which we live has certain functions to perform in serving the needs of its people. Accordingly, one of the functions of a society is to ensure that such learning takes place. Every society, in one way or another, makes provision for the education and training of people in order that the variety of functions necessary for its survival can be carried out. *Education and training goals* are those human activities that contribute to the functioning of a society, including the functioning of an individual *in* the society, and that can be acquired through learning.

Public Schools

Goal setting for public schools is serious business, and societies judge the suitability of their schools against performance of students in other schools and other cultures. Within the United States, for example, goal setting happens at many different levels. In 1988, Congress created a 26-member National Assessment Governing Board (NAGB) to set policy for the National Assessment of Educational Progress (NAEP), commonly called the "Nation's Report Card." NAGB establishes the goals and frameworks for different subject areas around which NAEP develops tests. NAEP then conducts regular assessments of sample schools to find out what students know and can do. From this information, policy makers set goals and develop programs, such as the federal program called "No Child Left Behind (2001)." Often these statistical reporting committees directly influence public school curriculum, because funding follows compliance.

Industry and the Federal Government

"Historically, both public and private organizations have acknowledged that people are their most valuable resource. Organizations are recognizing that a commitment to and investment in providing their staff continuous learning opportunities is a business strategy that makes sense" (Office of Human Resources Management [OHRM] Report, 2003a).

In corporate America, goals are generally established for training entry-level employees, for providing continuing education to increase the proficiency level of all employees, and for training at more advanced levels. At the more advanced level, training is likely to occur when new or emerging processes, technologies, or functions are adopted by the organization. The underlying goal of most industry training programs is to improve the performance of employees and to encourage and support them to reach their full potential so that they may make valued contributions to the organization.

To help the federal sector address a critical human-capital challenge, namely strategic planning and investment in the development and training of its workforce, the Office of Management and Budget (OMB) developed Circular No. A-11, which directs all agencies to develop training goals and measures annually, beginning in fiscal year 2002 (OHRM Report, 2003b). To support this directive, the U.S. Office of Personnel Management (OPM) developed *A Guide to Strategically Planning Training and Measuring Results*. This guide is designed to help agency Human Resources Development (HRD) professionals and planners integrate training goals into strategic performance plans that are aligned with mission requirements in order to accomplish agency goals.

Military

The overall goal of military training is to prepare servicemen and women for performing in conflict situations. The military is by far one of the most demanding professions in the world, and the rigorous training each service member receives is intended to produce highly motivated individuals who set high goals for themselves. As the Army puts it, soldiers must strive to "be all you can be." Military training instills a mindset that requires the service member to work toward an objective until it is achieved, no matter how difficult the challenge. The competitive military environment demands winners (Vet Jobs, 1999).

Goals as Educational Outcomes

The reflection of societal needs in education and training goals is typically expressed in statements describing categories of *human activity*. Preferably, a goal is stated not in one word, such as "reading," but as a phrase, for example, "reading with enough fluency to focus on the meaning of what they have read," or "possesses positive reading habits and attitudes" (National Assessment Governing Board, 1993). Goals are the desired outcomes of our educational and training systems. The question to be answered is, What skills, knowledge, and/or attitudes should students have at certain stages in their educational or training development?

To be useful to teachers and trainers, these educational and training goals must be analyzed with regard to the *capabilities* that would make possible the kinds of activities expressed in the goals. It is these capabilities that represent the proximate goals of instruction. For example, a proximate goal of reading with fluency is that the learner will be able to "paraphrase the main idea of a paragraph." To carry out the activities required for maintaining reading, students must possess certain kinds of capabilities (knowledge, skills, and attitudes). For example, before they can paraphrase the main idea, they have to be able to locate it and infer the author's intent. In most cases these skills are learned through deliberately planned instructional activities. A capability such as reading comprehension, for example, obviously serves several purposes in supporting other kinds of learning.

Goals as Training Outcomes

What is the difference between education and training? Often it is the purpose or specificity of the desired outcomes. Whereas education develops potential capabilities and dispositions, effective training depends upon acceptable performance of the task being taught. However, training organizations that focus primarily on skill development also have broader goals within their organizational context. A goal for training in the military might be to reduce the risk of battlefield injury, or to produce effective and efficient infantry. These goals must also be broken down into individual capabilities and attitudes, such as the soldier will be able to assemble a weapon by feel, in the dark, in five minutes or less. A related attitude is soldiers choose to observe safety rules when handling a weapon.

Courses and Their Objectives

As noted in the previous chapter, the scope of a design project can vary from large systems to individual lessons. However, it is common to design instruction for a *single course* rather than for larger units of a total curriculum. There is no necessary fixed length of a course or no fixed specification of what is to be covered. A number of factors may influence the choice of duration or extent of content. Often, the length of time available in a semester or year is the primary determining factor. In the military, a course might be one week, eight hours per day.

In any case, a course is usually defined rather arbitrarily by the title understood within the local environment of the particular institution, for example, "American History," "Beginning French," "Freshman English," "Reconnaissance," "Air Traffic Control," "Database Design," and so on. The ambiguity in meaning of courses with such titles is evident. One assumes that "American History" in grade 6 is not the same as "American History" in grade 12, but the course title gives no clue. Is "Freshman English" concerned with composition, literature, or both? Is "Database Design" creating data tables, forms, and reports, or solving real-world information management problems? These are by no means idle questions, because they represent sources of ambiguity for students, particularly when they are planning programs of study.

Ambiguity in the meaning of courses with title or topic designations can readily be avoided when courses are described in terms of the *course objectives* (Mager, 1975; Popham & Baker, 1970). Examples of objectives in many subject areas are described by Bloom, Hastings, and Madaus (1971). Thus, if the course objective for "Freshman English" is for the student to be able to "compose an essay on an assigned single topic, in acceptable printed English, within an hour," it is perfectly clear to everyone what a portion of the course is all about. It will not help students, in any direct fashion, to "identify imagery in modern poetry" or to "analyze the conflicts in works of fiction." However, it will, if successful, teach them the basic craft of writing an essay. Similarly, if an objective of "Database Design" is that the student be able to "create a database solution for an identified performance problem," the learning requirement is fairly clear. It will not be confused with an objective that states that the student is to "explain how a database works."

Most courses have several high-level course objectives. For example, a course in social studies may want the students to be able to: (1) describe the context of (specified) historical events (information/concepts); (2) evaluate the sources of written history (analysis and problem solving); and (3) show a positive liking for the study of history (attitudes). A course in science may wish students to develop the ability "to formulate and test hypotheses (problem solving)," to "engage in scientific problem solving (rule using)," and to "value the activities of scientists (attitudes)." Each of the objectives within a single course may be considered equally worthwhile. The main point is that they each represent different valid learning requirements or expected outcomes. Instruction must be sensitive to how the objectives interrelate, and what kinds of instructional activities are most likely to facilitate achievement.

Different Types of Learning Outcomes   That there are different types of learned capabilities has been known for many years. The military talks about knowledge, skills, and attitudes; Bloom and others recognized three domains (motor, cognitive, and affective). Gagné believed that instructional planning could be vastly simplified by categorizing learning objectives into one of five major categories (Gagné, 1985). Each category represents a different class of human performance, and as will be seen later, each category also requires a different set of instructional conditions for effective learning. A few of these five categories have subcategories that are useful for instructional planning, as the next chapter will show. But for the moment, in taking a fairly general look at instructional planning, five categories provide a comprehensive view.

FIVE CATEGORIES OF LEARNING OUTCOMES

Table 3.1 describes five categories of learning outcomes, each of which will be defined and discussed briefly in the paragraphs below. These outcomes are made possible by the acquisition of learned capabilities, which are viewed as changes in the learner's stored memory. The instructional conditions that facilitate these changes and a fuller description of each type of learning will be presented in Chapters 4 and 5.

Intellectual Skills

Intellectual skills are best described as things we do with symbols, like putting things into categories, applying rules and principles, and solving problems. These skills enable individuals to interact with their environment in terms of symbols or conceptualizations. Learning begins with the basics of reading, writing, and arithmetic, and progresses to whatever level is compatible with an individual's interests and intellectual ability. Intellectual skills make up the most basic and pervasive structure of formal education. They range from such elementary skills as language (e.g., composing a sentence) to the advanced technical skills of engineering (e.g., finding the stresses in a bridge) and economics (e.g., predicting the effects of currency devaluation).

TABLE 3.1   **FIVE KINDS OF LEARNED CAPABILITIES**

Capability	Examples of Performance
Intellectual Skill	Identifying the diagonal of a rectangle
	Demonstrating use of objective case of pronoun following a preposition
Cognitive Strategy	Using an image link to learn a foreign equivalent to an English word
	Rearranging a verbally stated problem by working backward
Verbal Information	Stating the provisions of the Fourth Amendment to the U.S. Constitution
	Listing the events of instruction
Attitude	Choosing to read science fiction
	Choosing running as a regular form of exercise
Motor Skill	Jumping rope
	Printing the letter E

Learning an intellectual skill means acquiring the capability to *do* something. Generally, this kind of learning is called *procedural knowledge* (Anderson, 1985). Such learning contrasts with learning *that* something exists or has certain properties, which is called *verbal information* or *declarative knowledge.* Learning how to identify a sonnet by its rhyme pattern is an intellectual skill, whereas learning what the sonnet says is an instance of verbal information. A learner may, of course, learn both, and often does, but it is possible for a person to learn how to do the first (identify a sonnet) without being able to do the second (state what a particular sonnet says). Likewise, as teachers know well, it is possible for a student to learn the second without being able to do the first. For these reasons, it is important to maintain this distinction between knowing how to *do* and knowing *that,* even while recognizing that a particular unit of instruction may involve both skills as expected learning outcomes.

Another example of an intellectual skill may be given here. A student of the English language learns at some point in his studies what a metaphor is. If instruction is adequate, the student learns to create metaphors to convey meaning descriptively. (In Chapter 4, we identify this particular subcategory of intellectual skill as *rule using.*) In other words, the student has learned to apply or transfer knowledge of metaphor, which increases the ability to communicate ideas. This skill, then, has become a component of further learning and now may contribute to the learning of more complex intellectual skills, such as writing illustrative sentences, describing scenes and events, and composing essays.

If one wishes to know whether the student has learned this intellectual skill, one must observe *performance.* Usually this is done by asking the student to "show what a metaphor is" in one or more specific instances. In this case, the student might be asked to use a metaphor to describe (1) a cat's movements, (2) a cloudy day, or perhaps (3) the moon's surface.

Cognitive Strategies

Cognitive strategies are special and very important kinds of skills. They are the capabilities that govern the individual's own learning, remembering, and thinking behavior. For example, they control behavior when reading with the intent to learn and the internal methods used to "get to the heart of a problem." The phrase *cognitive strategy* is usually attributed to Bruner (Bruner, Goodnow, & Austin, 1956). Rothkopf (1971) has named these cognitive strategies "mathemagenic behaviors," and Skinner (1968) "self-management behaviors." One expects that such skills will improve over a relatively long period of time as the individual engages in more and more study, learning, and thinking. A good example of a cognitive strategy, shown in Table 3.1, is the use of images as links to connect words in the learning of foreign-language vocabulary (Atkinson, 1975). Jeroen van Merriënboer et al. (2003) defines cognitive strategies used in complex learning tasks as *problem-solving strategies.* In order to develop these strategies, he indicates that "supportive information" is helpful. Supportive information might consist of models, cases, and examples of problems and their solutions that help the learner develop mental models of the component processes of the complex behavior.

It appears that most cognitive strategies are *domain specific*. For example, there are strategies for aiding the solution of word problems in arithmetic, for helping the composition of effective sentences, and many others that focus on particular domains of learning tasks and do not normally transfer to other domains. However, some cognitive strategies are more general, like study strategies that can be used for many different types of learning, such as the Survey, Question, Read, Recite, Review (SQ3R) text-reading strategy.

However, learning a cognitive strategy such as SQ3R is apparently not completed on a single occasion. Instead, this kind of capability develops over a fairly long period of time. Presumably, the learner must have a number of experiences with induction in widely different situations for the strategy to become dependably useful.

Cognitive strategies are often developed from experience. Pejtersen, Dunlop, and Fidel (1999) classified five strategies students use in retrieving information from the Web: browsing, analytical, empirical, known site, and similarity. Though the students had been taught Web-search strategies by a teacher and a librarian, as individuals they still approached search tasks in different ways. Pejtersen et al. concluded that if the student's approach is successful, that is, if it satisfies the situation, it becomes a pattern of behavior in similar situations.

Metacognition is a special type of cognitive strategy. Metacognition is the "cognition of cognition" or the self-monitoring of the cognitive process. Strategies such as reflection and self-regulation are metacognitive processes, and they are important when considering how distance learners, for example, will monitor their progress in a course. Support for metacognitive processes might include reflective questions in the instructional materials that help students to attend to components of the learning task. For example, "Are the objectives of this assignment clear to you?" and "Can you describe to another person the gist of the chapter you just read?" The degree to which these types of questions support metacognitive processes is not very well researched.

Verbal Information

Verbal information is the kind of knowledge we are able to state. It is *knowing that*, or *declarative knowledge*. All of us have learned a great deal of verbal information or verbal knowledge. We have readily available in our memories many commonly used items of information, such as the names of months, days of the week, letters, numerals, towns, cities, states, countries, and so on. We also have a great store of more highly organized information, such as many events of or nation's history, the forms of government, the major achievements of science and technology, and the components of the economy. The verbal information we learn in school is in part "for the course only" and in part the kind of knowledge we are expected to be able to recall readily as adults.

The learner usually acquires a great deal of information from formal instruction. Much is also learned in an incidental fashion. Such information is stored in the learner's memory, but it is not necessarily "memorized" in the sense that it can be repeated verbatim. Something like the gist of paragraph-long passages is stored in memory and recalled when the occasion demands. The examples given in Table 3.1 refer to the ability to recall what the Fourth Amendment says and the ability to recall the events of instruction from memory. Students of science, for example, learn a large amount of verbal information. They learn the properties of materials, objects, and living things. These science facts alone are rather lower-level learning, however, the ability to recall them from memory aids the learning of higher-order intellectual skills.

For example, a student may learn that "the boiling point of water is 100 °C." One major function of such information is to provide the learner with directions for how to proceed in further learning. Thus, in learning about the change of state of materials from liquid to gaseous form, the learner may be acquiring an intellectual skill (that is, a *rule*) that relates atmospheric pressure to vaporization. In working with this relationship, a student may be asked to apply the rule to a situation that describes the temperature of boiling water at an altitude of 9,000 feet. At this juncture, the *information* given in the example must be recalled in order to proceed with the application of the rule. One may be inclined to say this information is not particularly important; rather, the learning of the *intellectual skill is* the important thing. There is no disagreement over this point. However, the *information is essential* to these events. The learner must have such information available to learn a particular application.

Inert Ideas   Alfred North Whitehead is credited with coining the term *inert ideas* or *inert knowledge* (Whitehead, 1929). Inert ideas are "ideas received into the mind without being utilized, or tested, or thrown into fresh combinations." It is clear that verbal information that is not used or practiced is quickly forgotten, because it has no meaningful context associated with it. We agree with Whitehead. Information is remembered better when it is used, contiguously with some stimulus, so that it can be encoded and retrieved.

Information is important for the transfer of learning from one situation to another. For example, a student of government may hit upon the idea that the persistence of bureaucracy bears some resemblance to the growth of an abscess in the human body. If he or she has some information about abscesses, such an analogy may make it possible to think of causal relationships pertaining to bureaucracies that would not otherwise be possible. A variety of cognitive strategies and intellectual skills may now be brought to bear on this problem by the student, and new knowledge is thereby generated. The initial transfer in such an instance is made possible by an "association of ideas," in other words, by the possession and use of certain classes of information.

Finding out whether students have learned some particular fact or some particular organized items of information is a matter of observing whether they can communicate them. The simplest way to do this, of course, is to ask for a statement of the information either orally or in writing. This is the basic method commonly employed by a teacher to assess what information has been learned. In the early grades, assessing the communications children can make may require the use of simple oral questions. Pictures and objects that the child can point to and manipulate may also be employed.

Motor Skills

Another kind of capability we expect human beings to learn is a *motor skill* (Fitts & Posner, 1967; Singer, 1980). The individual learns to skate, to ride a bicycle, to steer an automobile, to use a can opener, to jump rope. There are also motor skills to be learned as part of formal school instruction, such as printing letters (Table 3.1), drawing a straight line, or aligning a pointer on a dial face. Despite the fact that school instruction is so largely concerned with intellectual functions, we do not expect a well-educated adult to be lacking in certain motor skills (such as writing) that may be used every day. A motor skill is one of the most obvious kinds of human capabilities. Children learn a motor skill for each printed letter they make with a pencil on paper. The function of the skill, as a capability, is simply to make possible the motor performance. Of course, these motor performances may themselves lead to further learning. For example, students employ the skill of printing letters when they are learning to make (and print) words and sentences.

The acquisition of a motor skill can be reasonably inferred when students can perform the act in a variety of contexts. Thus, if youngsters have acquired the skill of printing the letter E, they should be able to perform this motor act with a pen, a pencil, or a crayon, on any flat surface, constructing letters with a range of sizes. Obviously, one would not want to conclude that the skill has been learned from a single instance of an E printed with pencil on a particular piece of paper. But several Es, in several contexts, observably distinct from Fs or Hs, provide convincing evidence that this kind of capability has been learned.

Attitudes

Turning now to what is often called the *affective domain* (Krathwohl, Bloom, & Masia, 1964), we identify a class of learned capabilities called *attitudes*. All of us possess attitudes of many sorts toward various things, persons, and situations. The effect of an attitude is to amplify an individual's positive or negative reaction toward some person, thing, or situation. The strength of people's attitudes toward some item may be indicated by the frequency with which they *choose* or *avoid* that item in a variety of circumstances. Thus, an individual with a strong attitude toward helping other people will offer help in many situations, whereas a person with a weaker attitude of this sort will tend to restrict offers of help in fewer situations. The schools are often expected to establish socially approved attitudes, such as respect for other people, cooperativeness, personal responsibility, as well as positive attitudes toward knowledge and learning and an attitude of self-efficacy.

A student learns to have preferences for various kinds of activities, preferring certain people to others, showing an interest in certain events rather than others. One infers from a set of such observations that the student has *attitudes* toward objects, persons, or events that influence the choice of courses of action toward them. Naturally, many such attitudes are acquired outside of the school, and there are many that schools cannot appropriately consider relevant to their instructional function. As one possibility, though, school instruction may have the objective of establishing positive attitudes toward subjects being studied (for example, Mager,

1968). Often, too, school learning is successful in modifying attitudes toward activities that provide aesthetic enjoyment. One of the examples of Table 3.1 (on page 49) is a choice of reading a particular kind of fiction.

Considered as a human capability, an attitude is a persisting state that predisposes an individual's choice behavior. A positive attitude toward being healthy makes the student *tend* to choose to exercise on a regular schedule when possible. Of course, this does not mean he or she will always be exercising. Rather, it means that the probability of a choice to exercise is noticeably high. If one were able to observe the student over an extended period of time, one would be able to note that the choice of this activity was relatively frequent. From such a set of observations, it could be concluded that the student had a positive attitude toward exercising.

In practice, of course, making such a set of observations about a single student, not to mention a class of students, would be exceedingly time consuming and therefore expensive. As a result, inferences about the possession of attitudes are usually made on the basis of "self-reports." These may be obtained by means of questionnaires that ask students what choices of action they would make (or in some cases, *did* make) in a variety of situations. There are, of course, technical problems in the use of self-reports for attitude assessment. Because their intentions are rather obvious, students can readily make self-reports of choices that do not reflect reality. However, when proper precautions are taken, such as anonymous responses, such reports make possible the inference that a particular attitude has been learned or modified in a particular direction.

Thus, the performance that is affected by an attitude is the *choice of a course of personal action*. The tendency to make such a choice, toward a particular class of objects, persons, or events, may be stronger in one student than in another. A change in an attitude would be revealed as a change in the probability of choosing a particular course of action on the part of the student. Continuing the previous example, over a period of time or as a result of instruction, the probability of choosing to exercise may be altered. The observation of such change would give rise to the inference that the student's attitude toward exercising had changed, that is, had become "stronger" in the positive direction.

Attitude Training in the Military   Attitude and core-value instruction is the apex of military training. The values of loyalty, duty, respect, service before self, honor, integrity, and personal courage have been the hallmark of the American soldier for over 223 years (U.S. Army Posture Statement, 2000). Servicemen and women must learn to meet the demands and mission of the military profession even when it is hazardous. They must learn to make decisions that are in the best interest of the armed service and nation, without regard to personal consequences. They must learn to obey orders; to care for the safety, professional, personal, and spiritual well-being of people; and to show respect toward all people without regard to race, religion, or gender (U.S. Navy Core Values, 2003).

Over the years, the military has altered the instructional methods and strategies for core value and attitude training to reflect the generational differences in servicemen and women's attitudes toward career, family, and lifestyle. The way the military trained career-driven "baby boomers" (1943–1960) is different from the way they trained family/personal life-oriented "generation X'ers" (1961–1980), which is different from the way they train community and technology-minded "millennials" (born after 1980). Older members of the millenial generation are just now entering military service, and they bring with them variations on attitudes and commitments to military service, family life, and community values. This, coupled with a learning style conditioned by advances in digital technologies and other rapid technical and social changes in the larger culture, is requiring military leaders to again rethink instructional methods and strategies for core value and attitude training. Emphasis should be aimed at supporting the balance of work and family time to the extent compatible with mission readiness (Command Briefing Resources, 2000).

The military has always relied heavily on role modeling as a method for delivering core value instruction. Basic-training instructors demonstrate proper behaviors and continually articulate the military service philosophy, namely, that core values and mission dedication are common denominators to building mutual commitment, respect, and trust in any unit. In recent years, realistic simulation exercises and interactive war games have been introduced to reinforce core values and attitudes. For example, the Navy's "Battle Stations" has been specifically designed to galvanize the basic warrior attributes of sacrifice, dedication, teamwork, and endurance. The Army is currently developing "Crimson Storm," a first-person shooter game aimed at illustrating the negative impact of illegal drugs on the combat soldier.

Human Capabilities as Course Goals

A single course of instruction usually has objectives that fit into several categories of human capability. The major categories, which cut across the "content" of courses, are the five we have described. From the standpoint of the expected outcomes of instruction, the major reason for distinguishing these five categories is that they *make possible different kinds of human performance.* For example, a course in elementary science may foresee as general objectives such learning outcomes as (1) solving problems of velocity, time, and acceleration; (2) designing an experiment to provide a scientific test of a stated hypothesis; or (3) valuing the activities of science. Number one obviously names *intellectual skills* and, therefore, implies some performances involving intellectual operations the student can demonstrate. Number two pertains to the use of *problem solving*, because it implies that the student will need to generate this complex performance in a novel situation where little guidance is provided in the selection and use of rules and concepts previously learned. Number three has to do with an *attitude,* or possibly with a set of attitudes, that will be exhibited in behavior as choices of actions directed toward science activities.

The human capabilities distinguished in these five categories also differ from each other in another highly important way. They each require a *different set of learning conditions* for their efficient learning. The conditions necessary for learning these capabilities efficiently, and the distinctions among these conditions, constitute the subjects of the next two chapters. There, we give an account of the conditions of learning that apply to the acquisition of each of these kinds of human capability, beginning with intellectual skills and cognitive strategies and following with the remaining three categories.

DESIGNING INSTRUCTION USING HUMAN CAPABILITIES

The point of view presented in this chapter is that instruction should always be designed to meet accepted educational or training goals. When goals are matched with societal needs, an ideal condition exists for the planning of a total program of education. Were such an undertaking to be attempted, the result would be, as a first step, a list of activities, each of which would have associated with it an estimate of its importance in meeting the needs of the society.

Needs Analysis

The process of determining needs is called *needs analysis*. According to Kaufman, Herman, & Watters (2002), it is important to differentiate wants from needs. A need, according to Kaufman et al., is a gap between some desired state of affairs, and what currently exists. For instance, if it is desired that all third graders are reading up to grade level, and only 80 percent in fact are, there exists a gap between the desired situation and the current state of affairs. Needs analysis is an important concept because it not only identifies desirable goals, but it also attempts to quantify the current state of affairs so that progress towards meeting the goals can be measured.

When human activities derived from societal needs are in turn analyzed, they yield a set of *human capabilities*. These are descriptions of what human adults in a particular society ought to *know* and particularly what they ought to *know how* to do. Such a set of capabilities would probably not bear a close resemblance to the traditional subject-matter categories of the school curriculum. There would, of course, be a relationship between human capabilities and the subjects of the curriculum, but it would probably not be a simple correspondence.

Most instructional design, as currently carried out, centers upon *course* planning and design. We shall use such a framework in this book. However, we shall continue to maintain an orientation toward the goals of instruction. Learning outcomes cannot always be adequately identified, it appears, by the titles of courses. They *can* be identified as the varieties of learned human capabilities that make possible different types of human performances. Accordingly, the present chapter has provided an introduction to the five major categories of capabilities that will serve throughout the book as the basic framework of instructional design.

With the exception of motor skills, *all* of these categories are likely to be involved in the planning of any course. One cannot have a course without information, and one cannot have a course that doesn't affect attitudes to some degree. And most importantly, one cannot have a course without intellectual skills.

There are a couple of reasons why intellectual skills play a central role in designing the structure of a course of study. First, they are the kinds of capabilities that determine what the student can do and thus are intimately bound up with the description of a course in terms of its learning outcomes. A second reason is that intellectual skills have a *cumulative* nature; they build upon each other in a predictable manner. Accordingly, they provide the most useful model for the sequencing of course structure. In the next chapter, we begin to look more closely at intellectual skills: "What kinds are there?" "How can they be learned?" and "How does one know when they are learned?"

Summary

This chapter has shown that defining goals for education and training is a complex problem. In part, this is because so much is expected of education. Some people would like education to emphasize the importance of understanding the history of mankind, others would like it to perpetuate the present culture or present academic disciplines; some would stress the need to help children and young adults adjust to a rapidly changing society, and others would hope that education could prepare students to become agents improving themselves and the society in which they live.

One source of complexity in defining educational goals arises from the need to translate goals from the very general to the increasingly specific. Many layers of such goals would be needed to be sure that each topic in the curriculum actually moves the learner a step closer to the distant goal. Probably, this mapping has never been done completely for any curriculum. Thus, there tend to be large gaps from general goals to the specific objectives for courses in the curriculum. A major problem remains—the need to define course objectives in the absence of an entire network of connections between the most general goals and the specific course objectives.

Despite the involved nature of this problem, means are available for classifying course objectives into categories that then make it possible to examine the scope of types of human capabilities the course is intended to develop. One purpose of such taxonomies (sets of performance categories) is to evaluate the objectives themselves in their entirety. The taxonomy presented in this chapter contains the following categories of learned capabilities:

1. Intellectual skills
2. Cognitive strategies
3. Verbal information
4. Motor skills
5. Attitudes

The usefulness of learning each of these types of capabilities has been discussed and will be treated in greater detail in later chapters.

Uses of such a taxonomy, in addition to evaluating of the variety of capabilities a course is intended to produce in the learner, include the following:

1. Grouping specific objectives of a similar nature together and, thus, reducing the work needed to design a total instructional strategy
2. Grouping objectives to aid in determining the sequence of segments of a course of study
3. Grouping objectives into types of capabilities that can then be utilized to plan the internal and external conditions of learning estimated to be required for successful learning

Each performance objective of a course defines a unique performance expected as an outcome of the instruction. By grouping objectives into the five categories of capabilities that have been described, one also can assess the adequacy of coverage in each category while capitalizing upon the fact that the conditions of learning are the same for each objective within that category.

Identification of the conditions of learning for each type of human capability is the main topic of the next two chapters.

REFERENCES

Anderson, J. R. (1985). *Cognitive psychology and its implications* (2nd ed.). San Francisco: Freeman.

Atkinson, R. C. (1975). Mnemotechnics in second language learning. *American Psychologist, 30,* 821–828.

Bloom, B. S., Hastings, J. T., & Madaus, G. F. (1971). *Handbook on formative and summative evaluation of student learning.* New York: McGraw-Hill.

Bruner, J. S., Goodnow, J. J., & Austin, G. A. (1956). *A study of thinking.* New York: Wiley.

Command Briefing Resources (2000). Retrieved from: http://mfrc.calib.com/healthyparenting/cornell/generational/gn00.cfm.

Fitts, P. M., & Posner, M. I. (1967). *Human performance.* Belmont, CA: Brooks/Cole.

Gagné, R. M. (1985). *The conditions of learning* (4th ed.). New York: Holt, Rinehart and Winston.

Kaufman, R., Herman, J., & Watters, K. (2002). *Educational planning: Strategic, tactical, and operational.* Landham, MD: Scarecrow Press.

Krathwohl, D. R., Bloom, B. S., & Masia, B. B. (1964). *Taxonomy of educational objectives. Handbook II: Affective domain.* New York: McKay.

Mager, R. F. (1968). *Developing attitude toward learning.* Belmont, CA: Fearon.

Mager, R. F. (1975). *Preparing objectives for instruction* (2nd ed.). Belmont, CA: Fearon.

National Assessment Governing Board (1993). The National Education Goals Report. Retrieved on 12/12/2003 from: http://www.ed.gov/pubs/goals/report/goalsrpt.txt.

OHRM Report (2003a). A Commitment to Learning: Planning Training Strategically. Retrieved on 12/12/03 from: http://ohrm.doc.gov/employees/training/resources/smtms.htm.

OHRM Report (2003b). A guide for strategically planning training and measuring results. Retrieved on 12/12/03 from: http://tri.army.mil/LC/LCB/Bp/BPT/website/spguide.pdf.

Pejtersen, A. M., Dunlop, M., & Fidel, R. (1999). A Use Centered Approach to Evaluation of the Web. Paper presented at the ACM SIGIR Workshop on "Evaluation of Web Document Retrieval" at Berkeley, August 14–18, 1999, 8 pp.

Popham, W. J., & Baker, E. L. (1970). *Establishing instructional goals.* Englewood Cliffs, NJ: Prentice Hall.

Rothkopf, E. Z. (1971). Experiments on mathemagenic behavior and the technology of written instruction. In E. Z. Rothkopf & P. E. Johnson (Eds.), *Verbal learning research and the technology of written instruction.* New York: Teachers College.

Singer, R. N. (1980). *Motor learning and human performance* (3rd ed.). New York: Macmillan.

Skinner, B. F. (1968). *The technology of teaching.* New York: Appleton.

U.S. Army Posture Statement. (2003). Retrieved on 10/1/2003 from: http://www.army.mil/aps/2003/index.html

U.S. Navy Core Values. (2003). Retrieved on 10/1/2003 from: http://www.chinfo.navy.mil/navpalib/traditions/html/corvalu.html.

van Merriënboer, J. J. G., Clark, R. E., & de Croock, M. B. M. (2002). Blueprints for Complex Learning, The 4C/ID—Model. ETR&D, Vol. 50, No. 2. pp. 39–64.

Vet Jobs. (1999). Retrieved on 10/1/2003 from: http://66.45.115.142/emphire2.htm.

Whitehead, A. N. (1929). *The aims of education*. New York: Macmillan.

VARIETIES OF LEARNING

Intellectual Skills and Strategies

When one begins to think about the application of learning principles to instruction, there is no better guide than to ask the question, What is to be learned? We have seen that the answer to this question may, in any given instance, fall into one of five general categories: (1) intellectual skills, (2) cognitive strategies, (3) verbal information, (4) motor skills, or (5) attitudes. In this chapter, we intend to consider the conditions affecting the learning of intellectual skills, which are of central importance to school learning, and which in addition provide the best structural model for instructional design. It is a reasonable step to proceed, then, to a consideration of cognitive strategies, which are a special kind of intellectual skill deserving of a separate categorization. In Chapter 5, we will consider the learning requirements for the remaining three categories of human capabilities.

THE NEED TO CATEGORIZE TYPES OF LEARNING OUTCOMES

Most educators are familiar with Benjamin Bloom's categorization of three domains of learning (Bloom et al, 1956): cognitive domain, affective domain, and psychomotor domain. The cognitive domain was further divided into six types of learning: knowledge, comprehension, application, analysis, synthesis, and evaluation. Bloom conceived of this "taxonomy" as being hierarchical, with knowledge being the least complex type of objective on the hierarchy and evaluation being the most complex. The bottom three levels: knowledge, comprehension, and application, are sometimes referred to as lower-order learning skills, and the top three as higher-order learning skills. Bloom's taxonomy is slightly different from Gagné's classification scheme. First, Gagné considers verbal information a separate domain of learning and not a part of a skills hierarchy. Second, comprehension, application, analysis, synthesis, and evaluation are not reflected in similar ways in the Gagné intellectual skills domain. Gagné would probably see comprehension, application, analysis, synthesis, and evaluation as processes used to demonstrate learning, as opposed to types of learned capabilities. Table 4.1 attempts to compare Bloom's

| TABLE 4.1 | **A COMPARISON OF BLOOM'S TAXONOMY AND GAGNÉ'S TYPES OF LEARNING FOR THE COGNITIVE DOMAIN** |

Bloom	**Gagné**
Evaluation	Cognitive strategy, problem solving, rule using
Synthesis	Problem solving
Analysis	Rule using
Application	Rule using
Comprehension	Defined concepts, concrete concepts, and discriminations,
Knowledge	Verbal information

cognitive domain categories with Gagné's (1995) learning classification scheme. The table shows that comprehension, application, analysis, and synthesis, cut across many of Gagné's domains of learning.

Why try to categorize types of learning? One purpose is to clarify our thinking and improve the process of writing desired outcomes. It is not enough to say that a student will understand the process of long division. What level of "understanding" are we talking about? If we want students to be able to apply rules, not simply recall them, we should have a way of stating the learning objective so the intent is clearly understood by anyone who reads it. It would be clear also, that the application cannot be tested by asking the student to, "List the steps for doing long division." Even if students must first know the rules, this knowledge may be an insufficient condition for applying them. The purposes for developing a taxonomy of objectives, as stated by Bloom, were to, "help curriculum builders plan learning experiences and prepare evaluation devices; to clarify the meaning of a learning objective (what level of "understanding" is trying to be achieved); and to provide a framework for research on teaching and learning, in terms of remembering, thinking and problem solving" (Bloom et al., 1956, pp. 2,3).

Bloom's work preceded Gagné's development of the domains of learning outcomes, and the adoption of information processing theory as a theory of learning. Gagné was looking more at the structure of knowledge, as opposed to categories suggested by Bloom. Gagné differentiated between declarative knowledge (recall) and procedural knowledge (rule using). He did not see declarative knowledge as part of a hierarchy, although it was clearly a different type of learning that was important in facilitating the attainment of intellectual skills. However, he did believe procedural knowledge can best be explained as information relating to a hierarchy of rules, what he called "intellectual skills."

The Nature of a Hierarchy of Learned Capabilities

What Gagné means by a hierarchy of skills is that performance of the lower-level skills of the hierarchy are *prerequisites* for performance at the higher levels. Because problem solving involves the use of rules, the rules have to be learned prior to successful problem solving. Although this has implications for instructional sequencing, it does not mean that students can't first be presented with a problem they do not have the prerequisites to solve–this would be an instructional strategy. It does mean, however, that during the process of solving the problem they will be developing new rules, and that if they are successful, these rules should transfer to similar problems.

Gagné's (1985) taxonomy is less well known in education than Bloom et al.'s (1956). However, it holds a number of advantages for the instructional designer, as we will show.

An intellectual skill is a class of learned capabilities that makes it possible for an individual to respond to and describe the environment through symbols, for example, through language, numbers, and so on. Words "stand for" objects, actions, and relations among objects (for example, "above," "behind," and "within.") Likewise, numbers represent quantities, and symbols (for example, +, =, x^2) are used to represent relations among these quantities. Other kinds of symbols, such as lines, arrows, and circles, are frequently used to represent spatial relationships. Individuals communicate aspects of their experience to others by using such symbols. Symbol using is one of the major ways people remember and think about the world in which they live.

TYPES OF INTELLECTUAL SKILLS

The intellectual skills learned by the individual during school years are many, surely numbering in the thousands. One can appreciate this fact by thinking of a single domain—language skills. Topics of instruction such as oral reading, expressive reading, sentence composition, paragraph construction, conversing, and persuasive speaking contain scores of specific intellectual skills that must be learned. This is also true of skills within the various fields of mathematics. Many skills of spatial and temporal patterning form a part of such subjects as geometry and physics. In dealing with intellectual skills, one must be prepared to look at the "fine-grained" structure of human intellectual functioning.

In whatever domain of subject matter they occur, intellectual skills can be categorized by complexity. For example, suppose that a learner is shown two similar but different images and is instructed how to tell them apart. Later, when the images are presented again, the learner should be able to point out the differences. The kind of mental processing required is not very complex. One can infer that what has been learned in this situation, and can later be recalled, is a "discrimination."

Quite a different level of complexity is indicated by the following example: Following instruction, the learner is able to comprehend adjectives in the German language that he or she has never before encountered, by adding the suffix *lich* (as with gemüt–gemütlich). This kind of performance is often referred to as *rule governed* because the kind of mental processing it requires is "applying a rule." It is not necessary for the learner to state the rule. However, the learner is performing in a way that implies that he or she must have learned an internal capability, called a rule, that suggests the behavior is rule governed. Obviously, such a process is more complex than the process of discrimination referred to in the previous paragraph.

Different levels of complexity of mental processing, then, make possible the classification of intellectual skills. Such categories cut across and are independent of types of subject matter. How many levels of complexity of intellectual processing can be distinguished or need to be? For most instructional purposes, the useful distinctions among intellectual skills are shown in Figure 4–1.

Learning affects the intellectual development of the individual in the manner suggested by Figure 4–1. In solving problems for which instruction has prepared them, learners are acquiring some higher-order rules (that is, complex rules). Problem solving requires that they recall some simpler, previously learned rules and defined concepts. To acquire these rules, they must have learned some concrete concepts, and to learn these concepts, they must be able to retrieve some previously learned discriminations. For example, the reader who is confronted with the problem of figuring out the pronunciation of an unfamiliar printed word must bring to bear on this problem some previously learned rules (decoding skills), whose learning has in turn required the prerequisite of identifying the word components, called phonemes (defined concept), and printed letters (concrete concepts). The child who is learning to identify a letter such as a printed E must be able to see a difference (to discriminate) between an E and an F or even an L. The E is a symbol and it is also a concrete concept. It is in a class of letters that has certain physical characteristics that make it different from other letters. A child who cannot detect the differences between an "E" and a "D" can not be expected to detect differences in other letters.

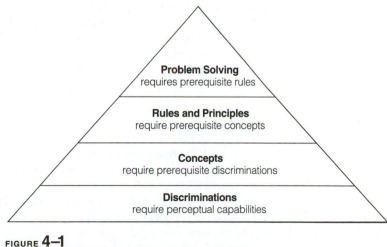

FIGURE **4–1**
LEVELS OF COMPLEXITY IN INTELLECTUAL SKILLS

Discriminations

A discrimination is the capability of detecting differences in stimuli along one or more physical or sensory dimensions. In the simplest case, the person indicates by responding that two stimuli are the same or different. Examples in secondary and adult education may occur with stimuli encountered in art, music, foreign languages, and science. Industrial examples pertain to the discrimination of differences in woods, metals, textiles, papers, forms of printing, and a host of others.

Discrimination is often a regular part of instruction for children in early school grades. Matching to a sample is another variant form of the discrimination task. The child may be asked to "select the block that has the same color as this one" from a group of blocks of various colors. In beginning music instruction, the child may be asked to learn to discriminate whether two successive tones are the same or different in pitch.

Discrimination is a very basic kind of intellectual skill. Deliberate practice in making discriminations is undertaken most frequently for young children. As far as most school learning is concerned, relevant discriminations are usually assumed to have been learned early in life. Every once in a while, however, one is surprised to realize that certain elementary discriminations may not have been learned and cannot be assumed. Does the learner of the French uvular and frontal *r* actually hear this distinction (that is, has it been learned as a discrimination)? Has the biology student using a microscope actually seen the distinction between the bright and dark boundary that will later be identified as a cell wall? Can the untrained adult discriminate between the taste of a Chardonnay and a Chablis?

In describing the characteristics of a discrimination, as well as other types of intellectual skills to follow, we need to account for three components of the learning situation:

1. The performance that is acquired or to be acquired. What is it that the learner will be able to do after learning that he or she was not able to do before?
2. The internal conditions that must be present for the learning to occur. These consist of capabilities that are recalled from the learner's memory and that then become integrated into the newly acquired capability.
3. The external conditions that provide stimulation to the learner. These may be visually present objects, symbols, pictures, sounds, or meaningful verbal communications.

The conditions of learning for discriminations are described in Table 4.2.

Concrete Concepts

A concept is a capability that makes it possible for an individual to identify a stimulus as a member of a class having some characteristic in common, even though such stimuli may otherwise differ from each other markedly. A concrete concept identifies an object property or object attribute (color, shape, and so on). Such concepts are called concrete because the performance they require is "recognition" of a physical object property.

Examples of object properties are round, square, blue, three, smooth, curved, flat, and so on. One can tell whether a concrete concept has been learned by asking

TABLE 4.2	CONDITIONS OF LEARNING FOR DISCRIMINATIONS
Performance	There must be a response that indicates that the learner can distinguish stimuli that differ on one or more physical dimensions. Often, this is an indication of "same" or "different."
Internal Conditions	On the sensory side, the physical difference must give rise to different patterns of brain activity. Otherwise, the individual must have available only the responses necessary to indicate that the difference is detectable, as in saying "same" and "different." Other possible responses include pointing, making a checkmark, or drawing a circle around a pictured object. An inability to learn a discrimination might indicate a disability, like color-blindness or tone deafness.
External Conditions	To teach discriminations, the instruction has to have the student practice seeing, smelling, tasting, hearing, or feeling differences among stimuli. The instruction might include the following: 1. Informing learners of what they will be working on. For example, "Today we are going to work on tasting differences between different spices." 2. Presenting stimuli and have the student indicate if they are the same or different. 3. Aid the discrimination by noting subtle differences. For example, "This tastes something like the last one but note how it is a bit more bitter." 4. Allow the student to practice making the discriminations with feedback, or example, having them match similar spices.

the individual to identify, by "pointing to" two or more members belonging to the same object-property class; for example, to identify "round" by pointing to a penny, an automobile tire, and the full moon. The operation of pointing may be carried out practically in many different ways; it is a matter of choosing, checking, circling, or grasping. Frequently, pointing is carried out by naming (labeling). Thus, the particular response made by the individual is of no consequence, so long as it can be assumed that he or she knows how to do it.

An important variety of concrete concept is object position. This can be conceived as an object property because it can be identified by pointing. It is clear, however, that the position of an object must be in relation to that of another object. Examples of object positions are above, below, beside, surrounding, right, left, middle, on, in front of. Obviously, one can ask that such positional characteristics be "pointed to" in some manner or other. Thus, object positions qualify as concrete concepts.

The distinction between a discrimination and a concept is easy to appreciate: The first is "responding to a difference"; the second is identifying something by name or other ways. A person may have learned to tell the difference between a triangle and a rectangle drawn on a piece of paper. These may be seen as different figures by choosing, pointing, or otherwise responding differentially. Such a performance permits only the conclusion that the person can discriminate between these particular figures. To test whether the concept *triangle* has been learned, however, one would need to ask the person to identify several figures exhibiting this property—figures that otherwise differ widely in their other qualities, such as size, color, border thickness, and so on. In other words, acquiring a concrete concept means that the individual is capable of identifying the class of object properties.

The capability of identifying concrete concepts is fundamentally significant for more complex learning. Many investigators have emphasized the importance of "concrete learning" as a prerequisite to "the learning of abstract ideas." Piaget (1950) made this distinction a key idea in his theory of intellectual development. The acquisition of concepts by definition (to be described next) requires that the learner be able to identify the referents of the words used in such definitions. Thus, to acquire the concept "rim" by way of the definition "the edge of a round thing," the learner must have as prerequisites the concrete concepts "edge" and "round." If the learner is not able to identify these concepts concretely, it will not be possible for him or her in any true or complete sense to "know the meaning" of rim. The conditions of learning for concrete concepts are described below in Table 4.3.

TABLE 4.3	CONDITIONS OF LEARNING FOR CONCRETE CONCEPTS
Performance	The student identifies a class of object properties, including object positions, by "pointing to" two or more members of the class. The "pointing" may be done in any of a number of ways (checking, circling, and so on) equivalent only in the sense that identification occurs. Examples: (1) Present a number of types of wine and ask for identification of the "dry" wine; (2) given a 10-word sentence containing many fonts, circle all the "o"s.
Internal Conditions	In acquiring a concrete concept, discriminations must be recalled. In addition, attributes of the concept being learned must be compared to the relevant attributes of the item to be categorized. Thus, an individual who is learning the concept of "dry " must be able to discriminate the taste of different wines, recognize the taste of a "dry" wine, and ignore the color.
External Conditions	Instruction for a concrete concept involves: 1. Informing the student what concept they will be learning. 2. Presenting instances (examples) of the concept, emphasizing relevant attributes. 3. Presenting potentially confusing nonexamples and explaining why they are not instances of the concept. 4. Allowing the student to practice application of the concept by identifying instances. 5. Providing spaced practice for retention and transfer.

Defined Concepts

Another kind of concept is one that cannot be identified by physical attributes, concepts like *love, mother, family, jealousy, empathy, conservative, democracy*. You can't pick them up, or identify them by pointing to them. Although we can classify instances of behavior or language into these categories, they are classified more from a definition than they are by their physical attributes.

The definition of a defined concept is a verbal statement of the attributes and relationships among them. For example, *Merriam-Webster's New Collegiate Dictionary*, 10th edition, defines *conservative* as "(a) of or relating to a philosophy of conservatism, (b) of or constituting a political party professing the principles of conservatism." It further defines *conservatism* as "(1) the principles and policies of a conservative political party, (2) a disposition in politics to preserve what is established, (3) the tendency to prefer an existing or traditional situation to change."

If you wanted to determine if someone fit the definition of a conservative what attributes would you look for? One might be a philosophy equivalent to leaving things alone or going back to the way things were. A second might be whether they prefer traditional situations to change. And, a third might be whether they belong to a political party (such as Republican) that prefers traditional situations to change. Now you can see how difficult it would be to point to a conservative unless there was a physical characteristic that they all shared (such as all conservatives wear gray coats and blue ties). However, by knowing something about the individual's philosophy, we might be able to categorize them as conservative (fitting that definition) or not.

For another example, consider the concept *alien*, a citizen of a foreign country. An individual who has learned the concept will be able to classify a particular person in accordance with the definition by showing that that person is currently in a country of which he is not a citizen and that he is a citizen of some other country. The demonstration may involve verbal reference to the definition, and this is an adequate demonstration when one assumes that the individual knows the meaning of the words *citizen*, *other*, and *country*. Should it be the case that such knowledge cannot be assumed, it might be necessary to ask for the demonstration in other terms, such as a response to a verbal scenario. Demonstration of the meaning distinguishes this kind of mental processing from the kind involved in memorized verbal information, such as the statement, "An alien is a citizen of a foreign country."

Some defined concepts have corresponding concrete concepts that carry the same name and possess certain features in common. For example, many young children learn the basic shape of a triangle as a concrete concept. Not until much later in studying geometry do they encounter the defined concept of triangle, "a closed plane figure formed by three line segments that intersect at three points." The concrete and defined meanings of *triangle* are not exactly the same, yet they overlap considerably.

Another example of a defined concept is "boundary line," the definition of which may be stated as "a line marking where an area ends." This concept must be demonstrated for an external observer to know that it has been learned. Such a demonstration by the learner would consist, essentially, of (1) identifying an area, either by pointing to a piece of ground or a map, or by drawing one on paper;

(2) identifying a line that shows the limits of the area; and (3) demonstrating the meaning of "end," by showing that passage of a moving object is brought to a stop at the line.

Why doesn't one just ask the question, What does "boundary line" mean? Why describe this elaborate procedure? As mentioned previously, only by ensuring that the individual is capable of operations identifying the referents of the words can one be confident that the meaning of a defined concept has been learned. In practice, of course, the procedure of obtaining verbal responses to questions is often used. But such a procedure is always subject to the ambiguity that the learner may be repeating a verbalization and, therefore, may not know the meaning of the concept after all. It is for this reason that we use the phrase "give an example of . . ." rather than a simpler task such as, "state the definition of. . . ." We want to imply that the learner has the ability to apply the defined concept rather than simply recall the verbal information. The conditions of learning for defined concepts are described in Table 4.4.

TABLE 4.4	CONDITIONS OF LEARNING FOR DEFINED CONCEPTS
Performance	The learner applies the defined concept by *classifying* instances and noninstances of the concept. For example, a student might be instructed to demonstrate his or her understanding of "conservative" by finding a newspaper article that represents a conservative viewpoint and contrasting it with a newspaper article that represents a liberal viewpoint.
	It is important to realize that application of the concept goes beyond recalling its definition. Obviously, a student can learn to state a definition such as, "Mass is the property that determines the amount of acceleration imparted to a body by a particular force," without having an understanding of the concept.
Internal Conditions	To acquire a concept by definition, the learner must retrieve all of the component concepts included in the definition, including the concepts that represent relations among them (such as *end* in the case of "boundary line").
External Conditions	Instruction would most likely follow a pattern consisting of 1. Identification of the concept or concepts they will be learning. 2. A presentation of the definition of the concept. 3. Examples and nonexamples that fit or do not fit the definition. 4. Practice is provided by having the learner classify instances and noninstances with corrective feedback. 5. Spaced practice for retention and transfer.

Rules or Principles

Rules are statements of relationships among concepts. For example, the spelling rule, "*i* before *e*, except after *c*, and when pronounced as an *a*, like in neighbor and weigh." This rule describes a series of relationships among letters and includes the component concepts "before," "except," "after," "when," and "like." A rule or principle has been learned when the learner can apply it in a consistent manner in a variety of specific situations. In other words, the learner shows that he or she is able to respond with a class of relationships among classes of objects and events.

There are many common examples of rule-governed behavior. In fact, most human behavior falls into this category. When we make a sentence using a given word such as girl, as in "The girl rode a bicycle," we are using a number of rules. For example, we begin the sentence with "The," not with "girl," employing a rule for the use of the definite article. The subject of the sentence is followed by a verb, or predicate to indicate what the subject did—that is, we say "The girl rode" and not "Rode the girl." The verb is followed by the object "bicycle," which, according to one rule, is placed in a particular order, and according to another, it is preceded (in this case) by the indefinite article "a." Finally, we complete the sentence by bringing it to a close, which in written form involves a rule for the use of a period. Since we have acquired each of these rules, we are able to construct any sentence of the same structure with any given words as subject and object.

Principles learned in science courses are also exhibited by the learner as rule-using behavior. For example, we expect students who have learned Ohm's law, $E = I \times R$, to apply the rule embodied in this statement. A question like the following may be asked: "Assuming that an electric circuit has a resistance of 12 ohms, and a voltage of 120 volts, how many amps would it draw?"

It may be apparent that being able to apply a rule isn't dependent upon being able to state it. For example, children construct oral sentences long before they learn grammatical rules. Conversely, being able to state a rule doesn't necessarily mean that the learner can apply it. A student might be able to state "voltage equals current multiplied by resistance" but not be apply the rule to a specific concrete problem.

Now that we have indicated what a rule is, we can admit that a defined concept, as previously described, is actually not formally different from a rule and is learned in much the same way. In other words, a defined concept is a particular type of rule whose purpose is to classify objects and events; it is a classifying rule. Rules, however, include many other categories besides classifying. They deal with such relationships as "equal to," "similar to," "greater than," "less than," "before," "after," and many others. The conditions of learning for rules are described in Table 4.5.

TABLE 4.5	CONDITIONS OF LEARNING FOR RULES
Performance	The rule is demonstrated by showing that it applies to one or more concrete instances. Examples: (1) The rule relating electrical resistance to cross-sectional area of a conductor can be demonstrated by the decrease in ohms when wire of larger diameter is selected for an electric circuit. (2) The rule governing the case of pronouns following prepositions can be demonstrated by making a correct choice of pronoun in the following sentence: "The secret was strictly between (she) (her) and (I) (me)." (3) The rule for multiplying fractions can be shown by application to an example such as 5/e × 2/a.
Internal Conditions	In learning a rule, the learner must retrieve each of the component concepts of the rule, including the concepts that represent relations. The instructor needs to assume that these concepts have been previously learned and can readily be recalled. In the example of resistance of a wire conductor, the learner must be able to retrieve such concepts as "cross-section," "area," "conductor," and "decrease."
External Conditions	The instructional conditions for teaching rules include the following: 1. A general statement about what will be learned (what the learner will be able to do) 2. Presentation of the rule to be learned as a verbal statement or list of procedures (much as we are doing here) 3. Guidance with learning by demonstrating application of the rule or procedure 4. Practice applying the rule (or components of the rule), with feedback 5. Opportunities for applying the rule in a variety of situations (spaced practice) to enhance transfer

Higher-Order Rules: Problem Solving

Is problem solving an instructional outcome or a process leading to an instructional outcome? One has a problem when the solution to a situation is not immediately evident. For example, someone wants to buy a pen I have for sale for 50 cents. The buyer gives me a dollar. I give them 50 cents back. Am I problem solving? No, I am rule using, because I already know how to make change for a dollar. Now, suppose they give me a Euro. How much change in U.S. currency should I give them? I don't know, because I don't have enough information to figure out how much change to return. If I am going to complete the transaction I will have to do some problem solving. In the process of solving the problem I will learn something.

Sometimes, the rules we learn are complex combinations of simpler rules. More-over, it is often the case that these more complex, or "higher-order," rules are invented for the purpose of solving a practical problem or class of problems.

The capability of problem solving is, naturally, a major aim of the educational process. Most educators would agree that the school should give priority to teaching students "how to think clearly." When students work out the solution to a problem that represents real events, they are engaging in the behavior of thinking. There are, of course, many kinds of problems, and some problems have many possible solutions. In attaining a workable solution to a problem, students also achieve a new capability. They learn something that can be generalized to other problems having similar formal characteristics. This means they have generated a new rule or perhaps a new set of rules. One might say they have "constructed" knowledge. However, the proof of learning is that this new rule can be recalled and applied in similar situations in the future.

Suppose that a small car has been parked near a low brick wall and is discovered to have a flat tire on one of its front wheels. No jack is available, but there is a 10-foot log and a piece of sturdy rope. Can the front of the car be raised? In this situation, a possible solution might be to use the log as a lever, the wall as a fulcrum, and the rope to secure the end of the lever when the car is in a raised position. This solution is invented to meet a particular problem situation. It is evident that the solution represents a "putting together" of certain rules that may not have been applied to previous similar situations by the individual who is solving the problem. One rule pertains to the application of force under the car to achieve a lifting of that car. Another rule pertains to the use of the wall as a fulcrum, and still another, is the rule regarding use of the log as a lever. All of these rules, in order to be used in an act of problem solving, must be assembled by the individual, which means they must have been previously learned. (Note once again that the rules need not be verbalized by the problem solver, nor have they necessarily been learned in a physics course.)

The invention of a complex rule can be illustrated with a problem in mathematics. Suppose a student has learned to add monomials such as $2x$ and $5x$, $3x^2$ and $4x^2$, $2x^3$; and $6x^3$. Now the student is shown a set of polynomials, such as:

$$2x + 3x^2 + 1$$
$$2 + 3x + 4x^2$$

The student is asked, "What do you suppose is the sum of these two expressions?" This question asks for the solution of a new problem, which (we assume) has not been previously encountered. Possibly, the student may make some false starts that could be corrected. The chances are, however, that previously learned subordinate rules will permit the student to think through the solution to this problem (for example, the rule that the variable a added to the variable a^2 results in the sum $a + a^2$, and the rule for adding monomials, such as $2a^2 + 3a^2 = 5a^2$. It is probably not a difficult problem for the student, therefore, to devise the complex rule: Add variables with the same exponents; express the sum as a set of terms connected by the + sign. Again, in this example, the problem solver has remembered and "combined" simpler rules into a more complex rule to solve the problem.

One type of problem solving involves discovery learning, where the learners are given a problem and left more or less on their own to solve it. While discovery learning takes place naturally, instruction aimed at helping students learn to solve problems can help the student by having students look for a rule and verbalize their solutions as they go along. (Gagné & Smith, 1962). Another technique used in teaching problem solving is guided discovery. Guided discovery provides hints to the student when they need them. Problem solving skills are generally tested with transfer problems. Transfer problems are problems like the original problem (they require the same rules), but previously unencountered by the student. Research has shown that guided discovery not only teaches problem solving faster than a method teaching the rule and example, it also leads to better transfer (Gagné & Brown, 1961).

Problem solving is taught by having the learner solve problems. The question is, how can we as instructional designers create situations that facilitate the acquisition of these skills? One method is planning for *cognitive apprenticeship*. Historically, apprenticeships are learning situations where a learner gets to work alongside an experienced individual. The instructional tactics include observation, coaching, practice, and feedback to the learner. "Cognitive apprenticeship, as we envision it, differs from traditional apprenticeship in that the tasks and problems are chosen to illustrate the power of certain techniques or methods, to give students practice in applying these methods in diverse settings, and to increase the complexity of tasks slowly, so that component skills and models can be integrated" (Collins, Brown, & Newman, 1989, p. 459).

Constructivist designers suggest centering instruction on realistic or "authentic" problems. They generally feel that authentic situations facilitate transfer. We agree with this proposition but would add that transfer and even remembering what was learned requires practice and performance by the student of their newly learned knowledge. Learning of this sort might be more effective in groups, as a collaborative activity, because learning is a social-cultural process (Coleman, Perry, & Schwen, 1997). We also agree with this proposition because the group work would facilitate discourse about the problem being solved. Group work on problem solving provides the social support and the pooling of knowledge (component rules) necessary to solve the problem. Groups will often solve problems faster and better than individuals. But, it is important to test students as individuals in a transfer situation to determine if they developed the problem-solving skill.

In general, a collaborative learning environment would seem to facilitate problem solving, and therefore knowledge construction. Looking more critically at the mechanisms within the group activities should provide information on how these activities support the problem-solving process. Table 4.6 presents the conditions of learning for problem-solving skills.

TABLE 4.6	CONDITIONS OF LEARNING FOR PROBLEM SOLVING
Performance	Performance requires the invention and use of a complex rule to achieve the solution of a problem novel to the individual. When the higher-order rule has been generated, it should also be possible for the learner to demonstrate its use in other physically different but formally similar situations.
Internal Conditions	In solving a problem, the learner must retrieve relevant subordinate rules and relevant information. It is assumed that these capabilities have been previously learned.
External Conditions	Instruction requires that students: 1. Be presented with novel problems for which they have the composite rules to solve. 2. Apply problem-solving strategies, because the instructional situation lacks direct instruction (otherwise the learned capability would be rule-using). The instructor should observe that they are monitoring their progress, recognizing dead ends, and choosing relevant rules from what they have learned. The instructor, through the processes of observation and coaching, aids the learner in achieving successive approximation of the goal skill. Here Vygotsky's notion of Zone of Proximal Development, becomes relevant. This zone represents the difference between where the student is and what he or she is capable of achieving in the presence of knowledgeable adults or in collaboration with more capable peers (Dixon-Krauss, 1996). In other words, the level of the problem presented should take into consideration the skills the learner brings to the task so that the learner can succeed. 3. Receive feedback in the form of encouragement in the previously mentioned process, and perhaps minor corrections of process. 4. Be encouraged to reflect on what they accomplished and verbalize how they did it. This should strengthen retention of the newly generated rule or procedure. 5. Be provided with practice on similar problems to encourage transfer. 6. Engage in problem solving, and therefore learning to solve problems, that is facilitated by collaborative group work.

COGNITIVE STRATEGIES

A very special kind of intellectual skill of particular importance to learning and thinking, is the cognitive strategy. In terms of modern learning theory, a cognitive strategy is a control process, an internal process by which learners select and modify their ways of attending, learning, remembering, and thinking (Gagné, 1985). Several of Bruner's writings (1961, 1971) describe the operation and usefulness of cognitive strategies in problem solving. More recently, many different strategies have been identified that relate to the entire range of cognitive processes of the learner (O'Neil & Spielberger, 1979).

Varieties of Learner Strategies

Although specific strategies may be used by the learner in dealing with all conceivable kinds of learning tasks, it is convenient to classify them into a few categories that indicate their control functions. The following categories are suggested by Weinstein and Mayer (1986).

Rehearsal Strategies   By means of these strategies, learners conduct their own practice of the material being learned. In simplest form, the practice is simply repeating to themselves the names of items in an ordered list (for instance, the U.S. presidents or the states). In the case of more complex learning tasks, such as learning the main ideas of a printed text, rehearsal may be accomplished by underlining the main ideas or by copying portions of the text.

Elaboration Strategies   In using the techniques of elaboration, the learner deliberately associates the item to be learned with other readily accessible material. In learning foreign-language vocabulary, for example, the foreign word may be associated with a mental image of an English word that forms an "acoustic link" with the word having the correct meaning (Atkinson, 1975; Levin, 1981). When applied to learning from prose texts, elaboration activities include paraphrasing, summarizing, note taking, and generating questions with answers.

Organizing Strategies   Arranging material to be learned into an organized framework is the basic technique of these strategies. Sets of words to be remembered may be arranged by the learner into meaningful categories. Relations among facts may be organized into a table, making possible the use of spatial arrangement cues to recall the material. Outlining the main ideas in prose passages and generating new organizations for the ideas is another method. Learners are able to acquire strategies that organize passages of text into several particular kinds of relations among ideas, such as "comparison," "collection," and "description" (Meyer, 1981).

Comprehension Monitoring Strategies   These strategies, sometimes referred to as *metacognitive strategies* (Brown, 1978), pertain to the student's capability of setting goals for learning, estimating the success with which the goals are being met, and selecting alternative strategies to meet the goals. These are strategies having the function of monitoring, the presence of which becomes evident in reading for understanding (Golinkoff, 1976). Students have been taught to develop their own statements and questions to be used in guiding and controlling their performance in the comprehension of prose (Meichenbaum & Asarnow, 1979).

Affective Strategies   These techniques may be used by learners to focus and maintain attention, to control anxiety, and to manage time effectively. Such strategies can be taught by making students aware of their operation and providing ways for them to practice their use (Dansereau, 1985; McCombs, 1982).

Other Organizational Systems   West, Farmer, and Wolff (1991) organize cognitive strategies into families, including chunking, spatial, bridging, and multipurpose. Each of these broad categories includes subclasses of cognitive strategies. For example, under the multipurpose category are rehearsal and mnemonic strategies. In turn, each subclass contains one or more specific strategies; for example, mnemonic strategies include key word, chain, and loci. Altogether these authors identify and categorize over 28 different strategies that have been the subject of research studies.

One might speculate that cognitive strategies serve particular functions during the process of information processing. Table 4.7 lists stages of the information-processing model presented in Chapter 1 in the left column, and strategies that may

TABLE 4.7   **FUNCTIONS OF COGNITIVE STRATEGIES IN SUPPORT OF STAGES OF INFORMATION PROCESSING**

Learning Processes	Supportive Strategies
Selective Perception	Highlighting Underlining Advance organizers Adjunct questions Outlining
Rehearsal	Paraphrasing Note taking Imagery Outlining Chunking
Semantic Encoding	Concept maps Taxonomies Analogies Rules/Productions Schemas
Retrieval	Mnemonics Imagery
Executive Control	Metacognitive strategies (see goal schemas, Chapter 9)

support each of those stages in the right column. For example, selective perception for a verbal learning task may be focused by underlining or highlighting important words. Selective perception for intellectual skills tasks may be facilitated by creating an expectation about the outcomes of the learning task. This expectation may be accomplished through the use of outlining, adjunct questions, or advance organizers.

Strategies may support other stages of information processing. We know, for instance, that information is lost from short-term memory unless it is rehearsed. We also know that the capacity of short-term memory is limited to approximately seven separate items. It would seem that the strategies of imagery and paraphrasing might serve a rehearsal function. The strategy of outlining may serve both functions of selective perception and rehearsal. Chunking strategies may also be employed to reduce the number of separate items held in short-term memory by organizing them into more general categories.

Semantic encoding is the process involved in moving information from short-term to long-term memory. This process involves making the information meaningful by tying it to previously learned information structures (schemas) or establishing new structures. Linkages of this sort would seem to be facilitated through the use of concept maps whereby the learner is enabled to see the structure of the material to be learned. Concept maps may be especially helpful where the existing structure is weak or nonexistent. Analogies, on the other hand, are only likely to work by linking new information with existing structures. Still another aid to encoding may be schemas in the form of stories that provide an elaborated context for the new information to be learned. Retrieval is the process of moving information from long-term to short-term memory. While in short-term memory, it may be combined with newly perceived information to bring about new kinds of learning. It then may be acted on or reencoded and returned to long-term memory. It is likely that the mnemonics and imagery support the retrieval process.

Executive control processes include metacognitive strategies. These are processes that activate and modulate the flow of information during learning. These strategies probably govern the learner's selection of cognitive strategies in an unstructured learning environment. Think-aloud protocols have been used to determine what learners do during the process of solving problems. What they do depends upon their expectancies or goals and upon strategies they have used in the past to achieve these goals. The particular strategies that will be selected are governed by goal schemas (Gagné & Merrill, 1990). For example, if a student is going to study for a test (taking the test would be the goal), he or she will probably use a different strategy than that used for preparing to teach a skill (teaching would be the goal). Goal schemas and integrated goals are discussed more fully in Chapter 9.

We consider cognitive strategies as learned capabilities that are the outcomes of instruction. One might consider cognitive strategies as instructional techniques for use in designing instruction, especially with regard to presenting stimulus materials to the learner. As previously noted, there are a number of different strategies that seem more or less appropriate at different stages in the instructional process. Embedding the strategies in the instructional materials is not the same as teaching the strategies. The embedded strategies serve a specific function, whereas the learned strategies allow the students to provide this function for themselves. However, it may be necessary to have the students apply the strategies within a content area in order to learn them. For example, consider outlining as a cognitive strategy. Outlining probably serves the function of providing a selective focus and of structuring main and subordinate relationships in textual discourse. Students who must construct an outline of a text are probably learning something different from students who study the text using a prepared outline. But what are they learning? What test would show the acquired differences? Do students who construct the outline become better at outlining? Are they better able to differentiate between superordinate and subordinate concepts? Do they apply the skill across subjects as a learning strategy? These and similar questions require answers from empirical research.

It is possible for designers to view the use of cognitive strategies in materials as helpful to the learner because they serve a supplemental or redundant function in some phase of the learning process. However, if the goal is to teach the learner cognitive strategies (as outcomes) designers must take account of the conditions necessary for learning these skills, just as they would with any other type of learning outcome.

Learning Cognitive Strategies

A cognitive strategy is a cognitive skill that selects and guides the internal processes involved in learning and thinking. Notice that it is the object of the skill that differentiates cognitive strategies from other intellectual skills. Concepts and rules are oriented toward environmental objects and events, such as sentences, graphs, or mathematical equations. In contrast, cognitive strategies have as their objects the learner's own cognitive processes. Undoubtedly, the efficacy of an individual's cognitive strategies has a crucial effect upon the quality of information processing. Learners' cognitive strategies may determine, for example, how readily they learn, how well they recall and use what has been learned, and how fluently they think.

Statements of educational goals often give the highest priority to cognitive strategies. Many statements of goals for school learning give a prominent place to "teaching students how to think." Although it would be difficult to find disagreement with the importance of such a goal, it seems wise to temper one's enthusiasm with a few facts concerning the feasibility of reaching it. First, one should realize that genetic factors, not amenable to the influence of education, are likely to play an important part in the determination of creative thought (see Tyler, 1965; Ausubel, Novak, & Hanesian, 1978, Chap. 16). In other words, there are bound to be enormous differences in intellectual capacity among people, which can never be completely overcome by environmental influences such as education. Second, the internally organized nature of cognitive strategies means that the conditions of instruction can have only an indirect effect upon their acquisition and improvement. In the case of other types of intellectual skills, one can plan a sequence of learning events so as to increase the probability of certain internal events; and these in turn determine the learning of the cognitive strategy. Accordingly, the design of instruction for cognitive strategies has to be done in terms of "favorable conditions." Generally, the favorable conditions are those that provide opportunities for development and use of cognitive strategies. In other words, to "learn to think," the student needs to be given opportunities to think.

Derry and Murphy (1986) describe a system of learning-strategies training that begins with direct instruction of such strategies as reading comprehension monitoring, problem solving, and control of affect. Following the initial training, the same strategies are practiced in a variety of learning situations over an extended period, using distinctive cues that remind the learner in each instance of an appropriate useful strategy. The method thus incorporates the idea of spaced and varied practice, which is considered to be desirable for the learning of these higher-order strategies. The conditions that facilitate learning of cognitive strategies are presented in Table 4.8.

TABLE 4.8   CONDITIONS OF LEARNING FOR COGNITIVE STRATEGIES

Performance	The performance of cognitive strategies cannot be observed directly but must be inferred from performances calling for the use of other intellectual skills. Investigators usually discover strategies by asking learners to "think aloud" while they are learning, remembering, or solving problems (Ericsson & Simon, 1980). However, inferences about the quality of reading comprehension reveal the use of comprehension strategies; inferences about the quality of learning new rules of trigonometry (for example) reveal the use of organizing strategies; and inferences about the quality of problem solving reveal the use of thinking strategies.
Internal Conditions	Prior knowledge (that is, intellectual skills and verbal information) relevant to the subject matter to be learned or thought about must be retrievable, just as is true for other intellectual skills. However, it should be noted that cognitive strategies often intrinsically possess a simple structure (for example, "underline main ideas," "divide the problem into parts").
External Conditions	Instruction involves the following steps: 1. Explain to the student what the strategy is, and the purpose or learning it. 2. Strategies may often be described or originally learned as a series of steps, suggested to learners by verbal communications or demonstrated to them in simple form. Even young children, for example, can respond appropriately to the suggestion that they use an organizing strategy like, "Put things that look alike into a group." 3. Strategies are more likely to be adopted if the learner invents them. 4. Dependable use of a strategy depends upon favorable outcomes. 5. Automaticity depends upon opportunities for practice.

METACOGNITION

The internal processing that makes use of cognitive strategies to monitor and control other learning and memory processes is known generally as *metacognition* (Flavell, 1979). In confronting problems to be solved, learners are able to select and regulate the employment of relevant intellectual skills and bring to bear task-oriented cognitive strategies. Such metacognitive strategies, which govern the use of other strategies, are also spoken of as "executive" or "higher level." Learners may also become aware of such strategies and may be able to describe them, in which case they are said to possess metacognitive knowledge (Lohman, 1986). Planning models for direct training in metacognitive knowledge are involved in many schemes for study skills and general problem solving.

Broadly speaking, there are two different viewpoints about the origins of metacognitive strategies (Derry & Murphy, 1986). One is that they may be acquired by learners through the communication of metacognitive knowledge (that is, by verbal information) followed by practice in their use. This approach is exemplified by courses in problem-solving strategies, such as that described by Rubinstein (1975). The second view proposes that metacognitive strategies arise from the generalization of a number of specific task-oriented strategies, usually after a considerable variety of problem-solving experiences by the learner. This latter view appears to be supported by the weight of evidence (Derry & Murphy, 1986), and we have therefore adopted it in our discussion.

Strategies for Problem Solving

Often, of particular interest in instructional design are those cognitive strategies called into play when the learner defines and thinks out a solution to a highly novel problem. Although such strategies are often of primary interest in educational programs, our knowledge of how to ensure their learning is weak (Gagné, 1980; Polson & Jeffries, 1985). A number of strategies employed by adults in solving verbally stated problems are described by Wickelgren (1974). These include (1) inferring transformed conceptions of the "givens," (2) classifying action sequences rather than randomly choosing them, (3) choosing actions at any given state of the problem that get closer to the goal ("hill climbing"), (4) identifying contradictions that prove the goal cannot be attained from the givens, (5) breaking the problem into parts, and (6) working backward from the goal statement. Strategies like these are obviously applicable to "brain teaser" problems of an algebraic or geometric sort.

Programs designed to teach problem-solving strategies are critically reviewed by Polson and Jeffries (1985). They point out the existence of three different models of problem solving that rest upon different assumptions, and are currently irreconcilable with each other. Model 1 makes the assumption that general problem-solving skills (such as those mentioned previously) can be directly taught and will exhibit generalization to other situations. Model 2 maintains that general problem-solving skills can be taught but not directly. Instead, general strategies are most likely to develop indirectly by generalization from task-specific strategies. There is, of course, dependable evidence that the latter kinds of strategies (such as strategies for solving mechanical problems or for constructing geometric proofs) can readily be acquired. Model 3 argues that direct instruction in general problem-solving strategies is effective in establishing only weak strategies that help problem solving very little, even though they are broadly generalizable ("break the problem into parts," is an example). Consequently, although the strategies viewed by model 3 are teachable, they are not very useful.

In estimating the value of general problem-solving strategies for an instructional program, one should take into consideration the findings of studies contrasting the capabilities of experts with those of novices in various fields (Gagné & Glaser, 1986). In general, these studies indicate that experts do not necessarily use better problem-solving strategies than do novices but that they approach problems with larger and better-organized knowledge bases. The organized knowledge of the expert includes verbal information as well as intellectual skills.

VARIETIES OF INTELLECTUAL SKILLS IN SCHOOL SUBJECTS

The range of human capabilities called *intellectual skills* includes the varieties of discriminations, concrete concepts, defined concepts, rules, and the higher-order rules often acquired in problem solving. An additional category of internally organized skills is cognitive strategies, which govern the learner's behavior in learning and thinking and, thus, determine its quality and efficiency. These varieties of learning are distinguishable by (1) the class of performance they make possible, (2) the internal and external conditions necessary for their occurrence, and (3) the complexity of the internal process they establish in the individual's memory.

Any school subject may at one time or another involve any of these types of learned capabilities. However, the frequency with which they are encountered in various school subjects varies widely. Examples of discriminations can be found in such elementary subjects as printing letters and reading music. In contrast, there are few examples of this type, and many more of defined concepts, in a history course. However, quite a few examples of discriminations also occur in the beginning study of a foreign language, which may be undertaken in the ninth grade. In the same grade, the writing of compositions very frequently involves defined concepts and rules but seems not to require the learning of discriminations or concrete concepts. In this case, the necessary learning of these simpler skills has been accomplished years ago.

Any school subject can be analyzed to reveal the relevance of all of these kinds of learning. But this is not always a practical course of action because the presentation of the subject in a particular grade may begin with the assumption that simpler kinds of learning have already been accomplished. Thus, discrimination of –/– from — is certainly relevant to the study of algebra. But one doesn't begin the study of algebra with the learning of discriminations, because it is assumed that students at this level already have these skills. However, a student in medical school may have to learn subtle discriminations of color and shape of skin lesions if they are going to classify types of skin cancer.

Adult education in technical and professional subjects sometimes exhibits objectives representing a limited range of intellectual skills, sometimes the entire range. For example, the processing of lumber and wood products requires training that may need to begin with discriminations of wood textures and proceed to concrete concepts of wood grain before instruction on the characteristics and uses of various woods can reach an advanced stage.

Is there, then, a structure of intellectual skills that represents the "path of greatest learning efficiency" for every subject in the curriculum? In theory, yes. Do we know what this structure is? Only vaguely. After all, teachers, curriculum specialists, and textbook writers try to represent structure in their lesson and curriculum plans. Nevertheless, most instructional sequences represent only one of many possible paths. Instruction, such as that presented in textbooks, is notoriously incomplete. The purpose of this book is to describe a systematic method for approaching the problem. The application of the method to be described can lead to descriptions of the "learning structure" of a subject. This structure may be represented as a kind of map of the terrain to be covered in progressing from one point in the course to the terminal objectives.

The mapping of learning structures may imply an instructional sequence for hierarchical skills, but there are many possible starting points. Mapping does not lead to "routinization" or "mechanization" of the process of learning any more than a road map leads to a single way to get to a destination. A map indicates starting points, destinations, and alternative routes in between; it does not tell how to make the journey. Making the "learning journey" requires a different set of internal events for each and every individual. In a fundamental sense, there are as many learning "routes" as there are individuals. Learning structures are simply descriptions of the accepted goals, or outcomes of learning, together with subordinate steps along the way.

SUMMARY

Starting with the need to identify goals as the desired outcomes of the educational system, Chapter 3 proposed that in attempting to design specific courses, topics, and lessons, there is a need to classify performance objectives into broad categories: intellectual skills, cognitive strategies, verbal information, motor skills, and attitudes. Doing so, it was shown, facilitates (1) review of the adequacy of the objectives, (2) determination of the sequencing of instruction, and (3) planning for the conditions of learning needed for successful instruction. The present chapter has begun the account of the nature of the performance capabilities implied by each of the five categories of learned capabilities, beginning with intellectual skills and cognitive strategies. For each of these two domains, this chapter has (1) described learned performances in terms of different subjects, (2) presented the kinds of internal conditions of learning needed to reach the new capability, and (3) suggested the external instructional conditions for facilitating learning.

For intellectual skills, several subcategories were identified: discriminations, concrete and defined concepts, rules, and the higher-order rules often learned by problem solving. Each represents a different class of performance, and each is supported by different sets of internal and external conditions of learning. Cognitive strategies were not broken down into subcategories as intellectual skills were. Research in the future may suggest that this can and should be done.

An important distinction is made between cognitive strategies relating to specific domains of knowledge (such as geometry or poetry) and those that are more general in their relevance. The latter are sometimes called executive or metacognitive strategies, because their function is to govern the use of other strategies, and they apply generally to information processing independently of specific knowledge domains. It may be that metacognitive strategies can be directly taught; more likely, they are generalized by learners from their experience with a variety of specific task-oriented strategies.

Chapter 5 gives a corresponding kind of treatment to the remaining kinds of learned capabilities: information, attitudes, and motor skills. The purpose of Chapters 4 and 5 is to move a step closer to the specification of a set of guidelines that apply the conditions of learning to the actual design of instruction for a lesson, a unit, a course, or an entire instructional system. They lead to suggestions of how to proceed with two aspects of instructional design: (1) how to take account of the prior learning assumed to be necessary for the learner to undertake the new learning, and (2) how to plan for the new learning in terms of the appropriate external conditions needed for the attainment of each type of learning outcome.

REFERENCES

Atkinson, R. C. (1975). Mnemotechnics in second language learning. *American Psychologist, 30,* 821–28.

Ausubel, D. P., Novak, J. D., & Hanesian, H. (1978). *Educational psychology: A cognitive view* (2nd ed.). New York: Holt, Rinehart and Winston.

Bloom, B., Krathwohl, D., et al. (1956). *Taxonomy of educational objectives. Handbook 1: Cognitive domain.* New York: McKay.

Brown, A. L. (1978). Metacognitive development and reading. In R. J. Spiro, B. C. Bruce, & G. W. F. Brewer (Eds.), *Theoretical issues in reading comprehension.* Hillsdale, NJ: Erlbaum.

Bruner, J. S. (1961). The act of discovery. *Harvard Educational Review, 31,* 21–32.

Bruner, J. S. (1971). *The relevance of education.* New York: Norton.

Coleman, S. D., Perry, J. D. , & Schwen, T. M. (1997) Constructivist instructional development: Reflecting on practice from an alternative paradigm. In C. Dills & A. Romisowski (Eds.), *Instructional development paradigms.* Englewood Cliffs, NJ : Educational Technology Publications.

Collins, A., Brown, J. S., & Newman, S. E. (1989). Cognitive apprenticeship: Teaching the crafts of reading, writing, and mathematics. In L. B. Resnick (Ed.), *Knowing, learning, and instruction: Essays in honor of Robert Glaser* (pp. 453–494). Hillsdale, NJ: Erlbaum.

Dansereau, D. F. (1985). Learning strategy research. In J. Segal, S. Chipman, & R. Glaser (Eds.), *Thinking and learning skills* (Vol. 1). Hillsdale, NJ: Erlbaum.

Derry, S. J., & Murphy, D. A. (1986). Designing systems that train learning ability: From theory to practice. *Review of Educational Research, 56,* 1–39.

Flavell, J. H. (1979). Metacognition and cognitive monitoring: A new area of psychological inquiry. *American Psychologist, 34,* 906–911.

Gagné, R. M., & Brown, L. T. (1961). Some factors in the programming of conceptual learning. *Journal of Experimental Psychology, 62,* 313–321.

Gagné, R. M., & Smith, E. C. (1962). A study of the effects of verbalization on problem solving. *Journal of Experimental Psychology, 63,* 12–18.

Gagné, R. M. (1980). Learnable aspects of problem solving. *Educational Psychologist, 15*(2), 84–92.

Gagné, R. M. (1985). *The conditions of learning* (4th ed.). New York: Holt, Rinehart and Winston.

Gagné, R. M., & Glaser, R. (1986). Foundations in research and theory. In R. M. Gagné (Ed.), *Instructional technology: Foundations*. Hillsdale, NJ: Erlbaum.

Gagné, R. M., & Merrill, M. D. (1990). Integrative goals for instructional design. *Educational Technology Research and Development, 38*(1), 23–30.

Golinkoff, R. A. (1976). A comparison of reading comprehension processes in good and poor comprehenders. *Reading Research Quarterly, 11,* 623–659.

Levin, J. R. (1981). The mnemonic '80s: Key words in the classroom. *Educational Psychologist, 16*(2), 65–82.

Lohman, D. F. (1986). Predicting mathemathanic effects in the teaching of higher-order thinking skills. *Educational Psychologist, 21,* 191–208.

Merriam-Webster's Collegiate Dictionary, 10th ed., s.v. "conservative."

McCombs, B. L. (1982). Transitioning learning strategies research into practice: Focus on the student in technical training. *Journal of Instructional Development, 5*(2), 10–17.

Meichenbaum, D., & Asarnow, J. (1979). Cognitive-behavior modification and metacognitive development: Implications for the classroom. In P. C. Kendall & S. D. Hollon (Eds.), *Cognitive-behavioral intervention: Theory, research and procedures.* New York: Academic Press.

Meyer, B. J. F. (1981). Basic research on prose comprehension: A critical review. In D. F. Fisher & C. W. Peters (Eds.). *Comprehension and the competent reader*. New York: Praeger.

O'Neil, H. G., Jr., & Spielberger, C. D. (Eds.). (1979). *Cognitive and affective learning strategies*. New York: Academic Press.

Piaget, J. (1950). *The psychology of intelligence*. New York: Harcourt, Brace & Jovanovich.

Polson, P. G., & Jeffries, R. (1985). Instruction in general problem-solving skills: An analysis of four approaches. In J. Segal, S. Chipman, & R. Glaser (Eds.). *Thinking and learning skills* (Vol. 1). Hillsdale, NJ: Erlbaum.

Rubinstein, M. F. (1975). *Patterns of problem solving*. Englewood Cliffs, NJ: Prentice Hall.

Tyler, L. E. (1965). *The psychology of human differences* (3rd ed.). New York: Appleton.

Weinstein, C. E., & Mayer R. E. (1986). The teaching of learning strategies. In M. C. Wittrock (Ed.). *Handbook of research on teaching* (3rd ed.). New York: Macmillan.

West, E. K., Farmer, J. A., & Wolff, P. M. (1991) *Instructional design implications from cognitive science*. Englewood Cliffs, NJ: Prentice Hall.

Wickelgren, W. A. (1974). *How to solve problems*. San Francisco: Freeman.

VARIETIES OF LEARNING

Information, Attitudes, and Motor Skills

Courses and lessons are not always aimed only at developing intellectual skills or cognitive strategies, as discussed in Chapter 4. A topic, course of study, or even an individual lesson usually teaches many kinds of learning outcomes. In this chapter we shall describe the conditions applicable to the learning of *verbal information*, the establishment or changing of *attitudes*, and the acquisition of *motor skills*. The importance of these very different learning outcomes varies depending on the instructional content. For each, we will consider three important aspects of the learning situation, namely:

1. The *performance* to be acquired as a result of learning
2. The *internal conditions* that need to be present for learning to occur
3. The *external conditions* that bring essential stimulation to bear upon the learner

VERBAL INFORMATION (KNOWLEDGE)

Verbal information, according to theory, is stored as networks of propositions (Anderson, 1985; E. D. Gagné, 1985) that conform to the rules of language. Another name for it, intended to emphasize the performance capability, is *declarative knowledge*. The major function of verbal information is to provide learners with a structure or foundation upon which to build other skills. Think of this as "building learning on learning." For example, in the vocabulary field, simple words must be learned before they can be used in sentences.

Differentiating between "Data," "Information," and "Knowledge"

In the study of knowledge, a number of descriptions about the relationships among data, information, and knowledge have been developed.

Data is a stimulus or entity, like a number. For example, the thermometer reads 40 degrees Fahrenheit (40 °F)—this is data. This data must be processed within a context of use to become information. For example, data that it is 40 degrees outside, and information that freezing is 32 °F or less, would lead to the proposition that it isn't freezing outside. The memorized verbal information allows a whole series of responses that were not memorized as facts. That is, the student did not have to memorize the independent facts that 33, 34, 35, 36, etc., degrees are not freezing temperatures. The declarative knowledge that freezing occurs when the temperature drops to 32 °F allows the individual to apply a rule (also learned as a proposition), that any temperature above 32 °F is not freezing.

When an individual can apply verbal information we often consider them knowledgeable. Knowledge is an *expansion* of information. Unlike information, knowledge is a dynamic mix of information in context, experience, insight, and values (Brooks, 2000). Knowledge, shown at the bottom of Bloom's taxonomy, is the foundation for other kinds of learning. It is also very important in R. M. Gagné's (1985) conceptualization of conditions of learning because these propositions form the knowledge structure upon which concepts, rules, and problem-solving skills depend.

Transforming Information into Knowledge in the Digital Age

In today's digital world, many people confuse *finding information* with *using* it. For example, the Internet gives people fast access to a great deal of information at school, at work, and at home. However, a large majority of people isn't able to transform the information into *usable knowledge* by finding, creating, editing, managing, analyzing, critiquing, sorting, and cross-referencing the information. Some people believe the difference between knowledge and information is the most widespread misunderstanding in the current use of information technology. It is pretty well accepted that information, if it is not used regularly in a meaningful context, is quickly forgotten, whereas information that is transformed into knowledge is more readily retained.

The use of technology to find information provides some powerful tools for teachers and the designers of learning activities that involve the learner in using verbal information. Online newspapers are an excellent example of how digital or electronic retrieval strategies can help learners transform vast amounts of information into meaningful knowledge. An unlimited amount of space and the ability to update information instantly allows journalists to expand the boundaries of news. While online newspapers deliver primarily the same information as their print predecessors, the capabilities of electronic media permit readers to *restructure* the information into a context that is useful and meaningful to them (Letham, 2003). Most online newspapers let readers manipulate the news in a way that goes beyond simple information gathering. In doing so, the information becomes useful knowledge, that is, knowledge that is *relevant* to the reader's personal needs and interests. The more information that is available to readers from a variety of sources, and the more control they have over the context, the more complete a picture they get on how a story connects to other events or beliefs in society. Most online papers provide retrieval tools and other interactive techniques that let readers view information outside of the restraints of sections. Examples include:

- Search engines, where a reader can enter keywords and receive all of the articles related to this topic, whether they fall into the politics, business, style, or the metro section.
- Links to external sites that let readers view the news through the eyes of another author and fill in any gaps in the story with supplemental information (Letham, 2003). This type of structure challenges readers not only to interact with the content, but also to evaluate news outside of the context intended by the journalist, and in doing so, place it in a new light.
- Links to back issues that help readers to better understand the current issues with respect to previous happenings.
- Analysis tools that help readers to see how people other than the author view the news. Analyses provide different viewpoints and place the information in an alternative context (Letham, 2003).
- Forums that allow readers to contribute *their own* ideas to the site. This service gives minority opinions a voice in the media and exposes readers to ideas, values, and belief systems that may differ from their own (Letham, 2003). While readers may not choose to *accept* other viewpoints, they are forced to *reevaluate* their own set of beliefs and how the news fits into those beliefs.

School Instruction and Verbal Information

While much information is learned and stored in memory as a result of formal school instruction, an enormous amount is acquired outside of school from searching the Internet, reading books, and through radio and television. For this reason, no special means of relaying information needs to be provided in order for a large amount of learning to occur. The communications provided by the various media bring about learning in many people, provided that they possess the basic intellectual skills for interpreting the information.

In school learning, there are many circumstances in which teachers or trainers want to *make certain* that information is learned. While literate individuals or sophisticated learners might be able to gain this information from accessing a Web site, the *amount* of information they gain is likely to vary greatly, depending on each individual's interests and previous experience. In contrast, a formally planned course delivered in a traditional school setting will be more likely to deliver *to all students* certain information that is essential for further study of the subject. Planned instruction in school subjects is necessary to ensure that information is delivered to, and understood by, every student.

There are two primary reasons for ensuring that *all* students are learning certain information. First, particular information may be needed for the student to continue learning a topic or subject. While some of the necessary information may be looked up on the Internet or in a book, a great deal of it might need to be recalled and used again and again as the student pursues study within the subject.

There is typically a body of information that is basic in the sense that future learning will be more efficient once the basic information is acquired and retained.

A second reason for learning certain information is that much of it may be continually useful to the individual *throughout life*. Everyone needs to know the names of letters, numbers, common objects, and a host of facts about themselves and their environment in order to communicate effectively. A great deal of factual information is acquired without any formal planning. In addition, an individual may acquire unusual quantities of factual information in one or more areas of particular interest. Distinguishing between information that is *more* or *less* essential is a familiar problem with designing school curricula. Some of the information might be used by individuals throughout their lifetimes, while other information might be personally interesting but not *essential*. Because there seems to be no reason to limit the information people want to learn because of their particular interests or desires, this former category can present a problem for teachers and trainers as they strive to ensure that everyone is learning the essential information.

Specialized and Generalized Knowledge

As noted previously, when information is organized into bodies of meaningfully interconnected facts and generalizations, it is usually referred to as *knowledge*. Obviously, the information possessed by individuals within their own particular field of work or study is usually organized as a *body of* knowledge. For example, we expect a chemist to have learned and stored a *specialized* body of knowledge about units and measurements; and similarly, we expect a cabinetmaker to possess a body of knowledge about woods, and joints, and tools. Given this specialized knowledge, the question of whether or not it is valuable to acquire *general* knowledge remains. Most societies believe it is important to pass on the *accumulated* knowledge of their society from one generation to the next. Information about the origins of the society, tribe, or nation, its development through time, its goals and values, and its place in the world, is generally considered a body of knowledge that should be included in each individual's education.

In the past within our own society, there was a body of general knowledge, fairly well agreed upon, that was considered desirable for the "educated class" (those who went to college) to learn. It was composed of historical information about Western culture extending back to early Greek civilization, along with related information from literature and the arts. As mass education progressively replaced class education, there was an accompanying reduction in the amount of general cultural knowledge considered necessary for all students to learn. In the early 1990s the "back-to-basics" movement revived interest in teaching general cultural information as a contributor to societal stability.

What function does general cultural knowledge serve in the life of the individual? Such knowledge serves the purpose of communication, particularly in those aspects of life pertaining to citizenship. Knowing the facts about the community, the state, and the nation and the services they provide, as well as the responsibilities owed them, enables the individual to participate as a citizen. Cultural and historical knowledge may also contribute to the achievement and maintenance of the individual's "identity" or sense of self-awareness of their origins in relation to those of the society to which they belong.

A much more critical function of general knowledge can be proposed, although evidence concerning it is incomplete. This is the notion that knowledge is the *vehicle* for thought and problem solving. In Chapter 4, we saw that thinking, in the sense of problem solving, requires certain prerequisite intellectual skills as well as cognitive strategies. These are the tools individuals possess that enable them to think clearly and precisely. How does one think *broadly*? For example, how can a scientist think about the social problem of the isolation of aged people? How can a poet capture in words the essential conflict of youthful rebellion and alienation? These individuals need to possess bodies of knowledge shared by many other people to solve these problems. The thinking that takes place is "carried" by the associations, metaphors, and analogies of language within these bodies of knowledge. The importance of a "knowledge background" for creative thought has been discussed by many writers, including Polanyi (1958) and more recently by Glaser (1984).

In summary, it is evident that a number of important reasons can be identified for the learning of information, whether this is conceived as facts, generalizations, or as organized bodies of meaningful knowledge. Factual information is needed in learning increasingly complex intellectual skills of a subject or discipline. Such information may in part be looked up, but it is often more conveniently stored in memory. Certain types and categories of factual information must be learned because it is necessary for communication pertaining to the affairs of everyday living. Information is often learned and remembered as organized bodies of knowledge. Specialized knowledge of this sort may be accumulated by individuals while they are pursuing a field of study or work. General knowledge, particularly that which reflects a cultural heritage, is desirable and essential for people to be able to communicate and function in society. In addition, it seems likely that the bodies of general knowledge are the foundation for reflective thinking and problem solving.

Learning Verbal Information

Verbal information is presented to learners in various ways. It may be delivered to their ears through oral communications or to their eyes through printed words and illustrations. There are many interesting research questions relating to the effectiveness of communication media (Bretz, 1971; Clark & Salomon, 1986), and some of the implications for instructional design will be discussed in a later chapter. At this point, however, we will focus on a set of dimensions for verbal information learning that cut across various communication media.

Verbal information may vary, in amount and in organization, and some variations along these dimensions appear to be more important than others are for instructional design. The three verbal learning situations are: (1) the learning of *labels* or *names*, (2) the learning of isolated or single facts which may or may not be part of larger meaningful communications, and (3) the learning of organized information. The latter two are often referred to as declarative knowledge.

Learning Labels

To learn a label simply means to acquire the capability to make a consistent verbal response to an object or object class in such a way that it is "named." The verbal response itself may be of almost any variety, for example "x-I," "petunia," "pocket dictionary," or "spectrophotometer." Information in this form is simply a short verbal chain. Substantial research on the learning of verbal paired associates can be found in many texts (for example, Hulse, Egeth, & Deese, 1980; Kausler, 1974).

Learning to name or "label" an object is quite distinct from learning the *meaning* of the name. The latter implies the acquisition of a *concept*, which has been described previously. Teachers and trainers are well acquainted with the distinction between "knowing the name of something" and "knowing what the name means." A student knows a label when he or she can simply say its name. To know the object as a concept (that is, know its meaning), the student must be able to identify examples and nonexamples that define and delimit its class.

In practice, the name of a concept is often learned at the same time, or just prior to, when the concept itself is learned. While the task of learning names is generally easy for one or two objects at a time, it gets increasingly difficult when several different names for several objects or many names for many objects must be learned at once. This situation arises in school learning when students are asked to learn the names of a set of objects, such as the members of Congress. At this point, students may be simply memorizing the names, and there is no harm in that. Some students even enjoy doing it. In any case, label learning is a highly useful activity. Among its other uses, it establishes the basis for communication between the learner and the teacher or between the learner and another source of information.

Learning the sets of names can often be aided by the use of *mnemonic techniques*, most of which have been known for many years. In associating words in pairs, such as *dog-car*, the learner may make up a sentence, "The *dog* chased the *car*." This strategy usually brings about remarkable improvements in paired associate learning (Rohwer, 1970). The learning of foreign-language vocabulary is another example where mnemonic techniques can be put to good use (Pressley, Levin, & Delaney, 1982). The strategy called the *keyword method* involves the use of learner-generated images to cue the retrieval of English equivalents to foreign words. For example, for the Spanish word *carta*, the keyword *cart* might be used as part of an image serving as a link: "The cart was used to deliver the *letter*."

Learning Facts

A fact is a verbal statement that expresses a relation between two or more named objects or events. For example, "The book has a blue cover." In normal communication, the relation expressed by the fact is assumed to exist in the natural world; that is, the words that made up the fact have *referents* in the environment of the learner. The words refer to the objects and to the relation between them. In the example given, the objects are *book* and *blue cover*, and the relation is *has*. It should be noted that a fact, as used here, is defined as the *verbal statement* and *not* the referent or referents to which it refers. (Alternative meanings of a common word like *fact* may readily be found in other contexts.)

Students learn many facts in connection with their studies in school. Some of these are isolated in the sense that they are unrelated to other facts or bodies of information. Others form a part of a connected set, that is, they are related to each other in various ways. For example, children may learn the fact, "the town siren is sounded at noontime," and this may be a fairly isolated fact that is well remembered, even though it is not directly related to other information. Isolated facts may be learned and remembered for no apparent reason. For example, in studying history, a student may learn and remember that Charles G. Dawes served as vice president in the administration of Calvin Coolidge at the same time they might learn the names of everyone else who ever served as a vice president of the United States. Most frequently, though, a specific learned fact is related to other facts in a total set or in a larger body of information. For example, a student may learn a number of related facts about Mexico in the sense that the facts all pertain to aspects of Mexico's geography, economy, or culture. Such facts may also be related to a larger body of information including facts about the culture, economy, and geography of other countries, including the student's native country.

Whether isolated or connected with a larger set, learned facts are of obvious value to the student for two major reasons. First, they are essential to everyday living. Examples are the fact that many stores and banks are closed on Sunday, or the fact that molasses is sticky, or the fact that the student's birthday is the tenth of February. The second and more obvious reason for the importance of learned facts is that they are used in further learning. For example, to find the circumference of a circle, one needs to know the value of *pi*. To complete a chemical equation, one needs to know the valence of certain elements.

When a student needs facts in order to learn certain skills or additional information, the facts can be *looked up* on the Internet or in reference books or tables when the skill or additional information is *ready* to be learned. There are many times when looking up facts is proper and desirable. The alternative is for students to learn the facts and store them in their memory so they can retrieve them whenever they need them. This alternative is often selected because of its convenience and efficiency. Facts that are likely to be used again and again might as well be stored in memory because constantly having to look them up would be a nuisance. However, instructional designers need to decide which of a great many facts in a given course are (1) of such *infrequent* usage that they might as well be looked up, (2) of such *frequent* reference that learning them would be efficient, or (3) of such *fundamental importance* that they ought to be remembered for a lifetime. The conditions of learning for verbal information are presented in Table 5.1.

Learning Organized Knowledge

Larger bodies of interconnected facts, such as those pertaining to events of history or to categories of art, science, or literature, are also learned and remembered. As is the case with learning single facts, the networks of propositions that constitute the new knowledge become linked to larger propositional networks that already exist in memory.

The key to remembering bodies of knowledge appears to be having them

TABLE 5.1	CONDITIONS OF LEARNING FOR VERBAL INFORMATION
Performance	The performance that indicates that a fact has been learned consists of *stating*, either orally or in writing, relations that have the syntactic form of a sentence.
Internal Conditions	For acquisition and storage of facts, an organized network of declarative knowledge needs to be accessed in memory, and the newly acquired fact must be related to this network (E. D. Gagné, 1985). For example, to learn and remember that Mount Whitney is the highest peak in the continental United States, an organized network of propositions (which may differ for each individual learner) needs to be accessed. This network of propositions might include a classification of mountain peaks and ranges, a set of categories of mountains in the United States, and information about the range of mountains that includes Mount Whitney. The learner associates the new fact with a number of other facts within this larger network.
External Conditions	Externally, a verbal communication, picture, or other cue is presented to remind the learner of the larger network of organized knowledge with which the new fact will be associated. The new fact is then presented, usually by means of a verbal statement. The communication may also suggest the association to be acquired, as in conveying the idea that Mount Whitney "sticks up highest" in the Sierra Nevada range. *Imagery* of the mountain and its name may help learners retain the fact. It might be advantageous to *elaborate* on the new fact by presenting other facts that relate to Mount Whitney or to mountain ranges. It is also advantageous for learners to rehearse the new fact by repeating it in *spaced reviews*. Spaced reviews are opportunities for the learner to use the newly learned information in various contexts.

organized in such a way that they can be readily retrieved. Organizing verbal information requires generating new ideas that relate sets of information already stored in memory. When such organizing is carried out during the learning process, later retrieval of information is aided, because affective cues are provided for retrieval (E. D. Gagné, 1985). For example, besides having a theoretical rationale, the periodic table of chemical elements also helps chemistry students remember the names and properties of a large number of elements. Similarly, U.S. history students might acquire a framework of historical periods into which many individual facts can be fitted for learning and remembering. The more this *previously acquired* information is organized, the easier it is for learners to acquire and retain *new* facts that can be related to the organized structure. The conditions of learning for organized knowledge are presented in Table 5.2.

Cues need to be as *distinctive* as possible so that they will not interfere with

TABLE 5.2	CONDITIONS OF LEARNING FOR ORGANIZED KNOWLEDGE
Performance	The substance of paragraphs or longer passages of connected prose appears to be learned and retained in a way that preserves the *meaning* but not necessarily the *detailed* facts (Reynolds & Flagg, 1977). General ideas appear to be recalled better than more specific ones (Meyer, 1975) and details are often "constructed" by the learner in accordance with a general *schema* (Spiro, 1977) that represents the gist of the story or passage.
Internal Conditions	As with individual facts, the learning and storage of larger units of organized verbal information occurs within the context of a network of interconnected and organized propositions previously stored in the learner's memory. Newly learned knowledge may be *subsumed* into larger meaningful structures (Ausubel, Novak, & Hanesian, 1978), or new information might be *linked* to a network of propositions already in the learner's memory (R. M. Gagné, 1985).
External Conditions	The external conditions that favor the learning and retention of organized sets of verbal information pertain primarily to the provision of *cues*. Such cues enable the learner to search successfully for and retrieve information at a later time.

other stored propositions. Cues can be made distinctive by introducing readily memorable stimuli (such as rhymes) within the material to be learned. Organizing ideas into tables or spatial arrays is another method of making cues distinctive (Holley & Dansereau, 1984). *Elaboration* is another technique that enhances retrieval. By adding related information to the new ideas to be learned, more cues are added for retrieval. The cues may be within the learner's environment; for example, parts of a room might be used to help the student recall the sequence of ideas in a speech. More frequently, though, cues are retrieved from the learner's memory as words, phrases, or images.

Another external condition that plays a part in the retention of meaningful prose is the adoption of an *attentional strategy* by the learner. Suggestions of "what to look for" or "what to remember" made to a learner before learning begins have the effect of activating a cognitive strategy for learning. A suggestion may be given directly or indirectly by questions inserted in a text (Frase, 1970) or through the use of an *advance organizer* (Ausubel, Novak, & Hanesian, 1978; Mayer, 1979), such as a brief passage given before text to be learned. This helps orient learners toward what they need to remember in a subsequent passage.

Repetition has long been known to have a marked effect on remembering information. This is true whether one is dealing with isolated facts or with larger bodies of information. Repetition is most effective when learners use *spaced reviews* to recall the information. The mental process the learner uses to retrieve information from memory significantly affects what is remembered.

LEARNING ATTITUDES

Attitudes are a very different kind of learning outcome in that they are related to *emotion* and *action* more than to knowledge. Arising from beliefs and accompanied by emotions, attitudes directly influence a choice of personal action on the part of the individual. A formal definition of attitude is, "an internal state that affects an individual's *choice of personal action* toward some object, person, or event" (R. M. Gagné, 1985). Attitudes are complex human states that affect behavior toward people, things, and events. Many investigators have studied and referred to attitudes as a system of beliefs (Festinger, 1957). These views support the *cognitive* aspects of attitudes. Other writers refer to their *affective* components—the feelings they give rise to or that accompany them, as in liking and disliking. Learning outcomes in the "affective domain" are described by Krathwohl, Bloom, and Masia (1964).

There are several theories concerning the nature and origin of attitudes. A comprehensive review of the major theories and their implications for instruction is presented by Martin and Briggs (1986). These authors describe procedures for instructional design that integrate affective and cognitive objectives.

An attitude is inferred from observations (or often, from reports) of an individual's behavior; it is important to remember that an attitude is a disposition to behavior, it is *not* the behavior itself. For example, if one observes a person dropping a gum wrapper in a wastebasket, an inference cannot be made from that single instance alone that the person has a positive attitude toward disposing of personal trash, or a negative attitude toward pollution, and certainly not an attitude toward gum wrappers. A number of instances of behavior of this general class need to be observed in a number of different situations to make inferences about that person's attitude. The inference is that some internal predisposition affects a whole class of specific instances in which the individual is making a *choice*.

Measuring Attitudes

Attitudes are best measured by unobtrusive observation of the *personal actions* of an individual. In some instances, measurements can be done by observing the frequency of a choice behavior over a period of time. For example, during basic training a military instructor might record observations of a recruit over a weekly period, recording the number of times the recruit helped other recruits as opposed to interfering with their activities. The recordings can help to measure the recruit's "attitude toward *helping others*." However, direct indicators of choice such as this cannot always be obtained. For example, it would be difficult to obtain behavioral measures of a recruit's "attitude toward family life" or "attitude toward senior citizens" because choices in these areas are made outside of the basic-training environment. Therefore, attitude measures are frequently based upon *self-reports* of choices in situations described in questionnaires. Typical questions might ask the recruit, "When you have a weekend off, how much time will you choose to spend with your family?" This method of attitude measurement, emphasizing choices of action, has been described in the work of Triandis (1964).

School Learning

The importance of attitudes in school learning can't be overemphasized. Students' attitudes toward attending school, cooperating with the instructor and fellow students, paying attention to the teacher, and learning itself significantly impact the learning process.

A second large class of attitudes is those that institutions (such as schools) aim to establish as a result of instruction. Attitudes of tolerance and civility toward other people are often mentioned as goals of formal education. Positive attitudes toward learning new skills and knowledge are highly valued. Specific interest in various subjects of instruction, such as science, literature, salesmanship, or labor negotiations, are also highly valued. Finally, schools and other societal institutions are expected to contribute to and influence broader attitudes, known as *values*. Values are attitudes that pertain to such social behaviors as *fairness, honesty, charitableness*, and the more general term *morality* (see R. M. Gagné, 1985, pp. 226–228).

Regardless of the great variety exhibited by the content of these types of attitudes, they all resemble each other in their formal properties. That is to say, whatever the particular content of an attitude, it functions to affect "approaching" or "avoiding." In so doing, an attitude influences a large set of specific behaviors. There are some general principles of learning that apply to the acquisition and changing of attitudes.

Military Training

As mentioned in Chapter 3, attitude and core value instruction are the apex of military training. The attitudes and values that American servicemen and women must possess and display must be beyond reproach. Our military services strive to produce leaders who idealize the values of loyalty, duty, respect, selfless service, honor, integrity, and personal courage. Because military officers lead the men and women of our country into combat to win our nation's wars, servicemen and women must place utmost trust in their leaders if they are to have the courage to fight and win on the battlefield.

Discipline is an integral core value of the military. Military discipline is defined as, ". . . an outward manifestation of mental attitudes and state of training that renders obedience and proper conduct instinctively at all times, under all conditions" (U.S. Army, 2003). While military discipline is most readily displayed in military training, every aspect of military life is affected by it. Military discipline is generally recognized in an individual or unit by smartness of appearance and action; by cleanliness and neatness of dress, equipment, and quarters; by respect for senior officers; and by prompt execution of lawful orders. Disciplinary training programs in each of the services rely on direct methods, such as positive and negative reinforcement and human modeling to condition the mind and body of soldiers, sailors, and airmen and women to respond quickly to orders and to build self-confidence in their ability to direct the actions of subordinates.

Attitude Learning

The conditions that favor the learning of attitudes and the means of bringing about changes in attitudes are complex. A number of contrasting views on the effectiveness of methods for changing an individual's attitudes are reviewed by Martin and Briggs (1986). Instructional methods for establishing desired attitudes differ considerably from those for intellectual skills and verbal information (R. M. Gagné, 1985).

How does the individual acquire or modify certain attitudes or values? According to a great deal of evidence, one way that this is *not* done, is solely through the use of persuasive communication (McGuire, 1969). Most adults recognize the ineffectiveness of repeating such maxims as "Be kind to others," or "Learn to appreciate good music," or "Drive carefully." Even more elaborate communications often have equally poor effects, such as those that make emotional appeals or those that are developed by a careful chain of reasoning. More sophisticated means than these are required to change attitudes.

Direct Methods   There are direct methods for establishing and changing attitudes, which sometimes occur naturally and without prior planning. On occasion, direct methods can also be employed deliberately.

A conditioned response of the classical sort (see R. M. Gagné, 1985, pp. 24–29) may establish an attitude toward some particular class of objects, events, or persons. Many years ago, Watson and Rayner (1920) demonstrated that a child could be conditioned to "fear" (that is, to shrink away from) a white rat the child previously had accepted and petted. This type of response was also made to other small furry animals. The unconditioned stimulus used to bring about the change in the child's behavior was a sudden sharp sound made behind the child's head when the animal (the conditioned stimulus) was present. Although this finding may not have specific pedagogical usefulness, it is important to realize that attitudes can be established in this way and that some of the attitudes students bring to school may be dependent upon earlier conditioned experiences. A tendency to avoid birds or spiders or snakes, for example, may be an attitude that was established through prior conditioning. In theory, almost any attitude might be established in this way.

A direct method of attitude learning that is useful in school situations is based upon the idea of arranging *contingencies of reinforcement* (Skinner, 1968). According to Skinner, initial learning can be established by following a new skill or knowledge with a reward. During learning, a student who begins to *like* the reward (called a *reinforcer*) will also begin to like the new skill or knowledge. Following this principle, one might make a preferred activity for a military recruit, such as engaging in conversation with a senior officer, contingent upon his or her properly saluting the officer before speaking. Continuing this practice in a variety of situations will likely result in the recruit *always* saluting an officer before speaking. The recruit will also come to enjoy the newly learned way of communicating with senior officers because of the success they experienced in doing it properly. In other words, an attitude toward saluting senior officers will take a positive turn.

Generalizing from the learning principle of reinforcement contingencies, it appears that *success* in learning an activity is likely to lead to a positive attitude toward that activity. Recruits often quickly acquire positive attitudes toward small arms operation and maintenance when they begin to get good at it. Recruits develop positive attitudes toward safety when they realize that they are able to recognize conditions in which fellow recruits can be injured.

An Important Indirect Method An excellent and widely used method of establishing or changing attitudes is *human modeling* (Bandura, 1969, 1977). The model can be real or imagined. This method is considered an *indirect* method because the process of learning takes longer than direct methods.

Students can observe and learn attitudes from many kinds of human models. In early childhood, one or both parents serve as role models of acceptable behavior. Older siblings or other family members may also play this role. During formal school years, teachers become models for behavior, from kindergarten through graduate school. But the varieties of human modeling are not confined to school. Public figures may become models, as may prominent sports people, or famous scientists, or artists. People who function as human models do not need to be seen or known personally—they can be seen on television or in movies or on the Internet. They can even be read about in books. Printed literature and information on the Internet has enormous potential for establishing attitudes and values.

The human model must be someone whom learners *respect*; or as some writers would have it, someone with whom they can *identify*. In addition, desirable characteristics of the model must be perceived as *credible* and *powerful* (R. M. Gagné, 1984). People need to observe the model as he or she makes the desired choices of personal action, as in exhibiting kindness, rejecting harmful drugs, or cleaning up litter. A teacher may dispense praise consistently and impartially. Having watched the behavior, whatever it may be, the learner also must see that the model experienced *pleasure* from the behavior. Bandura (1969) referred to this as *vicarious reinforcement*. A sports figure may receive an award or display pleasure in breaking a record; a scientist may exhibit satisfaction in discovering something new or even in getting closer to such a discovery; a teacher may show pleasure in helping a slow-learning child to acquire a new skill.

The essential characteristics of attitudes and the conditions for their learning, using human modeling, are summarized in Table 5.3. The essential conditions must be present even when a human model can't be directly observed, for example, when a learner is viewing television, reading a book, or accessing a Web site.

A variation of human modeling is *role-playing,* where an individual performs the actions of an *imagined* rather than an *actual* person. For example, a student might play the role of a fair-minded work supervisor and make the choices the imaginary supervisor would make. Human modeling also takes place during *class discussions* where social or personal problems are discussed. In these situations, attitudes can be influenced by more than one point of view toward the desired choice of personal action.

Because a person's attitudes can change over time, models that the student comes in contact with over the years bear a tremendous responsibility for the

TABLE 5.3	CONDITIONS OF LEARNING FOR ATTITUDES
Performance	As mentioned previously, an attitude is indicated by the choice of personal actions. These actions can be categorized as showing either a positive or negative tendency toward some objects, events, or persons.
Internal Conditions	A learner must respect and identify with the human model. If not, respect and identification needs to be established. Additionally, in order to imitate the behavior, learners need to have the prerequisite intellectual skills and knowledge related to the behavior. For example, if people are going to elect not to use harmful drugs they need to know the common names of the drugs, and the situations in which they might be available. It should be noted that prerequisite knowledge does not *in itself* engender the attitude.
External Conditions	Established with the following sequence of steps: 1. The model is presented in an appealing and credible way 2. The learner recalls appropriate prerequisite knowledge (choice alternatives and potential outcomes) 3. The model communicates or demonstrates the desired choice of personal action 4. The model displays pleasure or satisfaction with the outcome of their behavior leading to vicarious reinforcement of the target behavior

determination of socially desirable attitudes and the development of *moral behavior* (R. M. Gagné, 1985, pp. 226–227). Teachers should appreciate their important role as human models because of the large amount of time spent by students in their presence. "Good" teachers are often remembered as the ones who modeled positive attitudes.

Some Guidelines for Changing Attitudes

Take the following guidelines into consideration when designing instruction for attitude objectives:

1. Provide learners with information about alternative choices. One of the problems in changing attitudes is that learners may not know of available options. For instance, if you are trying to convince managers to choose to use collaborative management principles, they first need to be aware of those principles.
2. Provide learners with the pros and cons associated with the desired behavior. A lot of behavior occurs out of habit, and learners need to know the consequences of the desired behavior, especially if the consequences are long-term. Information about the costs and long-term benefits can be presented as

verbal information, and simulation can be designed to show the learner long-term consequences.

3. Provide relevant models for the desired behavior. "Do as I say," is not as effective as "Do as I do." The reason that advertising companies get sports heroes to promote their products is that human models form a very important part of the choice behavior. The more salient the human model is for the learner, the greater the likelihood the learner will adopt the behavior.

4. Make sure the environment supports the desired behavior. If an employer wants an employee to choose to return all customer calls before leaving for the day, time must be left at the end of the day to do this. If an environmental conflict appears to be unmodifiable, the person is not likely to adopt the desired behavior.

5. If possible, fit the desired behavior into a larger framework of values. Attitudes are reflective of values. For instance, if individuals value themselves as an important part of an organization, they will make different choices than if they feel unimportant. For example, an employee might choose to work over-time to meet an unusual deadline as a part of the overall value he or she places on "responsibility as a professional."

6. Identify and teach the skills that make the desired behavior possible. People cannot choose to eat low-cholesterol food if they are unable to identify which foods contain cholesterol.

7. Recognize and reward the desired behavior when it is exhibited. If teachers want students to "choose to be self-directed," they must recognize and reward this behavior.

8. Don't inadvertently punish the desired behavior. This is the corollary to the previous guideline. For example, employers should avoid "rewarding" productive employees with more work since it inevitably leads to resentment.

9. Reinforcement should be provided such that the employee will *want* to do more and become even *more* productive.

10. Let learners set their own goals with regard to the desired behavior. There are several different stages in acquiring effective behavior. These include *awareness, acceptance*, and *valuing*. In addition, behaviors are relatively resistant to change, and changes tend to occur very slowly. Allowing learners to set their own goals, report on their own progress, and periodically reevaluate their goals will help them develop greater confidence as they move toward adapting desirable behavior.

11. Use alternative instructional strategies such as simulation, role-playing, collaborative processes, or other interactive experiences in which benefits from the desired behavior become obvious. These types of experiences complement and supplement modeling experiences.

12. Don't inadvertently pair a behavior you want to change with an unrelated behavior. For example, attitudes toward smoking are not directly related to attitudes toward dieting. Because habits and other attitudes often form "behavior complexes" in humans, the most important behaviors should be identified and prioritized.

LEARNING MOTOR SKILLS

Sequences of unitary motor responses are often combined into more complex performances called *motor skills*. Sometimes these are referred to as *perceptual motor skills* or *psychomotor skills*, implying that the performance of motor skills involves the senses and the brain as well as the muscles.

Characteristics of Motor Skills

Motor skills are learned capabilities that underlie performances whose outcomes are reflected in the rapidity, accuracy, force, or smoothness of bodily movement. In school, these skills are interwoven throughout the curriculum at every age and include such diverse activities as using pencils and pens, writing with chalk, drawing pictures, painting, using a variety of measuring instruments, and, of course, engaging in various games and sports. Basic motor skills such as printing numbers on paper are learned early on and are assumed to be present thereafter. In contrast, a motor skill like tying a bowline knot might not have been learned at an early age and it would conceivably constitute a reasonable objective for instruction at a later age.

As motor skills are practiced, they appear to give rise to a centrally organized *motor program* that controls the skilled movements without feedback from the senses (Keele, 1973). However, this is not the whole story. The increased smoothness and timing that result from practicing of a motor skill are considered by Adams (1977) to be dependent on feedback that is both internal and external. Internal feedback takes the form of stimuli from muscles and joints that make up a *perceptual trace*, a kind of motor image that acts as a reference against which learners know if they make a mistake on successive practice trials. External feedback is often provided by *knowledge of results*, an external indication to the learner of the degree of error. For example, when people are learning to play golf, they can usually tell by the way they keep their head down and eye on the ball whether or not they're swinging the club correctly. If they swing and miss, the external condition (golf ball remains on the tee) reflects the problem. As practice proceeds, improvement in the skill comes to depend increasingly upon the internal type of feedback and to a lesser degree upon externally provided knowledge of results.

Motor skills can usually be divided into a series of steps or *separate skills* that constitute the total performance, in the sense that they occur simultaneously or in a temporal order. For example, swimming the crawl involves the separate skills of fluttering the feet and arm movement through the water (both of which are carried out at the same time), as well as the skill of turning the head to breathe, which occurs in a sequence following an arm stroke. Thus, the total performance of swimming is a highly organized and precisely timed activity. Learning to swim requires the *integration* of separate skills of varying degrees of complexity. The separate skills must be learned as well as the integration of the skills.

Learning to integrate skills that were previously learned has been recognized by researchers as a highly significant aspect of the total learning required. Fitts and Posner (1967) use the computer analogy of *executive subroutine* to express its organizing function. Suppose an individual who is learning to drive an automobile has already mastered the skill of driving backward, of turning the steering wheel to direct the motion of the car, and of driving forward at minimal speed. What does the person still need to learn in order to turn the car around on a straight two-lane street? The learner needs to master a procedure in which the separate skills are combined in a suitable order so that by making two or three backward and forward motions, combined with suitable turning, the car is headed in the other direction.

This instructive example of turning a car around shows the importance of the intellectual component of a motor skill. Obviously, the executive subroutine is not in itself a *motor* skill at all—instead, it is a *procedure* and as such it conforms to the qualities of a procedural *rule* as described in Chapter 4. The rule-governed aspect of motor-skill performance is what controls the sequence of action—which movement is executed first, which second, and so on (R. M. Gagné, 1985, pp. 202–212).

Swimming provides an interesting comparison. It, too, has an executive subroutine pertaining to the timing of flutter kicks, arm movements, and head turning to breathe. But in this case, the smooth performance of the separate skills is usually being improved by practice at the same time that the executive routine is being exercised. Many studies have been performed to find out whether practicing the separate skills of various motor skills first is more advantageous than practicing the whole skill (including the executive subroutine) from the outset (Naylor & Briggs, 1963). No clear answer has emerged from these studies, and the best that can be said is that it depends on the skill. We do know that both the executive subroutine and the separate skills must be learned. Practice on either without the other has consistently been shown to be ineffective for learning the total skill.

Learning Motor Skills

Learning motor skills is done through repeated practice. There is no easy way of avoiding practice if one wants to improve the accuracy, speed, and smoothness of motor skills. It is interesting to note that practice even continues to bring about improvement in motor skills over very long periods of time (Fitts & Posner, 1967; Singer, 1980), as performers in sports, music, and gymnastics are well aware. Table 5.4 presents the conditions of learning for motor skills.

Sometimes, verbal instructions are used: "Bend your knee and put the weight on your left foot." In fact, any of the kinds of verbal communication intended for encoding a procedure (see Chapter 4) may be used. A checklist can be presented with the sequence of required movements with the expectation that it will be learned as a part of practice. Pictures or diagrams are often used to show the required sequence. For the improvement of accuracy, speed, and quality of *separate skills* (as well as the *total skill*) the learner must practice and repeat the movements required to produce the desired outcome. The skill is improved by continued practice with the accompaniment of informative feedback (Singer, 1980).

TABLE 5.4	CONDITIONS OF LEARNING FOR MOTOR SKILLS
Performance	The performance of a motor skill embodies the intellectual skill (procedure) that constitutes a movement sequence of muscular activity. When observed as a motor skill, the action meets certain standards (either specified or implied) of speed, accuracy, force, or smoothness of execution.
Internal Conditions	The executive subroutine that governs the procedure of the motor skill must be retrieved from prior learning or must be learned as an initial step. For example, the separate skills of "backing" and "turning" in an automobile must be previously acquired and retrieved to enter into the skill of "turning the car around on a street." As for the separate skills that make up the total skill, they will depend upon the retrieval of individual responses or unitary motor chains.
External Conditions	To learn the *executive subroutine*, an instructor will provide one of several different kinds of communication to the learner.

Short example:
Given a jump rope, the student will execute jumping rope to the criterion of 100 continuous jumps.

Part skills:
1. Jump straight up and down with knees slightly bent.
2. Swing the rope with your wrists at your hips and your arms held close to your body.
3. Time the jump so that the rope doesn't hit your feet.

Executive subroutine:
Swing the rope as it comes by your nose; jump about an inch. This could be learned as a rhyme:

> Swing the rope,
> 'Round it goes,
> Jump an inch,
> As it passes your nose.

SUMMARY

This chapter has been concerned with a description of three different kinds of learning: verbal information, attitudes, and motor skills. Although they have some features in common, they are in fact very different. First, they differ in the kinds of outcome performances, which they make possible:

1. *Verbal information:* Verbally state facts, generalizations, and organized knowledge.

2. *Attitude:* Choose a course of personal action.
3. *Motor skill:* Execute a performance of bodily movement.

Second, as our analysis of the conditions of learning has shown, these three kinds of learning differ from each other in the conditions necessary for their effective achievement. For verbal information, the key condition is the provision of external cues that relate the new information to a *network of organized knowledge* from prior learning. For attitude, one must either ensure direct reinforcement of personal action choices or depend upon *human modeling* to bring about vicarious reinforcement of the learner. And for motor skills, besides the early learning of the executive subroutine and provision for the integration of separate skills, the important condition is *practice* with frequent feedback to the learner.

While the kinds of performances associated with these capabilities and the conditions for their learning are different from those pertaining to intellectual skills and cognitive strategies, they are not less important. The storage and accessibility of verbal information, particularly in the form of organized knowledge, is a legitimate and desirable objective of instruction in both formal and informal education and training settings. The establishment of attitudes is widely acknowledged to be a highly significant objective in many fields, the military in particular. Motor skills, although they often appear to contrast with the cognitive orientation of school learning, individually have their own justification as fundamental components of basic skills, of art and music, of science, and of sports.

Third, the features of these learned capabilities, as compared with intellectual skills, differ with respect to the internal conditions that must be assumed and the external conditions that must be arranged for instruction to be effective. Included in these differences are the *enabling prerequisite* relationships that intellectual skills have with each other, as compared to the *supportive* effects of prior learning on verbal information, attitudes, and motor skills. (R. M. Gagné, 1985, pp. 286–272). This characteristic has particular implications for *sequencing instruction*, as will be seen in a later chapter.

The system of instructional design being developed in this book is one that suggests that first priority be given to intellectual skills as central planning components. That is, the fundamental structures of instruction are designed in terms of what the student will be *able to do* when learning has occurred, and this capability in turn is related to what has previously been learned. This strategy of instructional design typically leads to the identification of intellectual skills as a first step, followed by analysis and identification of their prerequisites. Added at appropriate points to this basic sequence are the cognitive strategies that the basic skills make possible. In other cases, the primary objective of instruction might be a particular body of verbal information, the changing of an attitude, or the mastery of a motor skill. These cases also require analysis to reveal the supportive effects of prior learning and the typical instances where multiple objectives must be learned.

Several of the following chapters directly address procedures for designing instruction. In large part, the techniques we describe are derived from the knowledge of varieties of learning outcomes that we have detailed, and represent direct applications of this knowledge.

REFERENCES

Adams, J. A. (1977). Motor learning and retention. In M. H. Marx & M. E. Bunch (Eds.), *Fundamentals and applications of learning*. New York: Macmillan.

Ausubel, D. P., Novak, J. D., & Hanesian, H. (1978). *Educational psychology: A cognitive view* (2nd ed.). New York: Holt, Rinehart and Winston.

Bandura, A. (1969). *Principles of behavior modification*. New York: Holt, Rinehart and Winston.

Bandura, A. (1977). *Social learning theory*. Englewood Cliffs, NJ: Prentice Hall.

Bretz, R. (1971). *A taxonomy of communication media*. Englewood Cliffs, NJ: Educational Technology Publications.

Brooks, C. C., (2000). Knowledge management and the intelligence community. *Defense Intelligence Journal, 9*(1): 15–24.

Clark, R. E., & Salomon, G. (1986). Media in teaching. In M. C. Wittrock (Ed.), *Handbook of research on reaching* (3rd ed.). New York: Macmillan.

Festinger, L. (1957). *A theory of cognitive dissonance*. New York: Harper & Row.

Fitts, P. M., & Posner, M. 1. (1967). *Human performance*. Monterey, CA: Brooks/Cole.

Frase, L. T. (1970). Boundary conditions for mathemagenic behavior. *Review of Educational Research, 40,* 337–347.

Gagné, E. D. (1985). *The cognitive psychology of school learning*. Boston: Little, Brown.

Gagné, R. M. (1985). *The conditions of learning* (4th ed.). New York: Holt, Rinehart and Winston.

Glaser, R. (1984). Education and thinking: The role of knowledge. *American Psychologist, 39,* 93–104.

Holley, C. B., & Dansereau, D. F. (1984). *Spatial learning strategies: Techniques, applications, and related issues*. New York: Academic Press.

Hulse, S. H., Egeth, H., & Deese, J. (1980). *The psychology of learning* (5th ed.). New York: McGraw-Hill.

Kausler, D. H. (1974). *Psychology of verbal learning and memory*. New York: McGraw-Hill.

Keele, S. W. (1973). *Attention and human performance*. Pacific Palisades, CA: Goodyear.

Krathwohl, D. R., Bloom, B. S., & Masia, B. B. (1964). *Taxonomy of educational objectives. Handbook 11: Affective domain.* New York: McKay.

Letham, D. (2003). Exploring online journalism. Retrieved on 10/1/03 from: http://www.georgetown.edu/faculty/bassr/511/projects/letham/sitetxt.htm.

Mager, R. F. (1968). *Developing attitude toward learning*. Belmont, CA: Fearon.

Martin, B. L., & Briggs, L. J. (1986). *The affective and cognitive domains: Integration for instruction and research*. Englewood Cliffs, NJ: Educational Technology Publications.

Mayer, R. E. (1979). Can advance organizers influence meaningful learning? *Review of Educational Research, 49,* 371–383.

McGuire, W. J. (1969). The nature of attitudes and attitude change. In G. Lindzey & E. Aronson (Eds.). *Handbook of social psychology* (Vol. 3, 2nd ed.). Reading, MA: Addison-Wesley.

Naylor, J. C., & Briggs, G. E. (1963). Effects of task complexity and task organization on the relative efficiency of part and whole training methods. *Journal of Experimental Psychology, 65,* 217–224.

Polanyi, M. (1958). *Personal knowledge.* Chicago: University of Chicago Press.

Pressley, M., Levin, J. R., & Delaney, H. D. (1982). The mnemonic keyword method. *Review of Educational Research, 52,* 61–9 1.

Rohwer, W. D., Jr. (1970). Images and pictures in children's learning: Research results and educational implications. *Psychological Bulletin, 73,* 393–403.

Singer, R. N. (1980). *Motor learning and human performance* (3rd ed.). New York: Macmillan.

Skinner, B. F. (1968). *The technology of reaching.* New York: Appleton.

Triandis, H. C. (1964). Exploratory factor analyses of the behavioral component of social attitudes. *Journal of Abnormal and Social Psychology, 68,* 420–430.

U.S. Army. (2003). Retrieved on 10/01/03 from: http://wwwfac.wmdc.edu/ROTC/Main.html.

Watson, J. R., & Rayner, R. (1920). Conditioned emotional reactions. *Journal of Experimental Psychology, 3,* 1–14.

THE LEARNER

Whatever it is that gets learned can be identified as one or another of the capabilities, or as some combination of them, that are described in Chapters 4 and 5. For example, learners may be expected to learn a set of intellectual skills involving mathematical operations as well as a positive attitude toward the use of these operations. Or, they may be asked to acquire some organized verbal information about the history of the zipper fastener plus some intellectual skills about how to assemble such a fastener. Young learners who encounter a zipper fastener for the first time will doubtless need to learn the motor skill required for its operation.

This range of learning tasks is undertaken by learners who themselves exhibit diversity that is enormous in scope and detail with respect to native ability, background knowledge and experience, and motivation to learn. The learners who approach new learning tasks are all quite different in their characteristics as learners. In the face of these many individual differences, the procedures of instructional design must do the following things:

1. Utilize a rational means of reducing the great diversity of individual learner characteristics to a number small enough to make instructional planning feasible.
2. Identify those dimensions of common learner characteristics that carry different implications for instruction and that can lead to design differences that influence learning effectiveness.
3. Once common learner characteristics have been taken into account, provide a design appropriate for those learner variations that can be shown to make a difference in learning results.

We intend in this chapter to address these procedures and in so doing to convey the knowledge that will lead to good decisions in instructional design. Our discussion will be based upon considerations of what learners are like, what factors influence learning, and how to design instruction for individual differences. The focus in all of these contexts is on the psychological and environmental principles that support a learner-centered approach to instructional design.

LEARNER CHARACTERISTICS

Learners possess certain qualities that relate to instruction—for example, they are able to hear orally delivered communications, read communications printed on the page, and decide whether or not they want to read. Each of these common qualities varies in degree from learner to learner—one person may be able to read pages of printed text rapidly, whereas another reads slowly and haltingly, and still another refuses to even try. These differences might be assumed to be a result of individual differences in ability and motivation, but environmental and developmental factors can also affect learner performance. A task force sponsored by the American Psychological Association (APA Work Group, 1997) reviewed literature from many areas of psychological study to identify key elements from the research that are related to learner characteristics and learning environments with the aim of developing a set of learner-centered psychological principles. They produced 14 psychological characteristics and principles that are divided into four factors (Table 6.1): cognitive and metacognitive, motivational and affective, developmental and social, and individual differences.

These various factors and principles help define internal qualities of learners that are of concern to instructional designers because they affect the entire information-processing chain of learning and students' motivation to learn. These are qualities that may pertain to sensory input; to the internal processing, storage, and retrieval of information; and finally to the organization of learner responses. Furthermore, there are sets of factors and principles that affect what is learned. These include motivational, developmental and social, and individual difference variables.

The Nature of Learner Qualities

Some qualities of the individual that relate to learning are innately determined. For example, visual acuity, although artificial lenses may aid it, is a fundamental property of a person's sensory system that is "built in" and that cannot be changed by learning. Such a property needs to be considered in instruction but only in regard to accommodating the learners' perceptual requirements.

Other learner qualities, however, may affect learning at junctures of information processing that are more critical to instructional planning. For example, it has been proposed that the capacity of the working memory, where to-be-learned material is taken in and processed for memory storage, may have innate capacity limits. The number of items that can be "held in mind" at any one time is shown by the immediate memory span of seven, plus or minus two. The speed with which previously learned concepts can be retrieved and identified may be measured, for example, by requiring individuals to indicate as rapidly as possible whether pairs of letters match when the letters are physically different (as *A,a* or *B,b*). Because of the physical difference, the letters must be retrieved as concepts in order to be matched (Hunt, 1978). The speed and efficiency of this process is another individual quality that may be innately determined.

| TABLE 6.1* | LEARNER-CENTERED PSYCHOLOGICAL FACTORS AND PRINCIPLES (APA, 1997–) |

Cognitive and Metacognitive Factors

1. Nature of the learning process.
   The learning of complex subject matter is most effective when it is an intentional process of constructing meaning from information and experience.

2. Goals of the learning process.
   The successful learner, over time and with support and instructional guidance, can create meaningful, coherent representations of knowledge.

3. Construction of knowledge.
   The successful learner can link new information with existing knowledge in meaningful ways.

4. Strategic thinking.
   The successful learner can create and use a repertoire of thinking and reasoning strategies to achieve complex learning goals.

5. Thinking about thinking.
   Higher order strategies for selecting and monitoring mental operations facilitate creative and critical thinking.

6. Context of learning.
   Learning is influenced by environmental factors, including culture, technology, and instructional practices.

Motivational and Affective Factors

7. Motivational and emotional influences on learning.
   What and how much is learned is influenced by the learner's motivation. Motivation to learn, in turn, is influenced by the individual's emotional states, beliefs, interests and goals, and habits of thinking.

8. Intrinsic motivation to learn.
   The learner's creativity, higher-order thinking, and natural curiosity all contribute to motivation to learn, personal choice and control.

9. Effects of motivation on effort.
   Acquisition of complex knowledge and skills requires extended learner effort and guided practice. Without learners' motivation to learn, the willingness to exert this effort is unlikely without coercion.

Developmental and Social Factors

10. Developmental influence on learning.
    As individuals develop, they encounter different opportunities and experience different constraints for learning. Learning is most effective when differential development within and across physical, intellectual, emotional, and social domains is taken into account.

11. Social influences on learning.
    Learning is influenced by social interactions, interpersonal relations, and communication with others.

Individual Differences Factors

12. Individual differences in learning.
    Learners have different strategies, approaches, and capabilities for learning that are a function of prior experience and heredity.

13. Learning and diversity.
    Learning is most effective when differences in learners' linguistic, cultural, and social backgrounds are taken into account.

14. Standards and assessment.
    Setting appropriately high and challenging standards and assessing the learner and learning progress— including diagnostic, process, and outcome assessment—are integral parts of the learning process.

*Original contents reformatted for this context.

Source: Copyright © 1997 by the American Psychological Association.

For these and other learner characteristics that are genetically determined, instructional design cannot have the aim of altering these qualities by means of learning. Instead, instruction must be designed in such a way as to avoid exceeding human capacities. For example, in the early stages of learning to read, it is possible that some decoding tasks, such as learning words with many letters, may exceed children's working memory capacity. For readers in general, long sentences place demands upon working memory that may exceed the limits of capacity. The design technique to be used in such instances is to use words, sentences, diagrams, or other varieties of communication that stay well within the capacity of the working memory and thus avoid testing its limits.

Qualities That Are Learned

Besides qualities that may be innate, and therefore resistant to change by learning, there is a large set of characteristics that are learned. Many of these have critical effects upon learning. It is these that constitute the internal conditions described in previous chapters in connection with each of the learning varieties.

Intellectual Skills   The typical intellectual skill, a rule, is considered to be stored as a set of concepts that are syntactically organized. Specifically, it is believed by Newell and Simon (1972) that a rule has the functional form called *production*. An example of production is:

> IF the goal is to convert x inches to centimeters,
> THEN, multiply x by 2.54.

Concepts can similarly be represented as productions, as in the following example:

> IF the closed two-dimensional figure has all sides equal,
> THEN, classify the figure as a polygon.

Obviously, we are describing procedures, and that is why the phrase *procedural knowledge* is customarily used to refer to stored sets of intellectual skills. It is also true that productions, considered as stored entities, have the syntactic and semantic properties of propositions. The complex rules that are typical intellectual skills are composed of simpler rules and concepts. The latter are usually learned as prerequisites to the skill that is the targeted instructional objective. When retrieved from memory, the complex skill readily activates these simpler prerequisite skills, because they are actual components. The example in Figure 6–1 shows the component skills that have entered into the learning of the target skill of "pronouncing multisyllable printed words."

Cognitive Strategies   Because strategies are mental procedures, they are a form of intellectual skill. Accordingly, they may be conceived as *productions* and may be represented in that manner. For example, youngsters may acquire a cognitive strategy that enables them to "self-edit" their writing of sentences and, by so doing, generate sentences that are more mature. Thus, an original sentence such as, "John went to the store," when acted upon by a strategy of question asking, may be expanded to, "In the morning, John walked to the hardware store in the center of town."

The production (strategy) in this case may be represented as follows:

IF the goal is to revise a sentence to achieve full communication,
THEN, add component phrases that answer when, how, where, and why.

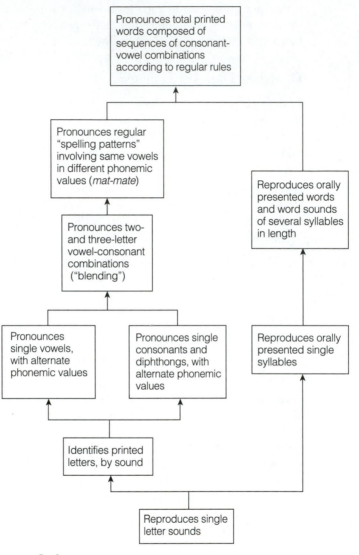

FIGURE **6–1**
A LEARNING HIERARCHY SHOWING PREREQUISITE SKILLS FOR THE SKILL OF PRONOUNCING MULTISYLLABLE PRINTED WORDS

Two characteristics of cognitive strategies are particularly notable. First, they are procedures that govern the selection and use of intellectual skills. Thus, the strategy of "self-editing" can be used only when the intellectual skill of sentence making and phrase making are already known. And second, cognitive strategies can range from relatively simple to complex. In the self-editing example, the structure of the strategy is not itself complex—it is simply a matter of asking specific questions such as "when, how, where, and why?" In other contexts, such as playing chess or analyzing the system dynamics of an organization, the cognitive strategies become more complex and place a greater challenge on a person's cognitive processing capacities. This is called "cognitive load" (Pass & van Merriënboer, 1994), and recent approaches to instructional design now focus on how to create instruction that accommodates the learning of complex cognitive skills (van Merriënboer, 1997). Typically, cognitive strategies have broad application. In the case of self-editing, the strategy is applicable to virtually any sentence of whatever subject. Yet, cognitive strategies are domain specific—the self-editing strategy is relevant to sentence editing and revision but generally not sufficient for something like reviewing a research article or critiquing a movie, which require more comprehensive and complex sets of guidelines.

Verbal Information Knowledge in verbal or declarative form may be stored as individual propositions (facts), or as networks of propositions, and organized around central ideas or generic concepts. As indicated in Figure 6–2, the fact that

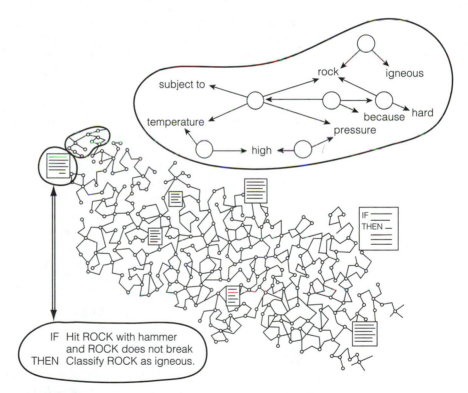

FIGURE 6–2

A NETWORK OF INTERRELATED PROPOSITIONS

Many items of verbal information and interspersed intellectual skills (productions), shown here as boxes. (From E. D. Gagné, *The cognitive psychology of school learning*, copyright 1985 by Little, Brown; Boston. Reprinted by permission.)

"igneous rock is very hard because it has been subjected to high temperature and pressure" is connected with a very large network of other interrelated propositions (E. D. Gagné, 1985). Furthermore, elements of this complex network make connections at various points with productions (intellectual skills) (see Figure 6–2).

When a search of memory makes contact with a single proposition, other interconnected propositions are "brought to mind" as well. The process is known as *spread of activation* (Anderson, 1985) and is considered to be the basis for the retrieval of knowledge from the long-term memory store. When the learner attempts to recall a single idea, the initial search activates not only that idea but many related ones also. Thus, in searching for the name Helen, for example, one may be led by spreading activation through Troy and Poe and Greece and Rome and the Emperor Claudius to the Battle of Britain and to many things in between. Spreading activation not only accounts for what we perceive as random thoughts, as in free association, but is also the basis for the great flexibility that is apparent when we engage in reflective thinking.

Attitudes   An attitude in memory appears to be somewhat complex and, therefore, difficult to represent in a schematic fashion. For an attitude, what is stored in memory would appear to include several motivational elements, both cognitive and emotional, such as (1) the choice of personal action, as exhibited by a human model; (2) a representation of a standard of conduct for the self that reflects the standard of the human model; and (3) a feeling of satisfaction derived from reinforcement of the chosen action or from vicarious reinforcement, as described in Chapter 5. Overlaid on these stored memories may be an emotional disposition arising from a given situation, as when a person experiences an internal propensity to resist contrasting ideas or dissonant beliefs.

Attitudes, too, are likely to be embedded within a complex of interconnected propositions. It has often been observed that internal states affecting choices of personal action are strongly influenced by situational factors. It may be supposed, therefore, that attitudes occur within propositional networks that are organized by situation. A person may have an attitude of neatness, for example, that applies to the situation of storing kitchen tools but does not apply to the storage of papers on a desk. When memory of the situation is revived, retrieval of the objects and events usually brings with it a revival of the attitude as well. The number 911 is an excellent illustration of such retrieval and of situational specificity. Almost all Americans can represent this number to themselves as "nine-eleven" or "nine-one-one." For many years, only the second representation would have occurred to people, and it would evoke a sense of security, that help is on the way, because of its association with a more-or-less universal phone number for emergency assistance, at least within the United States. However, since the attacks on the World Trade Center on September 11, 2001, people have been equally likely to see this number as "nine-eleven," which evokes fear, horror, and anger, the polar opposites of their original associations with this number. Now, other elements of a given situation will affect which attitudes and emotions will be evoked by this number.

Of particular importance to one's representation of a given set of attitudes are specific memories associated with someone who serves as a personal model. This human model is remembered in reference to personal action choices, and as an admirable person who is both credible and powerful (R. M. Gagné, 1985). Memory storage also includes the model's action choices: The model may be remembered as rejecting harmful drugs, or as liking running for exercise, or as preferring to listen to classical music. When these memories are retrieved along with the situational factors appropriate to each, conditions become right for the choice of personal action that reveals an attitude.

Motor Skills   The core memory of a motor skill appears to consist of a highly organized and centrally located motor program (Keele, 1968). Such a program is established by practice, attains automaticity, and becomes only incidentally responsive to variations in external stimulation and in kinesthetic feedback, as when a driver unthinkingly corrects the steering wheel after feeling the car drifting off course. In addition, a motor skill has some prerequisites, as is the case with intellectual skills. One set of simpler components of a motor skill may be its part skills—sometimes easy to identify, and sometimes not. In threading a needle, for example, one can detect the part skills of (1) holding the needle steady, (2) inserting the thread in the hole, and (3) grasping the end of the thread after insertion.

Even more essential as an aspect of motor skill storage is its procedure, or executive subroutine, usually learned as the earliest component of a motor skill (Fitts & Posner, 1967). The basic sequence of movement, having no requisite smoothness and timing, has the character of an intellectual skill (a procedural rule). Such a procedure may have been acquired as a prerequisite to the motor skill or learned in an early stage of practice. When a motor skill has been unused for many years, the executive subroutine is likely to remain intact, even though the performance has become hesitant and rusty.. A person will remember how to finger a clarinet, even though the musical quality of the performance may show the effects of years of disuse.

Having learned a skill to the level of automaticity helps explain why the skill, such as riding a bicycle, isn't totally lost even after years of disuse. But what explains the continued development of a skill to exceptionally high levels of expertise, even after one achieves the level of automaticity? Both Ericsson's extensive research and literature reviews on this topic (for example, Ericsson, Krampe, & Tesch-Roemer, 1993; Ericsson, 1998) show that most expert performers started practicing at younger ages, sought out teachers and instruction earlier, and perhaps most importantly, engaged in higher levels of deliberate practice with full concentration than less accomplished performers in the same domains.

QUALITIES THAT INFLUENCE LEARNING

There are numerous qualities that influence the amount and quality of learning. Some of these, such as intrinsic motivation, developmental factors, and individual differences in capabilities, are internal characteristics of the learner. Others, such as environmental effects on stimulation and attention, social norms and values, and standards and assessments, are external. In keeping with the categories established by the APA Work Group (1997), we can group these factors under motivation and affective factors, developmental and social factors, and individual difference factors.

Motivational Factors

One characteristic that should be taken into consideration when designing instruction is learner motivation. Motivation is defined by Good and Brophy (1990) as " a hypothetical construct to explain the initiation, direction, intensity and persistence of goal-directed behavior" (p. 360). In other words, there are forces that cause a learner to engage in study behavior, focus attention on a particular learning goal, or do extra work on an assignment. Motivation cannot be measured directly, but we infer motivation by observing the student's behavior.

Causes of motivation are classified as either extrinsic (external) or intrinsic (internal) to the learner. One type of intrinsic motivation is curiosity. Another, quite different intrinsic motivator is need for achievement. By understanding what internal factors motivate people, we can design instruction to be motivating. We can build in questions to arouse curiosity, or in the case of need for achievement, we can add opportunities for personal goal setting and competition. Like the external events of instruction, external conditions activate motivational processes or states. However, not all individuals are motivated by the same things. That is, a particular situation may motivate one individual because of prior learning, experience, or expectations, but not another. However, investigators of motivation have described many principles or conditions that seem generalizable enough to warrant their consideration in the design of instructional materials. Keller (1987, 1999) has developed a model of motivational design called *ARCS*, an acronym for the following categories of motivational conditions: attention, relevance, confidence, and satisfaction. The ARCS model has two major parts. The first is a synthesis of propositions and guidelines from many different motivation theories. The second is a motivational design process that incorporates the various motivational factors in a process analyzing students' motivational conditions as a basis for prescribing appropriate motivational strategies. As shown in Table 6.2, each ARCS category implies certain questions that a designer might ask in attending to the problem of learner motivation. For example, under the category of attention, the teacher or designer might capture the student's interest by showing a cartoon or colorful graphic. To make the lesson highly relevant, one might have the learner set his or her own goals for the topic to be studied. To build learner confidence, there should be a provision for practice with a high degree of success; and to give the learner a feeling of satisfaction, the instruction should provide for a reward for good performance. These are only a few specific suggestions that can be derived from applying Keller's model. The objective of the ARCS model is to make the theory and research in the field of motivation more easily applied in actual instruction. The objective in attending to motivation within instructional design is to get the students to give the time and intensity of effort necessary in order to learn the required knowledge and skills.

TABLE 6.2	MOTIVATIONAL CATEGORIES OF THE ARCS MODEL*

Categories and Subcategories	Process Questions
Attention	
A.1. Perceptual arousal	What can I do to capture their interest?
A.2. Inquiry arousal	How can I stimulate an attitude of inquiry?
A.3. Variability	How can I maintain their attention?
Relevance	
R.1. Goal orientation	How can I best meet my learners' needs? (Do I know their needs?)
R.2. Motive matching	How and when can I provide my learners with appropriate choices, responsibilities, and influences?
R.3. Familiarity	How can I tie the instruction to the learners' experiences?
Confidence	
C.1. Learning requirements	How can I assist in building a positive expectation for success?
C.2. Success opportunities	How will the learning experience support or enhance the students' beliefs in their competence?
C.3. Personal control	How will the learners clearly know their success is based on their efforts and abilities?
Satisfaction	
S.1. Natural consequences	How can I provide meaningful opportunities for learners to use their newly acquired knowledge/skill?
S.2. Positive consequences	What will provide reinforcement to the learners' successes?
S.3. Equity	How can I assist the students in anchoring a positive feeling about their accomplishments?

*Adapted from Keller (1987).

Developmental and Social Factors

Developmental psychology provides insight into the cognitive development of children and how to accommodate their learning patterns in the design of instruction. Piaget (1963) identified four distinct stages of development from infancy to the middle teen years. In the first, *sensorimotor*, a child begins to learn such things as object permanence (objects do not go out of existence when they are out of sight) and goal-directed behavior (that systematic actions result in predictable results, as in how to get the blocks out of a container). At approximately two years of age, children enter the *preoperational* stage in which they develop the concept of language as symbols that represent objects and actions; but they have not yet acquired what Piaget calls "operations." Operations are actions a person can carry out mentally and also reconstruct in a reverse order, instead of actually having to perform the actions in a physical, hands-on, manner. The following stage, *operational*, is from approximately seven to 11 years of age. This is when children acquire the well-known principle of *conservation*. The preoperational child is likely to say that a tall, thin cylinder has more liquid in it than a short, wide cylinder, even though both have the same volume. The operational child can conserve the perception of quantity from one situation to the next, even though the representation is different. The final stage, *formal operation*, occurs after age 11. It includes the ability to solve abstract problems in logical ways and to become more concerned about social issues and engage from "nonegocentric" perspectives. Instruction is most successful at these early ages if the developmental characteristics of the learners are considered.

In contrast to Piaget was Vygotsky (1978), whose developmental and learning theory is more socially oriented and whose work has a strong influence in contemporary expressions of constructivist learning theory. Piaget believed that the developmental process was primarily internal to the learner, and that children are primarily focused on themselves during the early stages of cognitive development. In contrast, Vygotsky identified children's verbalizations of their actions and their cognitive strategy development as being directly influenced by their interactions with more capable members of their culture. At any given point of development, there are tasks and cognitive processes that are very comfortable for the child, but there are also those areas that are at the outer edge of a child's readiness. The child can perform and develop in these challenging areas with the assistance and encouragement of others or with compensating supports in the learning setting. Vygotsky called these outer areas "zones of proximal development." These are areas where well-designed instruction and teaching are particularly effective because they are within the child's potential reach. The kinds of help that facilitate a child's development were called *scaffolding* by Jerome Bruner (Wood, Bruner, & Ross, 1976). Scaffolding refers specifically to assisting a child to increase cognitive capacities and skills within a zone of proximal development. The term is now used broadly to refer to any kinds of cues, prompts, explanations, job aids, or other traditional tactics that will help a person learn.

Individual Difference Factors

The list of learner-centered psychological principles that were formulated by the APA Study Group includes a variety of individual and environmental influences on what is learned: inherited characteristics, learning style preferences, acquired learning strategies, social and cultural values and beliefs, and expectations as defined in the standards represented by externally defined goals and assessment tools used in learning environments. Many of these individual difference factors are integrated into the various parts of this book, especially in the sections on instructional design processes and strategies.

With respect to assessments, self-evaluation of learning performance also has an influence on student motivation and performance. Instructional designers can incorporate self-evaluation tactics in their designs. These require learners to assess the quality of their own performance and to keep a record of their judgments. It appears that students can judge their behavior reasonably accurately (Rhode, Morgan, & Young, 1983), and when self-evaluation is combined with goal setting and self-recording of study time, self-evaluation can have positive effects on learning (Morgan, 1985). However, if students become too worried about succeeding or have poor self-concepts in relation to achievement, then self-evaluation can have negative effects.

MEMORY ORGANIZATION

The unitary things that are learned and stored in long-term memory may be conveniently thought of as propositions (both declarative and procedural), images, and attitudes. These unitary entities are organized into interconnected networks that may be searched out and retrieved by the learner to serve the requirements of some activity or of further learning.

The networks representing various kinds of learned capabilities often assume a form called a *schema,* in which ideas are organized in terms of a general topic or use function. As writers on the subject have pointed out (Rumelhart, 1980; Schank & Abelson, 1977), we carry around with us knowledge structures organized in terms of such general topics as "going to a restaurant" and "shopping in a supermarket."

An even more general conception of the stored capabilities of human learners is the notion of *ability*. Abilities are measured by psychological tests, which sample the quality of performance in a number of areas of activity. Some well-known ability areas are verbal, numerical, visual, and spatial. These are usually differentiated into more specific abilities, such as verbal fluency, numerical reasoning, memory for visual form, spatial orientation, and the like (Cronbach, 1970; Guilford, 1967). Still other general characteristics of human learners belong in the affective and personality domains. They are often referred to as *traits* and include such qualities as anxiety and motivation to learn (Tobias, 1986). The importance of abilities and traits as human qualities lies in the possibility that they may affect learning differently depending upon differences in the nature of instruction. Thus, learners with high verbal ability may respond well to instruction consisting of tersely written printed text. Learners who are very anxious may learn best from instruction that has a highly organized structure. These are simply examples and will be further discussed in a later section.

SCHEMAS

A schema is an organization of memory elements (propositions, images, and attitudes) representing a large set of meaningful information pertaining to a general concept (Anderson, 1985). The general concept may be a category of objects like house, office, tree, and furniture. Or the concept may be of an event, as in going to a restaurant or watching a baseball game. Regardless of subject, a schema contains certain features common to the set of objects or events contained in that category. Thus, the schema for *house* contains information on certain well-understood features, such as construction material, rooms, walls, roofs, windows, and the function of human dwelling. These features are called *slots*, to imply that the values they take are there to be "filled in" (how many windows, what kind of roof, and so on).

Event schemas have similar properties, including slots. Thus, the slots to be filled in a restaurant schema (Schank & Abelson, 1977) include such actions as entering the restaurant, deciding where to sit, examining a menu, ordering from the waitstaff, eating food, receiving the bill, paying the bill, leaving a tip, and leaving the restaurant. Thus, everyone who has had sufficient experience in dining in a restaurant carries around in memory a schema of roughly this sort, containing slots into which new facts from new experiences are fitted. Obviously, depending on his experience, one person's "restaurant schema" will differ from that of another person. Schemas may differ in their comprehensiveness as well as in the details stored in their slots. These differences may have a particular importance to the planning of instruction whose content is related to the schemas.

In approaching learning from newly presented instruction, learners come to the task with various schemas already in their memories. Thus, in beginning a lesson on the period of U.S. history encompassed by the presidential terms of Franklin Delano Roosevelt, learners are likely to have available schemas that contain such interconnected concepts as the Great Depression, the New Deal, and World War II. These and other features are filled out with more elaborate historical information by the new lesson. In learning to solve arithmetic word problems, youngsters may solve certain problems by reference to schemas of *change, combine,* or *compare* (Riley, Greeno, & Heller, 1983). For instance, a *combine* schema is applicable to the kind of problem that states: "Joe and Charles have 8 pennies together; Joe has 5 pennies; how many pennies does Charles have?" A learner schema of *air pollution*, besides containing information about the oxides of sulfur and nitrogen and their possible origins, is likely to include also an attitude that influences personal choices of action toward votes on legislation pertaining to this subject.

West, Farmer, and Wolff (1991) differentiate between *knowledge (state)* schema and *process* schema. West (1981) believes that schemas control perception. That is, an individual sees an event or stimulus only in reference to a schema. The schema directs attention to relevant stimuli (or perhaps more accurately, makes a stimulus relevant); and in conjunction with existing knowledge, it gives meaning to an event. This view implies that learning is a highly personal act. However, to the extent that schemas are learned as a function of growth experiences in a more or less homogeneous society, we might expect that individuals will possess and activate similar process schemas. For example, in the United States, we are taught a procedure for subtraction that involves a component procedure we call *borrowing*. However, in Australia, children are taught a different algorithm for subtraction that does not involve borrowing. So, with regard to arithmetic, the word subtraction would evoke one process schema in the United States, and quite a different one in Australia.

What the instructor should realize is that individuals do possess different knowledge and process schemas. Therefore, what may be obvious to most students may not make any sense at all to another. A careful analysis of a particular individual's knowledge schema may show that there are important prerequisite skills or knowledge missing which make it difficult or impossible to give the present stimulus meaning. The instructional solution in this case is to teach the prerequisites previous to the primary instructional intervention.

Abilities and Traits

In addition to the organization resulting from specific instances of learning and experience, it has long been apparent that human performance is affected in quality by even more broadly influential structures called *abilities*. Over a period of many years, these factors relating to how well new problems can be solved have been differentiated from the original purpose of assessing general ability (Cronbach, 1970). In general, the abilities that can be assessed by psychological testing tend to be stable characteristics of each human individual, persisting over long periods of time, and not readily changed by regimens of instruction or practice focused upon them.

Other qualities of the performing human individual reflect personality and are usually referred to as *traits*. These aspects of human performance, like abilities, are also persistent over relatively long periods and are not readily influenced by instruction aimed at changing them. Examples of traits are *introversion, conscientiousness, impulsiveness*, and *self-sufficiency*. So many traits have been assessed in so many ways, that it is difficult and perhaps pointless to keep track of them. Nevertheless, the possibility exists that differences in one or more traits will exhibit an influence on learning that makes desirable the adaptation of instructional approaches to these differences. For example, perhaps anxious learners will be better served by instruction that differs from the kind used with the nonanxious learner.

Differential Abilities It is still an unanswered question as to whether it is most useful to measure individual differences in general ability (or intelligence) or to measure a number of differential abilities. Scores on the latter kinds of tests show positive correlations with each other, and low-to-moderate correlations with measures of intelligence obtained from tests of general ability (such as the Stanford-Binet or the Wechsler Scales). Such abilities, therefore, are not truly distinctive one from another. And those who favor a view of intelligence as a general ability take satisfaction in noting that the various measures of different abilities all contain a g factor (for general intelligence). Various factors of differential ability have been proposed and investigated. Among the best-known systems for classifying abilities are those of Thurstone (1938) and Guilford (1967). Some of the best-known differential abilities are contained in the following list, which includes an indication of the kind of system used to measure each.

> Reasoning: Completing nonsense syllogisms
> Verbal comprehension: Comprehension of printed prose
> Number facility: Speeded tests of addition, division
> Spatial orientation: Identifying rotated figures
> Associative memory: Recalling object or number pairs
> Memory span: Immediate recall of digit lists

There are several varieties of commercially available tests designed to measure abilities of these sorts, among others. A description of ability tests may be found in Anastasi (1976), Cronbach (1970), and Thorndike and Hagen (1985).

Traits   The tendencies of people to respond in characteristic ways to a broad variety of particular situations give rise to the inference that they possess certain relatively stable personality traits (Cronbach, 1970; Corno & Snow, 1986). Many kinds of personality traits have been defined and studied in students of a variety of ages and types. In recent years, a great deal of research has been done on a few traits that appear to have strong conceptual relation to human abilities as well as to academic achievement. Some of the most widely studied traits of this sort are motivational characteristics such as achievement motivation (McClelland, 1965), anxiety (Tobias, 1979), locus of control (Rotter, 1966), and self-efficacy (Bandura, 1982).

Research on achievement-related traits often takes the form of a search for *aptitude treatment interactions (ATI)*. The hypothesis being investigated is that some variety of instruction (called a *treatment*) will differ in its effectiveness for learners scoring high and learners scoring low on a trait. In line with this idea, studies have shown such relationships with several of the traits mentioned previously (Cronbach & Snow, 1977; Snow, 1977). Thus, learners with high achievement motivation appear to achieve better than those with low motivation when the instruction permits a considerable degree of learner control (Corno & Snow, 1986). Another example of ATI comes from studies of the anxiety trait. Anxious students who were given the option of reviewing instruction on videotape were found to learn more than anxious students who viewed the same tapes in groups without the review option (Tobias, 1986). Some students feel that external factors (such as luck) are responsible for the results of their learning, whereas others attribute outcomes to their own efforts. This personality difference is called locus of control (Rotter, 1966). Students with an internal attribution might be expected to work harder and to have an active orientation to learning; this hypothesis may account for findings of ATI with respect to this trait.

Summary of Memory Organization

The unitary things that are learned and stored in human memory may be conceived of as *learning outcomes* and are called *learned capabilities* (R. M. Gagné, 1985). These learning capabilities are intellectual skills, verbal information, cognitive strategies, attitudes, and motor skills. They can be acquired through learning in a reasonably short time as a result of suitably designed instruction. These unitary capabilities (such as particular concepts, rules, or verbal propositions) are stored in memory as part of larger complexes called *schemas*.

A *schema* is a network of memory entities associated with each other through propositions, relating to an organizing general concept. There are event schemas (shopping in a supermarket), object and place schemas (your living room), problem schemas (elapsed clock time), and many others in the repertory of the average person. Schemas are characterized by commonly existing features, sometimes called *slots*, into which newly learned information is fitted. Thus, a supermarket schema may contain such slots as grocery cart, produce area, bread counter, meat counter, refrigerator, check-out counter, and the like. Newly acquired information about any particular shopping experience tends to be stored in these slots.

In addition to the large complexes of learned information and skills represented by schemas, there are even more general dispositions that can be revealed by psychological tests—*abilities and traits*. These features of human performance, although influenced by learning over long periods of time, are usually considered relatively stable characteristics that are not readily affected by instruction. An ability like spatial orientation may, however, have an effect on the ease with which particular learners acquire the skills of map reading. Likewise, a personality trait such as anxiety may affect the readiness for learning of certain learners when faced with a task that has severe time constraints. Relations of this sort are studied in investigations of aptitude treatment interaction (ATI). In practical terms, this type of research seeks ways in which instruction can be adaptively designed to allow for individual differences in abilities and traits.

In order for students to become successful learners, as described in the APA list of learner-centered psychological principles (APA Work Group, 1997) described earlier in this chapter, they must have the capacity for constructing meaningful and functional schemas that enable them to engage in strategic thinking and build meaningful constructions of knowledge. In other words, learning capabilities such as intellectual skills, verbal information, cognitive strategies, attitudes, and motor skills are the building blocks for developing complex cognitive skills in support of schema development and successful learning.

LEARNERS AS PARTICIPANTS IN INSTRUCTION

Learners come to learning situations and to new learning tasks with certain performance tendencies already present. In the simplest case, learners may approach instruction on some subject or topic they already know. More frequently, however, the new material may be only partially known, and gaps in knowledge may need to be filled. Frequently also, learners may have background knowledge or knowledge that is prerequisite to the learning of new material. Besides these direct relationships between the stored effects of prior learning and new learning, there may be more general ability differences in learners, or in groups of learners, that can profitably be taken into account in the design of instruction.

Designing Instruction for Learner Differences

As might be expected from our previous discussion, each of the kinds of learner characteristics carries different implications for the design of instruction. The most direct effects of the memory storage of prior learning can be seen in the entities called *learned capabilities*, which include intellectual skills, verbal information, cognitive strategies, attitudes, and motor skills. Retrieval of these previously acquired kinds of memories by the learner has a specific influence on the learning of new material. Similar effects result from the recall of organized information in the form of schemas, which may provide direct support to the accomplishment of a new learning task. Effects that are more indirect, however, are provided by learner abilities and traits. These dispositions do not enter directly into the new learning, but they may greatly influence the ease with which learning processes are carried out.

When a new learning task is undertaken, the learner begins with several varieties of memory structures already in place, which are available for retrieval as part of the processing of the new learning. The kinds of effects exerted by what has been learned previously depend primarily on the objective of the new learning (R. M. Gagné, 1980). It will be clearest, therefore, to consider how new learning is affected by prior learning in terms of the expected outcomes of the new learning. We shall deal with this question in the following paragraphs, in terms of the learning outcomes that may be the principal objectives of new learning.

New Learning of Intellectual Skills

The learning of intellectual skills is most clearly influenced by the retrieval of other intellectual skills that are prerequisite. Usually, these are simpler skills and concepts that, when analyzed, are revealed to be actual components of the skill to be newly learned (R. M. Gagné, 1985). Results of analysis of this sort may be expressed as a *learning hierarchy*, an example of which is shown in Figure 6–3. For the skill of calculating velocity from a position-time graph, the various skills in subordinate boxes are prerequisites. As the studies of White (1973) have shown, the retrieval of these prerequisite skills has a direct supporting effect on the learning of the targeted intellectual skill. In fact, the absence of any of the skills in a subordinate box markedly decreases the ease of learning the superior skill to which it is connected. Clearly, for intellectual skills, the most direct effect of prior learning is through the retrieval of other intellectual skills that are prerequisite components.

To be the most effective for new learning, prerequisite skills must be thoroughly learned, that is, learned to *mastery*. Presumably, this degree of learning makes the prerequisite skills easier to recall and, therefore, more readily accessible for new learning. Another condition that affects ease of retrieval is the number of cues available to the memory search process. Aids to memory search are provided by the cues of a schema. Accordingly, embedding the prerequisite skill (or skills) within the organized network of a schema may be expected to have a beneficial effect on instruction.

How will the presence of abilities and traits affect the learning of intellectual skills? This question deserves a separately headed section since its answer applies generally to other kinds of learning outcomes as well as to intellectual skills.

Effects of Abilities and Traits on New Learning

Human abilities are likely to affect new learning by contributing strategic techniques of processing the learning task and its material. For example, the ability called *numerical facility*, when possessed in a high degree, makes the processing of mathematics material easier and more rapid than it is for those whose numerical facility is low. The *verbal comprehension* ability has a similar facilitative effect on the processing of material presented in the form of connected prose. *Spatial orientation* as an ability aids in the processing of learning tasks that include information presented as figures and spatial arrays. In each case, the ability contributes to learning in an *indirect* fashion by making the learning process easier. This effect contrasts with that of learned capabilities and of schemas, which enter directly into the new learning in a substantive manner.

Traits may also be expected to have an indirect effect upon the learning of intellectual skills (and other learning outcomes). Learners who are very anxious may be reassured by frequent feedback on their performances during practice of a newly learned skill, and they accordingly learn more readily than under conditions

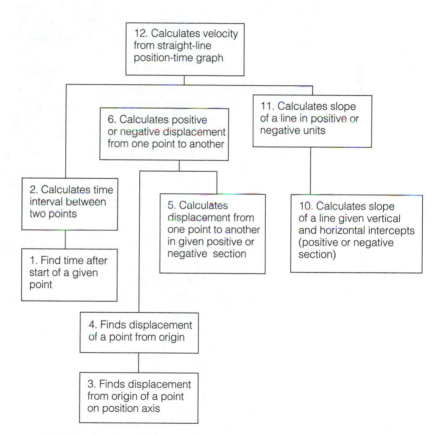

FIGURE **6–3**

A LEARNING HIERARCHY SHOWING RELATIONSHIPS OF PREREQUISITE SKILLS TO THE TASK

Calculating velocity from a straight-line graph of position and rime (subordinate skills 7, 8, and 9 were found to be invalid prerequisites and are not shown here). (Based on a description in R. T. White & R. M. Gagné (1978). Formative evaluation applied to a learning hierarchy, *Contemporary Educational Psychology, 3,* 87–94.) Reprinted with permission of Elsevier.

of infrequent feedback. Learners with high achievement motivation may learn rapidly when challenged by discovery learning, whereas learners with low achievement motivation may perform poorly.

An account of abilities and traits in instruction by Corno and Snow (1986, p. 618) conceives of their effects in the following manner. Abilities and traits in the individual learner give rise to an *aptitude complex* for performance in a particular situation. This complex engenders an attitude of *purposive striving*. Together with the learner's intellectual abilities, this prevailing attitude affects the quality of learning; along with personality traits, purposive striving influences the quantity of learning activity ("level of effort" and "persistence"). The combined effect of these factors of quality and quantity is to determine *learner engagement*, which in turn leads to *learner achievement*. Quite evidently, Corno and Snow see abilities and traits as having indirect effects upon learning. That is, these qualities of individuals influence how they go about learning, although they do not enter into the substance of the learning itself.

Bearing this point in mind, how can instructional design take abilities and traits into account? Corno and Snow suggest two alternatives: (1) by circumventing lack of aptitude, and (2) by developing aptitude. The first of these may be simply exemplified by instructional design that uses easily read text and elaborate learning guidance for learners exhibiting a lack of aptitude in verbal comprehension. Developing aptitude is the other route, and it involves instruction and practice in cognitive strategies (O'Neil, 1978; Snow, 1982). Although much progress has been made in this area of investigation, a conservative view is that cognitive strategies applicable to specific task domains are readily learnable, but generalizable strategies may require many years to develop.

New Learning of Cognitive Strategies   As is true for intellectual skills, cognitive strategies in their initial learning call upon previously learned memories. One would expect that there might be readily identifiable prerequisite skills whose retrieval would aid the learning of new cognitive strategies. For example, could a strategy such as "remembering a list of names by associating each name in order with an object of furniture in its place around a familiar room" be aided by retrieval of some prerequisite skills? The answer is, of course, that prerequisite skills do in fact, support this cognitive strategy. But note the fact that these prerequisite skills are often very simple and well known. The prerequisite skills are simply (1) identifying familiar furniture pieces, (2) imaging familiar furniture pieces, and (3) matching the sounds of names and objects (such as *hair* and *chair*). Actually, it would seem that the more general the cognitive strategy, the simpler its prerequisites. For example, a general problem-solving strategy is to "work the problem in steps backward from the goal." To acquire this strategy, the learner must make use of previous skills of the following sort: (1) the ability to identify the problem goal, and (2) the ability to place a set of steps in backward order.

Do schemas come into play as recalled entities in the new learning of a cognitive strategy? Again, as in the case of intellectual skills, a schema may provide cues for the retrieval of a strategy and its prerequisite skills. The familiar room in the list-learning strategy is itself a schema and is useful because it is easy to retrieve from memory. The "working backward" strategy, or others more specifically oriented toward task domains, may be retrieved because it is analogous to the strategy employed in another, different problem. The entire schema representing the previously encountered problem may be retrieved to reveal the analogy.

As for abilities and traits, they may be assumed to operate in the manner described in the previous section. They have indirect effects on the learning of new cognitive strategies. Some investigators propose that the aim of instruction in cognitive strategies is to bring about *aptitude development*. In that case, instruction may begin with a task that uses an ability that has been only partially developed and proceed to develop it further. For example, the ability to "mentally rotate figures" (spatial visualization) might be initially assessed as poorly developed in particular individuals. By instruction composed mainly of practice and feedback, the development of this ability could be attempted. Kyllonen, Lohman, and Snow (1981) successfully conducted a demonstration of training in spatial visualization.

New Learning of Verbal Information   The new learning and storage of verbal information requires a number of intellectual skills relevant to the understanding and use of language. These are skills including the employment of synonyms and metaphors in word meanings, the rules of syntax in the formation of sentences, and the logical sequencing of ideas among related propositions. It is these basic skills of language comprehension and usage that strongly affect how readily learners will acquire new knowledge of the declarative variety and, ultimately, what quantity of such knowledge will be available in their long-term memories.

The learning of new verbal information is strongly affected by retrieval of previously learned information. The cues provided by the to-be-learned information are believed to activate concepts in the long-term memory that spread to other items in a propositional network—the process known as *spreading activation* (Anderson, 1985). Presumably, the more such ideas have been subject to elaborative processing, the more readily will the retrieval of knowledge take place. And the greater the elaboration of knowledge—that is, the larger and more intricate the complex of ideas is that can be retrieved from prior learning— the more readily new verbal information will be learned and remembered.

The complex of previously learned verbal information that is retrieved to incorporate new information occurs most often in the form of a schema. This form of verbal information carries the meaning of an organizing concept (such as "taking an airplane trip"). Schemas contain slots into which new information is fitted, and these help to ensure later recall. Therefore, designing instruction of the verbal information sort requires the designer to determine what schemas are already available to the prospective student. Learning new information about Queen Elizabeth I, for example, is best undertaken with a readily accessible schema that includes at least previously learned information about British royal succession during that era.

As you might expect, the most important set of abilities affecting the learning of new verbal information falls in the category of *verbal comprehension*. Measures of this ability appear to evaluate cognitive strategies relating to the facile understanding and use of language. Obviously, measures of verbal comprehension also assess, in part, the intellectual skills of word usage and syntactic and semantic language facility, as previously mentioned. It is little wonder, then, that this ability has been shown in many studies to predict the ease with which new verbal knowledge is acquired (Cronbach, 1970). If it were possible to obtain only a single ability test score for a group of students about to learn new verbal information, verbal comprehension would be the one to choose.

New Learning of Attitudes   When learners acquire new attitudes, the retrieval of certain relevant intellectual skills and verbal information may be essential. For example, an attitude regarding safety in handling certain chemical substances may require the kinds of intellectual skills that make possible the estimation of concentrations of those substances. The attitude involved in following a dietary prescription may require the use of previously learned intellectual skills that make possible the calculation of caloric intake. For a number of reasons, verbal information may also be of importance to the learning of modification of attitudes. If a human model is used to communicate the choice of personal action (see Chapter 5), previously learned information must be available that identifies the model as a familiar, respected person and attests to his or her credibility.

The most typical form for essential verbal information in the learning of attitudes is the schema. In this case, schemas have the function of representing the situation or situations in which the attitude will be displayed. For example, an attitude toward association with people of different ethnic origins is evidenced by choices of action made in a number of situations (R. M. Gagné, 1985). Is the association likely to be in a large crowd, in an intimate family group, or on the job? Each of these possibilities is a different situation in which the attitude might be displayed. Schemas representing each of these situations must be accessible in memory for the new (or reactivated) attitude to be learned. Another example of the necessity of situational schemas may be illustrated by the attitude "declining to drive after drinking." The social situations that make this attitude a desirable one are what need to be represented as schemas—parties with friends, extended after-dinner meetings, and the like. The attitude of refusing to drive will be most effective if the situational schemas can be readily recalled at the time of learning.

Are there abilities and traits that make attitude learning easier or more rapid? Abilities have perhaps no different effects on attitude learning than they do for other types of learned capabilities. An ability, like verbal comprehension, facilitates the understanding and learning of verbal communications used in instruction. As for traits, it is possible that traits, such as sociability and external locus of control, may affect the ease with which learners acquire an attitude communicated by a human model. Little evidence is available on these relationships, however, and they are judged not to be of great significance. In any case, it is evident that these effects are of the indirect sort previously described.

New Learning of Motor Skills   Two kinds of prior learning are likely to be of importance in the new learning of motor skills. One kind consists of the *part skills* that are components of the total skill being acquired. The kicking part of swimming the crawl may have been learned separately for retrieval and use in combination with other part skills in the learning of the total skill. When children learn to print letters, the drawing of curved parts and straight-line parts may be previously learned as part skills. If already present as a result of prior learning, they may be retrieved and integrated with the total letter-printing skill.

The other kind of prior learning essential to learning a new motor skill is actually an intellectual skill—*a procedural rule* (see Chapter 5). This is the aspect of motor skill learning that Fitts and Posner (1967) identified as an early cognitive learning stage. The skill of throwing darts at a target, for example, requires retrieval of the procedure of holding the dart, balancing for the throw, aiming, and releasing the dart. Whatever degree of skill may come from practice, the procedure must always be followed for skill improvement to occur. Although itself an intellectual skill, the procedure may occur and be retrieved as part of a schema. It is reasonable to suppose, for example, that the tennis backhand and the golf swing may be conceived as schemas.

Abilities have their usual function in the learning of motor skills. Abilities such as *speed of movement* and *motor coordination* may be found to aid the learning of some motor skills. Also, motor skill learning can often be shown to be affected by spatial abilities such as *spatial visualization* and *space relations*. Correlations between these abilities and motor skill learning are usually found to be low to moderate in value.

SUMMARY

Learner characteristics that affect the learning of new instructional material assume several kinds of organization in human memory. The learned capabilities of intellectual skills, cognitive strategies, verbal information, attitudes, and motor skills have direct effects on the learning of new instances of these same kinds of capabilities. Another kind of memory organization is represented by the notion of *abilities*, which are measured by psychological tests (such as those of Reasoning and Number Facility). These are measures of human qualities that predict how well certain general types of performances will be accomplished by different individuals. Still, other characteristics of human learners fall in the domain of traits (such as anxiety, locus of control). Abilities and traits affect new learning in indirect ways.

Relations between characteristics of the learner and the ease and effectiveness of learning have a number of implications for the practical task of instructional design. The designer needs to take account of the outcomes of learning, as described in the preceding chapter, and be cognizant of how these different outcomes may be brought about in different learners. After all, various types of learners may be addressed by instruction. They may be children or adults and may, therefore, differ in the amount of prior learning they have experienced. They may have different learned capabilities, different schemas, and different abilities and traits. The main implications of these differences are summarized in Table 6.3.

TABLE **6.3**   INSTRUCTIONAL DESIGN FOR DIFFERENT LEARNER CHARACTERISTICS

Learner Characteristics	Design Procedure for New Learning
Intellectual Skills	Stimulate retrieval of (1) prerequisite skills as components of new skill, (2) subordinate skills essential to cognitive strategies, and (3) basic skills involved in verbal information learning, attitude learning, and motor skill learning.
Cognitive Strategies	Provide for retrieval when available.
Verbal Information	Stimulate recall of propositions that may cue retrieval of newly learned intellectual skills. Provide retrieval of a meaningful context (schema) for new learning of verbal information. Stimulate retrieval of situational context for attitude learning.
Attitudes	Activate for learning motivation.
Motor Skills	Recall essential part skills.
Schemas	Activate retrieval of schemas consisting of complex networks of propositions to aid new learning of intellectual skills, cognitive strategies, verbal information, attitudes, motor skills.
Abilities	Adapt instruction to differences in ability whenever possible. Example: Use easily read printed text for learners low in verbal comprehension.
Traits	Adapt instruction to learner differences in traits when possible. Example: Provide detailed learning guidance and frequent feedback for learners of high anxiety.

As can be seen from the table, intellectual skills and cognitive strategies are usually of help to new learning, and their retrieval needs to be provided for in design. Stimulating the recall of verbal information makes provision for cue retrieval and the activation of a meaningful context within which new information can be subsumed. Previously acquired positive attitudes contribute to motivation for learning. Motor skills that are part skills need to be retrieved as components of the learning of new skills.

Many of these previously learned capabilities are incorporated into meaningful complexes called schemas. These networks of meaningful propositions and concepts are of considerable importance to new learning. Instructional design procedures include provisions for detecting the presence of relevant schemas and activating them by means of questions, advance organizers, or other devices.

Instruction for new learning can be adapted for learner differences in abilities and traits to the extent that feasibility considerations permit. When instructions are verbal in nature, ease of verbal comprehension is of particular importance in the instructional design.

REFERENCES

Anastasi, A. (1976). *Psychological testing* (4th ed.). New York: Macmillan.

Anderson, J. R. (1985). *Cognitive psychology and its implications* (2nd ed.). New York: Freeman.

APA Work Group of the Board of Educational Affairs (1997, November). *Learner-centered psychological principles: A framework for school reform and redesign.* Washington, DC: American Psychological Association.

Bandura, A. (1982). Self-efficacy mechanism in human agency. *American Psychologist, 37,* 122–148.

Corno, L. J., & Snow, R. E. (1986). Adapting teaching to individual differences among learners. In M. C. Wittrock (Ed.). *Handbook of research on teaching* (3rd ed.). New York: Macmillan.

Cronbach, L. J. (1970). *Essentials of psychological testing* (3rd ed.). New York: Harper & Row.

Cronbach, L. J., & Snow, R. E. (Eds.). (1977). *Aptitudes and instructional methods.* New York: Irvington.

Ericsson, K. A., Krampe, R. T., & Tesch-Roemer, C. (1993). The role of deliberate practice in the acquisition of expert performance. *Psychological Review, 100*(3), 363–406.

Ericsson, K. A. (1998). The scientific study of expert levels of performance: general implications for optimal learning and creativity. *High Ability Studies, 9*(1), 75–100.

Fitts, P. M., & Posner, M. I. (1967). *Human performance.* Monterey, CA: Brooks/Cole.

Gagné, E. D. (1985). *The cognitive psychology of school learning.* Boston: Little, Brown.

Gagné, R. M. (1980). Preparing the learner for new learning. *Theory into Practice, 19*(1), 6–9.

Gagné, R. M. (1985). *The conditions of learning* (4th ed.). New York: Holt, Rinehart and Winston.

Good, T. L., & Brophy, J. E. (1990). Basic concepts of motivation. In T. L. Good & J. E. Brophy (Eds.). *Educational psychology: A realistic approach* (4th ed.). New York: Longman.

Guilford, J. P. (1967). *The nature of human intelligence.* New York: McGraw-Hill.

Hunt, E. B. (1978). Mechanics of verbal ability. *Psychological Review, 85,* 271–283.

Keele, S. W. (1968). Movement control in skilled motor performance. *Psychological Bulletin, 70,* 387–403.

Keller, J.M. (1987). Development and use of the ARCS model of motivational design. *Journal of Instructional Development, 10*(3), 2–10.

Keller, J. M. (1999). Motivation in cyber learning environments. *International Journal of Educational Technology, 1*(1), 7 – 30.

Kyllonen, P. C., Lohman, D. F., & Snow, R. E. (1981). *Effects of task facets and strategy training on spatial task performance* (Tech. Rep. No. 14). Stanford, CA: Stanford University, School of Education.

McClelland, D. C. (1965). Toward a theory of motive acquisition. *American Psychologist, 20,* 321–333.

Morgan, M. (1985). Self-monitoring of attained subgoals in private study. *Journal of Educational Psychology, 77,* 623–630.

Newell, A., & Simon, H. A. (1972). *Human problem solving.* Englewood Cliffs, NJ: Prentice Hall.

Pass. F. G., W. C., & van Merriënboer, J. J. G. (1994). Variability of worked examples and transfer of geometrical problem solving skills: A cognitive load approach. *Journal of Educational Psychology, 86,* 122–133.

Piaget, J. (1963). *Origins of intelligence in children.* New York: Norton.

O'Neil, H. F., Jr. (1978). *Learning strategies.* New York: Academic Press.

Rhode, G., Morgan, D. P., & Young, K. R. (1983). Generalization and maintenance of treatment gains of behaviorally handicapped students from resource rooms to regular classrooms using self-evaluation procedures. *Journal of Applied Behavior Analysis, 16,* 171–188.

Riley, M. S., Greeno, J. G., & Heller, J. I. (1983). Development of children's problem-solving ability in arithmetic. In H. P. Ginsburg (Ed.). *The development of mathematical thinking.* New York: Academic Press.

Rotter, J. B. (1966). General expectancies for internal versus external control of reinforcement. *Psychological Monographs, 80 (Whole No. 609).*

Rumelhart, D. E. (1980). Schemata: The building blocks of cognition. In R. J. Spiro, B. C. Bruce, & W. F. Brewer (Eds.). *The theoretical issues in reading comprehension.* Hillsdale, NJ: Erlbaum.

Schank, R. C., & Abelson, R. P. (1977). *Scripts, plans, goals, and understanding.* Hillsdale, NJ: Erlbaum.

Snow, R. E. (1977). Individual differences and instructional theory. *Educational Researcher, 6*(10), 11–15.

Snow, R. E. (1982). The training of intellectual aptitude. In D. K. Ketterman & R. J. Sternberg (Eds.). *How and how much can intelligence be increased.* Norwood, NJ: Ablex.

Thorndike, R. L., & Hagen, E. (1985). *Measurement and evaluation in psychology and education* (5th ed.). New York: Wiley.

Thurstone, L. L. (1938). Primary mental abilities. *Psychometric Monographs, No. 1.*

Tobias, S. (1979). Anxiety research in educational psychology. *Journal of Educational Psychology, 71,* 573–582.

Tobias, S. (1986). Learner characteristics. In R. M. Gagné (Ed.). *Instructional technology: Foundations.* Hillsdale, NJ: Erlbaum.

van Merriënboer, J. J. G. (1997). *Training complex cognitive skills: A four-component instructional design model for technical training.* Englewood Cliffs, NJ: Educational Technology Publications.

Vygotsky, L. S. (1978). *Mind in society: The development of higher mental process.* Cambridge, MA: Harvard University Press.

West, C. K. (1981). *The social and psychological distortion of information*. Chicago, IL: Nelson Hall.

West, C. K., Farmer, J. A., & Wolff, P. M. (1991). *Instructional design: Implications from cognitive science*. Englewood Cliffs, NJ: Prentice Hall.

White, R. T. (1973). Research into learning hierarchies. *Review of Educational Research, 43*, 361–375.

Wood, D., Bruner, J., & Ross, S. (1976). The role of tutoring in problem solving. *British Journal of Psychology, 66*, 181–191.

Defining Performance Objectives

The next two chapters discuss the topics of performance objectives and task analysis. These two topics, or rather what they have traditionally represented, have been the source of controversy among information theory-based instructional design models and constructivist design models (cf. Wilson, 1997). What we shall provide in this chapter is a discussion of the reasons for defining objectives, with consideration of constructivist concerns.

If instruction is to be evaluated and improved based on student performance, it seems logical that there be some consideration of what performance the instruction is designed to elicit. Following this line of reasoning it is essential that the desired outcomes of the designed instruction be clearly and unambiguously stated. Furthermore, defining learning outcomes is an important step in the curriculum development process because it makes the intentions of the course of study visible to the administrators, teachers, parents, and students, and it helps to identify assumptions about what knowledge and skills the students need to bring to succeed.

Advocates of constructivist models of instructional design take issue with the predefinition of learning objectives because they take the position that objectives can only partially represent what we know, and therefore expressing them as the content of instruction might act to constrain what the learner will seek to learn. This position could affect the perceived importance of analysis. Wilson (1997) states:

> The role . . . of analysis is fairly modest. Analysis provides an overall framework for instruction, and provides extra help on some tricky parts, such as identifying likely misconceptions of previous knowledge that may undercut students' efforts to understand the content (pp. 72–73).

Wilson further states that the role of the designer is, "to design a series of experiences—interactions or environments or products—intended to help students learn effectively" (p. 73). This is entirely consistent with our definition of instructional design, and we feel it even increases the need to define accurately what it is we will help the student learn.

In constructivist learning environments, the student is often a participant in determining goals and directions for learning, which can be a somewhat fluid process. As the objectives evolve, the instruction can be adapted for the learner until it meets his or her needs.

There has been a degree of polarization in some parts of the literature of this field in terms of characterizing learning goals and environments as constructivist or instructivist. Many traditional instructional designers reject the constructivist perspective, while many constructivists reject the instructivist approach. Our position is that both approaches are means to ends, not ends in themselves. One can design environments that aim to assist learners in building knowledge and skills in accordance with constructivist goals just as one can design environments to achieve a greater degree of structured knowledge growth. In this book we focus on the design of intentional learning, and we are suggesting that this is best done when learning objectives are stated before designing learning activities. Accordingly, in this text, we continue to include rigorous consideration of analysis and objectives as a foundation for increasing the likelihood of building learning environments that accomplish predetermined academic outcomes.

These outcomes are variously referred to as *behavioral objectives, learning objectives,* or *performance objectives.* We define a performance objective as a precise statement of a capability that, if possessed by the learner, can be observed as a performance. The question the designer must be able to answer before starting the development of any instruction or learning experience is, "What will these learners be able to do after the experience, that they couldn't (or didn't) do before?" or "How will the learner be different?"

One purpose of performance objectives is to communicate the aims of instruction (to students, administrators, other teachers, and parents) and provide a foundation for the development of instructional activities and assessment of learning. Although objectives might differ in the ways they are written, they all express the same idea, and that is what the learner should know, do, or feel. Creating good and meaningful objectives is sometimes a difficult task, because the designer and content expert must continually determine which objectives are important.

As has often been suggested, the procedure for overcoming the ambiguity of course purpose statements, and thereby achieving greater precision, starts with general statements of goals for instruction, followed by specific indicators of performance that reflect those goals. The question now is, How will we know when this goal has been achieved? For example:

> How will we know that the student "understands the concept
> *commutative*"?
> How will we know that the student "appreciates allegory in
> *A Midsummer Night's Dream*"?
> How can we discern that the student "comprehends spoken French"?
> How can we know that the student "reads short stories with enjoyment"?

Statements regarding instructional purposes may be quite successful in communicating general goals to fellow teachers, yet they are often not sufficiently precise for designing instruction. They simply do not tell how a person could observe whether the student has accomplished the goals. On the other hand, specific learning objectives may be of interest to a parent who wants to know what is expected of their child. And it is likely to be of interest to students who want to be able to tell when their performance is on-track.

COMMUNICATING EXPECTATIONS USING OBJECTIVES

An *objective* is useful when it communicates to the learner what they should be able to do after instruction. The statement is less useful if it is ambiguous. Consider the following instances:

1. *"Realizes that most plant growth requires sunshine."* Such a statement doesn't communicate what the learner is to do. Does it mean that the student should be able to explain the purpose of sunshine in plant growth, or simply to know that sunshine is one of the necessary factors?
2. *"Demonstrates how sunshine affects plant growth by explaining the process of photosynthesis."* This statement implies that the teacher must observe instances in which the student explains the process of photosynthesis, including the role of light. The observation assumes the relation between sunshine and plant growth. The objective also clarifies how the student will show that they have learned—by explaining the process. The main point is that it informs us of what sort of observation is required.

How to Write Objectives That Communicate

We suggest that a performance objective has five components:

1. Situation (context in which the learned outcome will be performed)
2. The type of learning being performed (a "learned capability" verb classifying the type of learning)
3. The content or object of the performance
4. The observable part of the behavior (action verb)
5. The tools, constraints or special conditions applied to the performance (acceptable performance)

Notice how the following objective contains all five components:

> In a computer laboratory situation, given a simple set of specifications for a data table [situation], the student will demonstrate [learned capability verb] the construction of a database table in Microsoft Access™ [object] by typing it into the computer [action verbs], using the appropriate data types, and selecting an appropriate key [tools, constraints and/or special conditions].

Do objectives *have* to include all five of these components? No, but the more components included the more precise the communication. We would say the most important components are the learned capability verb and object; in other words, the above objective could be written as "demonstrate the construction of a database table," and the other components would be inferred. One common mistake in writing performance objectives is including the instruction in the situation, such as, "After reading the chapter the student will be able to...." The performance desired should be independent of instruction. If the students can demonstrate the desired performance, they have already learned the skill.

Components of Objectives

One purpose for unambiguous objectives is to enable the designer to determine which *conditions of learning* should be included in the instructional materials. The five-component objective is more specific than the definitions suggested by other authors (Mager, 1975; Popham & Baker, 1970). The reason for greater specificity is to communicate more information about the type of learning outcome that is desired. We cannot directly observe that someone has developed a capability. We can only infer that a new capability has been attained by observing learner performance on a task that employs that capability. Often, the particular performance (action) exhibited by the learner is confused with the capability. The five-component method of writing objectives seeks to avoid this confusion by using two different verbs: one to define the capability, and a second to define the observable action. (See Table 7.1 for examples of verbs.). Each component of a five-component objective serves an express purpose as described in the following paragraphs.

Situation   What is the stimulus *situation* faced by the student? For example, when asked to "type a letter," is the student given parts of the letter in longhand copy? Is the letter to be produced from an auditory message or from notes? Obviously, if the student's performance is highly dependent on the situation, the objective should specify the features of this situation so that it is included as part of the instruction.

Sometimes, it may be desirable for the objective to include a description of the environmental conditions under which the behavior is to be performed on the job. For example, in the case of typing a letter, is this to be done in a quiet room with no other disturbances, or is it more likely that it will be in a busy office with phone interruptions, people walking by, or other tasks coming in? For many types of learned behavior, the environment in which the behavior is performed may not be terribly important. However, for other performances, for example when putting on a gas mask, it may be critical.

Learned Capability Verb   Some of the problems with the use of behavioral objectives arise from ambiguity about what type of learning outcome the demonstrated behavior actually represents. For example, the statement, "Using Microsoft Word, the student will be able to, type a business letter in 15 minutes or less" is ambiguous. It might mean, "types a copy of a letter from handwritten draft (a motor skill)," or it might mean a quite different capability, "demonstrating the use of Microsoft Word (a rule-using skill)." It might even mean type a response to a customer inquiry (possibly a problem-solving skill). This ambiguity can be reduced by including within the objective an indicator of the type of learned capability being demonstrated.

There are nine different *learned capability verbs* as shown in Table 7.1. These pertain to attitudes, cognitive strategies, verbal information, and motor skills, described in previous chapters, and to each of the five subordinate types of intellectual skills. These verbs may be used to *classify* each of the nine types of learning outcomes. By including one of these verbs in the objective, the type of learning desired is more clearly communicated, and the conditions of learning appropriate to that type of learning outcome are more likely to be applied.

Object   The *object* component contains the new content to be learned. For example, if the learned capability is the procedure for adding two three-digit numbers (a rule), the learned capability and its object might be stated as "demonstrates (the learned capability verb) *the addition of two three-digit numbers* (the object)." Other examples are given in objectives that follow.

Action Verb   The *action verb* depicts how the performance is to be completed: "executes a copy of a business letter *by typing*," describes the action (typing) one would observe to infer that the motor skill of typing was developed. For the problem-solving objective, "generates a business letter by typing a reply to a customer

TABLE 7.1   STANDARD VERBS TO DESCRIBE HUMAN CAPABILITIES, WITH EXAMPLE OF PHRASES INCORPORATING ACTION VERBS

Capability	Capability *Verb*	Example (Action *Verb* in Italics)
Intellectual Skill		
Discrimination	discriminates	discriminates by *matching* French sounds of *u* and *ou*
Concrete Concept	identifies	identifies by *naming* the root, leaf, and stem of representative plants
Defined Concept	classifies	classifies by *writing* a definition, the concept family
Rule	demonstrates	demonstrates the addition of positive and negative numbers by solving example problems *in writing,* showing all work
Higher-Order Rule (Problem Solving)	generates	generates *in writing* a business plan, including an estimate of ROI
Cognitive Strategy	adopts	adopts, *explaining the strategy used*, a strategy of imagining a U.S. map to recall the states
Verbal Information	states	states *orally* the major issues in the presidential campaign of 1932
Motor Skill	executes	executes by *backing* a car into a driveway
Attitude	chooses	chooses golf as a leisure activity, *evidenced by playing*

inquiry," the observable behavior is also typing, but we are really interested in the content of the letter as well as the motor skill. There are innumerable action verbs: matching, writing, speaking, discussing, pointing, selecting, drawing, and so on. Table 7.1 demonstrates how the learned capability verbs and action verbs work together to describe a task. We will describe the process of writing performance objectives shortly, but keep one rule in mind: *Never use one of the nine learned capability verbs as an action verb.* This will avoid confusion when sequencing the objective later on.

Tools, Constraints, or Special Conditions   In some situations, the performance will require the use of special tools, certain constraints, or other special conditions. The letter example specifies typing with Microsoft Word. Notice that the objective is not aimed at the acquisition of skill with MS Word; instead, it is a special condition placed on the performance of typing the letter. An example of a constraint could be a criterion of performance; a letter might have to be completed within a specified time, with fewer than three errors. As is true of the situation, the indication of any special conditions or tools may imply other prerequisite skills that must be learned before the target skill can be adequately evaluated.

Generating Five-Component Objectives

Constructing a five-component objective is a problem-solving task. There are many rules that must be applied. The first problem to be solved is deciding what type of learning outcome the instruction aims to produce. This next section will discuss how five-component objectives would be written for each of the nine types of learning, beginning with the five subordinate kinds of intellectual skills.

Discrimination   *Discrimination* performance always involves being able to see, hear, or feel sameness or differences between stimuli. There are many reasons persons cannot discriminate; for example, a person who is color-blind cannot discriminate red from blue. However, even persons who are physically able must learn important discriminations. For example, sighted people must be able to discriminate a *b* from a *d* if they are to learn to read. Objectives for this type of skill would read like the following. (The acronym LCV is used for *learned capability verb*.)

> [Situation] Given three pictures, two the same and one different, [LCV] discriminates [object] the picture that is different [action] by pointing to it.

Another discrimination objective might be:

> [Situation] Given printed letter *b* and the spoken instruction to select other letters that look the same from a set containing *d, p, b,* and *q,* [LCV] discriminates [object] *b* [action] by circling it. Notice that the learner was not told to circle the letter b—this would be a concept skill.

Not all discriminations are visual; they may also be aural, tactile, or olfactory. For example, a discrimination objective that might be appropriate for someone becoming a chef might be:

> [Situation] Given a piece of fresh beef as a reference, [LCV] discriminates [object] the smell of fresh beef from the smell of beef that is on the verge of spoiling [action] by indicating that the smells are the same or different.

The assessment of this discrimination would be to see if the learner could discriminate differences among the smells of the beef. This is a prerequisite skill for identifying spoiled meat (concrete concept skill).

Notice that in the previous objective the situation did not include a description of the environment in which the action is to take place. Is it important that this be specified? Maybe in an operating kitchen there are likely to be many smells of food in preparation that would make the discrimination more difficult than it would be in an isolated situation.

One other important point to make is that discriminations are often prerequisites for concepts. For instance, if the future chef cannot discriminate the smell of the spoiling beef, it would be impossible to learn to identify spoiled beef by smell.

Concrete Concept   A *concrete concept* requires that students be able to identify one or more instances of a class of items by its physical attributes. For example, how would you know if students understood the concept *cell wall*? You could ask them to describe a cell wall. If they could describe it you might infer that they indeed knew the concept. However, a better way might be to have them trace the cell wall on an illustration, or point out the cell wall while looking through a microscope. All these are acceptable ways to demonstrate that the learner understands the concept *cell wall*.

The learned capability verb [LCV] used in conjunction with concrete concepts is *identify*. Of course, in order to identify anything, the student must first be able to discriminate critical physical attributes. How could blind persons acquire the concept *cell wall*? While they might learn it as a defined concept, there would be no way they could identify that component of a cell because they lack the prerequisite visual discrimination capability.

An example of a concrete concept objective requiring multiple discriminations might be:

> [Situation] Given a set of 10 radiographic negatives of the abdomen, [LCV] identifies [object] the gall bladder on the negatives [action] by circling it with a wax pencil.

Many concepts are first learned as associations of physical objects with names; for example, we see a wood pencil and immediately know it is a pencil. Children learn animals by word associations with pictures, that is, they can identify an elephant long before they actually see a real elephant. However, many concepts take multiple physical forms. For instance, take the concept *chair*. Would a child learning to identify a dining-room chair identify a collapsed folding chair as a chair? Often, physical items are associated with their functions as much as their physical attributes. We might define the attributes of a chair as something an individual sits on, along with the associated physical characteristics. Of course we differentiate chairs from stools, which have a similar function but different physical characteristics.

Defined Concept   A *defined concept is* a class of objects or events that are associated by a definition that expresses the relationships among the concept's attributes and its function (Gagné, 1985). For example, the sociological concept *nuclear family* is a class of objects that includes parents and children, and that meets the criterion of a definition—"a family group that consists only of father, mother, and children" (*Merriam-Webster's Collegiate Dictionary,* 10th edition). Note that this rule contains other defined concepts (family, group, mother, father, and children, and the relational concept "only").

The LCV we associate with defined concepts is *classify* since what the learner has to do is put some instance into one or more categories, based on a verbal definition, or use the concept appropriately in a given context. Defined concepts make up a large portion of the vocabulary of a discipline or field of study, and students are expected to learn these concepts appropriately in conversation about the discipline.

Boundary is an example of a defined concept that is often first learned as a concrete concept, for example, "the fence is the boundary of our property." However, it has a more technical definition, "something (as a line, point, or plane) that indicates or fixes a limit or extent" (*Merriam-Webster's Collegiate Dictionary,* 10th edition). A learning objective for the concept boundary might look like this:

> [Situation] When asked to explain what a boundary is, [LCV] classifies [object] *boundary* [action] by verbally describing or visually illustrating a boundary.

Another way to approach the objective would be to see whether the student could recognize the attributes of the *boundary* concept, as in the following:

> [Situation] Given lines that do, and lines that do not indicate the extent of an area, [LCV] classifies [object] *boundaries* [action] by tracing those that conform to the definition.

Still another way to observe whether students possess a defined concept is to have them use it properly in a sentence; for example, "The boundary of a lake is marked by the line of its shore."

Rule Using: Rules, Principles, and Procedures   Rule using is an internal capability that governs one's behavior and enables one to demonstrate a relationship among concepts in a class of situations (Gagné, 1985). The inferred capability is that of demonstrating an appropriate response to a class of stimulus situations possessing established relationships. For example, a student applies a rule when confronted with the stimulus (236/4 = n). The same rule applies when the stimulus is different (515/5 = n). Rules are often given names. In this case, the rule might be called "short division," and the student possessing the capability of applying this rule would be able to show mastery by solving any number of short-division problems.

The learned capability verb we suggest for rules is *demonstrate*. A typical example of an objective for rule outcomes is:

> [Situation] Given a set of 10 numerical expressions indicating short division *(abc/d),* [LCV] demonstrates [object] division procedure [action] by writing the answers [tools and constraints] with 90% accuracy, using no special aids.

Is the objective representative of the examples of short division given above? It is not specific enough if the problems are to be limited to the type shown. A more accurate object statement would be "short division of three-digit numbers by a one-digit number, with no remainder." Are the rules different for division by a number that leaves a remainder, or when there is a multi-digit divisor? To the extent they are, it is desirable to be specific so that the components of the task can be accurately described and appropriate instruction accordingly designed.

To learn this rule, the student must be familiar with other rules of multiplication and subtraction. To multiply, the student must be familiar with rules of addition. Long division would be classified as a complex rule because it requires the use of previously learned concepts and rules.

Problem Solving   Gagné (1985) defines problem solving as an activity in which the learner selects and uses rules to find a solution in a novel situation. What the learner constructs during the process of *problem solving* is a new higher-order rule. The new rule is a synthesis of other rules and concepts and may then be used by the learner to solve other problems of the same type.

One problem in writing learning outcomes associated with problem-solving skills is separating the process of problem solving from a specific solution of the problem. It is possible that a problem has many acceptable solutions. The desired outcome is the process or rule learned during the process of solving a problem, that is, the student must generate this higher-order rule and also apply it in order to achieve a solution to a novel problem. When writing problem-solving objectives it helps to focus on what is being constructed by the learner.

The verb we associate with problem solving is *generate*. An example of a problem-solving objective is:

> [Situation] Given an archeological artifact and information about the location where it was found, the learner will [LCV] generate [object] a hypothesis about the age of the artifact, and the nature of the culture that might have produced it [action] in writing [special conditions] including a supporting rationale for the hypothesis.

Problem-solving objectives are not always easy to write, mainly because problem-solving skills are usually not formally taught. Instead, most teachers present problem-type situations and then verify whether or not the student has the problem-solving skill. A source of confusion among novice designers may occur in differentiating between rule-using and problem-solving objectives. The distinction can be kept clear by asking, "Do I want the learner to apply a rule I teach them, or generate a rule or procedure for solving a problem?" If the former, it is rule-using, if the latter, it is problem solving.

Cognitive Strategy   A *cognitive strategy* is an internally directed control process that regulates and moderates other learning processes. Gagné (1985) describes a number of types of cognitive strategies, including those that control attending, encoding, retrieval, and problem solving. Bruner (1971) distinguishes between the skills of problem solving and *problem finding*, the latter of which is a cognitive strategy requiring the location of "incompleteness, anomaly, trouble, inequity, and contradiction" (p. 111). Again, it is important to differentiate between the product of a cognitive strategy and the statement of the strategy itself as an outcome of instruction. For example, most persons can memorize a list of 10 items if given enough time. However, some can memorize the list much faster and remember it longer. Perhaps this is the result of their having a more efficient and effective encoding strategy. Research has demonstrated (Rohwer, 1975) that encoding strategies that facilitate learning can readily be suggested to the learner.

When learners acquire new ways of focusing their attention, encoding material to be learned, or retrieving previously learned knowledge, they may be using novel cognitive strategies that they have discovered themselves. Otherwise, strategies may be acquired by being directly described to learners and subsequently practiced. Generally, students apply existing strategies that have worked in the past. The learned capability verb we use for cognitive strategies is *adopt*. That is, learners must not only learn the strategy, they must adopt it as a way of learning:

> [Situation] Given a list of 10 items to be memorized, [LCV] adopts [object] the key-word mnemonic technique [action] for memorizing the list, using no mechanical aids, within 30 seconds, and with a retention of at least 49 hours.

Notice that this objective does not give the student the mnemonic. Instead, it implies that the student will adopt a mnemonic using an already known technique. Can a student actually "originate" a cognitive strategy? Sure. We learn many cognitive strategies without realizing it, but if we are creating instruction to teach cognitive strategies, as we might for a study-skills course, the learning goal would be to adopt the strategies being taught.

Verbal Information   Verbal information refers to information (names, facts, propositions) that can be *recalled* in a variety of forms. It is also called *declarative knowledge* (Anderson, 1985). According to Gagné (1985), a distinction should be made between the learning of *verbal chains* and the learning of verbal information. A verbal chain is a type of association learning, where each element of the chain must be previously learned before the entire chain can be reconstructed. Individuals can learn extremely long verbal chains and recall them verbatim, without having any comprehension of what the words mean. An essential characteristic of verbal information learning, on the other hand, is that it consists of propositions that are semantically meaningful.

The verb we associate with verbal information is *states*. We differentiate the learned capability of stating from the actions of stating, either "in writing" or "orally." An example of a verbal information objective is:

> [Situation] Given a verbal question, [LCV] states [object] three causes of the Civil War [action] orally or in writing [constraints] without references.

Could students memorize three causes of the Civil War as a verbal chain and lead the teacher to conclude that they had mastered the above objective? Yes, and many students probably do this, because the teacher doesn't require that they present the information in any other way. However, the fact that the student may recall something verbatim does not necessarily mean that it is stored in memory as a set of meaningful propositions. A modification of this objective would be to add the condition, "In your own words," to the objective. The proof of this would come when the student is required to use the same information in some meaningful way. For example, the student might learn that hamsters eat lettuce. If a teacher asked, "What do hamsters eat?" the student might answer "lettuce" as a memorized or rote response. However, the same answer to a different question, "What will you feed the hamster?" shows that the student has acquired the information in a meaningful way.

Motor Skills   Some behaviors require their expression in coordinated, precise muscular movements. Examples of these kinds of performances would be gymnastic skills such as a back flip or a jack-knife dive. Less obvious are common skills like walking or riding a bicycle. Forming a letter on paper or using a pen requires the coordinated use of muscles, and most teachers recognize that some students have greater proficiency at this skill than do others. The LCV we associate with motor skills is *execute.* For example:

> [Situation] Off a 3-meter board [LCV] executes [object] a jack-knife dive [action] by diving [constraints] with smooth and continuous movement, entering the water in a vertical position with minimal splash.

Notice that the statement of the action, "by diving," is redundant but there is only one way to demonstrate execution of the dive.

Study the following objective: "Given a blood pressure apparatus, the student executes the procedure of taking someone's blood pressure." Is this a motor skill? Probably not, because the student already has the requisite motor skills and is only applying a procedure (rule learning). However, "Given a hypodermic syringe, the student executes an intravenous injection, missing the vein no more than one time in twenty" is a motor skill, in that precision, timing, and eye-hand coordination are required.

Attitude   An attitude is stated as a desired choice behavior. For example, a description of behavior might be "the student will choose to vote when the opportunity presents itself." Obviously, the concept of choice means that people are free to "not vote" if they so desire. There are many determinants of attitudes, including situational factors. For instance, one person may choose to vote if it is physically convenient but choose not to vote if it is inconvenient. We might wish, as a learning outcome, to specify an attitude change that would foster the attitude, "will choose to vote even if it is inconvenient."

The learned capability verb used to classify attitude objectives is *choose.* A typical attitude objective that could be the focus of an educational program might be:

> [Situation] When harmful drugs are being used by peers, [LCV] chooses [action] to refuse [object] drugs when offered.

Martin and Briggs (1986) point out that many cognitive behaviors have affective components. For example, mathematical operations are taught as cognitive skills, but it is hoped that the learner will *choose* to feel that mathematics knowledge is important to learn (for reasons other than a course grade). If designers attempt to specify the attitudinal components, they will likely pay attention to the context in which the cognitive skills are presented, attempting to make the newly learned skill meaningful (relevant) for the learner and building as much reinforcement into the learning situation as possible.

Statements of Objectives and Criteria of Performance

Some systems of writing performance objectives (Mager, 1975) require the inclusion of a criterion of performance in the objective. In the five-component system we are suggesting the criterion statement is optional, because it is something that will be considered later in the overall assessment plan (Chapter 13). However, if the criteria of performance for a given task are already known at the time of writing the objective, the criterion statement can become a component of the objective, falling under the category of "tools, constraints, and special conditions." It would be perfectly acceptable to have an objective like the following:

> Given a 3-page handwritten manuscript, executes typing of the manuscript within 20 minutes with fewer than six errors.

EXAMPLES OF OBJECTIVES

One of the first questions from new learners of the five-component format is, "Is it really practical to require that all five components be specified?" Our answer is that an objective statement is written for the purpose of unambiguous communication of intent. If you can communicate unambiguously without all five components, then do so. For example, take the objective, "States the names of the 50 states and capitols in the United States of America." This seems like a pretty unambiguous statement, and all that is included is the learned capability verb and the object. There is nothing wrong with the objective as stated, but it leaves some of the components open for interpretation. The following examples show how the five-component format can be used in a number of different subject areas to make vaguely stated objectives more specific.

Examples in Science Instruction

Suppose that the instructional designer formulates in a written statement the purposes to be accomplished by a course of instruction. If it is a science lesson, the following purposes might be considered. These have been abstracted from a list of objectives for junior high school science instruction prepared by the Intermediate Science Curriculum Study (1973).

1. Understanding the concept of an electric circuit
2. Knowing that a major advantage of the metric system in science is that its units are related by factors of 10
3. Taking personal responsibility for returning equipment to its storage places

Objective No. 1—The Concept of an Electric Circuit   Objective 1 is a fairly straightforward purpose for instruction. The first question to be asked by an instructional designer is, "What kind of capability am I looking for here?" Do I mean by "understanding" something like "stating what an electric circuit is?" No, that would not be convincing, because it might merely indicate that the student had acquired some verbal information which she could repeat, perhaps in her own words. Do I mean "distinguishing an electric circuit from a noncircuit when shown two or more instances?" No, I cannot be sure that the student has the understanding I wish in this case because she may simply be able to pick up the cue of an open wire in the instances shown her and respond on that basis. What I actually want the student to do is to show me *that she can use a rule for making an electric circuit* in one or more specific situations. The rule to be learned has to do with the flow of electric current from a source through a connected set of conductors and back to the source. The student could be asked to exhibit this performance in one or more situations. The result of this line of reasoning is an objective statement that puts together the necessary components as follows:

> [Situation] Given a battery, light bulb, and socket, and pieces of wire, [LCV] demonstrates [object] the making of an electric circuit [action] by connecting wires to battery and socket and [constraint] testing the lighting of the bulb.

Objective No. 2—Knowing Something about the Metric System   The statement of purpose in Objective 2 implies that some verbal information is to be learned. Again, the first question to be asked by the instructional designer is, "What do I mean by 'knowing' this fact about the metric system? What will convince me that the student 'knows'?" In this instance, the designer may readily come to the conclusion that "knowing" means being able to state the particular fact about the metric system. Accordingly, the identification of the required capability as verbal information is fairly straightforward. The resulting objective can then be constructed as follows:

> [Situation] Given the question, "What major advantage for scientific work do the units of the metric system have?" [LCV] states [object] the "tens" relationship among units [action] by writing [constraints] in his own words.

Objective No. 3—Taking Responsibility for Equipment   In thinking over the instructional purpose for Objective 3, the designer will immediately realize that it is not concerned with whether the students are able to put equipment back in its place but rather with whether they tend to do so on all appropriate occasions. The word *responsibility* implies that the actions of a student may occur at any time and are not expected to result from any specific direction or questions. The designer must ask, "What would convince me that the student is 'taking responsibility' of this sort?" The answer to this question implies that the objective in this case deals with choices of personal action, in other words, with an attitude. The standard method of constructing the objective would, therefore, take this form:

> [Situation] Given occasions when laboratory activities are completed or terminated [LCV] chooses [object] to return [action] returning equipment to its storage places.

An Example from English Literature

A second example of the procedure for constructing statements of objectives comes from a hypothetical course in English literature. Suppose that a set of lessons in such a course had the following purposes:

1. Identifying the major characters in *Hamlet*
2. Understanding Hamlet's "To be, or not to be" soliloquy
3. Being able to recognize a metaphor

Objective No. 1—Identifying the Major Characters in **Hamlet**

Objective 1, according to our model, involves using definitions to classify. In this case, the student is being asked to classify characters in *Hamlet* in accordance with their functions within the plot of the play. Under most circumstances, it would be assumed that doing this by way of verbal statements would be convincing. That is, the student answers a question like "Who was Claudius?" by defining Claudius as the king of Denmark, Hamlet's uncle, who is suspected by Hamlet of having killed his father. The objective can be constructed as follows:

> [Situation] Given oral questions about the characters of *Hamlet* (such as "Who was Claudius?") [LCV] classifies [object] the characters [action] by defining their relationship to the plot.

Objective No. 2—Understanding Hamlet's Soliloquy

Objective 2 has a much more interesting and presumably more important instructional purpose. The instructional designer needs to ask, "How will I know if the student *understands* this passage?" In all likelihood, the answer to this question is to "ask the student to express the thoughts of the passage in words that simplify or explain their meaning." (An example would be explaining that "To be, or not to be" means "to remain living or not.") To accomplish such a task, the student must solve a series of problems, bringing a number of intellectual skills to bear upon them, such as rules for using synonyms, rules for defining, and the concepts of figures of speech. In sum, the student will be asked to generate a paraphrase of the soliloquy. It is, then, a problem-solving task, or more precisely a whole set of problems, in which subordinate rules must be applied to the generation of higher-order rules. The rules cannot be exactly specified, of course, because one does not know exactly how the student will solve each problem.

As a result of this analysis, the following objective might be composed:

[Situation] Given instructions to interpret the meaning of Hamlet's "To be, or not to be" soliloquy in simple terms [LCV] generates [object] an interpretation of the soliloquy [action] in writing.

Objective No. 3—Recognizing Metaphors

Even in its expression, Objective 3 has the appearance of representing a somewhat less complex purpose than Objective 2. It may be evident, also, that if students are able to generate a paraphrased soliloquy, they must be able to detect the metaphoric meaning of such phrases as "to take arms against a sea of troubles." In this simpler example of a purpose, then, question for the instructional designer is, "What will convince me that the student can 'recognize' a metaphor?" Obviously, a metaphor is a concept, and since it is not something that can be denoted by pointing, it must be a *defined* concept. The performance to be expected of the student, then, will be one of classifying a *metaphor in accordance with a definition.*

The resulting objective might be stated as follows:

[Situation] Given a list of phrases, some of which are metaphors and some not, [LCV] classifies [object] the metaphors [actions] by picking out those that conform to the definition, rejecting those that do not.

An alternative objective (and possibly a better one) for this instructional purpose would be:

[Situation] Given a phrase containing a verb participle and an object (as "resisting corruption") [LCV] classifies [object] a metaphor [action] by selecting an example that accords with the definition (as "erecting a bulwark against corruption").

An Example from Social Studies

A course in social studies in junior high school might have the following purposes:

1. Knowing terms of office for members of the two houses of Congress
2. Interpreting bar charts showing growth in agricultural production
3. Applying knowledge of the "judicial review" process of the Supreme Court

Objective No. 1—Terms of Office for Congress

The intended outcome in this case is information. It is, of course, rather simple information. As an objective, this purpose may be stated as follows:

[Situation] Given the question, "In what terms of office do members of both houses of Congress serve?" [LCV] states [object] the terms for House and Senate members [action] orally.

Objective No. 2—Interpreting Bar Charts

Intellectual skills are often important in social studies. For example, interpreting charts is a rule-using skill. There may be several such skills of increasing complexity to be learned. Consequently, particular attention has to be paid to the description of the situation. More complex charts may require several intellectual skills or a combination of them. This objective may be illustrated by the following example:

[Situation] Given a bar chart showing production of cotton bales by year during the period 1950–1960 [LCV] demonstrates [object] finding years of average production [action] by checking appropriate bars.

Objective No. 3—Applying Knowledge of Judicial Review
The statement of this goal is somewhat ambiguous. It might best be interpreted as one of solving problems pertaining to the Supreme Court's judicial review function and exhibiting knowledge by so doing. Such an objective might be stated in the following way:

[Situation] Given the statement of an issue of constitutionality contained in a fictitious act of Congress and reference to the constitutional principle to be invoked, [LCV] generates [object] a proposed judicial opinion [action] in written form.

USING OBJECTIVES IN INSTRUCTIONAL PLANNING

When instructional objectives are defined in the manner described here, they reveal the fine-grained nature of the instructional process. This in turn reflects the fine-grained characteristics of what is learned. There may be scores of objectives for the single topic of a course and several for each individual lesson. How does the instructional designer employ these objectives in the development of topics, courses, or curricula? And how does the teacher use objectives? Can the teacher, as the designer of an individual lesson, make use of lengthy lists of objectives? Many such lists are available, it may be noted, for a variety of subjects in all school grades.

Objectives and Instruction

The instructional designer, or design team, faces the need to describe objectives as part of each individual lesson. Typically, there will be several distinct objectives for a lesson. Each may then be used to answer the question, "What kind of a learning outcome does this objective represent?" The categories to be determined are those corresponding to the major verb indicating the type of learned capability. That is, the objective may represent verbal information, an intellectual skill in one of its subvarieties, a cognitive strategy, an attitude, or a motor skill. Having determined the categories of a lesson's objectives, the designer will be able to make decisions about the following matters:

1. Whether the lesson's purpose has been adequately represented
2. Whether the lesson has a suitable "balance" of expected outcomes
3. How the lesson might be taught
4. How learning will be assessed

The Balance of Objectives

The objectives identified for each lesson are likely to represent several different categories of a learning outcome. It may be possible to identify a primary objective—one without which the lesson would seem hardly worthwhile. However there are bound to be other objectives that must be learned prior to the desired objective. Thus, the lesson that has an intellectual skill as its primary objective is likely to be supported by other objectives, classifiable as cognitive strategies, information, or attitudes. As an example, one might expect a lesson having as its primary objective the intellectual skills of "demonstrating chemical equations for the oxidation of metals" to also include objectives pertaining to information about common metallic oxides and favorable attitudes toward chemistry. How to reflect these several objectives in lesson design is a subject for later chapters. The first step, however, is to see that a reasonable balance of the expected outcomes is attained.

Designing Instruction

Clearly, then, the systematic design of lessons making up a topic or course will result in the development of a sizeable collection of statements of objectives. This collection will grow as lessons are developed and assembled into topics. Decisions about the correspondence of these objectives with original intentions for the topic and course, and judgments about the balance of objectives, can also be made with reference to these larger instructional units. As in the case of the individual lesson, these decisions are made possible by the categorization of objectives into types of capabilities to be learned.

The teacher's design of the single lesson also makes use of individual statements of objectives and the classes of capabilities they represent. The instructional materials available to the teacher (textbook, manual, or whatever) may identity the objectives of the lesson directly. More frequently, the teacher may need to (1) infer what the objectives are and (2) design the lesson so that the objectives represented in the textbook are supplemented by other objectives. For purposes of planning effective instruction, the determination of categories of expected learning outcomes is as important to the teacher as it is to the design team. The teacher, for tomorrow's lesson, needs to make decisions about the how best to teach it and how to relate it to previous learning.

Objectives and Assessment

Fortunately, the lists of individual objectives developed in a systematic design effort have a second use. Descriptions of objectives, as we have said, are descriptions of what must be observed to verify that the desired learning has taken place. Consequently, statements of objectives have direct implications for assessing student learning (see Chapter 13). The teacher may use objective statements to design situations within which student performance can be observed. This is done to verify that particular outcomes of learning have in fact occurred. Consider the objective: "Given a terrain map of the United States and information about prevailing winds, demonstrates the location of regions of heavy rainfall by shading the map [applying a rule]." This description more or less directly describes the situation a teacher can use to verify that the desired learning has taken place. A student or group of students could be supplied with terrain maps and prevailing wind information, and be asked to perform this task. The resulting records of their performances would serve as an assessment of their learning the appropriate rule.

With comparable adequacy, statements of objectives can serve as bases for the development of teacher-made tests. These in turn may be employed for formal kinds of assessment of student performance, when considered desirable by the teacher. Alternatively, they can be used as "self-tests" that students employ when engaging in individual study or self-instruction.

The classes of objectives described in this chapter constitute a taxonomy that is applicable to the design of many kinds of assessment instruments and tests. A somewhat different, although not incompatible, taxonomy of objectives is described in the works of Bloom (1956) and Krathwhol, Bloom, and Masia (1964). The application of this latter taxonomy to the design of tests and other assessment techniques is illustrated in many subject-matter fields in the volume edited by Bloom, Hastings, and Madaus (1971). This work describes, in detail, methods of planning assessment for most areas of the school curriculum. Further discussion of methods for developing tests and test items, based on the categories of learning outcomes described in this chapter, is contained in Chapter 13.

SUMMARY

The identification and definition of performance objectives is an important step in the design of instruction. Objectives serve as guidelines for developing the instruction and for designing measures of student performance to determine whether the course objectives have been reached.

Initially, the aims of instruction are frequently formulated as a set of purposes for a course. These purposes are further refined and converted to operational terms by the process of defining the performance objectives. These describe the planned outcomes of instruction, and they are the basis for evaluating the success of the instruction in terms of its intended outcomes. It is recognized, of course, that there are often unintended or unexpected outcomes, judged, when later observed, to be either desirable or undesirable.

This chapter has presented a five-component guide to writing performance objectives. The five components are:

1. Situation
2. Learned capability
3. Object
4. Action
5. Tools and constraints

Examples are given, showing how these components can be used to make unambiguous statements of objectives for different school subjects. The examples chosen also illustrate objectives for various categories of learned capabilities.

Special attention is drawn to the need for care in choosing action verbs suitable both for describing the learned capability inferred from the observed performance and for describing the nature of the performance itself. Table 7.1 presents a convenient summary of the learned capability verbs and examples of action verbs.

The kinds of performance objectives described for the various categories of learned capabilities play an essential role in the method of instructional design presented in this book. Precisely formulated definitions of objectives within each category serve as a technical base from which unambiguous communications of learning outcomes can be derived. Different communications of objectives, conveying an approximate common meaning, may be needed for teachers, students, and parents. At the same time, precisely defined objectives relate the same common meanings to the construction of tests for evaluation of student performance, as discussed later in Chapter 13.

REFERENCES

Anderson, J. R. (1985). *Cognitive psychology and its implications* (2nd ed.). New York: Freeman.

Bloom, B. S. (Ed.). (1956). Taxonomy of educational objectives. Handbook 1: Cognitive domain. New York: McKay.

Bloom, B. S., Hastings, J. T., & Madaus, G. F. (Eds.). (1971). *Handbook of formative and summative evaluation of student learning.* New York: McGraw-Hill.

Bruner, J. S. (1971). *The relevance of education.* New York: Norton.

Gagné, R. M. (1985). *The conditions of learning* (4th ed.). New York: Holt, Rinehart and Winston.

Intermediate Science Curriculum Study. (1973). *Individualizing objective testing.* Tallahassee, FL: ISCS, Florida State University.

Krathwhol D. R., Bloom, B. S., & Masia, B. B. (1964). *Taxonomy of educational objectives.* Handbook II: Affective domain. New York: McKay.

Mager, R. F. (1975). *Preparing objectives for instruction* (2nd ed.). Belmont CA: Fearon.

Martin, B., & Briggs, L. J. (1986). *The affective and cognitive domains: Integration for instruction and research.* Englewood Cliffs, NJ: Educational Technology Publications.

Popham, W. J., & Baker, E. L. (1970). *Establishing instructional goals.* Englewood Cliffs, NJ: Prentice Hall.

Rohwer, W. D., Jr. (1975). Elaboration and learning in childhood and adolescence. In H. W. Reese (Ed.), *Advances in child development and behavior* (Vol. 8). New York: Academic Press.

Wilson, B. (1997). Reflections on constructivism and instructional design. In C. R. Dills & A. J. Romiszowski (Eds.), *Instructional design paradigms.* Englewood Cliffs, NJ: Educational Technology Publications.

ANALYSIS OF A LEARNING TASK

Instructional design often begins with identification of the purpose of the course and an analysis of the learning objectives. The question initially asked by the designer is not, "What will the students study?" but rather, "What will students know or be able to do after they have learned?" This chapter explores two analysis procedures that yield the systematic information needed to plan and specify the conditions for instruction: (1) *information-processing analysis*, and (2) *learning-task analysis*. Both types of analysis begin with an investigation of the purposes of the course, and the development of target learning objectives.

In this chapter we describe the two kinds of objectives involved in instructional design: (1) those to be attained at the end of a course of study (*target objectives*), and (2) those to be attained during a course of study (*enabling objectives*). The enabling objectives are either prerequisites for the target objectives, or they are supportive (facilitate learning for other objectives). We begin by describing how to determine the target objectives and then describe a "top-down" procedure for determining the enabling objectives.

The chapter concludes with a discussion of a requirement for instructional design jointly conceptualized by Gagné and Merrill (1990) that identified learning goals based upon *multiple integrated objectives* as they occur in lessons and courses. Gagné and Merrill proposed that the integration of multiple objectives be conceived in terms of a more comprehensive activity in which the human is engaged, called an *enterprise*.

SCOPE OF THE ANALYSIS

The broad scope of the task(s) must be carefully considered during instructional task analysis. Is the analysis related to a course (generally covering many skills), or is it related to a lesson (generally focused on a particular skill)? While the process of task analysis is the same for both, the scope of the analysis and the number of steps in the analysis can differ significantly.

Starting with a course, the designer must first identify the *purpose* of the course. At this stage it isn't necessary to formulate specific five-component objectives; however, many of the same guidelines apply:

1. State the purpose of a course in terms of what the student will be like *after* the instruction, not what he or she will be doing *during* the course. For example, the statement "To provide the learner experience in performing titration with chemical apparatus" describes what the student will be doing in the course, not what he or she will be learning. What is the ultimate *purpose* of experience with titrations? One desirable course outcome might be, "To be able to determine the concentration of an unknown substance using titration."

2. Avoid the tendency to identify purposes that are too far removed or too far in the future. Purposes should be stated in *expected current outcomes* of instruction. For example, rather than a purpose such as "Develops new compounds useful to society," it would be more realistic to say, "Understands how compounds are formed through chemical reactions." There is nothing wrong with the lifelong goal, but it is probably not going to occur as the result of a single course.

In summary, a good way to begin the task analysis process for a course is to define the course purpose. Examples of acceptable course purposes include:

1. Understands the process of instructional design.
2. Can play a musical instrument of his or her choice.
3. Reads and enjoys short stories.
4. Composes a screenplay.

As discussed in Chapter 7, course purposes can be translated into more specific learning outcome statements, such as:

1. Demonstrates the application of an instructional design model to develop an instructional module.
2. Executes the performance of a musical score in an orchestra.
3. Chooses to read and report on short stories.
4. Generates an outline, storyboard, and script for a screenplay of a short story.

These examples show how *course purposes*, even though originally broadly stated, can be classified by type of outcome and be made more specific in terms of the expected learning performances.

TYPES OF TASK ANALYSIS

There are two major types of task analysis. The first is generally referred to as a *procedural task analysis* but is also sometimes called an *information processing analysis*. The second is called a *learning-task analysis*.

Procedural Task Analysis

A procedural task analysis describes the steps for performing a task, for example, the steps to change a tire. A specific example of a procedural task analysis for making sentences with indefinite pronouns is shown in Figure 8–1.

Procedural task analysis involves breaking tasks down into steps the learner must perform to complete the task. Notice that the task shown in Figure 8–1 has both observable steps (write indefinite pronoun) and mental steps (recall action verb and make a decision whether to use a singular or plural form). The analysis goes beyond the observed behaviors. The analysis also accounts for the intellectual skills that are components of the total task, thus the name "information-processing analysis."

The distinction between choice and action implies that more than a series of steps needs to be identified; it needs to distinguish different *kinds* of steps. Thus, a more traditionally represented flowchart would be one like that shown in Figure 8–2.

Although the conventions of flowcharts vary, the symbol of a trapezoid is often used to represent an *input*, a rectangle an *action*, and a diamond a *choice* or *decision*.

Another example of an information-processing analysis is shown in Figure 8–3, for the task of subtracting two-place numbers. Information-processing diagrams of a number of other tasks in mathematics learning are described by Resnick (1976) and by Greeno (1976). An analysis of reading, including both decoding and comprehension skills, has been made by Resnick and Beck (1977). The application of this type of analysis to the task of balancing a checkbook has been described by Merrill (1971). A more complete discussion of this and alternative task-analysis techniques may be found in Jonassen, Hannum, and Tessmer (1989).

Uses of Information-Processing Analysis

Two primary kinds of information come from information-processing analysis. First, it provides a clear description of the *target objective*, including the steps involved in the procedure. For example, Figure 8–3 describes the performance of

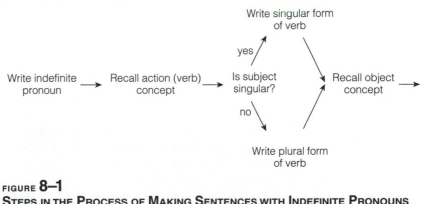

FIGURE 8–1
STEPS IN THE PROCESS OF MAKING SENTENCES WITH INDEFINITE PRONOUNS AS SUBJECTS

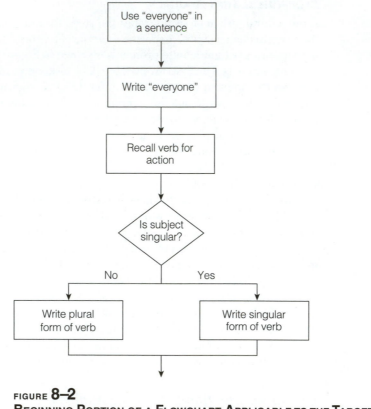

FIGURE **8–2**
**BEGINNING PORTION OF A FLOWCHART APPLICABLE TO THE TARGET OBJECTIVE:
WRITING SENTENCES WITH THE PRONOUN "EVERYONE" AS SUBJECT**

subtracting in a way that reveals its sequential steps. This description conveys more information than the objective statement, "Given two numbers, demonstrate the process of subtraction." The instructional designer can specify the sequence of the performance by developing a flowchart.

A second use of information-processing analysis is the depiction of individual steps that might not otherwise be obvious. This is particularly true for decision steps that are internally processed rather than overtly demonstrated. For example, the decisions indicated by the diagram in Figure 8–3 imply that the learner must be able to distinguish the larger from the smaller of two numbers in order to carry out the task of subtraction. This is a specific skill that must be acquired if it is not known already. It becomes one of the target objectives that make up the total task of subtracting two-place numbers.

After an information-processing analysis is completed, the component skills can be written as five-component objectives. These become the target objectives for the lesson or lessons. Writing five-component objectives requires the instruc-

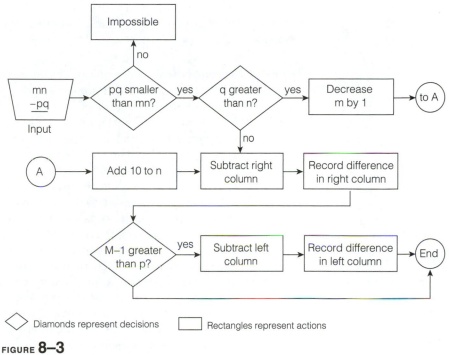

Diamonds represent decisions   Rectangles represent actions

FIGURE **8–3**

AN INFORMATION-PROCESSING ANALYSIS OF THE SUBTRACTION OF TWO-PLACE NUMBERS

(From R. M. Gagné, Analysis of objectives. In L. J. Briggs (Ed.), *Instructional design,* copyright 1977 by Educational Technology Publications, Englewood Cliffs, NJ. Reprinted by permission.)

tional designer to classify the target skills according to type of learning outcome. This makes it possible to perform the second kind of task analysis, a learning-task analysis.

Learning-Task Analysis

Once the target objectives have been specified, an analysis to identify prerequisite competencies or enabling skills can be performed. Both target objectives and enabling objectives need to be considered during instructional design.

In the most general sense, a prerequisite is a task that is learned prior to the learning of a target objective and it "aids" or "enables" learning. A task can be both a target objective for a particular lesson and, at the same time, an enabling objective for a subsequent lesson, because it is a prerequisite to the task to be learned later. For example, the target objective of finding the diagonal distance across a rectangular plot of land has as prerequisites the skills of (1) measuring the distance along the sides of the rectangle and (2) applying the rule for computation of the hypotenuse of a right triangle. These two enabling capabilities may have been learned some years prior to the lesson designed to teach the target objective (finding the diagonal distance), or they may have been learned immediately before or even during the lesson itself.

Types of Prerequisites   Prerequisite objectives can be classified into one of two types: *essential* prerequisites and *supportive* prerequisites.

Examples of essential prerequisites may be found by analyzing the task of "supplying the definite article" for a noun in writing a sentence in the German language. In acquiring this capability, a student must learn the prior tasks of (1) identifying gender, (2) identifying number (singular or plural), and (3) applying grammatical rules of case. Such capabilities may have been learned during formal instruction or, in an incidental fashion, by experience with the language. Learning in an incidental fashion is not relevant to the systematic design of instruction. What is relevant is that the "subordinate" capabilities are part of the total skill of supplying the definite article. This means that they are essential prerequisites, not merely helpful or supportive. These component skills must be learned if the total task of supplying the definite article is to be learned and performed correctly.

A prerequisite may, however, be simply supportive. The prerequisite may aid new learning by making it easier or faster. For example, a positive attitude toward learning to compose proper German sentences may be acquired by having students interact with German pen-pals over the Internet.

Such an attitude is likely to help the learner learn the foreign language. It is supportive of the learning, but not essential. If the learner had previously acquired a cognitive strategy for remembering the gender of German nouns, such as associating each newly encountered noun with a visual image, that strategy would also be a supportive prerequisite because it makes learning easier and faster.

For each category of task (as identified by task classification), one can identify both essential and supportive prerequisites that are considerably different for each task category. Keeping the differences straight is important for instructional design, and it's one of the major reasons for classifying tasks and determining of task categories before identifying prerequisites. In the following sections, our discussion of prerequisites begins with those that are essential and proceeds to describe some that are supportive.

PREREQUISITES IN LEARNING INTELLECTUAL SKILLS

Intellectual skills, like other kinds of learning, are affected by both essential and supportive prerequisites, with essential prerequisites being more directly involved.

Essential Prerequisites for Intellectual Skills

As previously stated in Chapter 4, intellectual skills are hierarchical, with problem solving at the top, requiring rules composed of defined concepts and concrete concepts, which require discriminations. A target objective representing an intellectual skill is typically composed of two or more subordinate and simpler skills. The simpler skills are prerequisites to learning the target objective in the sense that they must be learned first, before the objective is "put together." The learning of prerequisites may have occurred previously, although it often occurs just prior to learning the objective.

An example of the meaning of essential prerequisites is provided by Gagné (1977) for the task of subtracting whole numbers. Such a task may be represented by problems such as the following:

(a) 473	(b) 2132	(c) 953	(d) 7204
−342	−1715	−676	−5168

A common method for subtracting is performed by borrowing. The four examples illustrate four prerequisite skills (rules) that are involved in the skill of subtracting whole numbers. Example (a), the simplest, is "subtracting one-place numbers in columns, without borrowing." Example (b) is "subtracting when several borrowings are required." Example (c) is "successive borrowing in adjacent columns"; borrowing must be done in the first column on the right so that 6 can be subtracted from 13, and again in the next column so that 7 can be subtracted from 14. Example (d) requires use of a rule for borrowing when there is a "0" at the top of a column.

Each of these prerequisite skills represents a rule that is involved in the total skill of subtracting whole numbers. The task in example (d) cannot be learned in any complete sense without the prior learning of the subordinate skills. That is why they are called *essential prerequisites*.

Other examples of prerequisites for intellectual skills may be found by examining the results of the information-processing analyses described earlier in this chapter. The analysis of subtraction includes the borrowing skill, which is comparable to Example (a). When the objective is writing sentences with the subject *everyone*, the essential prerequisites indicated by the diagram of Figure 8–2 are (1) identifying verb names for actions and (2) using rules to make verbs singular or plural.

Hierarchies of Prerequisite Skills   Although learning-task analysis is often concerned with the prerequisite of a target objective, the analysis may be applied to the enabling skills as well, because these skills themselves have prerequisites. It is possible to continue the learning-task analysis until a point is reached where the identified skills are quite simple (and perhaps assumed to be known by all students).

When a learning-task analysis is carried out on successively simpler components of a target objective, the result is a learning hierarchy (Gagné, 1985). This outcome may be displayed as a diagram containing boxes with the successively identified subordinate skills (that is, essential prerequisite skills). Figure 8–4 is an example of a learning hierarchy for the target objective of "subtracting whole numbers." At the top level of analysis, this learning hierarchy incorporates the four prerequisite skills of subtraction previously described. These are numbered VII, VIII, IX, and X in Figure 8–4. Analyzing from the top-down of skills X, IX, VIII, and VII, identifies the simpler Skill VI, "subtracting when a single borrowing is required, in any column." Skill VI is an essential prerequisite to the more complex skills of borrowing (VIII, IX, and X). Skill VI can also be analyzed to reveal the prerequisites

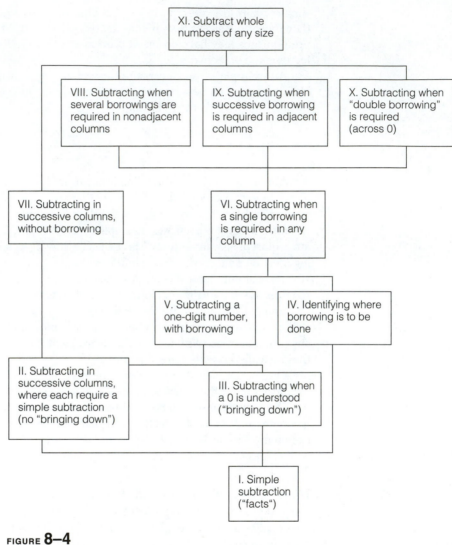

FIGURE **8–4**
A LEARNING HIERARCHY FOR SUBTRACTING WHOLE NUMBERS

described in the boxes labeled IV and V. The process may be continued to the level of simple subtraction "facts" (I).

The learning hierarchy displays a pattern of progressively simpler intellectual skills. These skills are enabling objectives for a given target objective (which is also an intellectual skill), and they are also composed of other subordinate skills. In designing instruction for intellectual skills, the enabling skills that are the most important are the *immediate prerequisites*. The most important part of the learning-task analysis is with any two adjacent levels in the learning hierarchy. The reasons for preparing a fully worked-out learning hierarchy that displays the entire pattern of enabling skills on several levels are that it serves as a guide for designing a sequence of instruction (Cook & Walbesser, 1973), and it can help the student and teacher as they plan instructional assignments.

Conducting a Learning-Task Analysis for Intellectual Skills   Intellectual skill analysis is carried out by "working backward" or "top-down" from a target objective. The purpose of the analysis is to reveal the simpler component skills that constitute the target objective. There is often a correspondence at the first level of analysis between the component steps in an information-processing analysis and the component skills in a learning-task analysis. The distinction between sequential steps and subordinate skills should be carefully maintained. Sequential steps are what an individual does when performing the task (the capability of which has been learned) and the subordinate skills are what the individual must learn in a sequence beginning with the simplest.

Subordinate skills for any given intellectual skill can be determined by asking, "What simpler skill(s) would a learner have to possess to learn this skill?" (Gagné, 1985). Once the first set of subordinate (enabling) skills is identified, the process can be repeated by addressing the same question for each subordinate skill. In doing so, the subordinate skills become simpler and simpler. Normally, the process stops when one decides, on the basis of knowledge about student characteristics, that the skills at the lowest level of the hierarchy are already known and do not have to be learned. This stopping point varies with the educational background of the students. For example, a learning hierarchy on grammatical rules in a foreign language would have many more levels for students who had not previously learned the grammatical rules of their native language.

Supportive Prerequisites for Intellectual Skills

A number of kinds of learning, when undertaken on a prior basis, may be supportive in the acquisition of an intellectual skill. This means that the previously acquired capability may be helpful, although not essential, for the learning of a target skill.

Verbal information, for example, is often useful to the learner in acquiring intellectual skills, presumably because it facilitates the verbal communications that are a part of instruction. Some good examples of the relation of verbal information to the learning of an intellectual skill occur in a study by White (1974). White developed and validated a learning hierarchy for the intellectual skill "finding velocity at a prescribed point on a curved graph relating position (of an object) and time." In its initial form, the trial hierarchy included capabilities of the information sort, such as "states that the slope of a position-time graph is velocity" and "states units of slope in units labeling axes." The results of White's investigation showed that although these capabilities may have been helpful for intellectual skill learning, they were not essential. Further verification of the supportive nature of information, contrasting with prerequisites that are essential, is provided in a study by White and Gagné (1978).

During the instructional design process it is sometimes necessary to consider several kinds of supportive prerequisites. Depending on the how the instruction is being delivered, these can be introduced in a single lesson, or they can be presented in the sequence of a larger topic or course. The three types of supportive prerequisites for intellectual skill learning are described below.

Information as Supportive Prerequisites   As previously shown, verbal information may support intellectual skills simply by aiding communication. For example, labels might be used for concepts during rule learning. Another possible function of verbal information is to provide cues for retrieval of an intellectual skill (Gagné, 1985). Normally, when intellectual skills are being learned a fair amount of information is included at the same time. The information supports the learning process, and the key is to not "mix" intellectual skills and information during the instructional design process.

Cognitive Strategies as Supportive Prerequisites   The learning of intellectual skills is supported by the use of cognitive strategies. For example, if students who are learning to "add positive and negative integers" possess the cognitive strategy of imagining a "number line," their learning of the requisite rules may be facilitated. Cognitive strategies speed up the learning of intellectual skills, make them easier to recall, and aid their transfer to novel problems.

Attitudes as Supportive Prerequisites   The supportive effect of positive attitudes on the learning of intellectual skills is widely recognized. Presumably, the attitudes a learner has toward a subject strongly influence the ease with which the subject is learned, retained, and put to use (Mager, 1968). The relationship between attitude and learning is readily observed in students' conduct toward a subject like mathematics. Evidence concerning the effects of "affective entry characteristics" on achievement in school subjects is reviewed by Bloom (1976), and a review of the literature by Martin and Briggs (1986) showed attitude learning to be strongly related to the learning of cognitive skills.

LEARNING-TASK ANALYSIS AND OTHER LEARNING TYPES

The rationale of learning-task analysis can also be brought to bear on learning tasks other than intellectual skills, namely the learning of cognitive strategies, information, attitudes, and motor skills. The purpose of analysis is the same—to identify essential and supportive prerequisites. However, the processes for these applications are quite different. For example, capabilities like information and attitude are not learned by putting together subordinate parts, as is the case with intellectual skills. Consequently, prerequisites tend to be of a supportive rather than an essential nature. Table 8.1 summarizes the essential and supportive prerequisites resulting from analysis of the five types of learning outcomes.

Type of Learning Outcome	Essential Prerequisites	Supportive Prerequisites
Intellectual Skill	Simpler component intellectual skills (rules, concepts, discrimination)	Attitudes, cognitive strategies, verbal information
Cognitive Strategies	Specific intellectual skills	Intellectual skills, attitudes, verbal information
Verbal Information	Meaningfully organized sets of information	Language skills, cognitive strategies, attitudes
Attitudes	Intellectual skills (sometimes) Verbal information (sometimes)	Other attitudes, verbal information
Motor Skills	Part skills (sometimes) Procedural rules (sometimes)	Attitudes

(From *Analysis of objectives* (p. 141) by R. M. Gagné, 1977. In L. J. Briggs (Ed.), *Instructional design*, Englewood Cliffs, NJ: Educational Technology Publications. Copyright 1977 by Educational Technology Publications. Reprinted by permission.)

Prerequisites: Cognitive Strategies

The prerequisites for cognitive strategies of learning, remembering, and thinking are some very basic and simple mental abilities. For example, an effective cognitive strategy for remembering a list of items is to generate a different mental image for each item. The essential prerequisite in this case is the *ability to create visual images*, which is a very basic ability. An effective cognitive strategy for solving complex mathematical problems is breaking the problem into parts and seeking the solution to each part. The prerequisite ability is the *ability to divide a verbally described situation into parts*. This, too, is a fundamental kind of ability of a rather simple sort.

Whatever the essential prerequisites of cognitive strategies are, there is disagreement over how much they depend upon innate factors that develop as people mature and how much they are learned. A discussion of these issues is presented by Case (1978) and Gagné (1977), and the factor of maturation plays a prominent role in the developmental theory of Piaget (1970). In contrast, Gagné (1985) proposes that cognitive strategies of the executive type, for example, organizing things in a sequence, are generalizations from learned intellectual skills. It is interesting to note that either of these processes (maturation or learning) takes its effect on cognitive strategies over a considerable period of time, as viewed from the standpoint of intellectual development.

Supportive prerequisites for the learning of cognitive strategies include the intellectual skills that may be useful in learning the particular material or solving the particular problems presented to the learner. Relevant verbal information may also play this supportive role. Just as in learning other kinds of capabilities, favorable attitudes toward learning are likely to be helpful.

Prerequisites: Verbal Information

To learn and store verbal information, the learner must have some basic language skills. A number of learning theories propose that information is stored and retrieved in the form of propositions. If this is the case, then the learner must already possess the essential prerequisite skills of forming propositions (sentences) in accordance with certain rules of syntax. These skills are likely to have been learned fairly early in life.

Verbal information, whether of single items or longer passages, appears to be most readily learned and retained when it occurs within a larger context of meaningful information. This context may be learned immediately before the information is to be acquired, or it may have been learned previously. The provision of this meaningful context has been described as a learning condition in Chapter 5 and is classified as a supportive prerequisite of information learning.

Attitudes support the learning of verbal information in much the same way they support other kinds of learning. A number of different cognitive strategies have been found to support the learning of word lists (see Gagné, 1985; Rohwer, 1970). Particular strategies also aid the retention of prose passages, such as remembering the gist of a textbook chapter (Palincsar & Brown, 1984).

Prerequisites: Attitudes

To acquire particular attitudes students may need to have learned particular intellectual skills or particular sets of information. In this sense the learned capabilities are essential prerequisites to attitude learning. For example, if a positive attitude toward "truth in labeling" of packaged foods is to be acquired, the learner may need to have (1) the intellectual skills involved in comprehending the printed statement on the label, and (2) a variety of verbal information about food ingredients.

As Table 8.1 indicates, attitudes may be mutually supportive of each other or one attitude might support the acquisition of another attitude. For example, preference for a political candidate makes it easier for a person to prefer the political views of that candidate's party. In a more general sense, the degree to which a human model is respected affects the readiness with which the model's attitude is adopted.

Besides its essential role in a specific sense, verbal information also has a supportive function in establishing attitudes. Knowledge of the situations in which the choice of personal action will be made contributes to the ease of attitude acquisition. For example, an attitude such as "don't drive after drinking" is more readily acquired if the individual understands the social situations (such as peer pressure) that would tempt one to undertake such behavior.

Prerequisites: Motor Skills

As described in Chapter 5, motor skills are often composed of several part skills, and efficient learning takes place when the part skills are practiced individually and then combined in practice of the total skill. In such instances, the part skills function as essential prerequisites for learning the total skill.

Another component of a motor skill that has this role is the *executive subroutine* (Fitts & Posner, 1967), which is sometimes learned as an initial step. For example, swimming the crawl involves an executive subroutine that selects a sequence of movements for arms, legs, body, and head. Even before the total skill is practiced the swimmer may receive instruction in the correct execution of this sequence. In Table 8.1, these subroutines are referred to as *procedural rules*. When learned separately and prior to the skill itself they are classed as essential prerequisites.

Positive attitudes toward learning a motor skill, and toward the performance it makes possible, are often significant supportive prerequisites.

Instructional Curriculum Maps

We have described the diagramming of skills in the intellectual skills domain by showing hierarchical relationships among the skills, discriminations as prerequisites for concepts, concepts as prerequisites for rules, and rules as prerequisites for problem solving. These relationships can be diagrammed as shown in Figure 8–5.

It is more difficult to visualize a diagram of the relationships among objectives from different domains, such as the relationship between intellectual skills and attitudes. Briggs and Wager (1981) described a system called *instructional curriculum mapping* for illustrating these relationships. Instructional curriculum mapping represents the functional relationships among instructional objectives. It starts by identifying the target intellectual skills objective and asking the question, "What other objectives are related to the attainment of this objective?" (either essential skills or supportive prerequisites). Hierarchical relationships of essential prerequisites among intellectual skills are drawn in much the same way as shown in Figure 8–5.

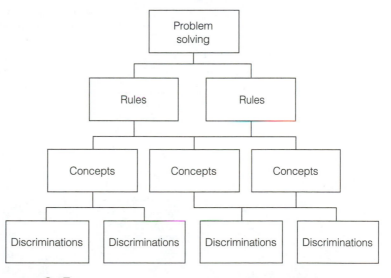

FIGURE **8–5**
HIERARCHICAL RELATIONSHIPS AMONG OBJECTIVES IN THE INTELLECTUAL SKILLS DOMAIN

Supportive objectives are shown in Figure 8–6 connected to the target objective, with an indication in each case that they are not from the same domain.

For example, the target intellectual objective in a computer literacy course might be, "The student will be able to demonstrate the use of MS Word" (a complex rule-using skill). A related target attitude objective might be, "The student chooses to use a computer as a word processor to type assignments rather than to write them by hand." The student will learn the intellectual skills necessary to apply the skills, but these skills alone may be insufficient to formulate the attitude. Supporting objectives related to the purposes for using a word processor might help. Examples of such supporting objectives might be:

1. States the different functions of a word processor, such as editing, spell checking, grammar checking, printing, and saving.
2. States advantages of using a word processor—easy revision of drafts, adding in graphics, electronic transfer of files, etc.
3. States advantages of typed over handwritten material (neatness, formatting, cut and paste, graphics.

None of the verbal information objectives listed above are required to learn the intellectual skills associated with operating word processors; that is, they are not essential prerequisites. However, the student probably already knows a fair amount about the advantages of neatly presented work as a result of having come through the school system. The information supports the formulation of an attitude toward use of the computer as diagrammed in Figure 8–6. The triangle between the verbal

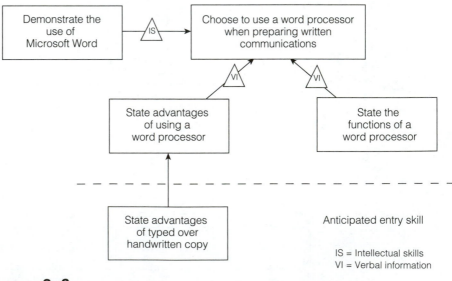

FIGURE 8–6
INSTRUCTIONAL CURRICULUM MAP (ICM) SHOWING SUPPORTIVE RELATIONSHIPS OF VERBAL INFORMATION OBJECTIVES TO AN ATTITUDINAL TARGET OBJECTIVE

information objectives and the attitude objective illustrates the fact that this is an intersection of two different domains and alerts the designer that perhaps different conditions of learning will be needed to accomplish the target objective. The three verbal information objectives are not essential prerequisites to each other, but they may be taught in contextual (supportive) sequence. The relationships among objectives from the same domain are connected with solid lines.

Figure 8–7 shows the highest level of intellectual skill associated with this target objective, namely, rule using: "Demonstrates the use of a word processor by typing, editing, and printing the text."

This objective is functionally related to the target attitude objective as an essential prerequisite. The relationship is again diagrammed to show that there is a domain change by the inclusion of the *IS* (intellectual skill) symbol in the connecting line, meaning that the intellectual skill is functionally related to attainment of the attitude.

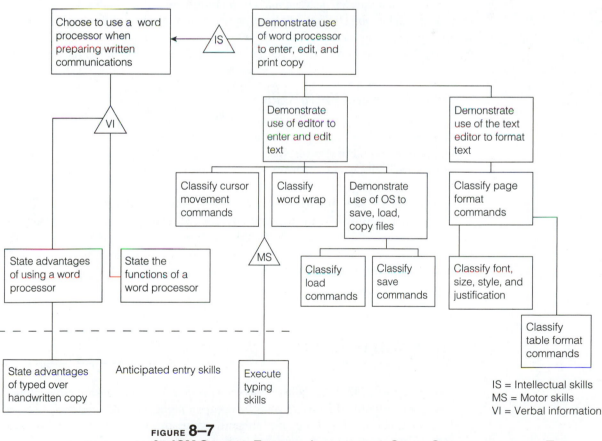

FIGURE **8–7**
AN ICM SHOWING ENABLING INTELLECTUAL SKILLS OBJECTIVES FOR THE TASK OF USING A WORD PROCESSOR

The triangle symbol, which indicates a change in domains, identifies skills from the facilitating domain. There may be several such domain changes in the development of instructional sequences within learning tasks. The particular symbols are not important. We have shown a triangle with *VI* in it for "verbal information," a triangle with an *IS* in it for "intellectual skills," and a triangle with *MS* in it for "motor skills." What is important is that the domain change be recognized because it might have important design implications.

The objective "Demonstrates use of word processor" is an intellectual skill with other prerequisite intellectual skills, including the concepts of *editor, word wrap, filer, blocks, formatting,* and others. Objectives related to these concepts are diagrammed in a hierarchical manner in Figure 8–7.

Notice that the motor skill of typing is prerequisite to using the word processor. Being able to touch-type might also be a skill that would help the learner take advantage of using a word processor, however, touch-typing skills are not essential to learning the use of a word processor.

The technique of instructional curriculum mapping facilitates the designer's task of relating objectives to one another when they are from different domains. It also lets the designer see when there are holes in the instruction and/or if there are extraneous "dead wood" objectives that don't seem to relate to any target objectives.

Subordinate and Entry Skills

The terms *entry skill* and *subordinate objectives* generally apply to the description of objectives related to a particular lesson. For example, a single lesson might have one or more target objectives. *Enabling objectives* are subordinate to these objectives. Entry skills, which the learner is expected to have acquired before beginning the lesson, are also subordinate to the *target objective*. They are essential or supportive prerequisites, but they will not be *taught* during the lesson. *Entry skills* are identified in both hierarchy diagrams and instructional maps as those skills listed below the dotted line. This is illustrated in Figure 8–8. Identifying the entry skills in this manner makes it possible to construct a pretest to see whether the student has the skills necessary to take the lesson.

INTEGRATED GOALS

Gagné and Merrill (1990) jointly conceptualized a requirement for instructional design that identified learning goals based upon *multiple integrated objectives* as they occur in lessons and courses. Integrative goals are conceived as *incorporating* rather than supplanting the various single types of instructional outcomes (facts, concepts, rules, strategies). Gagné and Merrill proposed that the integration of

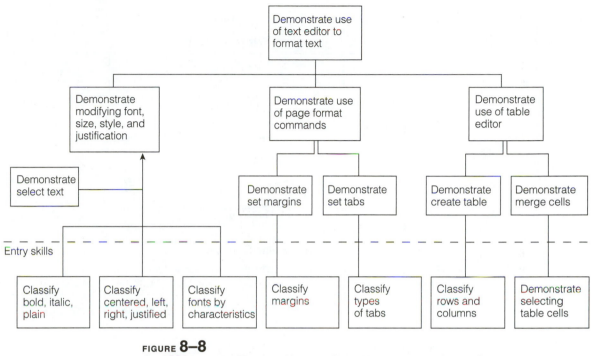

FIGURE **8–8**
AN ICM FOR THE TASK OF USING A TEXT EDITOR, WITH ENTRY SKILLS INDICATED

multiple objectives be conceived in terms of a more comprehensive activity in which the human is engaged, which they called an *enterprise*. For its execution, an enterprise may depend upon some combination of verbal information, intellectual skills, and cognitive strategies, all related by their involvement in the common goal. Depending upon the enterprise, motor skills and attitudes may also be involved. Enterprise schemas build upon one or more of the single types of learning outcomes in the sense that they are constituent parts of the more complex activity. Instructional designers need to identify the goal of a targeted enterprise, along with its component skills and knowledge, and then design instruction that enables the student to acquire the capability of achieving this integrated outcome.

Gagné and Merrill also proposed that different *integrated goals* of various enterprises are represented in memory as different kinds of cognitive structures. Each kind of enterprise is represented in memory by a schema that reflects the purpose or goal of the enterprise category, the various knowledge and skills required to engage in the enterprise, and a scenario that indicates when and how each piece of knowledge or skill is required by the enterprise. The general form of schemas representing such goals is diagrammed in Figure 8–9.

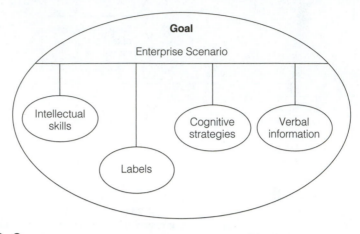

FIGURE **8–9**

GENERAL FORM OF AN ENTERPRISE SCHEMA

(From Gagné, R. M., & Merrill M. D. 1990, Integrative Goals for Instructional Design, *Educational Technology Research and Development 38* (1): 23–30. Reprinted with permission.*)*

SUMMARY

Task analysis refers to several different, interrelated, procedures that are carried out to yield the systematic information needed to plan and specify the conditions for instruction. The two procedures described in this chapter were (1) information-processing analysis and (2) learning-task analysis. Both types of analysis begin with target objectives for lessons or courses.

Information-processing analysis describes the steps taken by learners as they perform the task(s) they have learned. Included in these steps are: (1) input information, (2) actions, and (3) decisions. Of particular importance is the fact that this type of analysis usually reveals mental operations that are involved in the performance but are not directly observable as overt behavior. Together, the various steps in the performance may be shown in a flowchart. The results of the analysis exhibit (or imply) capabilities that must be learned as components of the performance described as the target objective.

These components are themselves instructional objectives, called *enabling objectives,* which support learning of the target objective. In addition, they may need to be analyzed further (in the manner of learning-task analysis) to reveal additional enabling objectives.

Task classification has the purpose of providing a basis for designing the conditions necessary for effective instruction. The objectives of instruction are categorized as intellectual skills, cognitive strategies, information, attitudes, or motor skills. As indicated in previous chapters, each of these categories carries different implications regarding the conditions necessary for learning, which can be incorporated into the design of instruction.

Learning-task analysis has the purpose of identifying the prerequisites of both target and enabling objectives. Two kinds of prerequisites are distinguished, essential and supportive. Essential prerequisites are the components of the capability being learned, and therefore, their learning must occur as a prior event. Other prerequisites may be supportive in the sense that they make the learning of a capability easier or faster.

Target objectives for intellectual skills may be analyzed into successive levels of prerequisites, in the sense that complex skills are progressively broken down into simpler ones. The result of this type of analysis is a learning hierarchy, which provides a basis for planning instructional sequences. Prerequisites for other categories of learning objectives do not form learning hierarchies, because their prerequisites do not relate to each other in the manner of intellectual skills.

A number of supportive prerequisites may be identified for particular types of target objectives. For example, task-relevant information is often supportive of intellectual-skill learning. Positive attitudes toward lesson and course objectives are an important source of learning support. Cognitive strategies of attending, learning, and remembering may be brought to bear by the learner in supporting these processes. These supportive relationships may be diagrammed through the use of instructional curriculum mapping.

Planning instruction for more than one objective may simply be a matter of designing instructional procedures for one after another in sequence. This is particularly evident in topics composed primarily of intellectual skills, in which a lesson, such as addition of simple fractions, may be followed by a lesson on improper fractions, and followed again by one on simplification of fractions. However, a linear sequence of single objective lessons may not be satisfactory for multiple objectives because it fails to assist the learner in the acquisition of interrelationships among the various component objectives. Instead, it seems possible that some integration of these objectives might be conceived as a way of expressing a combined goal. Such integration would not replace the multiple objectives that make up a module or course goal, but instead would actually incorporate the several different objectives.

When instruction is considered in the more comprehensive sense of a module, section, or course, it becomes apparent that *multiple objectives* commonly occur. Gagné and Merrill (1990) proposed that integrative goals are represented in cognitive space by *enterprise schemas*, whose focal integrating concept is the integrative goal. Associated with the integrative goal is an enterprise scenario and the various items of verbal knowledge, intellectual skills, and cognitive strategies that must be learned in order to support the required performances. These performances are brought together in a purposeful activity known as *enterprise.* Examples of enterprises are: operating an item of equipment, teaching a science topic, counseling someone about applying for a job, giving directions for how to use a weed cutter. The schema representing the goal of the enterprise and including the goal-related knowledge and skills is an *enterprise schema.*

Instructional design must specify the conditions for acquisition of an enterprise schema. Besides constituent knowledge and skills, this schema includes a scenario of declarative knowledge relating these skills to the goal. This scenario serves to remind the learner of the purpose for learning the various facts and skills—the relations they have with the enterprise to be accomplished. In view of these characteristics, the enterprise schema is seen as a factor of substantial positive influence in transfer of training.

REFERENCES

Bloom, B. S. (1976). *Human characteristics and school learning.* New York: McGraw-Hill.

Briggs, L. J., & Wager, W. W. (1981). *Handbook of procedures for the design of instruction.* Englewood Cliffs, NJ: Educational Technology Publications.

Case, R. (1978). Piaget and beyond: Toward a developmentally based theory and technology of instruction. In R. Glaser (Ed.), *Advances in instructional psychology* (Vol. l). Hillsdale, NJ: Erlbaum.

Cook, J. M., & Walbesser, H. H. (1973). *How to meet accountability.* College Park, MD: University of Maryland, Bureau of Educational Research and Field Services.

Fitts, P. M., & Posner, M. I. (1967). *Human performance.* Monterey, CA: Brooks/Cole.

Gagné, R. M. (1977). Analysis of objectives. In L. J. Briggs (Ed.), *Instructional design.* Englewood Cliffs, NJ: Educational Technology Publications.

Gagné, R. M. (1985). *The conditions of learning* (4th ed.). New York: Holt, Rinehart and Winston.

Gagné, R. M., & Merrill, M. D. (1990). Integrative goals for instructional design. *Educational Technology Research and Development. 38* (1), 23–30.

Greeno, J. G. (1976). Cognitive objectives of instruction: Theory of knowledge for solving problems and answering questions. In D. Klahr (Ed.). *Cognition and instruction.* Hillsdale, NJ: Erlbaum.

Jonassen, D. H., Hannum, W. H., & Tessmer, M. (1989). *Handbook of task analysis procedures.* New York: Praeger.

Mager, R. F. (1968). *Developing attitude toward learning.* Belmont, CA: Fearon.

Martin, B. L., & Briggs, L. J. (1986). *The affective and cognitive domains: Integration for instruction mid research.* Englewood Cliffs, NJ: Educational Technology Publications.

Merrill, P. F. (1971). *Task analysis: An information processing approach* (Technical Memo No. 27). Tallahassee, FL: Florida State University, CAI Center.

Palincsar, A. S., & Brown, A. L. (1984). Reciprocal teaching of comprehension fostering and comprehension-monitoring activities. *Cognition and Instruction, 1,* 117–175.

Piaget, J. (1970). Piaget's theory. In P. H. Mussen (Ed.). *Carmichael's manual of child psychology.* New York: Wiley.

Resnick, L. B. (1976). Task analysis in instructional design: Some cases from mathematics. In D. Klahr (Ed.), *Cognition and instruction*. Hillsdale, NJ: Erlbaum.

Resnick, L. B., & Beck, I. L. (1977). Designing instruction in reading: Interaction of theory and practice. In J. T. Guthrie (Ed.), *Aspects of reading acquisition*. Baltimore, MD: Johns Hopkins Press.

Rohwer, W. D., Jr. (1970). Images and pictures in children's learning. *Psychological Bulletin, 73,* 393–403.

White, R. T. (1974). The validation of a learning hierarchy. *American Educational Research Journal, 11,* 121–136.

White, R. T., & Gagné, R. M. (1978). Formative evaluation applied to a learning hierarchy. *Contemporary Educational Psychology 3,* 87–94.

DESIGNING INSTRUCTIONAL SEQUENCES

Learning directed toward achieving the goals of school education takes place on a number of occasions over a period of time. Learning a particular capability is preceded by learning prerequisite capabilities and followed by learning more complex capabilities. The specification of a set of capabilities is generally referred to as a *curriculum* or *course*.

A curriculum or course requires decisions about the sequencing of objectives. The goal of an educational or training institution is to establish sequences within courses that promote effective learning. The most obvious sequence follows the order of simple (prerequisite skills) to complex (target) skills, the latter of which take longer to accomplish. Another sequencing principle is one of sequencing objectives in increasing order by the degree of meaning in what is being learned. We know from cognitive learning theory (Anderson, 1985) that one very important determinant of what students will learn, and how fast they will learn, is what they already know. Reigeluth and Stein (1983) address the sequencing problem at a macro level in their "elaboration theory of instruction." The elaboration theory proposes that sequencing should be structured so that the student is first presented with an *epitome* (a generalization) of a concept, procedure, or principle to be learned. The student is then presented with an elaboration or extension of the epitome. The concepts, procedures, and rules are organized from simple to complex, general to specific.

The question of sequencing is encountered at several levels of curriculum and course design, and the issues differ between levels. The matter of effective sequences of instruction is closely related to course organization. This chapter describes a procedure for organizing a course from the top down, going from general to more specific objectives, and utilizing the functional relationships among the types of learning described in previous chapters. Three basic types of instructional sequences are discussed—*hierarchical, knowledge-based*, and *spiral*—and the chapter concludes with a discussion of how to integrate multiple and different kinds of objectives.

As discussed in Chapter 8, once the objectives or goals are specified for a given curriculum or course the major *course units*, each of which may require several weeks of study, are identified next. Under each unit, specific objectives to be reached by the end of the unit are identified. The highest level unit objectives are often the prerequisite skills for the end of course objectives because together they make the end of course performance possible. The unit objectives are then analyzed to identify the supporting or enabling objectives, which are grouped together into lessons. Finally, each group of lesson objectives is analyzed to identify any supporting or enabling objectives. The process stops when entry skills have been identified. Entry skills are objectives related to the objectives to be taught, that the student is expected to have already acquired.

Lessons are generally sequenced so the lower-level objectives are taught first. This is especially important with intellectual skills, because of their hierarchical relationships. More is known about the sequencing relationships among intellectual skills than about other types of learned capabilities. Objectives from other domains that support learning intellectual skills are often woven into the intellectual skills structure. This procedure assumes that intellectual skill objectives are the principal target objectives. However, if the terminal objective is an attitude rather than an intellectual skill, for example the terminal skill in an on-the-job safety course, then the intellectual skills that are supportive of it must be identified. The integration of objectives from different domains may be expressed in the form of instructional maps, as described in Chapter 8. Ultimately, individual lessons are planned to integrate related skills into an overall curriculum of lessons to accomplish the purposes of the course.

One problem with terminology is that the word course has many different meanings. For example, a course on cardiopulmonary resuscitation (CPR) is quite different from a course in computer literacy. The first has very definite criteria for judging mastery of the required skills. There would be substantial consensus among persons who teach CPR about the objectives, the criteria for performance, and the amount of time needed to teach the course. Also, the number of objectives in the CPR course is relatively small. In contrast, the curriculum for a computer literacy course is much broader; there is less agreement on terminal objectives, and the total number of objectives for such a course is quite large.

Another problem in defining a course is the constraint imposed by specifying a set number of hours of instruction. For example, a three-semester-hour course in a university typically represents 48 contact hours of instruction per semester. In public school, a course represents about 180 hours of formal instruction. In the military, a training course can range from one to 1,000 hours of instruction! The length of the course must be carefully considered in planning course and unit objectives.

There are no standard levels to be employed in organizing a course (except for the possible assumption that it consists of two or more lessons). Even a very large course can be described in five different levels of performance outcomes as follows:

1. *Lifelong objectives,* which imply the continued future use of what is learned, after the course *is* over
2. *End-of-course objectives,* which state the performance expected immediately after instruction is completed for the course
3. *Unit objectives,* which define the performance expected on clusters of objectives (topics) having a common purpose in the organization of the total course

4. *Specific performance objectives,* which are the specific outcomes attained during a segment of instruction and which are likely to be at the appropriate level for task analysis
5. *Enabling objectives,* which are either essential or supportive prerequisites for specific target objectives

AN EXAMPLE OF COURSE ORGANIZATION

Considering the nature of the content of this book, we've chosen to illustrate the levels of course organization for a graduate course in the design of instruction. Such a course would be part of a doctoral program in instructional systems design. Related courses in the curriculum would pertain to learning theory, research methods, statistics, varieties of instructional design, design theories, and models of instructional delivery. Students entering the course would typically have master's degrees, often in an area of teaching, such as science education, or in fields such as educational media or educational administration. Most of them would have completed an introductory course in the theory of the design of instruction.

Students are taught to design their own courses based on some identified instructional need or goal. Following the "general-to-specific" basis for course design, students are asked to state their course objectives at several levels.

The levels of objectives for the graduate course in the design of instruction may be illustrated as follows:

1. *Lifelong objective.* After completion of this course, the students will continue to add to their course design skills by (1) enrolling for other design courses and (2) seeking a variety of opportunities to apply design skills in circumstances that require them to modify learned models or to originate new models. Students will choose to employ or originate systematic course design procedures based on theory, research, and consistent rationales; they will choose to use empirical data to improve and evaluate their designs.
2. *End-of-course objective.* By the end of the course, the students will demonstrate the ability either to perform or to plan each step in a systems model of instructional design, from needs analysis to summative evaluation. (In our hypothetical course, efforts are concentrated on stages 4 through 9, as listed in Table 2.1.)
3. *Unit objectives.* Students will complete four successive assignments by completing stages of design representing the following course units:

   Unit A. The student will generate a course organization map showing lifelong objectives, end-of-course objectives, and unit objectives, with accompanying measures of learner performance for those levels of objectives at which the learners' work is to be evaluated.
   Unit B. The student will generate, in writing, a learning hierarchy for an intellectual skill objective and will also devise an instructional map

to show how the prerequisite skills in the hierarchy are to be sequenced in relation to each other and to objectives in other domains of outcomes.

Unit C. The student will generate, in writing, either a lesson plan or a module of instruction, writing a rationale for learning activities suggested.

Unit D. The student will generate a student assessment instrument, related to the unit objectives.

4. *Specific performance objectives* (for Unit C, above).

    1. State the objective(s) or enabling objective(s) for the lesson being planned.
    2. Classify the objective(s) by domain (and sub domain, if appropriate).
    3. List the instructional events to be employed and the rationale for each; also supply a rationale for omitted events (why they were omitted).
    4. Describe the content and activities for each event.
    5. Describe media or materials needed for each event.
    6. Give a rationale based on conditions of learning for decisions 4 and 5.
    7. Write the instructional plan or a set of prescriptions to develop the lesson.

Through the course the students are working with subject matter experts, analyzing and designing real courses. To facilitate learning the design process, the instructor has broken the instruction down into a number of units, and each unit has a detailed criteria sheet that requires the student to reflect on each step of the process. Students turn in their unit assignments with their criteria sheet for the instructor's feedback. The sequence for the course is somewhat temporal (first steps of the process are taught first), but within each step the lower-level objectives are taught before the higher-level objectives.

The levels of objectives just described are one way to organize a course. This organization progresses top-down from the course objectives to the to the level of objectives for individual lessons. However, the activities within the lessons must also be organized and sequenced; that is, the sequence of the instructional events that constitute the lesson must also be planned. This part of the planning depends a great deal on how much support will be given to the learners, because the choice of instructional events designed into the lesson means those not included will have to be provided by the learners themselves.

An example of four levels of sequence planning is illustrated by a curriculum in English writing at the level of junior high school (see Table 9.1). The sequence problem arises at the course level, and there may be a problem to be solved for the single-course topic, such as "writing the paragraph." A third and critically important level of the sequence question concerns the sequence of skills within the individual lesson, such as "constructing sentences with dependent clauses." Finally, there is the matter of the sequence of events that occur or are planned to occur to bring about the acquisition of an individual lesson component objective, such as "making subject and verb agree in number." Different considerations apply to each level.

TABLE 9.1 FOUR DIFFERENT LEVELS OF THE PROBLEM OF INSTRUCTIONAL SEQUENCE

	Unit	Example	Sequence Question
Level 1	Course or Course Sequence	Essay composition Short story Creative writing	What would be the optimal sequence of courses to teach prerequisite concepts and engage learner's attention?
Level 2	Topic or Units	Constructing a theme Writing a paragraph Creating transitions Character development	How will the major units of the course be sequenced to achieve the course goals?
Level 3	Lessons	Composing a topic sentence	How will the subordinate skills in composing a topic sentence be presented?
Level 4	Lesson Objectives	Identifying topic sentences, supportive sentences, and transition sentences	In what sequence will the objectives of the individual lesson be sequenced?

Sequence of the Course and Curriculum

Course sequence decisions deal mainly with answering the question, "In what sequence should the units be presented?" One wants to ensure that the prerequisite information and intellectual skills necessary for any given topic have been previously learned. For example, the topic of adding fractions is introduced in arithmetic after the student has learned to multiply and divide whole numbers because the operations required for adding fractions requires the simpler operations. In a science course, one is concerned that a topic like "graphically representing relations between variables" be preceded by the skill of "measuring variables." One would expect a student to understand the concept of "culture" before teaching a social studies topic on "comparing family structures across cultures."

A model for sequencing instruction in a course is referred to as *macrolevel* sequencing by Reigeluth and Stein (1983) in their account of the elaboration theory of instruction. The content of ideas with which this theory deals includes concepts, procedures, and principles. The theory proposes that instructional content be structured so that the student is first presented with a special kind of overview called an *epitome*, which includes a few general, simple, and fundamental ideas. Instruction then proceeds by presenting more detailed ideas that *elaborate* on the earlier ones. Following this is a *review* of the overview and a delineation of the *relationships* between the most recent ideas and those presented earlier. This pattern of overview, elaboration, summary, and synthesis is continued until the desired level of coverage of all aspects of the subject has been reached.

Course and curriculum sequences are typically represented in *scope and sequence* charts, which name the topics to be studied in a total course or set of courses and lay them out in matrices. This approach was utilized by Tyler (1949), and it makes a good first step in defining different levels of skills across content topics. For example, an introductory course on computers might be as represented in Table 9.2.

This scope and sequence matrix is by no means complete and represents only four types of learning outcomes; yet it demonstrates how the designer can structure topics and skills. It is especially useful to specify the affective outcomes that may be desired. In the computer course, it is evident that most of the outcomes are directed toward achieving intellectual skills. However, in the social issues unit, attitude outcomes are most important if the learner is to respond to using computers in a positive manner.

The target objectives of a unit can be related to the course objective or goal in a course level instructional curriculum map (ICM). Figure 9–1 shows such an ICM for an introductory computer course. In this example, the sequence in which Units 1 and 4 are taught is not critically important because the intellectual skills objectives are fairly independent. However, the skills in Unit 1 are prerequisite to the skills in Unit 2, and those in Unit 2 are prerequisite to those in Unit 3. Also, basic terminology and use of the computer (Unit 1) are prerequisite to the rule-using skills in Unit 5.

Sequence of Skills within the Topic

Systematic techniques greatly facilitate specifying a teaching sequence within a topic. A topic can, and often does, have several components. For example, a topic on computer hardware is likely to include objectives such as: (1) identify the components of a microcomputer, (2) demonstrate how to turn the computer on and

---

TABLE 9.2 **SCOPE AND SEQUENCE MATRIX OF TOPICS AND TYPES OF LEARNING OBJECTIVES FOR A COURSE ON COMPUTER USAGE**

	Types of Learning Objectives			
Topical Content	Verbal Information State	Defined Concepts Classify	Rule Using Demonstrate	Attitudes Choose
Components of Computers	Definitions— hardware, software, storage, operating system, network	External storage RAM memory input/output CPU	Machine set-up— connecting various devices	Caring for the computer— maintenance
Basic Operations	Definitions and purpose of operations like: application, file copy, shortcut, folder, copy, move, delete	System components: C: drive, CD network drives, removable drives, desktop, folders, files, recycle bin	Finding programs, finding files, creating folder, copying files, moving files,	Be comfortable with finding files, and moving files from one place to another
Language	Definition, purposes for, names of common languages	Commands, statements, editor compiler, interpreter	Input, run, debug, edit and save a program	Choose to value the ability to control computing operations
Social Issues	Five social issues	Examples of computer theft, fraud, copyright infringement, equity, vandalism	Using a virus scanner; proper citation of intellectual information	Be an ethical user of the computer

run an application, and (3) choose to handle the equipment and software so it won't be damaged. Notice that all three of these objectives are stated in performance terms. It would not be helpful to have objectives like "understand the computer" or "appreciate computer equipment." These statements are too ambiguous and may mean different things to different people.

Analyzing Topic Objectives to Determine Learning Outcomes   The use of performance objectives is particularly important at the unit level because the designer's objective is to determine what lessons are needed. This can get complicated when each unit objective has many essential subordinate and supportive prerequisites. At this point, we suggest that the outline be kept rather broad and that only the major objectives of the unit be specified. These objectives may include any or all of the types of learning outcomes. The specific unit objectives can be represented in an ICM, just as the course and unit objectives were represented. The unit map for the first unit in the computer course is shown in Figure 9–2.

This map has more detail, and it shows the relationships among the objectives within the topical unit. The relationship between the course map and the unit map may be compared to the relationship between a world globe and a series of flat maps of each country. The flat maps are going to show less scope than the globe but more detail.

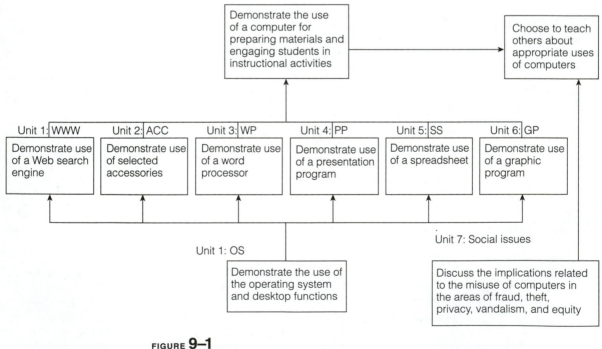

FIGURE **9–1**

INSTRUCTIONAL CURRICULUM MAP (ICM) FOR A COURSE ON COMPUTERS AND THEIR USES IN EDUCATION

The unit maps also show the relationships of the objectives from the different domains of learning outcomes. Some will be prerequisite to others, and therefore, they must be taught in the earlier lessons.

Identifying Lessons   A lesson is generally considered to occur in a given period of time; that is, the learner expects to spend a given amount of time on a lesson. Obviously, lesson times vary. A lesson for a small child may be shorter than one for an adult because the attention span of a child is shorter. Sometimes a designer will have a single lesson deal with a single learning outcome. The reason for this is that each type of learning outcome requires a different set of learning conditions, as described in Chapters 4 and 5. However, because the time it takes to teach a single

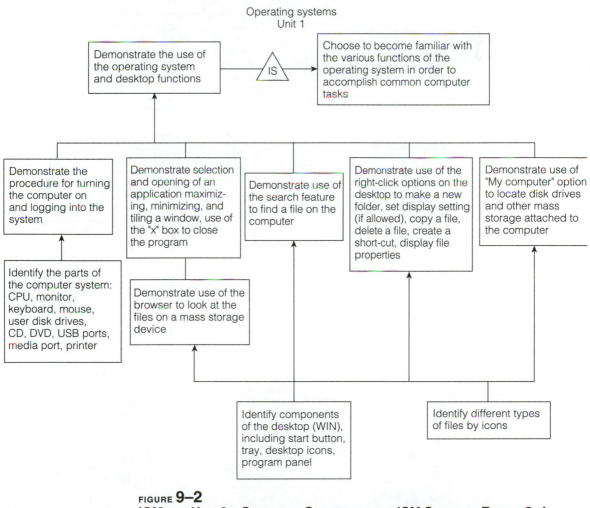

FIGURE **9–2**
ICM FOR UNIT 2—OPERATING SYSTEMS OF THE ICM SHOWN IN FIGURE 9–1

objective may be quite short, it is not feasible to think of every objective as having its own lesson. For this reason, specific objectives are often grouped into lessons.

It is probably more important to plan lessons around the order in which the performance objectives are best learned rather than worry about having different kinds of learning outcomes in the same lesson. In fact, once the decision is made to group different types of learning outcomes together, based on their functional relationships and the amount of time spent at a single sitting, the process of integrating the necessary conditions of learning becomes quite straightforward.

The unit map shown in Figure 9–3 shows how specific objectives within the previous map may be grouped into lessons. In this case, the unit has two lessons,

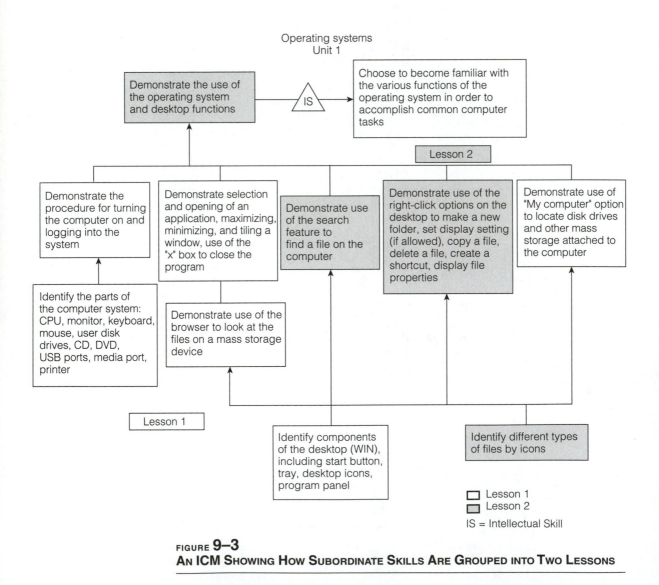

FIGURE **9–3**

AN ICM SHOWING HOW SUBORDINATE SKILLS ARE GROUPED INTO TWO LESSONS

each about one hour in length. If the instruction period were two hours long, the whole unit could possibly be taught in a single lesson.

The sequencing of lessons within units should be based on the prerequisite relationships among the objectives. Although these are very loose guidelines, they have the following requirements: (1) new learning is supported by previous learning; (2) a learning analysis should be performed to determine that the skills are being taught in sequential order; (3) sequences must be complete; and (4) irrelevant objectives are eliminated or taught at a different time.

Table 9.3 summarizes the major considerations regarding the sequential arrangement within a topic for each type of learned capability. The middle column of the table indicates sequencing principles applicable to the particular type of capability that represents the central focus of the learning. The right-hand column lists sequence considerations relevant to this learning but arising in other domains.

Sequence of Skills within Lessons

The next level for mapping is the lesson map as shown in Figure 9–4. A lesson map is to a unit map what a state road map is to a map of the United States. It contains less scope than the unit map and greater levels of detail. Although Chapter 12 is concerned with designing individual lessons, we introduce the lesson map here to show how it relates to the course and unit map.

The target objectives in the lesson map shown in Figure 9–4 have one or more objectives from the unit map. In addition, it has subordinate objectives related to the attainment of these target objectives. The subordinate objectives were obtained by asking the question, "What must the learner know to learn these new skills?" It is

TABLE 9.3   **DESIRABLE SEQUENCE CHARACTERISTICS ASSOCIATED WITH FIVE TYPES OF LEARNING OUTCOMES**

Type of Learning Outcome	Major Principles of Sequencing	Related Sequence Factors
Intellectual Skills	Presentation of the learning activity for each new skill should be preceded by prior mastery of subordinate skills	Verbal information may be recalled or newly presented to provide elaboration of each skill and conditions of its use
Cognitive Strategies	Learning and problem-solving situations should involve recall of previously acquired relevant intellectual skills	Verbal information relevant to the new learning should be previously learned or presented in instructions
Verbal Information	For major subtopics, order of presentation should be from simple to complex. New facts should be preceded by meaningful context	Prior learning of necessary intellectual skills involved in reading, listening, etc., is usually assumed
Attitudes	Establishment of respect for source is important. Choice situations should be preceded by mastery of any intellectual skills involved	Verbal information relevant to choices should be previously learned or presented in instructions
Motor Skills	Provide intensive practice on part skills of critical importance and practice on total skill	First of all learn the executive subroutine (procedure)

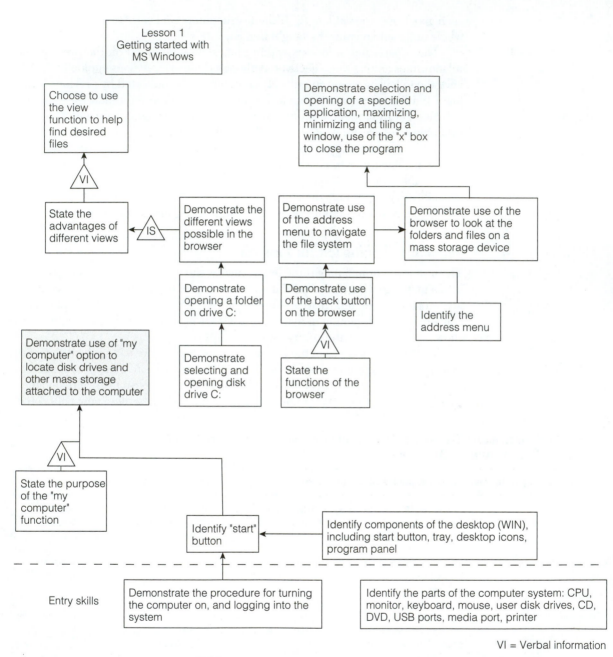

VI = Verbal information

FIGURE **9–4**
A LESSON-LEVEL ICM FOR THE FIRST LESSON SHOWN IN FIGURE 9–3

also necessary to ask, "What do the learners already know to help them learn of these new skills?" A learner's present general knowledge reflects his or her entry skills for the lesson. The designer must begin with information about the audience and make some assumptions about the skills they bring to a particular learning task. Usually, this means that the designer will have to make a detailed analysis of the intellectual skills involved in the lesson. This is the organizing factor, and the device for revealing the requirements for sequencing will now be described in greater detail.

During the process of constructing a lesson map, it may become obvious that the skills that need to be taught cannot be accomplished in a single instructional period. In this case, the map may be divided into two lesson maps, each representing a single period of instruction.

In some cases, the unit may center on a specific domain of learning such as motor skills, information, intellectual skills, attitudes, or cognitive strategies.

LEARNING HIERARCHIES AND INSTRUCTIONAL SEQUENCE

The nature of intellectual skills makes it possible to design precise conditions for their learning. When a proper sequence of prerequisite skills is established, learning intellectual skills becomes easy for a teacher or trainer to manage. In addition, the process of learning is highly reinforced for the learners because they suddenly realize they know how to do something they didn't know how to do before. The activity of learning takes on an excitement that is the opposite from "drill" and "rote recitation."

As described in Chapter 5, the learning hierarchy that results from a learning-task analysis is the arrangement of intellectual skill objectives into a pattern that shows the prerequisite relationships among them. An additional example of a learning hierarchy, this time for a skill in solving a type of physics problem, is shown in Figure 9–5.

Here, the lesson objective is one of finding the horizontal and vertical components of forces as vectors of a system in equilibrium. To learn to perform the task correctly, students must have some prerequisite skills; these are indicated on the second level of the hierarchy. Specifically, they must be able to: (1) identify the forces in the situation that are acting in opposition to each other when the body being acted upon is in equilibrium, (2) represent the opposing forces as sides of triangles that include vertical and horizontal sides, and (3) identify trigonometric relationships of the sides and angles of right triangles (sine, cosine, and so forth). Each of these subordinate skills also have prerequisites, which are shown below them in the hierarchy.

What is meant by a prerequisite? A prerequisite is a simpler intellectual skill, but such a characterization does not adequately identify it because one could name a number of intellectual skills that are simpler than the lesson objective described in the figure. A prerequisite skill is integrally related to the skill to which it is subordinate, in the sense that the latter skill cannot be achieved if the learner does not

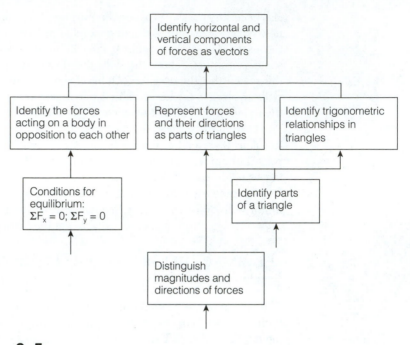

FIGURE **9–5**

A LEARNING HIERARCHY FOR THE TARGET SKILL OF IDENTIFYING HORIZONTAL AND VERTICAL COMPONENTS OF FORCES AS VECTORS

(From R. M. Gagné, *The conditions of learning*, 4th ed., copyright 1985, Holt, Rinehart and Winston, Fort Worth, TX. Reprinted by permission.)

have the prerequisite skill. Consider what students are doing when they demonstrate "horizontal and vertical components of forces as vectors." They must show the values and directions of the horizontal and vertical vector forces. The directions must "resolve" the forces that oppose each other to produce a state of equilibrium (prerequisite 1). And the values of these vectors must be obtained by using trigonometric relationships of right triangles (prerequisites 2 and 3). If the students do not have these prerequisites, they will not be able to perform the target (lesson) objective. Conversely, if students already know how to do each of the subordinate tasks, learning to do the lesson objectives will be easy and straightforward. The likelihood is that these students will learn to do it rapidly, perhaps even with the kind of immediacy implied by the word "discovery."

To identify a skill's prerequisites, one must ask, "What skill must the learner have to learn this (new) skill, the absence of which would make that learning impossible (Gagné, 1985). In other words, prerequisite intellectual skills are those that are critical to the rapid, smooth learning of the new skill. A way of checking whether one's first attempt to answer the preceding question has been successful is to examine the demands the new skill makes on the learner and identify where he or she could go wrong. Applying this to the lesson objective of Figure 9–5, one can see that students who are attempting to "identity horizontal and vertical components of forces as vectors" might fail if they aren't able to (1) identify the forces acting in opposition (at equilibrium), and (2) represent the forces as parts of triangles, or (3) identify trigonometric relationships in right triangles. Thus, the specification of prerequisite skills should provide a complete description of the previously learned skills necessary for readily acquiring the new skill.

The fact that prerequisite skills may be checked by considering ways in which the learner can fail serves to emphasize the direct relevance of learning hierarchies to the teacher's task of diagnosis. If one finds a learner who is having trouble acquiring a new intellectual skill, the first diagnostic question should probably be, "What prerequisite skills has this person failed to learn?" Responsible diagnosis attempts to discover what the learner needs to learn. The chances are high that this will be a prerequisite intellectual skill, as indicated by a learning hierarchy. If it is, suitable instruction can be designed to get the learner "back on track" in a learning sequence that continues to be positively reinforcing.

OTHER TYPES OF INSTRUCTIONAL SEQUENCING

Knowledge-Based Sequencing

Early work on adaptive navigation support in educational hypermedia applied the ideas of sequencing in Web-based instructional resources (Brusilovsky, 2000). Within today's digital (online) adaptive hypermedia applications, instructional design is accomplished, in part, by carefully planning the learner's sequence through the material (Thomson, 2000). This method of instructional sequencing is based upon the notion that certain patterns can be used to guide the design of instructional hypermedia applications (Thomson, 2000; Merrill, 1998). Research in this area spans several fields including software engineering, instructional design, hypermedia design, and human modeling.

While most hypermedia development processes provide no mechanism for including the sequencing of conceptual information in the application design, one model, called Applying Patterns to Hypermedia Instructional Design (APHID), documents the structure associated with the concepts in the domain of instruction as a concept map (Thomson, 2000). Instructional design is represented as organizational patterns on the concept map and then used during the development phase to automatically generate instructional hypermedia applications that are tailored to specific instructional goals (Thomson, 2000).

In the last few years, automatic sequencing of course material has become an important research issue, particularly with the standardization of metadata for educational resources and the introduction of the Internet for online learning. Sequencing can help to generate hypermedia documents that, at their best, match the learner's needs (Fischer, 2001). The concept of learner-centric, student-controlled interfaces capable of (1) launching individualized training content based on a student's learning requirements or what they are currently working on, (2) adapting to a student's individual learning style and preferences, and (3) mapping to a student's preexisting knowledge.

Sequencing Content for Online Learning   For online learning, the goal of curriculum sequencing is to provide the student with the most suitable individually planned sequence of knowledge units to learn, as well as a sequence of learning tasks (examples, questions, problems, etc.) to work with (Fischer, 2001). In other words, curriculum sequencing helps the student to find an "optimal path" through the learning material. Modern sequencing programs are expert systems that can do more than just select the "next best" task—they can classify all available tasks into "nonrelevant" and "relevant." For example, a task might be considered "nonrelevant" if it was already completed or if it is not ready to be learned because of the lack of prerequisite knowledge and experience. After excluding "nonrelevant" tasks, the sequencing engine searches for and finds the "best" of the relevant tasks. In hypermedia, where each learning task is represented by a separate page, an ability to distinguish "ready," "not-ready," or "best" tasks is a direct precondition for adaptive navigation support (Fischer, 2001). Adaptive navigation support is an interface that can integrate the power of machine and human intelligence—the user is free to make a choice while still seeing an opinion of an "intelligent" system. From this point of view, one can speculate that adaptive navigation support is a *natural* way to add some intelligence to adaptive hypermedia systems (Fischer, 2001).

The evolution of the Internet has impacted not only the number of adaptive educational hypermedia systems, but also on the *type* of systems being developed. All the early systems were essentially used in learning laboratories to explore new learning methods where adaptive learning was studied in an educational context. In contrast, a number of more recent systems provide complete frameworks, and even authoring tools, for developing online courses. The appearance of a number of adaptive learning authoring tools is not only indicative of the maturity of adaptive educational hypermedia, but also a response to a Web-provoked demand for user-adaptive distance education courses (Fischer, 2001).

Techniques for Knowledge-Based Instructional Sequencing   As described above, the use of a hypermedia allows flexibility in how instructional materials are sequenced. A designer can include supplemental learning support for students who need support without forcing *everyone* to use it. Or, a designer can provide learners with a choice of alternative learning pathways to follow as they progress in understanding from level to level (Distance Learning Resource Network, 2003). The one thing that hypertext does *not* do is relieve the designer of the obligation to provide some kind of structure. This is especially true when no particular sequence is implicit in the material itself. The structure suggested by the design should help students grasp relationships within the new material, as well as between the new material and things they already know.

One observable characteristic of hypermedia users is the *path* they take through an application. One sequencing technique for hypermedia instructional design, called record *browsing behavior*, captures a record of user browsing behavior through the hypermedia application and then allows for comparison of different users and classification of those users into groups (Thomson, 2000). Different users of the same hypermedia application should have similar paths through the hypermedia, if their purposes and skill levels are relatively equal and a user who is classified into one particular group is likely to benefit from pages viewed by other users who also belong to that group.

A second sequencing method for hypermedia instructional design, called *record material viewed*, considers not the *path* through the hypermedia, but the material *viewed* by the user (Yan, Jacobsen, Garcia-Molina, & Dayal, 1996). Each page the user accesses, along with the amount of time they spend on the page, is represented as part of a vector. The vectors for different users are then clustered, and the clusters are used as classifications for the users (Thomson, 2000).

Spiral Sequencing

Spiral sequencing is another way to conceptualize a curriculum. To visualize spiral sequencing think of a spring that circles upward from the base to the top. Around the circumference are different topics or kinds of skills that will be revisited at successively higher levels as the course progresses, see Figure 9–6. Spiral sequencing is particularly evident in foreign language courses, and many vocational skill courses where competency is built as the student refines their skills throughout the course.

Language Learning Models   A language course typically has a number of different kinds of skills represented as topics like vocabulary (verbal information), grammar (rule using), pronunciation (rule using and motor skills, and conversation (rule using and problem solving). The curriculum is a series of spirals that cut through each of the topics; each loop in the spiral contains objectives at an increasingly higher and complex level. The visual model that best represents this type of instructional sequencing progress is an expanding spiral, as shown in Figure 9–6. The expansion represents an inclusion of previous learning at every level. For

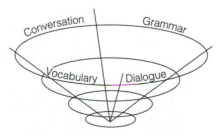

FIGURE **9–6**
SPIRAL SEQUENCING MODEL

instance, if at a low level the student learns a greeting, in Spanish, like "Buenos días, ¿Cómo está?" and a response like "Muy bien, gracias," this greeting is included in dialogue and practiced many times throughout the course. These techniques reinforce the notion that language learning is integrative, not merely cumulative. With spiral sequencing, each new element that is added must be integrated into the whole of what has gone before. (Saskatchewan Education, 1997).

Using this kind of progression is also a way of accommodating differences among students. For example, the first time a grammar structure is explicitly taught, some students may not be cognitively ready to learn it. As the structure comes up again and again, students who got it the first time will have their learning consolidated while others will have more opportunities to acquire it.

Structuring courses and sequencing material following this concept provides the opportunity for practice and repetition with gradually increased complexity. Such processes are very much congruent with research and theories which highlight the limitations of the novice learner (Berliner, 1988), the gradual increase in complexity of schemas as they are constructed (Sweller, 1993), and refinement of skill learning through practice and feedback (Fitts, 1964, 1968). In addition to languages, many vocational courses for skilled occupations also are best designed using a spiral model building from simple applications of a particular skill to more complex applications of the same skill.

Elaboration Theory A major theme in the theoretical framework of Bruner (1966) was that learning is an active process in which learners construct new ideas or concepts based upon their current/past knowledge. Bruner believed that curricula should be organized in a *spiral* manner so that students continually build upon what they have already learned, and structured so that they can most readily grasp the material. In the 1980s, a body of literature had accumulated in support of individual components of Bruner's spiral curriculum model, with the most popular being Reigeluth and Stein's (1983) *Elaboration Theory*, where spiral sequencing is described as learning gradually in several passes. Unlike topical sequencing, where a topic (or task) is taught to whatever depth of understanding (or competence) is required before moving to the next task, with spiral sequencing the learner masters a topic (or task) gradually in several passes. *Elaboration Theory* proposes that when structuring a course, it should be organized in a simple-to-complex, general-to-detailed, abstract-to-concrete manner, which is consistent with the rules for instructional mapping and intellectual skills sequencing suggested in this chapter.

Another principle involved following a learning prerequisite sequence, as applied to individual lessons within a course. In order for a student to develop from simple to more complex lessons, certain prerequisite knowledge and skills must first be mastered. This prerequisite sequencing provides linkages between each lesson as students spiral upwards in a course of a study. As new knowledge and skills are introduced in subsequent lessons, they reinforce what is already learned and become related to previously learned information. What the student gradually achieves is a rich breadth and depth of information that is not normally developed in curricula where each topic is discrete or unconnected (Dowding, 1993).

INTEGRATING MULTIPLE OBJECTIVES

As previously discussed in Chapter 8, it is not uncommon for a lesson to have several different kinds of objectives. Frequently, multiple objectives may be chosen for a course topic or for a comprehensive module within a course. For example, a lesson or topic may have as a primary objective the procedural rule for setting the chiming mechanism of a grandfather clock. Sequencing techniques for such instruction may find learning hierarchies useful for the identification of prerequisites. However, in teaching about the adjustment of chiming mechanisms, additional objectives may be desirable, such as verbal information about the varieties and characteristics of chiming mechanisms. Attitudes of carefulness, precision, and avoidance of hazards in working with clock movements may also be required. A curriculum map can be employed to show the interrelationships among the different kinds of objectives involved.

Planning for integrative goals may be done, in part, by identifying suitable sequences of objectives, utilizing such techniques as the learning hierarchy and the curriculum map. As described in Chapter 8, an additional aspect of such planning is the establishment of a schema representing the learning goal. This schema includes a scenario relating prior knowledge to the goal toward which learning is aimed. It serves the metacognitive functions of relating prior knowledge to the new learning, monitoring incoming communications for relevance, and enhancing the thoughtful abstractions that support the transfer of learning.

SUMMARY

This chapter opened with an account on how the organization of a total course relates to questions about the sequencing of instruction. Sequencing decisions are identified at the four levels of course, topic, lesson, and lesson component. We suggested ways for deciding upon instructional sequences at the levels of the course and the topic. Course planning for a sequence of topics is typically done by a kind of common-sense logic. One topic may precede another because it describes earlier events, because it is a component part, or because it provides a meaningful context for what is to follow.

In proceeding from course purposes to performance objectives, it may not always be necessary to describe all the intermediate levels of planning in terms of complete lists of performance objectives for the topic. The method suggested here involves choosing representative samples of objectives within each domain of learning outcomes.

The designing of sequences for intellectual skills is based upon learning-hierarchies. These hierarchies are derived by working top-down from target objectives; and in doing so, we can analyze the sequences of skills to be learned (see Chapter 8). The learning of a new skill is most readily accomplished when the learner is able to recall the subordinate skills that compose it. When an instructional sequence has been designed for an intellectual skill, related learning of other capabilities may be interjected at appropriate points, as when the learning of information is required or the modification of an attitude is desired. In other instances, instruction aimed at other capabilities may come before or after the intellectual skill represented in the learning hierarchy. Designing sequences for other types of learned capabilities also requires an analysis of prerequisite skills and the identification of supportive and enabling objectives.

The next three chapters describe how the plans for instructional sequence are carried into the design of a single lesson or lesson component. It is in the latter context that the events of instruction are introduced. These events pertain to the external supports for learning provided by the teacher, the course materials, or the learner. They depend upon previous learning that has been accomplished in accordance with a planned sequence.

REFERENCES

Anderson, J. R. (1985). *Cognitive psychology and its implications* (2nd ed.). New York: Freeman.

Berliner, D. C. (1988, February). *The development of expertise in pedagogy.* The Charles W. Hunt Memorial Lecture for the American Association of Colleges for Teacher Education, New Orleans, LA.

Bruner, J. S. (1966). *Toward a theory of instruction.* New York: W.W. Norton.

Brusilovsky, P. (2000). Adaptive Hypermedia: From Intelligent Tutoring Systems to Web-Based Education. Abstract retrieved on 2/02/04 from: http://www2.sis.pitt.edu/~peterb/papers/ITS00inv.html.

Distance Learning Resource Network. (2003). Retrieved on 2/2/04 from: http://www.dlrn.org/educ/course/unit2/session7/sequencing.html; Using a "Natural Order."

Dowding, T. J. (1993). The application of a spiral curriculum model to technical training curricula. *Educational Technology, 33*(7), 18–28.

Fischer, S. (2001). Retrieved on 2/02/04 from: http://www.cstc.org/cgi-bin/show_abstract.pl?number=159.

Fitts, P. M. (1964) Perceptual skill learning. In A.W. Melton (Ed.), *Categories of skill learning.* New York: Academic Press.

Fitts, P. M. (1968) Factors in complex skill training. In R. G. Kuhlen (Ed.), *Studies in educational psychology.* Waltham, MA: Blaisdell.

Gagné, R. M. (1985). *The conditions of learning* (4th ed.). New York: Holt, Rinehart and Winston.

Merrill, M. D. (1998, March/Apr). Knowledge analysis for effective instruction. *CBT Solutions,* 1–11.

Reigeluth, C. M., & Stein, F. S. (1983). The elaboration theory of instruction. In C. M. Reigeluth (Ed.), *Instructional-design theories and models.* Hillsdale, NJ: Erlbaum.

Saskatchewan Education (1997). *The Evergreen Curriculum.* Regina, SK: Saskatchewan Education.

Sweller, J. (1993). Some cognitive processes and their consequences for the organization and presentation of information. *Australian Journal of Psychology, 45,* 1–8.

Thomson, J. (2000). Generating Instructional Media with APHID. Proceedings from the 11th Conference on Hypertext and Hypermedia, San Antonio, TX.

Tyler, R. W. (1949). *Basic principles of curriculum and instruction.* Chicago: University of Chicago Press.

Yan, T. W., Jacobsen, M., Garcia-Molina, H., & Dayal, U. (1996, October 5). From User Access Patterns to Dynamic Hypertext Linking. Fifth International World Wide Web Conference, Paris, France.

THE EVENTS OF INSTRUCTION

THE NATURE OF INSTRUCTION

The issue to be addressed in this chapter is how one designs instruction that makes use of the principles that have been described for the different kinds of learning.

We all know from experience that different types of learning outcomes benefit from different types of instruction. In addition, there are certain methods or strategies of instruction that have been proven to facilitate learning. Perhaps you have heard the heuristic guidelines for giving a good speech: Tell the audience what you are going to tell them, tell them, and finally, tell them what you told them. This heuristic has become a model for designing and organizing the components of a speech. In this chapter we will present a model for designing instruction that has components and a suggested sequence, and is designed to facilitate information processing, and thus learning.

Instruction and Learning

The kinds of information processing to which we are referring are those involved in modern cognitive learning theories (Anderson, 1985; Estes, 1975; Klatzky, 1980). The sequence of processing, illustrated in Figure 10–1, envisaged by cognitive theories of learning is approximately as follows (Gagné, 1977, 1985):

1. The stimulation that affects the learner's receptors produces patterns of neural activity that are briefly "registered" by *sensory registers*.
2. This information is then changed into a form that is recorded in the *short-term memory*, where prominent features of the original stimulation are stored. The short-term memory has a limited capacity in terms of the number of items that can be held in mind. The items that are so held, however, may be internally rehearsed and, thus, maintained.
3. In a following stage, an important transformation called *semantic encoding*, takes place when the information enters the *long-term memory* for storage. As its name implies, in this kind of transformation, information is stored according to its meaning. (Note that in the context of learning theory,

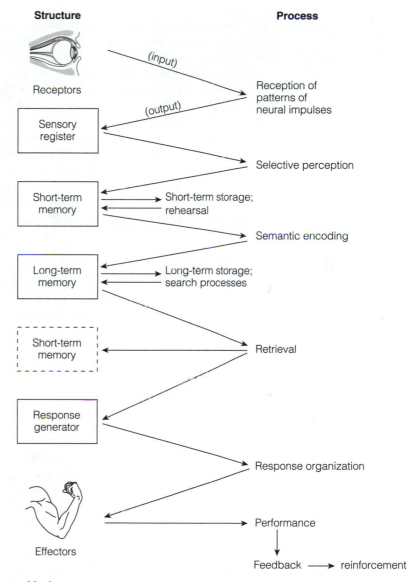

Structure   Process

(input)

Receptors   Reception of
                                       patterns of
(output)   neural impulses

Sensory
register
                                       Selective perception

Short-term   Short-term storage;
memory   rehearsal
                                       Semantic encoding

Long-term   Long-term storage;
memory   search processes

Short-term   Retrieval
memory

Response
generator
                                       Response organization

                                       Performance

Effectors
                                       Feedback ⟶ reinforcement

FIGURE **10–1**

**THE POSTULATED STRUCTURES OF COGNITIVE LEARNING THEORIES, AND THE
PROCESS ASSOCIATED WITH THEM**

information has a general definition that includes the five kinds of learned
capabilities distinguished in this book.)

4. When learner performance is called for, the stored information or skill must
   be searched for and *retrieved*.

5. It may then be transformed directly into action by way of a *response-generator*.

6. Frequently, the retrieved information is recalled to the *working memory* (another name for the short-term memory), where it may be combined with other incoming information to enable encoding of new learned capabilities.

7. Learner performance itself sets in motion a process that depends upon external *feedback* involving the familiar process of *reinforcement*.

8. In addition to the learning sequence itself, cognitive theories of learning and memory propose the existence of *metacognitive control* processes. These are processes that select and set in motion cognitive strategies relevant to learning and remembering. Control processes of this sort modify the other information flow processes of the learner. A control process may select a strategy of continued rehearsal of the contents of short-term memory for example, or a cognitive strategy of imaging sentences to be learned. They may exercise control over attention, over the encoding of incoming information, and over the retrieval of what has been stored.

Instructional Events

The processes involved in an act of learning are, to a large extent, activated internally. That is to say, the output of any one structure (or the result of any one kind of processing) becomes an input for the next, as Figure 10–1 indicates. However, these processes may also be influenced by *external* events, and this is what makes instruction possible. Selective perception, for example, may obviously be affected by particular arrangements of external stimuli. For example, highlighting, underlining, bold printing, and other visual enhancements may call attention to the features of a picture or text.

This leads to our definition of instruction as *a set of events external to the learner designed to support the internal processes of learning*. The events of instruction are designed to activate the processes of information processing, or at least to parallel their occurrence, and support the process.

The functions served by the various events of instruction in an act of learning are listed in Table 10.1, in the approximate order in which they are typically employed (Gagné, 1968, 1985). The initial event of *gaining attention* is one that supports the learning event of reception of the stimuli and the patterns of neural impulses they produce. Before proceeding further, another instructional event is designed to prepare the learner for the remaining sequence. This is Event 2, *informing the learner of the objective*, which is presumed to set in motion a process of executive control by means of which the learner selects particular strategies appropriate to the learning task and its expected outcome. Event 3 is also preparatory to learning and refers to the *retrieval of items of prior learning* that may need to be incorporated in the capability being newly learned. Events 4 through 9 of Table 10.1 are each related to the learning processes shown in Figure 10–1.

If all the events of instruction were each presented in the order that they are shown, it would represent one form of instructional strategy. However, these events of instruction do not have to be presented in this order, nor do all the events need to be included for every lesson. The students might be called upon to provide the activities of an event for themselves, giving them more of the responsibility for

TABLE 10.1   EVENTS OF INSTRUCTION AND THEIR RELATION TO PROCESSES OF LEARNING

Instructional Event	Relation to Learning Process
Gaining attention	*Reception* of patterns of neural impulses
Informing the learner of the objective	Activating a process of *executive control*
Stimulating recall of prerequisite learned capabilities	*Retrieval* of prior learning to working memory
Presenting the stimulus material	Emphasizing features for *selective perception*
Providing learning guidance	Semantic *encoding;* cues for retrieval
Eliciting performance	Activating response *organization*
Providing feedback about performance correctness	Establishing *reinforcement*
Assessing the performance	Activating *retrieval;* making reinforcement possible
Enhancing retention and transfer	Providing cues and strategies for *retrieval*

their own learning. Their role with regard to the events in instruction is to stimulate internal information processes, not to replace them. In designing instruction, the list of instructional events might be thought of as guidelines. In using these guidelines the designer asks, "Do these learners need support at this stage for learning this task?" With regard to order of presentation, the events might be considered as part of a cycle of information processing. The process is continuous and some stages probably happen very rapidly. It is likely that attention is maintained for a series of learning tasks, and so that event, once established, needs stimulation only occasionally.

We have found it helpful to think in terms of instructional activities and learning activities. *Instructional activities* are what the instructor (or instructional materials) will do, and *learning activities* are what the learners will do. Each of the events of instruction might represent one or more instructional or learning activities.

Gaining Attention   Various kinds of activities are employed to gain the learner's attention. Basic ways of commanding attention involve the use of novelty, as is often done with animation, a demonstration, or some unexpected event. Beyond this, a fundamental and frequently used method of gaining attention is to appeal to the learner's curiosity, for example, by means of a verbal question such as, "How do you think scientists can determine how old the Earth is?" In connection with a lesson on percentages, one student's interest may be captured by such a question as, "How do you figure a baseball player's batting average?" Naturally, one cannot provide a standard content for such questions—quite the contrary—because every student's interests are different. Although skill at gaining the attention of students, involving insightful knowledge of the particular students involved, is a part of the teacher's art, the ARCS model (described in Chapter 6) provides an expanded and systematic approach to stimulating and sustaining learner motivation.

A good preplanned lesson provides the teacher or trainer with one or more options for gaining attention. When instruction is individualized, the teacher is able to vary the content and form of the communication whenever necessary to appeal to individual student interests.

Informing the Learner of the Objective   Presenting students with learning objectives communicates an expectation of the knowledge and/or skills they are expected to perform. However, there are many objectives that may not be initially obvious to students in school. For example, if the subject under study is the Preamble to the United States Constitution, being able to recite it verbatim is not at all the same objective as being able to discuss its major ideas. If decimals are being studied, is it obvious to the student during any given lesson whether he or she is expected to learn to (1) read decimals, (2) write decimals, or perhaps, (3) add decimals? The idea is that telling learners what is expected will help them focus on learning that skill.

Lacking guidance, the learners will establish their own expectations, which is not necessarily a bad thing. However, the objective constructed by the student may not be consistent with what the teacher had in mind and could lead to a miscommunication. Providing the objective takes little time and may at least serve the purpose of preventing the student from getting entirely off track. Communicating the objective also appears to be an act consistent with the frankness and honesty of a good teacher. In addition, the act of verbalizing the objective may help the teacher to stay on target.

Stimulating Recall of Prerequisite Learned Capabilities   Much of new learning (some might say all) is building on what we already know. Learning a rule about mass (Newton's second law of motion) involves building on the ideas of acceleration and force as well as the idea of multiplying. In terms of modern mathematics, learning the numeric concept of *eight* involves the numeric concept of *seven*, the set *one*, and joining. Component ideas (concepts, rules) must be previously learned if the new learning is to be successful. At the moment of learning, these previously acquired capabilities must be highly accessible to be part of the learning event. The recall of previously learned capabilities may be stimulated by asking a recognition question or, better, a recall question. For example, when children are being taught about rainfall in relation to mountains, they might be asked, "Someone tell me what we know about warm air and water vapor," and, "What do we know about the temperature at the top of mountains?"

Presenting the Stimulus Material   The nature of this particular event is relatively obvious. The stimuli to be displayed (or communicated) to the learner are those involved in the performance that reflects the learning. If the learner must learn a sequence of facts, such as events from history, then there are facts that must be communicated, whether in oral or printed form. If the learner is engaged in the task of pronouncing printed words aloud, as in elementary reading, then the printed words must be displayed. If the student must learn to respond to oral questions in French, then these oral questions must be presented, because they are the stimuli of the task to be learned.

Although seemingly obvious, it is nevertheless of some importance that the proper stimuli be presented as a part of the instructional events. For example, if the learner is acquiring the capability of answering questions delivered orally in French, then the proper stimuli are not English questions or printed French questions. (This is not to deny, however, that such tasks may represent subordinate skills that have previously been used as learning tasks.) If the learner is to acquire the capability of using positive and negative numbers to solve verbally stated problems, then the proper stimuli are verbally stated problems and not something else. If one neglects to use the proper stimuli for learning, the end result may be that the student learns a different skill. An anecdote might illustrate this point. After much basic instruction at a military base a soldier looked perplexed when asked to solve the problem: $17 + 45 = $ ____. The instructor noticed and approached him to determine the problem. The soldier said he had never seen anything like that before. Indeed all of the instruction had him answering questions formatted vertically $\left[\begin{array}{r} 17 \\ + 45 \end{array} \right]$ and he did not recognize the horizontal presentation nor did he know how to change it to the vertical format.

Stimulus presentation often emphasizes features that determine selective perception. Thus, information presented in a text may contain italics, bold print, underlining, or other kinds of physical arrangements designed to facilitate perception of essential features. When pictures or diagrams are employed, important features of the concepts they display may be heavily outlined, circled, or pointed to with arrows. In establishing discriminations, distinctive features may he emphasized by enlarging the differences between the objects to be distinguished. For example, in programs of reading readiness, large differences in shapes (such as those of a circle and triangle) may be introduced first, followed by figures exhibiting smaller differences. Distorted features of *a, b,* and *d* may be initially presented in order that the smaller differences of these letters will eventually be discriminated.

Stimulus presentation for the learning of concepts and rules typically follows one of two patterns: the rule followed by an example, or an example followed by the rule. When the objective is the learning of a concept, such as circle, it is desirable to present not only large and small circles on the chalkboard or in a book, but also green circles, red ones, and ones made of rope or string. One might even have the children stand and join hands to form a circle. For young children, the importance of this event can hardly be overemphasized.

Comparable degrees of usefulness can be seen in the use of variety of examples as an event for rule learning. To apply the formula for area of a rectangle, $A = x \times y$, the student must not only be able to recall the statement that represents the rule, but must know that A means area, understand what area means, know that x and y are the dimensions of two nonparallel sides of the rectangle, and know that the $\times$ between x and y means to multiply. But even when all these subordinated concepts and rules are known, the learner must do a variety of examples to understand and use the rule. Retention and transfer are also likely to be enhanced by presenting problems stated in words, in diagrams, and in combinations of the two over a period of time.

Once such rules are learned, groups of them need to be selectively recalled, combined, and used to solve problems. Employing a variety of examples in problem solving might entail teaching the learner to break down odd-shaped figures into known shapes, like circles, triangles, and rectangles, and then to apply rules for finding the area of these figures as a way to arrive at the total area of the entire shape.

In the learning of both concepts and rules, one may proceed either inductively or deductively. In learning concrete concepts, like *circle* or *rectangle,* it is best to introduce a variety of examples before introducing the definition of the concept. (Imagine teaching a four-year-old child the formal definition of a circle before exposure to a variety of circles!) But for older learners who are learning defined concepts, a simple definition might best come first, such as "A root is the part of a plant below the ground." Assuming the learner understands the component concepts that are contained in the statement, this should be a good start, perhaps followed at once by a picture.

Providing Learning Guidance

The essence of learning guidance is to provide support for learners in making connections between what they know and what is being learned. In the previous event, learners encounter the content they are to learn; in this event they establish a context for it. Another word for learning guidance might be *scaffolding*. Scaffolding is cognitive support for the construction a learner might make. For example, suppose one wishes a learner to acquire the *defined concept* of prime numbers. A prime number is a defined concept because a number can't be categorized as a prime number simply by looking at it. It can only be classified by applying a rule for classification.

The instruction might begin by displaying a list of successive numbers, say, 1 through 25. The teacher might then ask the learner to recall that the numbers may be expressed as products of various factors: $8 = 2 \times 4$ or $2 \times 2 \times 2 = 8 \circ 1$, and so on. The learner could then be asked to write out all the factors for the set of whole numbers through 30. What is wanted now, as a learning outcome, is for the learner to "understand" that there is a certain class of numbers whose only factor (or divisor), other than the number itself, is 1. In the end, we want the learner to determine if a given number is a prime number, or whether it is the factor for another number, but first, we want them to be able to *classify* prime numbers.

The learner may be able to "see" this immediately. If not, he or she may be led to the discovery by a series of communications in the form of hints or questions. For example: "Do you see any regularities in this set of numbers?" "Do the original numbers differ with respect to the number of different factors they contain?" "In what way are the numbers 3, 5, and 7 different from 4, 8, and 10?" "In what way is the number 7 like the number 23?" "Can you pick out *all* the numbers that are like 7 and 23?"

These communications and others like them may be said to have the function of *learning guidance.* Notice that they do not tell the learner the answer; rather, they suggest the line of thought that will presumably lead to the desired "combining" of subordinate concepts and formation of a new concept, "numbers divisible only by themselves and 1." It should be apparent that the specific form and content of such questions and hints cannot be spelled out in precise terms. Exactly what the teacher or textbook says is not the important point. It is rather that such communications are performing a particular "scaffolding" function. They are stimulating a direction of thought and are thus helping to keep the learner on track. In performing this function, they contribute to the efficiency of learning.

The amount of learning guidance, that is, the number of questions and the degree to which they provide "direct or indirect prompts," will obviously vary with the kind of capability being learned (Wittrock, 1966). If what is to be learned is an arbitrary matter, such as the name for an object new to the learner (say, a pomegranate), there is obviously no sense in wasting time with indirect hinting or questioning in the hope that somehow such a name will be "discovered." In this case, showing the learner a variety of pomegranates—large ones, small ones, green ones, ripe ones, whole ones, and cut ones—or elaborating on the concept is likely to be better guidance in recognizing a pomegranate at a later time.

At the other end of the spectrum, however, are cases where less direct prompting is appropriate, because this is a logical way to discover the answer, and such discovery may lead to learning that is more permanent than that which results from being told the answer. Guidance for learning is an event that may readily be adapted to learner differences, as described in Chapter 6. Instruction that is highly didactic and that makes use of low-level questions like, "What were some of items the Inca's used in trade with other tribes?" is likely to find greatest appeal and effectiveness among learners of high anxiety, whereas low-anxiety learners may be positively affected by the challenge of difficult, or higher-level questions like, "How might the distribution of obsidian inform us about the trade routes of the Incas?" As previously noted, guidance taking the form of frequent pictures and oral communications may aid learners of low ability in reading comprehension, whereas these measures may be quite inefficient with skillful readers.

The amount of hinting or prompting involved in the learning guidance event will also vary with the kind of learners. Some learners require less learning guidance than do others; they simply "catch on" more quickly. Too much guidance may seem condescending to the quick learner, whereas too little can simply lead to frustration on the part of the slow learner. The best practical solution may sometimes be to apply learning guidance a little at a time and allow the student to use as much as he or she needs. Only one hint may be necessary for a fast learner, whereas three or four may help a slower learner. Providing adaptive learning of this sort can readily be made part of a total system of computer-based instruction (Tennyson, 1984).

In the learning of attitudes, a *human model* may be employed, as indicated in Chapter 5. Models themselves, as well as the communications they deliver, may be considered to constitute the learning guidance in attitude learning. Thus, the total instructional event in this case takes a somewhat more complex form than is the case with the learning of verbal information or intellectual skills. However, the same function of semantic encoding is being served.

Eliciting Performance   Presumably, having had sufficient learning guidance, the learners will now be at the point where the actual internal integrating event of learning takes place. Perhaps they look less confused, or some indication of pleasure has crossed their faces. They now understand it! In this event we ask them to show that they know how to do it. We want them not only to convince us, but to convince themselves as well.

Often the learner is first asked to recall an example of the performance they encountered in instruction. For example, if they have been learning to make plurals of words ending in *ix* and have been presented with the word *matrix,* the first performance is likely to be production of the plural *matrices.* In most instances, the instructor will follow this with a second example, such as *appendix* to make sure the rule can be applied in a new instance. Eliciting performance serves at least two functions. First, it causes the learner to recall from long-term memory what has been learned in short-term memory in order to perform the task. This will be important later when the learner has to recall the learning for future learning. Second, it provides the opportunity for feedback—confirmation that the "understanding" is accurate and sufficient.

Providing Feedback   It is incorrect to assume that the essential learning event is concluded once the learner has exhibited correct performance. One must be highly aware of the after effects of the learning event and their important influence on determining exactly what is learned. In other words, as a minimum, there should be feedback confirming the correctness or degree of correctness of the learner's performance.

In many instances, such feedback is provided by the event itself; for example, an individual learning to throw darts can see almost immediately how far away from the bull's eye the dart lands. But, of course, there are many tasks of school learning that do not provide this kind of "automatic" feedback. For example, consider the student practicing using the pronouns *I* and *me* in a variety of situations. Is the student able to determine which are correct and which are not? In such instances, feedback from an outside source, usually a teacher, may be an essential event.

There are no standard ways of phrasing or delivering feedback. In an instructional program, the confirmation of correctness is often printed on the side of the page or on the following page. Even standard textbooks for such subjects as mathematics and science customarily have answers printed in the back of the book. When the teacher is observing the learner's performance, the feedback communication may be delivered in many different ways—a nod, a smile, or a spoken word. Again in this instance, the important characteristic of the communication is not its content but its function: providing information to the learners about the correctness of their performance. However, if a learner's performance is not correct, corrective feedback (or remediation) may be necessary. Just knowing one's performance is not correct does not automatically mean he or she knows how to change it.

Assessing Performance   The immediate indication that the desired learning has occurred is provided when the appropriate performance is elicited. This is, in effect, an assessment of learning outcome. Accepting it as such, however, raises the larger questions of *reliability* and *validity* that relate to all systematic attempts to assess outcomes or to evaluate the effectiveness of instruction.

When one sees the learner exhibit a single performance appropriate to the lesson objective, how does the observer or teacher tell that he or she has made a *reliable* observation? How does that person know the student didn't do the required performance by chance or by guessing? Obviously, if the learner did it again, using a different example, we would have greater confidence of his or her learning. A first grader shows the ability to distinguish the sounds of *mat* and *mate*. Has the child been lucky, or can he or she exhibit the same rule-governed performance with *pal* and *pale*? Ordinarily, one expects the second instance of the performance to raise the reliability of the inference (concerning the student's capability) far beyond the chance level. Employing yet a third example should lead to a higher probability for the observer that the rule has been learned.

How is the teacher to be convinced that the performance exhibited by the learner is *valid*? This is a matter that requires two different decisions. The first is, does the performance in fact accurately reflect the objective? For example, if the objective is to "recount the main idea of the passage in your own words," the judgment must be made as to whether what the student says is indeed the *main* idea. The second judgment, which is no easier to make, is whether the performance has occurred under conditions that make the observation free of distortion. As an example, the conditions must be such that the student could not have "memorized the answer" or remembered it from a previous occasion. The teacher must be convinced, in other words, that the observation of performance reveals the learned capability in a genuine manner.

Enhancing Retention and Transfer   At this point, the knowledge or skill has been learned. The question is how to prevent forgetting, and how to enhance the learner's ability to recall the knowledge or skill at the appropriate time. When information or knowledge is to be recalled, the existence of the meaningful context in which the material has been learned appears to offer the best assurance that the information can be reinstated. The network of relationships in which the newly learned material has been embedded provides a number of different possibilities as cues for its retrieval.

Provisions made for the recall of intellectual skills often include arrangements for "practicing" their retrieval. Thus, if defined concepts, rules, and higher-order rules are to be well retained, course planning must make provision for systematic *reviews* spaced at intervals throughout weeks and months. The effectiveness of these spaced repetitions, each of which requires that the skill be retrieved and used, contrasts with the relative ineffectiveness of repeated examples given directly following the initial learning (Reynolds & Glaser, 1964).

As for the assurance of transfer of learning, it appears that this can best be done by setting some variety of new tasks for the learner, tasks that require the application of what has been learned in situations that differ substantially from those used for the learning itself. For example, suppose that what has been learned is the set of rules pertaining to "making the verb agree with the pronoun subject." Additional tasks that vary the pronoun and the verb may have been used to assess performance. Arranging conditions for transfer, however, means varying the entire situation more broadly still. This might be accomplished, in this instance, by asking the child to compose several sentences in which he or she supplies the verb and pronoun (rather than having them supplied by the teacher). In another variation of the situation, the student may be asked to compose sentences using pronouns and verbs to describe some actions shown in pictures. Ingenuity on the part of the teacher is called for in designing a variety of novel "application" situations for the purpose of ensuring the transfer of learning.

Variety and novelty in problem-solving tasks are also of particular relevance to the continued development of cognitive strategies. As has previously been mentioned, the strategies used in problem solving need to be developed by the systematic introduction of occasions for problem solving, interspersed with other instruction. An additional event to be especially noted in the presentation of novel problems to the student is the need to make clear the general nature of the solution expected. For example, "practical" solutions may be quite different from "original" solutions, and the student's performance can easily be affected by such differences in the communication of the objective (Johnson, 1972). One way of providing parameters for acceptable performance is by having examples of acceptable or exemplary work to which the learners can compare their work.

Instructional Events and Learning Outcomes   The events of instruction may be used in connection with each of' the five kinds of learned capabilities described in Chapters 4 and 5. In the case of some instructional events, such as gaining attention, the particular means employed to bring about the event is not necessarily different for intellectual skill objectives than for attitude objectives. However, for learning guidance, the specific nature of the event is likely to be very different indeed. As we have seen in the previous section, the encoding of an intellectual skill may be guided by verbal instructions, such as communicating to the learner a verbal statement of a rule to be learned. In contrast, effective encoding of an attitude often requires a complex event that includes observation of a human model. The requirement of differing treatments of instructional events extends also to Event 3, stimulating recall of prior learning, and to Event 4, presenting the stimulus material.

A summary of Events 3, 4, and 5 for each type of learned capability is contained in Table 10.2, along with examples of the function served by these events. For each kind of learning outcome, appropriate conditions of learning are listed under each of the three events. These descriptions are not intended to be all-inclusive, but rather examples of how the nature of the events might differ.

An inspection of the table will show that the particular form taken by each of these three instructional events depends upon the capability to be learned. For example, when an intellectual skill is to be learned, the stimulation of recall pertains to the retrieval of prerequisite concepts or rules, whereas if verbal information is to be learned, the recall of a context of organized information is required. Similar differences in the specific form of Event 3, as well as Events 4 and 5, may be noted throughout the table. Each of these treatments might be viewed as different "instructional strategies" to facilitate the type of learning desired. An interesting activity is to look at your favorite instructional strategies in terms of how they represent various events of instruction, and see which events are present and which are not.

TABLE 10.2 — **FUNCTIONS OF INSTRUCTIONAL EVENTS 3, 4, AND 5, WITH EXAMPLES FOR EACH OF FIVE KINDS OF LEARNING OUTCOMES**

Intellectual Skill

Event 3: Stimulate Recall of Prerequisite Knowledge or Skills Ask a question about prior learning so learner retrieves prerequisite rules and concepts to working memory.

Event 4: Present the Stimulus Display a statement of the rule or concept, with example, giving emphasis to features of component concepts.

Event 5: Provide Learning Guidance Present varied examples in varied contexts; also, give elaborations to furnish cues for retrieval.

Cognitive Strategy

Event 3: Stimulate Recall of Prerequisite Knowledge or Skills Recall task strategies and relevant intellectual skills.

Event 4: Present the Stimulus Describe the task and the strategy and show what the strategy accomplishes.

Event 5: Provide Learning Guidance Describe the strategy and give one or more application examples.

Verbal Information

Event 3: Stimulate Recall of Prerequisite Knowledge or Skills Recall familiar, well-organized bodies of knowledge related to the new learning.

Event 4: Present the Stimulus Display printed or verbal statements, emphasizing distinctive features.

Event 5: Provide Learning Guidance Elaborate content by relating to larger bodies of knowledge; use mnemonics, images.

Attitude

Event 3: Stimulate Recall of Prerequisite Knowledge or Skills Recall the situation and the actions involved in personal choice. Remind learner of human model.

Event 4: Present the Stimulus Human model describes the general nature of the choice of personal action to be presented.

Motor Skill

Event 3: Stimulate Recall of Prerequisite Knowledge or Skills Recall the executive subroutine and relevant part skills.

Event 4: Present the Stimulus Display the situation existing at the beginning of the skill performance. Demonstrate executive subroutine.

Event 5: Provide Learning Guidance Continue practice with informative feedback.

THE EVENTS OF INSTRUCTION IN A LESSON

In using the events of instruction for lesson planning, it is apparent that they must be organized in a flexible manner, with primary attention to the lesson's objectives. What is implied by our description of these events is obviously not a standard, routine set of communications and action. The events represent the functions to be carried out in instruction. These functions are adapted to the specific situation, the task to be accomplished, the type of learning represented in the task, and the students' prior learning.

It is now possible to consider how these events are exemplified within an actual lesson. We have chosen, as an example, a set of instructions to the designer of a computer-based lesson, showing the implications of each instructional event for frame-by-frame design (Gagné, Wager, and Rojas, 1981). The lesson is about a *defined concept* in use of the English language, namely, the part of a sentence called the *object*. Instructions to the designer are outlined in Table 10.3.

It will be evident that this lesson in English grammar may best be conceived as part of a longer sequence in which such prior concepts as *sentence, subject,* and *predicate* have already been learned. For learners without such previous experience, instruction in the concept *object* would need to begin with simpler prerequisite concepts. It may be noted that the lesson is carefully planned in the sense that it reflects each of the instructional events described in this chapter. Obviously, it is an exercise in which the designer's art has considerable opportunity to flourish within the framework of events that support the desired learning.

Comparison with Lessons for Older Students

As instruction is planned for middle and higher grades, one can expect the events of instruction to be increasingly controlled by the materials of a lesson or by the learners themselves. Thus, when the units of instruction that make up a course of study are structurally similar, as may be the case in mathematics or beginning foreign language, for example, the objectives for each succeeding unit may be evident to students and, therefore, may not need to be communicated. For reasonably well-motivated students, it is often unnecessary to make any special provisions for controlling attention, because this event, too, may be appropriately managed by the learners themselves.

Homework assignments, such as those that call for learning from a text, depend upon the learners to employ cognitive strategies available to them in managing instructional events. The text may aid selective perception by its inclusion of bold printing, topic headings, and other features of this general sort. The text may, and often does, include a context of meaningful material that provides for semantic encoding by relating new information to organized knowledge already in learners' memories. An important part of study, however, is the necessity for practicing appropriate performance, whether this is a matter of stating information in the learner's own words, applying a newly learned rule to examples, or originating solutions to novel problems. For these events of self-instruction, as well as for the judgment of correctness that gives an immediate sort of feedback, learners frequently must depend upon cognitive strategies available to them.

TABLE 10.3	EVENTS OF INSTRUCTION IN DESIGN OF A COMPUTER-BASED LESSON
Instructional Event	**Procedure**
1. Gaining attention	Present initial operating instructions on screen, including some displays that change second by second. Call attention to screen presentation, using words like "Look!" "Watch!" etc.
2. Informing learner of lesson objective	State in simple terms what the student will have accomplished once he or she has learned. *Examples:* "Joe chased the ball." 'The sun shines brightly." One of these sentences contains a word that is an object, the other does not. Can you pick out the object? In the first sentence, ball is the object of the verb chased. In the second sentence, none of the words is an object. You are about to learn how to identify the object in a sentence.
3. Stimulating recall of prior learning	Recall concepts previously learned. *Example:* Any sentence has a subject and a predicate. The subject is usually a noun, or a noun phrase. The predicate begins with a verb. What is the subject of this sentence? "The play began at eight o'clock." What verb begins the predicate of this sentence? "The child upset the cart."
4. Presenting stimuli with distinctive features	Present a definition of the concept. *Example:* An object is a noun in the predicate to which the action (of the verb) is directed. For example, consider the sentence, "The rain pelted the roof." The word "roof" is the object of the verb "pelted."
5. Guiding learning	Take a sentence like this: "Peter milked the cow." The answer is *the cow* and that is the *object* of the verb. Notice, though, that some sentences do not have objects. "The rain fell slowly down." In this sentence, the action of the verb "fell" is not directed at something. So, in this sentence, there is no object.
6. Eliciting performance	Present three to five examples of sentences one by one. State, "Type *'O'* if this sentence has an object; then type the word that is the object." *Examples:* "Sally closed the book. " "The kite rose steadily."
7. Providing informative feedback	Give information about correct and incorrect responses. *Example:* Book is the object of the verb closed in the first sentence. The second sentence does not have an object.
8. Assessing performance	Present a new set of concept instances and noninstances in three to five additional pairs of sentences. Ask questions requiring answers. Tell the learner if mastery is achieved and what to do next if it is not.
9. Enhancing retention and learning transfer	Present three to five additional concept instances, varied in form. *Example:* Use sentences such as, "Neoclassical expressions often supplant mere platitudes." Introduce review questions at spaced intervals.

Note: From "Planning and authoring computer-assisted instruction lessons," by R. M. Gagné, W. Wager, and A. Rojas, p. 23. *Educational Technology* (September 1981). Copyright 1981 by Educational Technology Publications. Reprinted by permission of the authors and copyright owners.

SUMMARY

This chapter is concerned with the events that make up instruction for learning outcomes as they may occur within a lesson. These are the events that are usually external to the learner, supplied by the teacher, text, or other media with which the learner interacts. When self-instruction is undertaken, as is more frequently expected as the learner's experience increases, the learner may bring about instructional events. However they originate, the purpose of these events is to activate and support the internal processes of learning.

The general nature of supporting external events may be derived from the information-processing (or cognitive) model of learning and memory, which is employed in one form or another by many contemporary learning investigators. This model proposes that a single act of learning involves a number of stages of internal processing. Beginning with the receipt of stimulation by receptors, these stages include (1) a brief registration of sensory events, (2) temporary storage of stimulus features in the short-term memory, (3) a rehearsal process that may be employed to lengthen the period of short-term storage to prepare information for entry into long-term memory, (4) semantic encoding for long-term storage, (5) search and retrieval to recall previously learned material, and (6) response organization producing a performance appropriate to what has been learned. Most theories include, either implicitly or explicitly, the process of (7) reinforcement as brought about by external feedback of the correctness of performance. In addition, this learning model postulates a number of (8) executive control processes that enable the learner to select and use cognitive strategies that influence other learning processes.

As derived from this learning model, instructional events are

1. Gaining attention
2. Informing the learner of the objective
3. Stimulating recall of prerequisite learning
4. Presenting the stimulus material
5. Providing learning guidance
6. Eliciting the performance
7. Providing feedback about performance correctness
8. Assessing the performance
9. Enhancing retention and transfer

These events can be applied to the learning of all of the types of learning outcomes we have previously described. Examples are given to illustrate how each is planned for and put into effect. The order of these events for a lesson or lesson segment is approximate and may vary somewhat depending on the objective. Not all of the events are invariably used. Some are made to occur by the teacher, some by the learner, and some by the instructional materials. An older, more experienced learner may supply most of these events by his or her own study effort. For young children, the teacher would arrange for most of them.

As these events apply to the various kinds of capabilities being acquired, they take on different specific characteristics (Gagné, 1985). These differences are particularly apparent in the following events from our list: Event 3, *stimulating recall of prerequisite knowledge and skills;* Event 4, *presenting the stimulus material;* and Event 5, *providing learning guidance.* For example, *presenting the stimulus* (Event 4) for the learning of discriminations requires conditions to which the differences in stimuli become increasingly fine. Concept learning, however, requires the presentation of a variety of instances and noninstances of the general class. Conditions of *learning guidance* (Event 5) required for the learning of rules include examples of applications, whereas these conditions for verbal information learning are prominently concerned with linking to a larger meaningful context. For attitude learning, this event takes on an even more distinctive character when it includes a human model and the model's communication.

An example is given of using the events of instruction for the design of a computer-based lesson of a defined concept in English grammar.

REFERENCES

Anderson, J. R. (1985). *Cognitive psychology and its implications* (2nd ed.). New York: Freeman.

Estes, W. K. (Ed.). (1985). *Handbook of learning and cognitive processes: Introduction to concepts and issues* (Vol. 1). Hillsdale, NJ: Erlbaum.

Gagné, R. M. (1968). Learning and communication. In R. V. Wiman, & W. C. Meierhenry (Eds.), *Educational media: Theory into practice.* Columbus, OH: Merrill.

Gagné, R. M. (1977). Instructional programs. In M. H. Marx & M. E. Bunch (Eds.), *Fundamentals and applications of learning.* New York: Macmillan.

Gagné, R. M. (1985). *The conditions of learning* (4th ed.). New York: Holt, Rinehart and Winston.

Gagné, R. M., Wager, W., & Rojas, A. (1981, September). Planning and authoring computer-assisted instruction lessons. *Educational Technology,* 17–26.

Johnson, D. M. (1972). A *systematic introduction to the psychology of thinking.* New York: Harper & Row.

Klatzky, R. L. (1980). *Human memory: Structures and processes* (2nd ed.). San Francisco: Freeman.

Reynolds, J. H., & Glaser, R. (1964). Effects of repetition and spaced review upon retention of a complex learning task. *Journal of Educational Psychology, 55,* 297–308.

Wittrock, M. C. (1966). The learning by discovery hypothesis. In L. S. Shulman & E. R. Keislar (Eds.), *Learning by discovery: A critical appraisal.* Chicago: Rand McNally.

TECHNOLOGY—AFFORDANCES

One of the original conceptions of educational technology was as a replacement for the teacher. In 1960, A. A. Lumsdain wrote:

> What are the possible applications of automation . . . to the process of instruction? It seems clear that automated instructional methods would include any means whatever by which the functions of a teacher in guiding or mediating the process of a student's learning are encoded so they can be removed or extended in time and space and reduplicated as desired. (p. 136)

We know today that replacement of the teacher isn't going to happen; however, the role of the teacher in the learning process is changing. One of the questions an instructional designer has to deal with is how to provide the external conditions of learning to the student. These external conditions include attention devices, advance organizers, new information, contexts for learning and practice, feedback, and transfer.

The explosive development of digital technologies in the last decade has fundamentally transformed how, what, when, and where people learn. Without a doubt, being a successful and contributing member of society today requires significantly different skills than in the past. Technology is affecting change in educational institutions, corporate America, and the federal government by posing new challenges to teachers and instructors, students and parents, and training developers and administrators. To take full advantage of the digital age, educators and training developers need to rethink approaches to learning, education, and training and determine how technology can support each (Resnick, 2002).

We are defining the term *affordances* as the properties or functions of technology that extend our learning and perceptual capabilities. These affordances may be economic, such as the rapidity that technology affords when searching data; social, such as affording asynchronous communication and collaboration; cognitive, such as affording information search and data sharing; or affective, afforded by a rich media mix that can present messages in attractive ways. Cognitive affordances encompass those criteria that relate to how people learn; social affordances encompass those criteria that relate to shared human activities; affective affordances relate to the motivational aspects of learning; and economic affordances relate to resources and other practical issues regarding instructional design and delivery. Cognitive affordances refer to the capabilities afforded a computer user, such as communication, information retrieval, computation, data manipulation, data conversion, and so forth.

This chapter explores each of the affordances and discusses how technologies, and in particular the Internet, are affecting learning and training processes, products, and outcomes. Addressed are the types of resources and technologies available to educators and trainers today, their relationship to the events of instruction and learning outcomes, and the challenges associated with their use.

LEARNING IN THE DIGITAL AGE

Information and communication technologies are transforming organizations and redefining the knowledge and skills required by society to succeed in the new millennium. At the individual level, being "digitally literate" (Gilster, 1997) means having the ability to understand and make use of information and communication technologies. This is essential to employment success, civic participation, and education and training. Digital technologies are revolutionizing how we work, live, play, and learn.

Effect of Computers on What People Learn

Curricula in our schools must be continually updated to reflect tasks and skills of the digital age. New technologies are changing not only what students *should* learn, but also what they *can* learn (Resnick, 2002). Many ideas and topics that have been left out of school curricula because of the limitations of traditional instructional media and delivery methods, such as a blackboard, paper and pencils, and books, can now be introduced. For example, computer simulations can be used to let children explore how systems work and the math behind certain phenomena, such as volcanoes, tornados, and earthquakes. Ideas previously introduced only at the university level can now be introduced much earlier in school learning, such as use of fractal mathematics to understand objects in the real world. Curricula need to be transformed to focus less on "things to know" and more on "strategies for learning the things you don't know" (Resnick, 2002). In the digital age, learning to become a more strategic learner, who knows how to draw on a vastly expanded world of information through the Internet, is significantly better than learning simply through rote memorization.

Critical and creative thinking, informed decision making, and real-world problem solving are examples of higher-order skills that students must further develop and broaden in the digital age. Sound reasoning skills must be learned to enable students to plan, design, execute, and evaluate solutions (Committee on Information Technology Literacy, 1999). Unlike reference libraries and printed books, the sheer vastness of information available online requires new skills at finding, sorting through, and evaluating information; rejecting extraneous material; validating information sources; and resolving conflicting information. People need to be technologically literate in order to use electronic resources such as Internet search engines and Internet development tools. Acquiring all of these skills fosters critical thinking.

Effect of Computers on How People Learn

Resnick (2002) believes school classrooms of the 21st century need to be reorganized so that students can become more active and independent, with the teacher serving as consultant rather than a lecturer. Instead of dividing the curriculum into separate disciplines such as math, science, language, social studies, the focus should be on themes and projects that cut across several disciplines in order to take advantage of the rich connections among the different domains of knowledge.

The Internet has become a primary source for research, and because so much of the content on the Internet is captured in text, reading is of increased importance. However, text is not the only source of information. The Internet is multimodal. It can deliver sound, graphics, and video or moving pictures as well. Students will need to sharpen their listening skills, their ability to read graphs, and their ability to follow a moving picture. Past editions of this book focused on media selection. We no longer see this as an issue since the computer has essentially created a convergence of media to the monitor or display screen. The term *multimodal* incorporates the idea that there are many types of stimuli that can be delivered through a single technology. When using multimodal delivery systems, it is important to consider which stimuli will be needed to facilitate learning.

Effect of Computers on Where and When People Learn

Schools are one of the slowest changing cultural institutions. School learning traditionally takes place between the ages of six and 18, grades K–12, Monday through Friday, 8:30 a.m. to 3:00 p.m. Classrooms were designed to facilitate the student's listening to the teacher present new information by way of speech and graphics drawn on the blackboard. Today, Resnick's (2002) more entrepreneurial approach to learning has students divided *not* according to age in separate grades or time, such as the typical hour-long class period. Instead, students of all ages would be encouraged to work together on projects for *extended* periods of time. This would enable them to learn from one another and to follow through more meaningfully on the ideas that arise through the learning process. Learning would become a lifelong experience. Formal learning could take place not only in schools but also in homes, community centers, and workplaces. Many educational reform proponents (Resnick, 2002) believe that schools are just a part of a broader learning ecosystem and that in the years ahead digital technologies will continue to open up new learning opportunities. In doing so, the technologies will support the development of new types of "knowledge-building communities" where children and adults can collaborate on projects around the world without the constraint of time.

IMPACT OF THE INTERNET

The Internet is an essential tool in our information-based society. Already a great deal of content is "Web-enabled" for delivery on the Internet. Internet technologies provide increasing options for citizens to conduct daily activities online. People are going online to conduct day-to-day activities, such as banking, buying and selling stock, shopping, personal correspondence, research, and to take train-ing courses. Businesses are using the Internet for activities such as marketing, recruiting, advertising, and providing customer service. Being computer savvy and digitally connected is becoming critical to our nation's educational, economical, governmental, and societal advancement. Increasing the number of Americans to use digital-age technologies, such as the Internet, has become a vitally important national goal. For this reason, America is turning toward educators and trainers to rethink the purpose and architecture of our educational infrastructures in very fundamental ways. This affords opportunities for instructional designers to use the Internet technology to develop integrated curriculum where knowledge learned in one area can be applied in another, increasing relevance and transfer.

Challenges of Technology

Technological innovations are both beneficial and problematic. For example, online learning generally reduces personal face-to-face contact between teachers and learners, and among learners themselves. This social aspect of learning is something that many learners highly value. Even with advances in synchronous communication, where interaction between participants is simultaneous through two-way audio or video, online learning is not a replacement for student-teacher and student-student interaction. Online learning can enhance social relationships through chat rooms, "threaded" discussions, and other collaboration techniques. The technology affords the possibility of increasing the quality of student-teacher communications. However, as noted previously, while digital technologies have the *potential* to change the purpose and function of the classroom considerably, there is still much resistance to change. Because the Internet is such a powerful instruc-tional tool, it must be subjected to the same development and implementation rules as traditional education and training; in other words, it requires good peda-gogical practices and good instructional design.

Because a larger percentage of Americans regularly use the Internet to con-duct daily activities, and corporate America has embraced the Internet as a leading resource for most business transactions, people who lack access, knowledge, and training on how to use it are at a great disadvantage. Eventually, they will find it more difficult to function in society. The gap between individuals who have reason-able opportunities to access technological tools, especially the Internet, and those who do not, is called the *digital divide*. While our government is intent on ensuring that citizens have reasonable opportunities to access technology, technological training is needed to develop the knowledge and skills required for citizens to use the technology to increase their quality of life.

Validating Content   Even advocates of Internet use in the classroom agree that the enormous network, which President Clinton called, "a commonplace encyclopedia for millions of schoolchildren," is actually an unwieldy, uneven, and often unreliable information source. While the Internet is the largest and most diverse information resource in the world today, and significant progress has being made to incorporate its wealth of information into online curricula, there is a significant challenge to create *valid* educational or instructional content (Golas, 2000). Factual knowledge is plentiful, but educators often question the real value of the information. Significant effort is needed to transform information into useful knowledge systems; this is the work of communities of learners (Riel & Polin, 2002).

For the most part, the Internet is not "instruction." It is a resource with a great deal of information. However, we began this book by defining instruction as an arrangement of external events to facilitate learning. How, then, does the Internet fit into the instruction process? We believe it fits in because it affords flexibility and convenience by allowing the learner to study when and where they want to, and it affords the learner access to a wide variety of resources, including other learners.

Lowering Costs   Education is always associated with expense. We want quality instruction at minimal cost. Media and computer technology are sources of instruction; however, there are questions of scale and return on investment (ROI).

Online learning is not necessarily less expensive to develop and implement than traditional instructional media, although it can be very cost-effective in the long run because it can reduce learning and training time and travel and accommodation costs previously required to send people to training. Additionally, online learning content can be updated, revised, and re-broadcast in far less time than conventional learning media, such as books. Online learning can be more expensive when multimedia strategies, such as video scenarios, complex interactive exercises, and 3D simulations are developed. Initial costs and maintenance costs associated with hardware, software, and networks add up quickly. Online learning also creates the need for specialized training for administrators, instructional designers, and technology implementers. These individuals need to be trained in design strategies, tools, processes, and standards.

Keeping Pace with Technologies   Because the Internet is changing so rapidly, moving from phone lines to cable and satellite venues and using broadband capabilities to handle emerging digital media convergence, the onus is on leaders from government, education, and industry to stay abreast of the changes and to recognize the technologies that will truly benefit society. There will be more change in the next 30 years than we saw in the entire 20th century, and this will be especially true as technologies converge and changes happen faster (Mehlman, 2003). Just as there are many terms used to describe Internet-based training, there are many instructional design strategies, technological capabilities, and development tools for online learning design, development, and delivery (see Chapter 15).

Effective Collaboration   The success of online learning programs will depend upon the capacity of schools, parents, children, and the training industry to collaborate effectively on a global scale. The Web and networking technologies have made it possible to connect learners, separated by time and space, with distributed instructional resources, that is, resources that go beyond the individual classroom. Online instructional resources include teachers, other learners, subject-matter experts, reference materials, simulations, and interactive practice exercises. Technological advances provide an environment in which students and teachers or instructors can function as both learners and facilitators of learning. Professional teacher development is an essential ingredient for making the most of digital content in the classroom (Trotter, 1999).

What Technology Is Not

Technology is *not* an end in itself; any successful use of training technology must begin with clearly defined educational objectives. In most places where new technologies are being used in education and training, they are there simply to reinforce conventional approaches to learning (Resnick, 2002). Every student in every school can have access to the Internet and to sophisticated learning tools, but these tools won't have any effect on learning if teachers don't know how to incorporate digital strategies and content into their classrooms.

Digital literacy is *not* a substitute for good parenting and effective teaching. Any effort to define and promote digital literacy must reinforce the unique and vital roles of parents and teachers. Technology can improve people's lives by making the world a safer, more interesting, more prosperous, and more equitable place; but it can also exacerbate problems. For example, encryption technologies that protect our privacy also conceal terrorist communications. The Internet lets children in North America explore the rain forests of Brazil and take science courses online, but it also gives them access to pornography and instructions on how to build bombs and conceal weapons.

Online learning provided by digital technologies is *not* a one-size-fits-all solution. For example, an asynchronous course can be taken anytime, anywhere, and is perfect for self-paced, supplemental, or refresher training, or for continuous learning. On the other hand, a synchronous course is delivered at a specified time, typically with an online moderator, and is an excellent way to reach geographically dispersed students.

There are two guiding principles for online learning. The first is "just-in-time," or "targeted delivery," where critical information or instruction is delivered precisely where and when it is needed, in just the amount it is needed, and often in a format preferred by the user. With "just-in-time" or "targeted delivery," excessive and extraneous information is avoided to ensure that the educational or instructional workload is manageable and meaningful to the user. The second guiding principle is modular learning, where information covering different topics is delivered to students as individual courses or units of instruction. With modular learning, students often progress through the course material at their own pace.

Online education and training is *not* a replacement for hands-on training or learning. It can help students visualize and bring to life information through 3D animation, video sound, and interactivity. However, educational media by themselves do not influence the achievement of students; they permit the delivery and storage of instructional messages but do not determine learning.

Digital literacy *is not* just about having Internet access and broad technical proficiency. It's about learning digital rights and wrongs. For example, respecting intellectual property rights, practicing security as second nature, and valuing others' privacy are all going to be critical to a functionally literate information society (Mehlman, 2003).

TECHNOLOGY IN SCHOOL LEARNING

Colleges and Universities

Near universal adoption of the Internet by the postsecondary community has set the stage for widespread use of online learning tools and pedagogy. Colleges and universities have embraced online learning as a means of enhancing the classroom experience and expanding educational opportunities for students. Despite a challenging fiscal climate, technology expenditures at colleges and universities grew by more than 9 percent between 2000 and 2001 to reach $4.7 billion (National Center for Educational Statistics, 2002).

According to a survey conducted by the International Data Corporation (IDC) in 2002, 90 percent of American colleges and universities will offer some level of online learning by 2005, and information technology (IT) spending by postsecondary institutions will grow by 10 percent every year until 2005. The higher education online learning market will be worth $5 billion by 2005, giving suppliers of hardware, software, support services, and communications technologies a major market for which to compete. Although colleges and universities will buy fewer institutional personal computers (PCs), the market for network servers will grow. Smaller institutions, in particular, will be contracting out IT support services and computer training at a significant rate.

High Schools

Raised amidst pervasive, multigigabit wireless networks, the high school class of 2030 will be a truly digital generation, more empowered and more challenged then any who have come before (Mehlman, 2003).

A study by Interactive Educational Systems Design (2003) found that over 40 percent of high schools offered online courses during the 2003 school year and 17 percent plan to offer them in the future. The study also found that 32 percent of our nation's public school districts will adopt online learning for the first time in 2003. Data from the National Center for Educational Statistics (2002) showed that 98 percent of all public schools in America had Internet access in 2001. Teachers in 94 percent of public schools monitored Internet use, and 74 percent of schools had blocking or filtering software. Almost two thirds of the schools implemented an honor code related to Internet use.

A study by CyberAtlas (2002) found that when buying online courses the most important factor taken into account by high schools is an accredited curriculum. Affordability, delivery ease, and speed were also important. According to the study, the main reasons cited by high schools for turning to online learning were cost effectiveness, providing educational equity, and resolving scheduling conflicts. However, the study also indicated that while 84 percent of teachers in America believed that computers and Internet access improved the quality of education, two thirds said the Internet was not well integrated into their classrooms.

According to a survey report from NetDay (2003), almost all teachers now have Internet access at the high schools where they work, and 80 percent have classrooms with Internet access. Despite these high numbers and the fact the almost half of teachers said the Internet had become an important tool for teaching over the last two years, the majority reported that they use the Internet at school for less than 30 minutes a day. Over three quarters of them said their main reason for not using the Internet was lack of time. Lack of equipment, access speed, and lack of technical support were also mentioned as barriers to increased use of the Internet. The study also found that most teachers do not use the Internet to communicate with students, parents, and other teachers; to organize activities; to build lessons; to complete project work; or to update lesson plans.

Lifelong Learning and Student-Centered Systems

Linn (1996) identified several features of online learning that support autonomous lifelong learning for students. Students are able to

- make effective decisions and create new ideas
- recognize when, how, and why they learn new material
- diagnose their strengths and limitations
- select activities compatible with their goals, strengths, and limitations
- develop independent projects tailored to their personal goals within an academic discipline
- take responsibility for their own learning
- monitor their own progress
- reflect on their understanding of the material
- seek guidance from peers as well as instructors
- create activities that support practicing learned skills
- understand disciplinary knowledge, practice, and culture through autonomous learning activities that include linking ideas, comparing alternatives, reflecting on progress, and critiquing ideas with guidance and support
- structure their courses to take advantage of the social nature of learning and social contributions to learning by engaging in collaborative practices

In the near future, student-controlled interfaces will be able to

- launch individualized training content based on a student's learning requirements or what they are currently working on
- adapt to a student's individual learning style and preferences
- map a student's preexisting knowledge to instructional content
- track emotional responses to help students refine their ability to interact more effectively with others

With student-centered systems, everything a student does or action he or she takes will feed the system with a better idea of what the student finds interesting. Student-centered systems will be capable of

- monitoring a student's level of interest, anxiety, and motivation and adapting to specific target audiences (language, cultural background, and learning abilities)
- collecting information about who the learners are, what they know, where they've been, and what they've accomplished throughout their *entire* learning career

Assessment tools will

- remind students where to focus their attention, what to work on next, and provide quick, context-sensitive, individualized feedback
- model an individual student's difficulties and tailor problems and explanations to address conceptions and misconceptions
- automatically track students' progress and provide statistical models of presentation sequences and paths and provide instant feedback to students, instructors, and administration on the problems with the curriculum and its presentation

TECHNOLOGY IN TRAINING

Demands to reduce training costs have led many corporations, government agencies, and the military to invest in digital technologies such as advanced distance learning. Traditional classroom courses are rapidly giving way to online learning over the Internet. The demand for accessible "just-in-time" asynchronous training and lower per-student costs are also helping to expand the online learning training market. Online learning utilizes the existing infrastructure of networks, intranets, and PCs, while conserving and helping better utilize other corporate or organizational resources. Books and classrooms aren't going away, but the Internet is fast becoming an integral aspect of learning in corporate America and our federal government. A new employee can begin study on his or her own and, once prepared, move into the active learning phase with an instructor or mentor.

In Industry

Immediate corporate access to sophisticated educational and training products is essential for organizations to compete successfully in the global marketplace. Training programs must be aligned with businesses strategies and meet the immediate learning needs of employees, suppliers, and customers. With corporate and government training budgets shrinking because of the current global economic downturn, training programs must consistently deliver a high return on investment. Employees need to learn more efficiently and be able to effectively transfer what they've learned to their rapidly changing work environments.

According to a report from eMarketer (2002), 24 percent of American organizations used online learning to train employees in 2002, up from 16 percent in 2001. Fifty-seven percent of the respondents relied on instructor-led training, down from 65 percent in 2001. Far less popular were traditional books and manuals, CD-ROMs, videotapes, and satellite broadcasts. According to Fulcrum Analytics (2002), access to adult education sites increased by 60 percent since 1997. These sites provide training, preparation for standardized tests, seminars, and graduate degrees, among other services.

According to a 2001 IDC study, the worldwide corporate online learning market will exceed $23 billion by 2004. The growth in the online learning is attributed to increased Internet use, faster and cheaper access to the Internet, and improvements in the quality of online learning products. North America is expected to maintain its dominance of the market, accounting for two thirds of worldwide revenues by 2004. IDC identified western Europe as the second fastest-growing market, predicting that corporate online learning revenues would increase by a compound annual growth rate of 97 percent from 1999 to 2004. A shift in content demand is expected, with non-IT courseware replacing IT training content as the largest market in online learning. By 2004, non-IT content will account for 54 percent of worldwide demand, up from 28 percent in 2000.

In the Federal Government

Our government is rapidly adopting new and better training technologies. This trend will continue and accelerate as our leaders require more effective management through improved selection, control, and evaluation of technological advancements. Digital technologies are seen as a way to create a government that works better, costs less, and gets results that Americans care about (Warnick, Jordan, & Allen, 1999).

For the first time, information age technologies are allowing federal agencies to search for and provide comprehensive information on topics of concern both to their employees and to the public. Faced with tighter budgets, government agencies have turned to online training to cut costs, making it an increasingly essential component of many professional development programs. Agencies need to know about the latest training tools and technologies and how to use them in order to build a knowledge-based workforce. As standards continue to evolve about how government organizations should collect and share information, with heightened emphasis on how to support many pressing national security concerns, there is increasing interest in incorporating knowledge management into government-wide enterprise architectures. An enterprise architecture is a plan to streamline and standardize computer systems within a government organization by using common hardware and software (Hasson, 2001). It's a blueprint of how an organization's systems should operate, such as identifying one e-mail package that the entire organization should use (Hasson, 2001).

The development of the National Information Infrastructure and the increase of personal computers at home and work are offering new opportunities for distributed (online) learning. Advances in networking technology and telecommunications are revolutionizing the availability and speed of information access over the Internet and other networks. As bandwidths and speeds increase, it will be possible to run distributed multimedia training applications over networks using sources of data and information from all over the world. Point-to-point videoconferencing technology will enable virtual classrooms to convene courses without regard to location. Homeland defense is significantly affecting workforce development and technical training in the military, federal law enforcement agencies, and corporate America. Organizations are turning to technologies to lower per student costs and to increase training effectiveness.

Section 508–Rehabilitation Act   The government has created an independent federal agency, called the Access Board, which is devoted solely to improving access to digital-age electronic and information technology to employees and members of the public who are disabled, including those with vision, hearing, and mobility disabilities. The Access Board developed standards under Section 508 of the Rehabilitation Act as amended by Congress in 1998. The law applies to all federal agencies and covers various means of disseminating information, including online learning, computer software, and electronic office equipment.

In the Military   Education and training are integral parts of every soldier's preparedness. Each branch of the military is relying heavily on digital technologies to train a force that is more responsive, more deployable, more agile, more versatile, more lethal, more survivable, and more sustainable than ever. Simulation technologies are advancing at a rapid pace, to the point where troops can be trained while weapon systems are still being built. In the past, highly realistic training was not possible until weapon systems came off of the production line and could be used to provide such training. Today, hands-on training using actual systems is being greatly reduced because of advances in digital simulation technologies. The maturity of 3D graphics technology and migration to PC platforms, are making desktop simulation systems widely affordable in the military.

American military operations require precise choreography of air, ground, sea, and space-based assets. Because of advances in simulation and digital technologies, the Army, Navy, Air Force, and Marine Corps are able to integrate their warfighting capabilities and coordinate which forces are deployed to support a mission, how they are transported, how they are supplied, how they will fight, and so on. The United States Joint Forces Command (USJFCOM) was established to meet these training objectives. USJFCOM trains military forces primarily through the use of computer simulations, where forces and capabilities are modeled to allow commanders to exercise decision-making processes.

Demands to reduce training costs have had a major impact on interactive distance learning technology in the military. Traditional classroom courses are rapidly giving way to online learning. The military has conducted extensive research and analyses on the effectiveness of distance learning. Barry and Runyan (1995) and Wisher (1999) reviewed the literature on the effectiveness of distance learning as applied to training and found that by using online learning as "pretraining," classroom-based training experiences were more meaningful, because students started at levels equal to their peers, and they were better prepared for the training they were to receive.

Electronic classrooms with access to the Internet or military intranets have become the mainstay of military training. Electronic classrooms often come equipped with interactive control stations for the instructor; desks with sunken, angled monitors to reduce eyestrain; a student discrete-response system; and audio and lighting systems tailored to the specific environment. Electronic classrooms take advantage of electronic data storage and communication and display technologies that permit new ways of creating and delivering instructor-led training. Instructors and students can interact with each other, and instructors can select the most appropriate medium to explain a certain point or process. Instructors can demonstrate procedures as students follow along, and students can practice on their individual computers. During practice exercises, instructors can monitor the students' screens and easily control their activities and provide feedback.

Learner-Centric Approaches Educational research literature points to clear research directions for learner-centric approaches within military training. The training approaches derive from psychological principles in cognition, motivation, social factors, and individual differences. The key research areas include

- the instructor's role in online training
- the use of online moderators
- learner perceptions
- methods for online collaboration
- interaction schemes
- use of collaborative tools
- affect of online communities
- impact of individual learning styles
- effectiveness of electronic classrooms

The Carroll model of school learning (Carroll, 1963) is helpful when considering the role technology plays in learning. According to Carroll's model, the degree of learning attained by a learner is a function of the amount of time they spend trying to learn, divided by the amount of time they need. As instructional designers, we try to reduce the amount of time learners need by developing good instruction. However, by using technology we can also allow more time for the learner who needs it. The Internet affords us access to other learners, so learners with a lower aptitude for a subject can be put into groups with learners with higher aptitudes, in effect leveraging the knowledge held by the higher-aptitude learners. Because the Internet can be accessed almost any time a student might want to study, students with different learning needs don't have to wait for access to a classroom teacher to answer a question.

Course Management Systems (CMS) There are a number of course development and delivery tools, like WebCT and BlackBoard, for "putting" courses onto the Internet. These tools are basically structured databases for holding course content, resources, and activities, that allow registered users access. These are generally designed to be collaborative learning environments, where student participation in the class is highly valued. One place for sharing ideas or communicating about a topic is the course "discussion board."

The source of content for the course may or may not be on the Internet. For example, it is common to have a text as the primary source of information for the course. However, other events of instruction, such as activities that allow for clarification of the text and practice activities, can be presented on the Web. Testing may be done either on or off the Web, depending upon security requirements.

Advanced Distributed Learning

The Advanced Distributed Learning (ADL) initiative, sponsored by the Office of the Secretary of Defense (OSD), is a collaborative effort between government, industry, and academia to establish a new distributed learning environment that permits the interoperability of learning tools and course content on a global scale. The ADL vision is to provide access to the highest-quality education and training, tailored to individual needs, delivered cost-effectively anywhere anytime. By working with industry and academia, the OSD is promoting collaboration in the use of tools, specifications, guidelines, policies, and prototypes that make courses

- accessible from multiple remote locations through the use of metadata, or data about data, and packaging standards
- adaptable by tailoring instruction to the individual and organizational needs
- affordable by increasing learning efficiency and productivity while reducing time and costs
- durable across revisions of operating systems and software
- interoperable across multiple software design and development tools and hardware platforms such as IBM PCs, Apple MacIntosh computers, or workstations
- reusable through the design, management, and distribution of tools and learning content across multiple applications

The ADL initiative is designed to accelerate large-scale development of dynamic and cost-effective learning software and systems to stimulate an efficient market for these products in order to meet the education and training needs of the military services and the nation's workforce of the future. ADL will achieve this through the development of a common technical framework for computer and Internet-based learning that will foster the creation of reusable learning content as "instructional objects." The ADL initiative is evolving the development and implementation of specifications and guidelines, such as the Sharable Content Object Reference Model (SCORM). SCORM defines the interrelationship of course components, data models, and protocols so that learning content objects are sharable across systems that conform to the same model. SCORM contains a collection of specifications adapted from various worldwide advanced distributed learning specifications that were developed by numerous consortia to provide a comprehensive suite of online learning capabilities enabling interoperability, accessibility, and reusability of Web-based learning content (ADL Co-lab, 2003).

FUTURE TRAINING TECHNOLOGIES

The future holds great promise in terms of the design, development, and implementation of digital technologies for education and training applications. Several of these advanced training technologies are described below.

Integrated Immersive Technologies

Integration of motion and haptic or "touch" interfaces, display and sound technologies, computer simulation and sensors, and next-level communication and information technologies are combining to provide scalable models for engaging in learning by doing (Golas, 2003). Next-level communication refers to systems that support the delivery of voice and high-speed Internet and digital video services. Data acquired automatically from students' interactions in immersive environments (that is, environments that provide the sensory experience of being in a computer-generated, simulated space) will be captured and used to optimize lesson/course progression. Simulated work experiences will be provided via shared applications from real-world 3D toolsets accessible on PCs. Assisted or augmented virtual-reality scenarios will provide an enhanced perspective of a problem and support role-playing activities.

Training applications for integrated immersive technologies include tasks where

- people can be injured or equipment damaged
- training under real-world conditions is very expensive or impossible
- students need to create 3D mental models from 2D data, such as air traffic control
- engineering and scientific course content is required, and revealing the math behind certain phenomena will facilitate learning

An example of the application of integrated immersive simulation technologies is the integrated virtual reality (VR) training program for combat casualty care developed by the Defense Advanced Research Projects Agency (DARPA). Researchers are using VR technologies for both part-task training and battlefield casualty team training. High-performance part-task training simulators allow medical personnel to rehearse a variety of procedures, including suturing, sinusoscopy, endoscopy, knee arthroscopy, catheter insertion, wound debridement, and vascular stent placement. DARPA's research in VR training provides a multisensory experience through the use of tactile sensor and virtual olfaction devices. Virtual olfaction devices allow the user to smell various odors, such as smoke or chemicals, without actually being exposed to the source of the odor. These and other technologies are just the beginning of a revolution in combat casualty care, and are providing a strong foundation for 21st century medical practices.

Wireless Computing

Wireless, optical, mobile, and wireline communications will make the delivery of interactive multimedia training available on hand-held or wearable computers with wireless Web access (Golas, 2003). Sophisticated voice recognition will become the standard method of input and output, enabling "real" conversation. During training, students will be able to communicate with devices that record their interactions, hypotheses, previous actions, and so on. Portable wireless devices will impact on-the-job training by providing guidance, feedback, and virtual responses during hands-on training activities. Miniature wireless position and orientation sensors will support high precision tracking of a student's movement in simulators. For example, if a sensor is attached to a student's hand, when the student moves his hand in the simulator to pick up a weapon, the simulation will respond with appropriate feedback that shows that the weapon is now in the student's hand.

Training applications for wireless computing include tasks where

- training must be available anywhere/anytime
- training must be integrated or embedded for immediate content delivery
- tetherless or augmented virtual reality systems are implemented (Tetherless VR systems do not attach the student to the computer system with wires or cables, unlike augmented VR systems, where the student is attached to the system by some type of hardware.)
- training must be delivered in field locations for such tasks as range instrumentation and forward observer exercises
- training is performed on-the-job on actual equipment under real-world conditions
- environmental constraints do not support the use of desktop computers.
- people are dispersed in teams, such as during first-responder and law-enforcement training

Ultra Broadband Simulation and Courseware

In the near future, ultra broadband technologies will be capable of achieving ultra-fast transmission speeds. Swift connections and prodigious data-transmitting capacity will transform Web-based training (Golas, 2003). Ultra broadband will support a network that consists of converged voice and data networks, private and public networks, and wireless and wireline networks. High-resolution video and immersive 3D shared environments will allow discussion, collaboration, and interaction among physically distant participants. Growth of the Internet will bring about the creation of massive distributed online archives of past lectures, interactive presentations, simulations, and proficiency tests. Textbooks will begin to be replaced. Information agents will manage, analyze, and display multimedia and multisource information. These agents will provide access to knowledge repositories and facilitate knowledge sharing, group authorship, and control of remote instruments. Server and client-based Intelligent Digital Assistants (IDAs) will work and act on behalf of the user as a personal assistant. During training, IDAs will act as advisors, content experts, consultants, and personal reporters.

Training applications for ultra broadband simulation and courseware include tasks where

- complex simulations, and a high degree of interactivity are required to achieve the learning objective
- performance support systems are required for complex systems
- distributed mission training must be supported
- next-generation virtual-reality games will be incorporated
- training is delivered via virtual private networks
- synchronous video conferencing is required
- novel modes of electronic commerce are required

Full motion video streaming is required. Streaming video is a sequence of moving images sent in compressed form over the Internet and displayed by the viewer upon arrival. With streaming media, a Web user does not have to wait to download a large file before seeing the video or hearing the sound. Instead, the media is sent in a continuous stream and is played as it arrives (Miller, 2003).

Distributed Intelligence

Distributed intelligent systems are computational entities, such as online robots or agents, that integrate perception, reasoning, and action to perform cooperative tasks under circumstances that might not be known in advance, and that dynamically change during task execution (Parker, 2002). The agents or robots are immersed in, and interact with, complex unpredictable environments through sensing and action. These include physical agents, such as mobile robots, as well as software agents, such as Web search engines. Significant research is being done today to design software that enables agents or robots to behave intelligently in unpredictable environments. Agent/robot design involves integrating research in many areas, including artificial intelligence, control theory, machine learning, robotics, and operations research.

Distributed intelligent systems have the potential to address many missions that are inherently distributed in space, time, and/or functionality. Specific application domains for distributed intelligent systems include

- homeland Security, surveillance, and reconnaissance
- planetary exploration
- search and rescue
- cleanup of hazardous waste
- mining and construction
- automated manufacturing
- industrial/household maintenance
- nuclear power plant decommissioning
- pipeline monitoring

Distributed training is similar to distributed intelligence in that distributed training systems support exercises delivered on networked desktop computers that emulate actual systems, where participants or "entities" are geographically dispersed while in a common synthetic environment (Golas, 2003). Distributed training provides ground force commanders greater situational awareness and distributed support, fostering faster decision making. Human-in-the-loop simulation tests will evaluate the effectiveness of visualization, speech recognition, context tracking, and dialogue management technologies within distributed training systems. The High Level Architecture (HLA) developed by the Defense Modeling and Simulation Office (DMSO) addresses the continuing need for simulation interoperability among new and existing simulations within the U.S. Department of Defense.

Training applications for distributed training include tasks where

- teams of people are trained using detailed synthetic environments and physics-based modeling to simulate real-world experiences
- virtual meetings and collaborative training environments are required
- training under real-world conditions on actual equipment is very expensive or impossible

INSTRUCTIONAL RESOURCES

Instructional resources refer to all of the ways in which instructional materials can be designed, developed, and implemented. Instructional resources include delivery methods, such as a teacher/instructor, computer, simulator, or actual system; instructional strategies, such as small group discussion, case studies, and mentoring; and instructional media, such as text and video. Existing media presentations are often selected as part of a larger instructional plan rather than being separately designed and developed (Gagné, Briggs, & Wager, 1992). Teachers, as well as teams of instructional designers, may carry out a comprehensive design of instruction that depends upon the selection and mix of various methods, strategies, and media. In today's digital world, these are often *combined* in a single course of instruction. This is referred to as blended learning.

Blended Learning

The term *blended learning* refers to a training product or program that combines several different delivery methods, such as collaboration software, online courses, electronic performance support systems, and knowledge management practices. Blended learning also describes learning that mixes various event-based activities, including face-to-face classrooms, synchronous online learning, and self-paced learning. There's no single formula that guarantees learning and in most cases a variety of learning strategies are developed in a course or learning event. For example, an instructor-led course can be integrated with

- online course materials and syllabus (document sharing)
- online or computer-based software, courseware, or tutorials
- group activities (in person or online)
- peer tutoring, collaboration
- e-mail or voice-mail discussions
- journal writing (reflective learning)
- calendar of events, course announcements, and bulletin boards
- chat-room discussions, threaded discussions, or guided discussions
- video teleconferencing, audio conferencing
- Web searches (critical evaluation)
- exploration activities or discovery learning
- online graphics, video, and voice clips
- online interactive quizzes and other assessments

The optimum choice and mix of these methods is based on the target audience, the content to be learned, and the availability of technologies. Sometimes students take one or more online learning lessons and only then meet, online or in person, for instructor-led learning. Sometimes synchronous training occurs at regular intervals, such as once a week in a video conference, and the rest of the time students work at their own pace from a combination of hard copy, digital media (such as a CD-ROM), or online materials.

Blended learning environments combine the elements of traditional classroom-based instruction with the tools of online distance delivery. This combination produces several benefits. For example, tools can be provided to facilitate communication outside of scheduled class time and office hours, which enhances student-student and faculty-student communication. Different learning styles and methods can be supported. For example, students will have time to reflect when they are participating in online discussions, and they can participate at a time and place that meets their needs. Online materials are available 24 hours a day, seven days a week, ensuring that students always have access to assignments and other handouts. Online testing can be used for student pretests and practice, and online discussion between class sessions can identify areas of student difficulty that need to be addressed in class. Course management and administration is simplified with an online grade book and tools for e-mail management. Historically, the military has made outstanding use of the blended learning approach. In the military, blended learning combines classroom-based learning, online learning, on-the-job training and periodic skills assessment.What is missing in the blended learning approach is the ability to capture knowledge over a period of time and then make it available in a just in time fashion (Battersby, 2002).

From Stanford University and the University of Tennessee, there are early reports of the effectiveness of blended learning. Stanford University increased student retention in their e-learning program by adding live events to motivate learners to complete self-study materials on time. The University of Tennessee uses a blended approach in their Physicians's Executive MBA program, showing a 50 percent savings in time and a 10 percent improvement in learning outcomes over traditional classroom learning (Singh, 2003).

INSTRUCTIONAL STRATEGIES, MEDIA, AND DELIVERY METHODS

Instruction is provided in a *learning situation*. The features of this situation impose constraints upon the instructional strategies, instructional media, and instructional delivery methods that will be the most effective.

Instructional Strategies

Instructional strategies are tools or techniques available to educators and instructional designers for designing and facilitating learning. There are many ways to teach or design an effective course or curriculum. Effective instruction depends on appropriately designed learning experiences that are facilitated by knowledgeable teachers or instructors, or by some other means of delivery, such as a computer. Because people have different learning styles or a combination of learning styles, instructional designers and teachers often design activities that address these different modes of learning in order to provide the best learning environment for each student.

In course design this is accomplished by utilizing multiple instructional strategies. Instructional designers and teachers should choose instructional strategies that are most effective for accomplishing a particular learning objective. Because of advances in interactive and multimedia technologies and PC-based hardware, many instructional strategies commonly implemented in traditional classroom settings can be successfully adapted to online learning and other more advanced instructional delivery methods. For example, large and small group discussion can now be accomplished via the Internet through synchronous and asynchronous delivery methods. With synchronous delivery, the teacher and the student interact with each other in "real time." Two-way video teleconferences and Internet chat rooms are examples of synchronous delivery methods. With asynchronous delivery, the interaction between a student and an instructor or other students does not take place simultaneously. For example, the teacher may deliver instruction via the Web, and the student's feedback, responses, or questions may be sent via e-mail messages at a later time.

Field and lab exercises that once could only be accomplished using actual equipment in an actual setting can now be accomplished through distributed mission training with simulators connected via wide area networks. Distributed mission training is a shared training environment that includes *live, virtual,* and *constructive* simulations that allow warfighters to train individually or collectively at all levels of war (George, Brooks, Breitbach, Steffes, & Bell, 2003). *Live* simulation involves real people operating real systems under realistic operational conditions. *Virtual* simulation involves real people operating or using simulated systems. *Constructive* simulation involves simulated people operating or using simulated systems. With distributed mission training, the combination of live, virtual, and constructive environments provides on-demand, realistic training opportunities for warfighters by overcoming many current constraints that limit training effectiveness (George et al., 2003).

Demonstrations that once were only possible in real life can now be modeled and delivered via virtual reality systems. Table 11.1 presents various instructional strategies and the instructional media and delivery methods that are the most effective choices for implementing those strategies.

TABLE 11.1   STRATEGIES, MEDIA, AND DELIVERY METHODS FOR EVENTS OF INSTRUCTION/LEARNED CAPABILITIES

Instructional Delivery Strategies:

Events of Instruction and Learned Capabilities*:	Instructional Delivery Methods:	Panel/Focus Group/Forum	Large/Small Group Discussion	Collaborative Learning	Self-directed/Discovery Learning	Mentoring	Peer Instruction	Demonstration	Lecture/Tutorial	Simulation	Practice	Typical Instructional Media:
4,6,8 I,M	Actual System Hardware			x**				x			x	Not applicable
4,6,7,8,9 I,M	Full Fidelity Simulator			x**				x		x	x	3D animation
4,6,7,9 I,M	Virtual Reality			x**				x		x	x	3D animation
4,6,7,8,9 I,M	Distributed Mission Training			x				x		x	x	2D/3D graphics/animation
5,7,8,9 I,M	Display/Debriefing Systems		x					x	x			2D/3D graphics/animation
4,6 I,M,V	Part-Task Training Device							x			x	Multimedia
4,5,6 I,M	Embedded Training				x				x	x	x	Multimedia
4,6 I,M	System Emulation							x		x	x	Not applicable
3,4,5,6,7,8 I,C	Intelligent Tutoring System/Cognitive Tools				x					x	x	Multimedia
4,6,7 I	Performance Support System				x						x	Multimedia
4,6,7,9 I,M,V	Simulator (Desktop/PC)			x**	x			x		x	x	Multimedia
4,6, I,V	Handheld Computer/PDA			x**	x			x			x	Text
1,2,3,4,5,6,7,8,9 I,V,C,A	Computer Based Training (CBT) (online)	x	x	x	x	x	x	x	x	x	x	Multimedia
1,2,3,4,5,6,7,8,9 I,V,C,A	CBT CBT (stand-alone)				x			x	x	x	x	Multimedia
1,2,3,4,5,6,7,8,9 I,V,C,A,M	Structured On-The-Job Training	x	x			x	x	x			x	Audio/text
4,5 I,V,A	Video Teleconference						x					Audio/video/text
1,2,3,4,5,6,7,8,9 I,V,A	Classroom/Teacher					x	x					Audio/multimedia

*Note: **Events of instruction:** 1. Gain attention. 2. Inform learner of objective. 3. Stimulate recall. 4. Present stimulus materials. 5. Provide learning guidance. 6. Elicit performance. 7. Provide feedback. 8. Assess performance. 9. Enhance retention and transfer. **Learned capabilities:** I=Intellectual Skills; V=Verbal Information; C=Cognitive Strategies; A=Attitudes; M=Motor Skills.

**Note: Can be connected via wide area or local area networks for collaborative learning.

Instructional Media

The term *instructional media* refers to the variety of ways instruction can be communicated, such as audio, video and film, text, photographs, animation, and graphics. The term *multimedia* refers to a combination of these media. Depending on the medium selected, instructional strategies can be adapted in order to optimize effectiveness. Multimedia content greatly improves learning for visual learners, and studies have shown that the use of multimedia in training programs can improve retention by as much as 50 percent (Hall, 1995). Multimedia materials have the added advantage of appeal to different learning modalities. PCs today are capable of displaying each form of media listed above and in Table 11.1.

Attributes of Different Media   Individual media have attributes that determine their capability for handling specific instructional strategies. Certain media are better than others in representing objects, facts, ideas, and processes; modeling behavior or human activities; showing spatial relationships; or developing motor skills. *Text* is particularly good for conveying large amounts of information and providing a means for easy review. *Text* is appropriate for learners with good reading skills and the ability to compare and handle abstract representations, abstract ideas, and develop arguments. *Graphics* support and enhance text or audio and provide more concrete representations. *Audio* narration in short segments can enhance learning, as can the presentation of other varieties of sound, such as environmental noises and music. *Video, film,* and *animation* are particularly good media for teaching procedural and interpersonal skills and for conveying concrete examples. They are also useful when presenting complex, real-life situations that require interpretation, or where illustrating ambiguities would support the learning objective. When the dynamic features of objects are a part of the essential content to be displayed, *video, film,* and *animation* are essential, for example, the movement of storm clouds and the internal operations of a gasoline engine. These media are particularly helpful when one wants to display the actions of a human being realistically to model appropriate and inappropriate behavior.

Instructional Delivery Methods

Instructional delivery methods are the actual mechanisms for delivering instruction. Table 11.1 lists types of delivery methods and the associated media, instructional strategies, events of instruction, and learned capabilities they *best* support. Most media selection models indicate that there is no one medium that is universally superior to all others for all types of desired outcomes and for all learners. For most situations, several strategies and methods can be combined to achieve effective learning. This conclusion is also supported by research on media utilization (Aronson, 1977; Briggs, 1968; Briggs & Wager, 1981; Clark & Salomon, 1986).

When selecting instructional delivery methods, initial consideration should be given to learned capabilities and the type of performance expected of learners as a result of instruction (the *learning outcome*) in order to avoid critical errors in the selection process. For example, text should not be developed for learners who are nonreaders. An audio recording should not be the sole medium for teaching intel-

TABLE 11.2 **IMPLICATIONS FOR INSTRUCTIONAL DELIVERY METHODS EXCLUSION AND SELECTION**

Learning Outcome	Exclude	Select
Intellectual Skills	• Delivery strategies that have no interactive features • Printed materials for nonreaders	• Methods that can provide feedback to learner responses • Audio and visual features for nonreaders
Cognitive Strategies	Same as intellectual skills	Same as intellectual skills
Verbal Information	• Actual equipment or simulators verbal accompaniments • Complex prose for nonreaders	• Methods able to present verbal with no messages and elaborations • Audio and pictorial features for nonreaders
Attitudes	Same as verbal information	Media that can model human behavior
Motor Skills	Methods that cannot allow direct practice under realistic conditions and provide for learner response and feedback	Methods that allow direct practice of skill with informative feedback

lectual skills. A lecture is not the appropriate method for training motor skills. The basic decisions based upon the type of learning situation lead to selecting strategies and methods that are capable of supporting instruction *most effectively*. When verbal information is the learning outcome, such as knowledge about the prevention of diseases, the instructional delivery method must be capable of presenting the material either in print or by narration. Attitudes are best presented by media that can display a human model, such as video and animation. Table 11.2 provides implications for delivery method exclusion and selection for each learning outcome. Perhaps the most obvious media differences arise over interactive quality. When intellectual skills are being learned, precise feedback about correct and incorrect performance is significant to learning. When concrete concepts or rules involving spatial arrangements or spatio-temporal sequences are being learned, pictures, as opposed to verbal descriptions, are essential.

Selecting Instructional Strategies, Media, and Delivery Methods

When selecting instructional strategies, media, and delivery methods instructional designers need to consider a variety of factors. Moore and Kearsley (1996) identified the following four major steps that most media selection models include: (1) identification of the media attributes required by the instructional strategies and learning activities; (2) identification of learner characteristics and the ability of particular media to support learner needs; (3) identification of learning environment characteristics that favor or preclude particular media; (4) identification of economic and organizational factors that affect the feasibility of using or supporting particular media. Media and delivery methods also need to be evaluated based on their capacity to motivate students, help students recall prior learning, provide new learning stimuli, activate the student's responses, providing timely feedback, and encourage or support practice (Moore & Kearsley, 1996).

There are many different logistical, psychological, sociological, and economic factors to consider when selecting media. Most of the time, an exclusionary process is used. In other words, use what is most immediately available and costs the least, if it will do the job. However, new ways of thinking about learning and how best to facilitate it will require new ways of thinking about media utilization. It is probably true that commercial media, such as television, offering lecture-type courses will not be a big player in public education. Distance online courses involving learning communities and mentored by knowledgeable teachers, seem more likely. However, every new technology has learning affordances, as we defined them, but also constraints. Those constraints may be cultural as much as economic, and any one fault may be a reason for to rule it out.

COGNITIVE TOOLS FOR LEARNING

Definition of Cognitive Tools

Cognitive tools are generalizable computer tools, or tools that can be used in a variety of settings and domains, that are intended to engage and facilitate cognitive processing (Kommers, Jonassen, & Mayes, 1992). They are both mental and computational devices that support, guide, and extend the thinking processes of their users (Derry, 1990), and they are knowledge construction and facilitation tools that can be applied to a variety of subject-matter domains. Jonassen (2002) argues that students cannot use these tools without thinking deeply about the content that they are learning, and if they choose to use these tools to help them learn, the tools will facilitate the learning process.

Computer technologies as cognitive tools represent a significant expansion to traditional conceptions of technologies (Steketee, 2002). In cognitive tools, information and intelligence is not encoded in the educational communications that are designed to efficiently transmit that knowledge to the learners. Jonassen (2002) suggests taking the tools away from instructional designers who use them to constrain the learners' learning processes through prescribed communications and interactions, and giving them to learners as tools for knowledge construction, rather than as media for conveying knowledge. Learners would use them as media for representing and expressing what they know and would begin to function as designers themselves, using the technology as tools for analyzing the world, accessing information, interpreting and organizing their personal knowledge, and representing what they know to others. The process of building knowledge bases using these tools, a process that Papert (Jonassen, 2002) referred to as *constructionism,* will engage the learners more and result in more meaningful and transferable knowledge in the learners.

With cognitive tools, students are encouraged to construct their own meaning of knowledge, rather than absorb ideas preconceived by others (Jonassen & Reeves, 1996). Salomon, Perkins, and Globerson (1991) make the distinction between working with computers to construct or facilitate learning, as opposed to working with computers to simply *receive* training. When computer technology is used as a teaching tool (which students learn *from*), rather than as a cognitive tool (which students learn *with*), a certain amount of intelligence on the part of the computer is implied (Steketee, 2002). In theory, computerized tutoring applications are intelligent enough to replace human teachers' diagnoses of the cognitive abilities and needs of their students (Reusser, 1993). Not only do these applications provide ready-made knowledge, they also decide how much of that knowledge students should learn and the pace at which they should learn it. This level of intelligence can be detrimental to learning if computer applications encourage students to abdicate their responsibility in the learning process and become passive recipients rather than active constructors of knowledge (Lajoie & Derry, 1993). In contrast, cognitive tools promote reflection (Norman, 1983), critical thinking (Jonassen & Reeves, 1996), and student-regulated knowledge construction (Jonassen & Rohrer-Murphy, 1999). Provided they are deployed within appropriate classroom environments, they facilitate cognitive and metacognitive thinking (Lajoie, 1993) and ultimately rely on students to determine the pace and direction of their learning.

Examples of Cognitive Tools

Cognitive tools and learning environments that have been adapted or developed to function as intellectual partners with the learner in order to engage and facilitate critical thinking and higher-order learning include, but are not necessarily limited to, databases, spreadsheets, semantic networks (knowledge representation schemes involving nodes and links between nodes where the nodes represent objects or concepts and the links represent the relationship between them), expert systems (systems that facilitate problem solving in a given *field* or application by drawing inference from a knowledge base developed from human expertise), multimedia courseware, computer conferencing, and to a lesser degree, computer programming and context-dependent tools. When students build knowledge bases with databases, expert systems, or semantic networking tools, they must analyze subject domains, develop mental models to represent them, and represent what they understand in terms of those models (Steketee, 2002).

Designing Cognitive Tools

Reusser (1993) contends that the design of effective cognitive tools should be based on current research in cognitive psychology. More specifically, they should acknowledge that knowledge is actively constructed by students, and that this knowledge is typically produced, shared, and transformed within groups of students working together to solve problems. Therefore, to be characterized as effective, cognitive tools must support the cognitive and social aspects of learning.

In addition to this, Lepper, Woolverton, Mumme, and Gurtner (1993) argue that the affective side of cognitive tools is also critical to successful learning, yet this issue remains largely unaddressed in the literature. The assumption is that if the cognitive and social issues are addressed, then high levels of motivation will naturally ensue. However, Keller (1979, 1983) and Perkins (1993) warn against making this assumption and argue that the cognitive tool and the learning environment must openly attend to the motivational state of the student by (a) providing appropriate levels of challenge, (b) enabling the student to maintain a sense of control, and (c) eliciting from the student a high level of curiosity.

Furthermore, Jonassen (1996) contends that cognitive tools should possess certain administrative features, such as automatic student registering and automatic scoring for quizzes or tests, in order to reduce the time teachers or students spend on these administrative functions, although these more practical aspects are not necessarily critical to effective learning. He also urges that cognitive tools should be affordable and available so they can be accessed by a large population of students.

The visual component is a vital characteristic of any cognitive tool. Through the manipulation of graphic interfaces, cognitive tools enable students to generate conceptual networks, diagrams, hierarchical structures, graphs, tables, symbol systems and more (Steketee, 2002). Not only do these visuals provide concrete representations of thought against which meaning can be indexed and explained, they also facilitate the intentional construction and externalization of mental models. Because mental models are typically constructed incidentally, that is, unsystematically and in an unstructured manner, they are generally not readily available for reflection nor are they easily manipulated (Wild, 1996). However, building mental models with cognitive tools is an intentional pursuit that requires active mental participation from students. As such, the understandings these computer-mediated mental models represent are more accessible, flexible, and, above all, useful (Steketee, 2002).

SUMMARY

Information and communication technologies are transforming organizations and redefining the knowledge and skills required by society to succeed in the 21st century. Digital literacy (Gilster, 1997) is essential to employment success, civic participation, and education, and training and digital technologies are revolutionizing how we work, live, play, and learn. The notion of *learning* with technology implies the development of an intellectual partnership where the student and computer work together to achieve learning outcomes; the *effects* of technology refers to the knowledge or skills acquired by the student as a result of learning from the computer (Steketee, 2002). Technological advances in modeling and simulation; display and sound devices; wireless, optical, mobile, and wireline communications; ultra broadband; virtual reality; and the Internet are fundamentally transforming how, what, when, and where people learn. Critical and creative thinking, informed decision making, and real-world problem solving are examples of higher-order skills that students must develop in the digital age. Being computer savvy and digitally connected is becoming critical to our nation's educational, economical, governmental, and societal advancement. Training technologies must possess cognitive, social, economic, and affective features if they are to contribute to quality learning outcomes.

There are many different logistical, psychological, sociological, and economic factors to consider when selecting media. Most of the time, instructional designers are driven to use media that are immediately available and the most cost-effective. However, new ways of thinking about facilitating learning requires new ways of thinking about media utilization. While commercial media, like television, will not be big players in public education, distance-learning courses via the Internet most likely will be. It is important to remember that every new technology has learning affordances, but also constraints. The constraints may be cultural or economic, and any one fault may be a reason for not adopting a particular medium.

This chapter looked at how technologies, and in particular the Internet, are affecting training processes, products, and learning outcomes in our schools, in industry, in the federal government, and in the military. The types of resources and technologies available to educators and trainers today were reviewed, as were several emerging technologies. Challenges associated with the use of technologies were discussed in relationship to the events of instruction and learning outcomes. Guidelines related to the selection of instructional media and delivery methods and how media and methods can be used to support various instructional strategies were provided. The chapter concluded with the definition, examples, and guidelines for designing cognitive tools for learning.

REFERENCES

ADL Co-lab (2003). Retrieved summer of 2003 from: http://www.adlnet.org.

Aronson, D. (1977). *Formulation and trial use of guidelines for designing and developing instructional motion pictures.* Unpublished dissertation, Florida State University.

Barry, M., & Runyan, G. B. (1995). A review of distance-learning studies in the U.S. Military. *American Journal of Distance Education,* 9 (3), 37–47.

Battersby, A. (2002). *Tying elearning together.* Retrieved summer 2003 from: http://www.mt2-kmi.com.

Briggs, L. J. (1968) Learner variables and educational media. *Review of Educational Research,* 38, 160–176.

Briggs, L. J., & Wager, W. W. (1981). *Handbook of procedures for the design of instruction* (2nd ed.). Englewood Cliffs, NJ: Educational Technology Publications.

Carroll, J. (1963). A model of school learning. *Teachers College Record,* 64, 723–733.

Clark, R. E., & Salomon, G. (1986). Media in teaching. In M. C. Wittrock (Ed.), *Handbook of research on teaching* (3rd ed.). New York: Macmillan.

Committee on Information Technology Literacy (1999). Retrieved summer 2003 from: http://www.cni.org/tfms/1999a.spring/handout/HLin-ppt.

CyberAtlas (2002). Retrieved summer 2003 from: http://www.nua.ie/surveys.

Derry, S. D. (1990). Learning strategies for acquiring useful knowledge. In B. F. Jones, & L. Idol (Eds.), *Dimensions of thinking and cognitive instruction*. Hillsdale, NJ: Lawrence Erlbaum.

eMarketer (2002). Retrieved summer 2003 from: http://www.nua.ie/surveys.

Fulcrum Analytics (2002). Retrieved summer 2003 from: http://www.nua.ie/surveys.

Gagné, R. M., Briggs, L. J., & Wager, W. W. (1992). *Principles of instructional design* (4th ed.). New York: Harcourt Brace.

George, G. R., Brooks, R. B., Breitbach, R. A., Steffes, R., & Bell, H. H. (2003) Air Force C2 training solutions in distributed mission training environments, a report from the synthetic battlefield. Retrieved January 2004 from: http://www.link.com/pdfs/itsec3.pdf.

Gilster, P. (1997). *Digital literacy*. New York: John Wiley & Sons.

Golas, K. C. (2003). Final report. *Southwest Research Institute planning document for training, simulation and performance Improvement technologies*.

Golas, K. C. (2003). Training, simulation & performance improvement division three and five year planning document. *Southwest Research Institute annual planning document*. San Antonio, TX.

Golas, K. C. (2000). Guidelines for designing online learning. *Proceedings of the Interservice Industry Training and Education Systems Conference*. Orlando, FL.

Hall, B. (1995). Return-on-investment and multimedia training: A research study. *Multimedia Training Newsletter*. Sunnyvale, CA.

Hasson, J. (2201). Retrieved January 2004 from: http://www.fcw.com/fcw/articles/2001/0625/cov-vabx-06-25-01.asp.

Howard, F. S. (1997). *Distance learning annotated bibliography*. Department of the Army technical report (TRAC-WSMR-TR-97-015). White Sands, NM: White Sands Missile Range.

Interactive Educational Systems Design (2003). Retrieved summer 2003 from: http://www.nua.ie/surveys.

International Data Corporation (2002). Retrieved summer 2003 from: http://www.nua.ie/surveys.

Jonassen, D. H. (1996). *Computers in the classroom: Mindtools for critical thinking*. Englewood Cliffs, NJ: Prentice Hall.

Jonassen, D. H. (2002). Learning as activity. *Educational Technology, 42*(2), 45–51.

Jonassen, D. H., & Reeves, T. C. (1996). Learning with technology: Using computers as cognitive tools. In D.H. Jonassen, (Ed.), *Handbook of research on educational communications and technology*. New York: Scholastic Press.

Jonassen, D. H., & Rohrer-Murphy, L. (1999). Activity theory as a framework for designing constructivist learning environments. *Educational Technology Research and Development, 47*(1), 61–79.

Keller, J. M. (1979). Motivation and instructional design: A theoretical perspective. *Journal of Instructional Development, 2*(4), 26–34.

Keller, J. M. (1983). Motivational design of instruction. In C. M. Reigeluth (Ed.), *Instructional theories and models: An overview of their current status* (pp. 383–434). Hillsdale, NJ: Erlbaum.

Kommers, P., Jonassen, D., & Mayes, T. (1992). *Cognitive tools for learning*. Berlin: Springer.

Lajoie, S. P. (1993). Computer environments as cognitive tools for enhancing learning. In S. Lajoie and S. Derry (Eds.), *Computers as cognitive tools,* Hillsdale, NJ: Erlbaum.

Lajoie, S. P. and Derry, S. J. (Eds.) (1993). *Computers as cognitive tools,* Hillsdale, NJ: Erlbaum.

Lepper, M. R., Woolverton, M., Mumme, D. L., and Gurtner, J. L. (1993). Motivational techniques of expert human tutors: Lessons for the design of computer-based tutors. In S. P. Lajoie and S. J. Derry (Eds.), *Computers as cognitive tools.* Hillsdale, NJ: Erlbaum.

Linn, M. C. (1996) Cognition and distance learning. *Journal of the American Society for Information Science, 47*(11), 827–842.

Lumsdaine, A. A. (1960). Teaching machines: An introductory overview. In A. A. Lumsdaine & R. Glaser (Eds.), *Teaching machines and programmed learning: A source book.* Washington, DC: National Education Association of the United States.

Mehlman, B. P. (2003). Technology administration ICT literacy: Preparing the digital generation for the age of innovation. Remarks delivered at the ICT Literacy Summit, Washington, DC.

Moore, M. G. & Kearsley, G. (1996). *Distance education: A systems view.* Belmont, CA: Wadsworth.

National Center for Educational Statistics (2002). Retrieved summer 2003 from: http://nces.ed.gov.

NetDay (2003). Retrieved summer 2003 from: http://www.nua.ie/surveys.

Norman, D. A. (1983). Some observations on mental models. In A. L. Stevens and D. Gentner (Eds.), *Mental models.* Hillsdale, NJ: Erlbaum.

Norman, D. A. (1988). *The psychology of everyday things.* New York: Basic Books.

Parker, L. E. (2002). Distributed algorithms for multi-robot observation of multiple moving targets. *Autonomous Robots, 12*(3), 231–255.

Perkins, D. N. (1993). Person-plus: A distributed view of thinking and learning. In G. Salomon (Ed.), *Distributed cognitions: Psychological and educational considerations* (pp. 88–110). Cambridge, MA: Cambridge University Press.

Resnick, M. (2002). Rethinking learning in the digital age. In G. Kirkman (Ed.), *The global information technology report: Readiness for the networked world.* London: Oxford University Press.

Reusser, K. (1993). Tutoring systems and pedagogical theory: Representational tools for understanding, planning and reflection in problem solving. In S. P. Lajoie & S. J. Derry (Eds.), *Computers as cognitive tools* (pp. 143–177). Hillsdale, NJ: Erlbaum.

Riel , M., & Polin, L. (2002). Communities as places of learning. In S. A. Barab, R. Kling, & J. Gray (in press) (Eds.), *Designing for virtual communities in the service of learning.* Cambridge, MA: Cambridge University Press.

Salomon, G., Perkins, D. N., & Globerson, T. (1991). Partners in cognition: Extending human intelligence with intelligent technologies. *Educational Researcher, 20*(3), 2–9.

Singh, H. (2003). Building effective blended learning programs. *Educational Technology, 43*(6), 51–54.

Steketee, C. (2002). Computers as Cognitive Tools. Retrieved summer 2003 from: http://members.iteachnet.org/pipermail/iteachnet-daily/2002-October/000050.html.

Trotter, A. (1999). Preparing teachers for the digital age. *Editorial Projects in Education, 19,* 37.

Warnick, W. L., Jordan, S. M., & Allen, V. S. (1999). *Advancing the virtual government: A survey of national digital library initiatives in the executive branch.* Washington, DC: DOE Office of Scientific and Technical Information.

Wild, M. (1996). Mental models and computer modeling. *Journal of Computer Assisted Learning, 12*(1), 10–21.

Wisher, R. A. (1999). Training through distance learning: An assessment of research findings. *Technical Report 1095.* Washington, DC: U.S. Army Research Institute.

DESIGNING THE INDIVIDUAL LESSON

The ultimate goal of instructional design is to produce effective instruction. When this goal is accomplished, it generally results in a lesson or set of lessons that make up a *module* that can be delivered by a teacher or trainer using instructional materials, such as visual presentations and worksheets, or through self-paced, self-instructional materials, such as an online course. A lesson or module is planned so that it can be completed in a single sitting, and courses of study consist of many lessons. In Chapter 9 , we described the process of defining and sequencing lesson objectives, and in Chapter 10 we discussed how the events of instruction facilitate information processing. In this chapter we discuss the selection and sequencing of events of instruction that facilitate learning, and the content of those events in lessons for different types of learning outcomes. Examples of lessons for different types of learning outcomes are presented and conditions of learning discussed. The chapter concludes with a discussion of how planning a lesson for multiple objectives can be accomplished using the events of instruction to guide the development of learning activities that serve many objectives.

In designing a lesson, the events of instruction are a template for including activities that support learning. The content of the events depends upon the type of learning outcomes being taught. A description of what will be done to support the event we call a prescription or instructional treatment.

LESSON PLANNING AND MODULE DESIGN

Frequently, teachers and trainers select rather than develop instructional materials. Also, in practice, they often "design as they teach"—that is, they design lessons at a high level in advance of teaching, or they prepare lesson plans outlining the lesson content, but they do not design all of the lessons in detail before beginning instruction. Because of practical circumstances, teachers and trainers (who are often subject-matter experts) usually plan lessons in only enough detail to be "ready" to deliver the instruction, because they can improvise some of the details as the lesson progresses. This is not entirely undesirable because it gives the teacher or trainer the flexibility to redesign "on the spot"—that is, to adjust procedures to the instructional situation and to responses of the learners (Briggs, Gustafson, & Tillman, 1991).

As will be discussed in Chapter 14, large groups allow less precision in instruction than what is possible in small groups. The unpredictability of student responses in a large group, coupled with restricted planning time, means that instruction is often planned and carried out with only a moderate degree of control over the conditions of learning. Small group or individualized instruction allows more control or adapting of the instruction to meet student needs. The ability to adapt instruction to an individual's entry-level skills and knowledge is provided by instruction that permits self-pacing and self-correction for each learner. These functions are possible in intelligent tutoring systems and with any materials that allow "branching" by the student to the most needed and helpful exercises contained in the instructional material. Such branching occurs in most computer-based training courses, or by the frequent use of self-tests that allow the learner to use the instruction in an adaptive manner.

Individualized, Self-Paced, and Adaptive Instructional Materials

The terms *individualized, self-paced,* and *adaptive instructional materials* are often used synonymously, although there are shades of differences in their meanings. We define *individualized instruction* as that which takes into consideration the particular needs of students. Such instruction begins with an analysis of the entry skills of the learner, and subsequent instruction is based precisely on that individual's needs. *Self-paced instruction* implies the learner is managing the learning process and is spending as much time as necessary to achieve the objectives. Self-paced instruction is generally associated with the procedures of mastery learning, in which achievement rather than time dictates the rate of the student's progress through the instruction. The term *adaptive instruction* refers to online learning-management systems that constantly monitor the progress of the student and change the instructional content based on that progress. Adaptive instruction involves complex record keeping and decision making and is facilitated by the use of computers. However, its procedures can be carried out manually for individuals or small groups. These types of instruction usually depend on the use of electronic instructional delivery methods, because all students in a class may be at different stages of learning at any particular point in time.

In summary, the object of instructional design is to produce a lesson or series of lessons that consider the delivery system being used as well as the needs of the learners. The nature of the lesson will depend on how it is to be used. In a teacher/trainer-based system, the lesson plan may be somewhat incomplete because the teacher can fill in the gaps. In contrast, individualized or self-paced instruction is more carefully planned and developed because there is often no immediate teacher or trainer available. The remainder of this chapter focuses on how the principles of instructional design described in previous chapters can be applied to the development of either a teacher/trainer-led or a self-paced, self-instructional lesson. Both forms of instructional delivery emphasize the following central themes:

1. Classifying objectives by using taxonomy of learning outcomes
2. Sequencing objectives to take prerequisites into account
3. Including the appropriate events of instruction that apply to all domains of outcomes
4. Incorporating the particular conditions of learning relevant to the domains of the objectives in the lesson

We now turn to further discussion of the sequencing of instruction and then to instructional events and conditions of learning. The chapter concludes with a discussion of the steps in lesson planning and an example of a lesson plan that incorporates the model commonly used by teachers who design and conduct instruction.

ESTABLISHING A SEQUENCE OF OBJECTIVES

In Chapter 9, we described top-down analysis of intellectual skills and considered the functional relationships among different domains of learning. We indicated a way of diagramming these relationships through the use of instructional curriculum maps (ICMs) and showed how ICMs can be used to identify different levels of curricula. Within each ICM is an implied sequence of instruction, and that sequence is based on principles underlying hierarchical prerequisite relationships and facilitative learning sequences. For example, Figure 12–1 shows a learning hierarchy ICM composed of objectives from only the intellectual skills domain.

Planning a Sequence for Intellectual Skill Objectives

The subordinate skills required to attain an intellectual skill objective can be derived as a learning hierarchy. For example, to establish the skill of subtracting whole numbers of any size, the learning hierarchy shows 10 essential prerequisites, as indicated in the boxes in Figure 12–1.

Assume that box I, simple subtraction facts, represents learning already accomplished by the students. The teacher needs to design a lesson or sequence of lessons to enable the learners to subtract whole numbers. Although several sequences of teaching the skills shown in boxes II through X might be successful, the implication of the hierarchy is that the bottom row of boxes should be taught first, then the next higher row, and so on. A sequence going in numerical order from box II to box X is likely to be the most effective sequence.

In summary, if you want to adopt a single sequence for all learners in a group, hierarchies should be arranged to allow options in a sequence of boxes within a horizontal row, but not in the sequence that goes vertically from the bottom up. This isn't to say that a student couldn't learn the task by a sequence that violates this rule of thumb. If a student does learn by a nonhierarchical sequence, it might

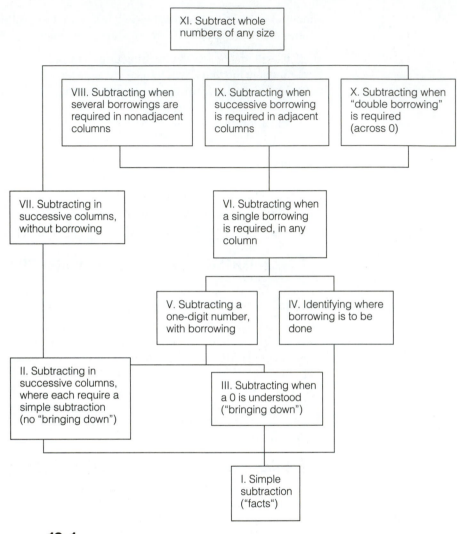

FIGURE **12–1**
A LEARNING HIERARCHY FOR SUBTRACTING WHOLE NUMBERS

be because they could already perform some of the skills or because they possessed sufficient cognitive strategies to discover some of the rules without receiving direct instruction in their application.

Determining a Starting Point   Continuing with the example of learning to subtract whole numbers, it is possible that some students may have learned some of the prerequisite skills. One student may already be able to perform the skills in boxes II and III; another may be able to perform II and V. Obviously, the designer needs to begin the instruction "where each student is." This is conveniently done in individualized instructional programs as described in Chapter 15, but it can also be done with a group by arranging other activities for the students who do not need some of the instruction planned for the group. An alternative is for students to sit through some of the instruction as a review, although this may not always be the best solution. A review of earlier skills may be needed at the beginning of each lesson to be sure there is ready recall when the new learning is undertaken. Generally speaking, intellectual skills that are learned are recalled well, as compared with the recall of facts or labels.

Achievement of Skills in Sequence   In planning the lessons to attain the final skill objective, XI, each student should display mastery of prerequisite skills before being asked to learn the next higher skill. For example, before tackling skill X, requiring double borrowing across a column containing a zero, you need to know that the learner can accomplish skills VI and VII, which require subtracting in successive columns without borrowing and borrowing in single and multiple columns.

The notion of mastery is of utmost importance when dealing with intellectual skills. The lessons must be designed so that each prerequisite skill can be performed with perfect confidence by the learner before attempting to learn more complex skills in the hierarchy. Any lesser degree of learning of prerequisites will result in puzzlement, delay, inefficient trial and error at best, and in failure, frustration, or termination of effort toward further learning at the worst. For this reason, allowing the student to choose the sequencing is not likely to be the most efficient procedure.

Provisions for Diagnosis and Relearning   Lesson planning that utilizes the hierarchy of intellectual skills may also help the trainer diagnose learning difficulties. If a student has a problem learning a given skill, the most likely reason is that they could not perform one or more prerequisite skills. Diagnostic information can be determined by requiring the student to recall the prerequisite skill. If they can't recall one or more of the skills, they will need to relearn them before proceeding to the next skill. The assessment of mastery for any given skill, occurring as a part of a lesson for that skill, may be followed by further assessment of prerequisite skills to ensure mastery is achieved. Designers can provide a "relearning loop" in the sequence of lessons, where the student has an opportunity to relearn and to display mastery of the necessary prerequisites before proceeding.

Sequence in Relation to Cognitive Strategies

It is difficult to know when cognitive strategies have been learned because often one cannot specify a particular sequence of prior learning leading up to the attainment of a cognitive strategy. Remember, students already possess some kind of cognitive strategy at the time instruction begins. Think of these strategies as automated rules for processing new information. When teaching a new cognitive strategy, students are actually being introduced to a new way of processing information. This means that they will have to learn to modify their existing strategy or simply forget it and adopt a new strategy.

The prerequisite skills essential for learning cognitive strategies are often simple skills established by prior learning. Examples are associating unrelated names by using them in a sentence, and breaking a complex problem into parts. Strategies such as these can easily be communicated to the learner through verbal statements. In addition, a sequence of instruction designed to improve cognitive strategies usually takes the form of repeated opportunities for the application of the strategies. Such opportunities can be interspersed with instruction and typically recur over relatively long periods of time. In this way, it is expected that gradual improvement in the application of the new strategy will be possible. In the case of metacognitive strategies (see Chapter 4), it does not seem likely that observable improvement will occur within a single lesson or two.

When cognitive strategies become the target of instruction, they often take the form of a sequence of steps or activities to be performed by the learner in order to help the learner process information in a new way. An example of such a procedure is the SQ3R (Survey, Question, Read, Recite, Review) technique for reading text materials (Robinson, 1970). The list of steps, and the explanation of the activity in each step, serve as an executive subroutine, much the same way a sequence of steps in a motor skill does. The instructional activity is to have the student practice the application of the executive subroutine. As the student applies the procedure over a period of time, performance will become more automatic and fluid. How do you know when the student has adopted the procedure as a cognitive strategy? One indicator is a self-report; another is direct observation of the manipulation of text as the student reads it. However, the best indicator is the decrease in time and increase in accuracy the student exhibits between early applications (while learning) and later applications (after "adopting"). Adoption implies that the strategy is now a part of the student's information-processing repertoire and that it can be applied efficiently and effectively.

Planning a Sequence for Verbal Information Learning

As indicated in Chapter 5, the most important prerequisite for learning verbal information is a meaningful context within which the newly learned information can be subsumed or, in some meaningful sense, associated. The principles applicable to sequencing differ somewhat, depending on whether the objective concerns learning a set of names (labels), learning an isolated fact, or learning the sense of a logically organized passage.

Names or Labels   Learning a set of names (such as the names of a number of trees) is facilitated by the use of previously learned organized structures, which the learner has in memory. The learner can use a variety of ways to encode the newly acquired information. Encoding might take the form of a simple association, as when a new French word *le journal* is associated with the English word *journal,* which thus becomes an association for *newspaper.* Or, it might involve the use of a sentence, such as one that associates *starboard* with *right* as in "the star boarder is always right." The method of encoding often involves the use of visual images, as is the case if the learner associates an image of a crow with a person's name, *Crowe*. Mnemonic techniques involving the use of images and the key-word method are reviewed by Pressley, Levin, and Delaney (1982). The imagery employed for encoding may be quite arbitrary, such as a learner associating the shops on a well-known street with newly acquired names that have nothing to do with the shops themselves (Crovitz, 1970).

Individual Facts   The learning of individual facts, as they might occur in a chapter of history text, also involves an encoding process. In this case, the encoding is usually a matter of relating the facts to larger meaningful structures—larger organized "bodies of knowledge" that have been previously learned.

Two kinds of procedures are available for instructional sequencing when one is dealing with factual information, and both should be used. The first is prior learning (in a sequence) of what Ausubel (1968) calls *organizers*. For example, to learn facts about automobiles, an organizing passage might first be presented to the student informing him about the major distinctive categories of automobile description—body style, engine, frame, transmission, and so on. This is followed by specific facts about particular automobiles.

The second procedure, not entirely unrelated to the first, involves the use of questions or statements to identify the major categories of facts for which learning is desired (Frase, 1970; Rothkopf, 1970). For example, if the names of persons described in a historical passage is the most important information to be learned, prior experience with questions about such names in a sample passage will facilitate learning and retention. Should the objective be to state dates, dates could be addressed in a prior passage.

Organized Information   Most frequently, to learn a verbal information objective, the student must be able to state a set of facts and principles in a meaningful, organized manner. Learning organized information of this sort is subject to an encoding procedure that calls upon previously learned structures in the student's memory. Anderson (1984) describes such a memory structure as a *schema*. He defines schema as an "abstract structure of information . . . [which may be] conceived as a set of expectations" (p. 5). These expectations are "slots" in the learner's knowledge structure into which new information can be integrated. For example, an objective in social studies might be to describe the process involved in the passage of a bill by the U.S. Congress. In this case, a schema would likely include at least the essential steps, such as drafting the bill, introducing the bill, and so on.

Sequencing of organized knowledge should take into account existing schemas into which the new knowledge can be subsumed. The teacher or trainer should structure the new information so that it builds on what the student already knows. An example is cited in the work of Ausubel (1968), where he speaks of the process of "correlative subsumption," where information about Buddhism is acquired following what was previously learned about a different religion, Zen Buddhism.

When learning new material about Buddhism, the learner compares the new information to what he or she already knows about Zen Buddhism. Because the information about both is similar, the new information is subsumed in the Zen Buddhism schema, which then becomes the Zen Buddhism/Buddhism schema.

Planning a Sequence for Motor Skill Learning

Prerequisites for learning a motor skill are learning the part skills and the executive subroutine (the procedural rule) that controls execution of the skills. The relative importance of these two prerequisites depends upon the complexity of the skill itself. For example, because dart throwing involves only a simple one-step rule, identifying and training part skills would not be useful; whereas because swimming requires mastery of several prerequisite skills, identifying and training the prerequisite skills would be very valuable.

Learning the executive subroutine should come early in the sequence of instruction for a motor skill, before the various part skills have been fully mastered. For example, learning to heave a shot put would have the learner-athlete acquire the executive subroutine (approaching the line, shifting his weight, bending his arm and body, and propelling the shot) before he has fully mastered all the part skills.

Particular part skills may themselves have important prerequisites. For example, when firing a rifle at a target, the concrete concept of a correct sighting picture is a valuable subordinate skill for the execution of the total act of target shooting.

Planning a Sequence for Attitude Learning

As is true for other kinds of learned capabilities, the learning or modification of an attitude calls upon previously acquired capabilities in the learner's memory. For example, a positive attitude toward reading poetry cannot be established without some knowledge of particular poems or without some of the language skills involved in interpreting the meaning of poetic writing.

An instructional sequence for learning an attitude often begins with the learning of intellectual skills and verbal information relevant to the attitude. It then proceeds to the introduction of a procedure to establish the positive or negative tendency that constitutes the attitude itself, as described in Chapter 5. For example, if the learner is to adopt a positive attitude toward associating with people of different races, the attitude must be based upon information concerning what the various "associations" (playing games with, working with, dining with, and so on) are about. Because attitude learning may require prior learning of intellectual skills and verbal information, it is often necessary to consider learning domain interactions as described by Martin and Briggs (1986). These interactions can be analyzed by means of "audit trails," in which the attitude to be acquired is related to other skills that facilitate its acquisition. The audit trail may include other attitudes, verbal information, or intellectual skills, and it provides a guide for the sequencing of experiences leading to attitude change (pp. 275–289).

When human modeling is used to modify attitudes, a prerequisite step in the sequence may be necessary. Since the "message" that represents the attitude needs to be presented by a respected source (usually a person), it may be necessary to establish or "build up" respect for this person. For example, a currently famous scientist is not likely to command the respect that a well-known scientist, such as Einstein, does; and Einstein, as a pictured model, is more likely to be respected if the learner knows about his accomplishments.

LESSON PLANNING FOR LEARNING OUTCOMES

The sequence of capabilities exemplified by the learning hierarchy (for intellectual skills) or by a set of identified prerequisites (for other types of outcomes) is used as a basis for planning a series of lessons. The implication for the design of a single lesson is that one or more prerequisite or supporting capabilities need to be available to the learner. Obviously, there is more than this to planning lessons. How does the student proceed from the point of having learned some subordinate knowledge or skills to the point of having acquired a new capability? It is within this interval, during which the actual learning occurs, that the events of instruction become essential. These events include the actions taken by the students and teacher to bring about the desired learning.

Instructional Events and Effective Learning Conditions

The most general purpose for the events of instruction is to arrange the external conditions of learning in such a way that learning occurs. Instructional events are typically incorporated into individual lessons or modules. The events apply to all types of lessons, regardless of their intended outcomes, and to all types of delivery methods, including a live instructor in the classroom and computer-based online learning. Just as it is necessary to sequence instruction in a particular way, it is also necessary to incorporate the events of instruction to ensure learning effectiveness.

Tables 12.1 and 12.2 consolidate several ideas that influence lesson design. First, they assume the general framework of instructional events, described in Chapter 10. Second, they describe procedures for implementing optimal learning conditions that are specifically relevant to each class of learning objective. These are the external conditions of learning. Third, they take into account the problem of lesson sequencing by representing the recall of prerequisite capabilities appropriate for each kind of learning outcome.

The result is a list of distinctive conditions for effective learning that need to be incorporated into the general framework of instructional events in order to accomplish learning objectives. It should be noted that the list pertains only to the following events of instruction: Event 3, stimulating recall of prior learning; Event 4, presenting the stimulus; Event 5, providing learning guidance; and Event 6, eliciting performance. The remaining instructional events are described in Chapter 10.

TABLE 12.1 **EFFECTIVE LEARNING CONDITIONS FOR INCORPORATION INTO LESSONS HAVING OBJECTIVES OF INTELLECTUAL SKILLS AND COGNITIVE STRATEGIES**

Type of Lesson Objective	Learning Conditions
Discrimination	Recall of responses Presentation of *same* and *different* stimuli, with emphasis on distinctive features Repetition of *same* and *different* stimuli, with feedback
Concrete Concept	Recall the discrimination of relevant object features Presentation of several instances ("it's like this") and noninstances, varying in irrelevant object qualities ("it's *not* like this") Identification of instances by student, with feedback
Defined Concept	Recall of component concepts Demonstration of the concept, using its definition Demonstration of concept example by student
Rule	Recall of subordinate concepts and rules Demonstration of rule, using verbal statement Demonstration of rule application by student
Higher-Order Rule	Recall of relevant subordinate rules Presentation of a novel learning task or problem Demonstration of new rule in problem solution by student
Cognitive Strategy	Recall of relevant rules and concepts Verbal statement or demonstration of strategy Practice of strategy in novel situations

Lessons for Intellectual Skill Objectives   Effective learning conditions for the varieties of intellectual skills are shown in Table 12.1. The list of conditions in the second column begins with a statement designating the recall of a previously learned capability, often from a previous lesson. The list then proceeds with conditions to be reflected in other instructional events (such as those of presenting the stimulus, providing learning guidance, eliciting the student performance, and so on). In interpreting the information in this column, it may be useful to review the statements of internal and external conditions of learning for these types of objectives, as described in Chapters 4 and 5.

Lessons for Cognitive Strategy Objectives   Conditions designed to promote effective learning for cognitive strategies are listed in the bottom portion of Table 12.1. The list pertains to the strategies of learning, remembering, and problem solving. External and internal conditions for learning cognitive strategies were discussed in Chapter 3.

TABLE 12.2	EFFECTIVE LEARNING CONDITIONS FOR INCORPORATION INTO LESSONS HAVING OBJECTIVES OF VERBAL INFORMATION, ATTITUDES, AND MOTOR SKILLS

Type of Lesson Objective	Learning Conditions
Verbal Information	
Names or Labels	Recall verbal associations Relate name to image or meaningful sentence (encoding by student) Use the name in context of other knowledge
Facts	Recall the context of related meaningful information Reinstate the fact in a larger context of verbal information Use the fact in context of other knowledge
Knowledge	Recall the context of related information Reinstate the new knowledge in the context of related information Use knowledge by relating it to other facts and bodies of knowledge
Attitude	Recall verbal information and intellectual skills relevant to chosen personal actions Establish or recall respect for "source" (usually a human model) Reward for personal action, either by direct experience or vicariously by observation of the human model
Motor Skill	Recall responses and part skills Establish or recall of executive subroutine (procedural rule) Practice the total skill

Lessons for Information, Attitudes, and Motor Skills   The design of instructional events for verbal information, attitudes, or motor skills should consider the conditions for effective learning shown in Table 12.2. The lists are derived from the fuller discussion of internal and external conditions of learning contained in Chapter 4.

STEPS IN LESSON PLANNING

Assuming that a teacher or trainer has organized a course into major units or topics and has planned the sequences of lessons for each, how does he or she proceed with the design of a single lesson?

Given the value of incorporating the events of instruction, we suggest that teachers and trainers use a planning sheet with the following four elements:

1. A statement of the objective of the lesson and its classification (i.e., domain of learning)
2. A list of the instructional events to be employed
3. A list of the media, materials, and activities by which each event is to be accomplished

4. Notes on teacher or trainer roles and activities for each event selected (the prescriptions for instruction)

Such a planning sheet might list the objective at the top, with a column for each of the other three items in the previous list. After the planning sheet is completed, the lesson can be fully designed and the supporting instructional materials produced. An example of a completed lesson-planning sheet is shown in Table 12.3. We now describe some varieties of circumstances related to the four elements of the planning sheet.

TABLE 12.3 **EFFECTIVE LEARNING CONDITIONS FOR INCORPORATION INTO LESSONS HAVING OBJECTIVES OF VERBAL INFORMATION, ATTITUDES, AND MOTOR SKILLS**

Objective: Shown a number of different kinds of geometric figures, the student will be able to identify the trapezoids by circling them.

Event	Method/Media	Instructional Treatment or Strategy
1. Gain Attention of Learner	Live instruction and chalkboard	Draw figures on chalkboard, emphasizing the variety of appearances of figures.
2. Inform Learner of Objective	Live instruction and chalkboard	Present several pairs of figures differing in critical attributes (4 sides, straight, 2 parallel), and tell the students they will be learning how to identify the trapezoids.
3. Stimulate Recall of Prerequisites	Instructor using overhead projector with transparencies or PowerPoint slides	Present pairs of lines that are straight, not straight, parallel, not parallel; figures that are 4-sided, 5-sided, 3-sided; closed, open. In the case of each pair, ask the student to identify the difference by telling or by pointing.
4. Present Stimulus Material and 5. Provide Learning Guidance	Instructor using overhead projector with transparencies or PowerPoint slides	Present a series of pairs of figures, each containing a trapezoid and some other figure. Ask students to identify the trapezoid in each case. When feature names are known, point out the presence or absence of the feature in each member of the pair (straight, nonstraight; parallel, nonparallel, etc.).
6. Elicit Performance	Worksheets	Present a worksheet with 20 plane figures, 8 of which are trapezoids, and other figures differing in one or more critical attributes. Have students circle the trapezoids.
7. Provide Feedback	Overhead projector and oral review by instructor	When students have finished the worksheet, project a copy on the overhead. Identify the trapezoid in each example; identify the absence of the critical feature in the figure that is not a trapezoid.
8. Assess Performance	Live instruction	Using a test similar to the worksheet, have students circle the trapezoid.
9. Enhance Retention and Transfer	Worksheets	Ask students to draw a trapezoid, beginning with each of three straight lines: 1 vertical, 1 horizontal, and 1 slanted. As materials are available, ask students to identify trapezoid shapes in pictures of objects (furniture, tools, etc.).

The Objective of the Lesson

As noted previously, some lessons may have a single objective, whereas others may have several related objectives. For example, the lesson presented in Table 12.3 is for a single objective that appears in a learning hierarchy for a complex intellectual skill objective. In delivering this lesson, the teacher must attend to its prerequisites and provide for transfer to subsequent objectives. The purpose of the lesson is to provide part of the instruction needed to accomplish the integrated goals, as discussed in Chapter 9.

Listing the Instructional Events

The events of instruction are based on a sequence of internal stages of information processing. The purpose of the external events is to facilitate the internal processes; therefore, it makes sense to present them in order. However, the events only serve as guidelines for lesson development. It may not be necessary to include all the events or to present them in a strict linear order. When designing a lesson, the teacher/trainer or instructional designer should consider the sophistication of the learners in terms of how self-directed they are as well as the nature of the objectives of the lesson. Under some circumstances, it may be necessary to spend an entire period on a single instructional event, for example, establishing motivation for a series of lessons. As much as one entire hour may be required to present a complex objective to the students, including a discussion or a demonstration of its subordinate parts, each of which will require the learners to respond to in some prescribed manner. In a course where objectives are written at the unit level and not at the lesson level, it may be reasonable to spend an hour or more clarifying the exact nature of the expected performance for each unit before the actual instruction for the unit is undertaken. This type of organization may be appropriate for a course whose major outcomes are problem-solving skills.

Choosing Media, Methods, and Strategies   It is at this step in instructional design that the greatest differences between designing teacher-led classroom instruction and self-paced, self-instructional materials are found. Self-paced, self-instructional courses require the designer to include all of the events of instruction. The model for teacher-led instruction is much less exact because the teacher can fill in the gaps. However, the basic principle of planning the external events of instruction is the same for both. For example, to gain the attention of the students for an objective in a genetics lesson, the teacher might look for a Web site that shows various species of animals whose distinctive features are so exaggerated that they look comical and then use it to lead up to the objective about how genes determine these differences. If a Web site can't be found, the teacher might use a series of color photographs or a videotape, to accomplish the event. When developing an online lesson on the same topic, the designer should go through the same process of determining how the event will be accomplished. In some cases, existing materials can be incorporated into the lesson; in many instances it requires the production of new materials.

Examples of Lesson Planning Sheets for Other Types of Learning Outcomes

Table 12.3 provides an example of how the events of instruction might be interpreted for a lesson that teaches a concrete concept. Tables 12.4 through 12.8 show examples of lesson-planning sheets for other types of learning including: defined concept, rule, problem solving, and verbal information and attitude. Notice how the conditions of learning presented in Tables 12.1 and 12.2 have been incorporated.

 TABLE 12.4   **EXAMPLE OF A LESSON FOR A DEFINED CONCEPT**

Objective: Given a text printed with no caps, the student will be able to classify proper nouns.

Event	Method/Media	Instructional Treatment or Strategy
1. Gain Attention of Learner	Live instruction and chalkboard	Put two sentences on the blackboard, using no caps. (Examples: the team's name was the wildcats. the woman's name was mrs. brown.) Ask students if they notice anything unusual about these sentences. Point out the words that are usually capitalized.
2. Inform Learner of Objective	Live instruction and chalkboard	Tell students this lesson is about proper nouns. A proper noun begins with a capital letter. Tell them they will be learning to identify which nouns are proper nouns, to be written with an initial capital letter.
3. Stimulate Recall of Prerequisites	Instructor using overhead projector with transparencies or PowerPoint slides	Remind students that a noun is the name of a person, place, or thing. Ask students to give examples of nouns in each of these categories. Reminder: The first word in a sentence is always capitalized—not important for this lesson.
4. Present Stimulus Material	Instructor using overhead projector with transparencies or PowerPoint slides	Write the definition of a proper noun on the overhead: A proper noun is a word that names a particular person, place, or thing.
5. Provide Learning Guidance	Instructor	Compare common nouns to proper nouns to show application of the definition "general noun" versus "particular noun." For example: boy-John; girl-Alice; mother-Mrs. Smith; building-Pentagon; monument-Lincoln Memorial.
6. Elicit Performance	Worksheets	Ask students to write some proper nouns next to a list of common nouns. Include the categories of people, places, and things.
7. Provide Feedback	Oral review by instructor with class participation	Inform students as to the correctness of their answers. Remind students, if necessary, that proper nouns are always capitalized.
8. Assess Performance	Written quiz	Have students underline the proper nouns in each of 10 sentences. Include the following conditions: sentences with no proper nouns, 1 proper noun at the beginning of the sentence, 1 proper noun embedded in the sentence, multiple proper nouns, pronouns.
9. Enhance Retention and Transfer	Worksheets	Have each student write 5 sentences that include proper nouns, for people, places, and things. Conduct a contest to see who can use the most proper nouns in their sentences.

TABLE 12.5   **EXAMPLE OF A LESSON FOR TEACHING A RULE**

Objective: Given the voltage in a circuit and the wattage of an appliance, the student will be able to find the amperage for the appliance using the formula: Amperage = Watts/Volts.

Event	Method/Media	Instructional Treatment or Strategy
1. Gain Attention of Learner	Videotape or animation	Show a scene where everyone is getting ready for work and school in the morning. Mom has her curling iron plugged in, Dad is ironing a shirt. Sally plugs in her hair dryer, and all of a sudden the screen goes blank. Ask if anyone knows what happened? (Answer: Sally's hair dryer overloaded the circuit and blew a fuse.)
2. Inform Learner of Objective	Instructor	State that the purpose of this lesson is to be able to figure out how much electricity (in amps) is needed by appliances.
3. Stimulate Recall of Prerequisites	Instructor using overhead projector with transparencies or PowerPoint slides	Ask students to recall that the typical voltage in a household circuit is 115 volts. (In using the formula, this may be rounded to 100 volts.) The wattage of an appliance is usually printed on the appliance's metal label. Fuses in electric circuits are rated according to amps (amount) of electricity they can carry; if this amount is exceeded, the fuse blows.
4. Present Stimulus Material	Instructor using overhead projector with transparencies or PowerPoint slides	Tell students the rule for calculating the amps used by an appliance is to divide the wattage of that appliance by the voltage of the circuit: Watts/Volts = Amps. Therefore, if Sally's hair dryer uses 1,200 watts, it is drawing 12 amps (1,200/100=12).
5. Provide Learning Guidance	Instructor and class participation	Use several different examples to illustrate the application of the rule Watts/Volts = Amps. (1) Ask the student if Sally's hair dryer would blow a fuse rated at 15 amps. (No, because the dryer uses only 12 amps.) (2) Ask students what happens if Mom plugs the iron into the same circuit. (Some will reply, "It will blow the fuse.") Ask how they could prove it. Give help when needed to find the amperage drawn by the iron (1,000 watts) and to find the total amps in the circuit with both the iron and the hair dryer turned on. (12 + 10 = 22 amps; the fuse will blow).
6. Elicit Performance	Worksheets	Ask students to find amps for a number of other appliances.
7. Provide Feedback	Oral review by instructor	Inform students as to the correctness of their answers and remediate incorrect answers. Watch for the inversion of the fraction Volts/Watts.
8. Assess Performance	Written quiz	Have students do 10 problems requiring the calculation of amps.
9. Enhance Retention and Transfer	Worksheets	Describe or picture the need for finding amperage in several different practical situations. Have students tackle a few problems to determine whether a fuse will blow or not. Have a contest to see how many electrical things (from a list, showing watts) students can plug into a 20-amp circuit without blowing the fuse.

TABLE 12.6   **EXAMPLE OF A LESSON FOR A PROBLEM-SOLVING SKILL**

Objective: Given a drawing of a plot of land, the student will be able to generate a plan for a sprinkler system that will cover at least 90% of the land, using the fewest amount of material.

Event	Method/Media	Instructional Treatment or Strategy
1. Gain Attention of Learner	Videotape or animation	Show pictures of sprinkler coverage of a rectangular plot of ground, one highly successful (90%) coverage, one unsuccessful (70% coverage), and one using too many sprinkler heads. Show these rapidly, inviting attention to their differences.
2. Inform Learner of Objective	Instructor	Tell students the problem to be solved is to design the most efficient sprinkler system for a plot of ground— one that covers at least 90% and uses the smallest amounts of pipe and sprinkler heads.
3. Stimulate Recall of Prerequisites	Instructor using overhead projector with transparencies or PowerPoint slides	Have learners recall applicable rules. Because the sprinkler heads they will use spray in circles and partial circles, rules to be recalled are: (1) area of a circle, (2) area of quarter and half circles, (3) area of rectangular areas, (4) area of irregular shapes made by the intersection of circular areas with straight sides.
4. Present Stimulus Material	Instructor using overhead projector with transparencies or PowerPoint slides	Restate the problem in general terms, and then add specific details: (1) rectangular lot 50 by 100 ft; (2) radius of the sprinklers, 5 ft; (3) water source in the center of the lot.
5. Provide Learning Guidance and 6. Elicit Performance	Instructor using overhead projector with transparencies or PowerPoint slides	Students will need to design tentative sprinkler layouts, draw them out, and calculate the relative efficiency of each. Guidance may be given by informing learners of various options if it appears that rules are not being applied correctly. For example, "Could you get more efficient coverage in the corner by using a quarter-circle sprinkler head?" Or "It looks as if you have a lot of overlap; are you allowing for a 10% noncoverage?" Ask the learners what rules they are following for placing the sprinkler.
7. Provide Feedback	Oral review by instructor	Confirm good moves, when in a suitable direction. If learners don't see a possible solution, make suggestions. For example, "Why don't you draw four circles that barely touch, calculate the area, then draw a rectangle around the circles and calculate the area of coverage to see how much you have?"
8. Assess Performance	Instructor	Present a different problem using the same type of sprinkler, with different lot shape and size. Check the efficiency of the students' solutions in terms of coverage and amount of materials used.
9. Enhance Retention and Transfer	Worksheets	Present several different problems varying in shape of lot, position of the water source, and area of sprinkler coverage. Assess how well students can generalize the problem solving to these new situations.

TABLE **12.7**   **EXAMPLE OF A LESSON FOR A VERBAL INFORMATION OBJECTIVE**

Objective: Given the question "What 'truths' were held to be self-evident, according to the framers of the Declaration of Independence?" the student will be able to state the truths in his or her own words.

Event	Method/Media	Instructional Treatment or Strategy
1. Gain Attention of Learner	Instructor	Say, "In 1776, the English colonies on this continent declared that they were independent of the country that established them—England. What reasons did they give for such an audacious declaration?"
2. Inform Learner of Objective	Instructor	Some of the reasons were found in truths held to be self-evident. In this lesson you'll learn what these "truths" were.
3. Stimulate Recall of Prerequisites	Chalkboard and handouts	The prerequisites in this case are gaining meaning from sentences, including the words in the sentences. Word meanings that might need to be defined are self-evident, endowed, unalienable, instituted, deriving. Syntactic sentence structures also need to be recognized and understood.
4. Present Stimulus Material	Handouts	Present the relevant prose passage from the Declaration of Independence.
5. Provide Learning Guidance	Provide room on handouts for list and evaluations	Ask students to number the "truths" in the passage, beginning with (1) "All men are created equal." Ask students to elaborate each of these "truths" to themselves, by associating each point with some other familiar ideas. (For example, the "right to life" might be associated with controversies about capital punishment, the "right to liberty" might be associated with the taking of hostages, and so forth.)
6. Elicit Performance	Have students read responses— elicit different responses	Ask students to answer the question "What truths are held to be self-evident?" without trying to repeat the passage word for word.
7. Provide Feedback	Instructor	Verify the learning and retention of the passage in terms of meaning. Give corrections when errors or omissions are made.
8. Assess Performance	Instructor	Ask for recall of the entire passage, scored in terms of "meaning units."
9. Enhance Retention and Transfer	Instructor	Verbal information is best remembered when it is practiced (used). Ask students what the English government's response might have been to each of the "truths" put forward in the Declaration. Another question might be, "Why did the colonies think that each of these rights was being violated?" Exercises of this sort require the use of the verbal information that has been learned.

TABLE 12.8 **EXAMPLE OF A LESSON FOR AN ATTITUDE OBJECTIVE**

Objective: The learner will choose to eat foods that are low in fat and low in calories in order to keep cholesterol levels low. (Note: This lesson is not for children; it is most appropriate for adults who are concerned about high cholesterol. Also, this class is ongoing with Events 6, 7, and 8 presented weekly.)

Event	Method/Media	Instructional Treatment or Strategy
1. Gain Attention of Learner	Video or animation	Present an image of a human heart with clogged arteries, alongside foods that are high in fat (butter, ice cream, pastry), and contrast picture of a human heart with no clogged arteries alongside foods that are low in fat (string beans, celery, fish). Ask, "Which heart do you want to have?"
2. Inform Learner of Objective	Videotape of a nurse talking	"The goal of this workshop is to understand how we can control our cholesterol levels through eating foods low in calories and fat." (The hidden agenda is that the student will choose to do so.)
3. Stimulate Recall of Prerequisites	Same	Remind the students (or instruct them) of the calories and fat content of common foods. Mention foods that are high in calories and fat and others that are low. Emphasize balancing the diet and exercising.
4. Present Stimulus Material	Instructor or video	The content of this lesson should be delivered by a person who serves as a model for good nutrition.
5. Provide Learning Guidance	Instructor or video	The model should be admirable and believable. He or she describes the shift in food choices made, the difference in weight that transpired, and the satisfaction that resulted. The messages delivered by the model might be "If I can do it, you can do it."
6. Elicit Performance	Overhead transparencies, PowerPoint slides, worksheets	Ask the students for reports of food eaten over the the past week. These should include mention of the occasions on which food choices are made (at meal times and between meals).
7. Provide Feedback	Instructor	Give positive feedback to indicators of desirable choices in self-reports of food eating. Feedback should confirm a desired choice (or movement toward a desired behavior) with praise or support.
8. Assess Performance	Instructor	Attitudes may be assessed using unobtrusive measures. Observe students over a period of weeks to see if unusual weight gains are avoided and if they use positive phrases in talking about their food choices.
9. Enhance Retention and Transfer	Worksheet	Attitudes are reinforced by support from the environment. The efforts of the individual can be aided by weekly meetings of a support group.

INTEGRATIVE GOALS: LESSON PLANNING FOR MULTIPLE OBJECTIVES

The occurrence of multiple objectives is common in instruction, and single lessons often come together to make up a larger unit. As discussed in Chapter 9, instruction should engage a student in a comprehensive purpose of the sort that Gagné and Merrill (1990) call an *enterprise*. For example, after instruction, the student might be expected to demonstrate new knowledge through the act of "denoting" or by elaborative discussion. A particular "denoting" goal might require the integration of many different types of learning outcomes including verbal information, attitudes, related concepts, and rules.

The instructional curriculum map, introduced in Chapter 8, is one way to analyze integrative goals into component objectives from differing domains. The issue to be addressed is how lesson design for multiple objectives from different domains differs from lesson design for single objectives. It is useful to draw instructional maps in the process of planning sequences of lessons. These maps may be drawn at several levels, corresponding to the three levels at which the question of sequencing arises in the design of a course. Such maps show the integration of objectives from the different domains and visually depict each objective's role in supporting attainment of a larger goal. Figure 12–2 illustrates a map for a lesson on the inheritance of sex-linked traits. In this lesson, it is easy to see that instruction on many of the objectives can be combined and presented together. For example, the teacher might group the information objectives (A and B) and present the content related to both of them at one time.

Planning Instructional Activities

The main difference between planning for multiple-objective and single-objective lessons lies in how the teacher or designer presents the events of instruction. Our model for lesson design proposes that the teacher or designer will determine a strategy for a lesson by grouping objectives and events of instruction into instructional activities. An instructional activity is something the teacher does, or has the student do. It represents one or more events of instruction for one or more objectives. For example, showing a videotape is an instructional activity. The purpose of that activity may be to motivate the learner, present the content, or both. Likewise, a game that divides a class into two teams that compete in applying rules learned may provide both motivation and the opportunity to show what they know (or "elicit performance," one of the events of instruction). A lesson consists of one or more instructional activities that occur in a predetermined framework. Even a self-paced, self-instructional lesson, such as one from an online course, is planned to be completed in some predetermined amount of time. For computer-based training, this is known as *student interaction time* or *number of courseware hours*. The designer's task is to figure out the instructional activities that will occur during the

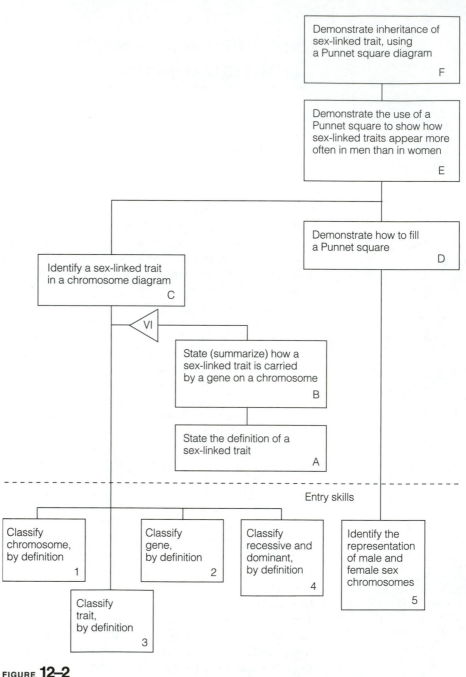

Demonstrate inheritance of sex-linked trait, using a Punnet square diagram

F

Demonstrate the use of a Punnet square to show how sex-linked traits appear more often in men than in women

E

Demonstrate how to fill a Punnet square

D

Identify a sex-linked trait in a chromosome diagram

C

VI

State (summarize) how a sex-linked trait is carried by a gene on a chromosome

B

State the definition of a sex-linked trait

A

Entry skills

Classify chromosome, by definition

1

Classify gene, by definition

2

Classify recessive and dominant, by definition

4

Identify the representation of male and female sex chromosomes

5

Classify trait, by definition

3

FIGURE **12–2**

INSTRUCTIONAL CURRICULUM MAP FOR A LESSON ON GENETICS: SEX-LINKED TRAITS

set period of time. To do this, one might construct a table like the one shown in Figure 12–3, which we call an objectives/time-line matrix.

The guiding principle in designing the lesson from the objectives/time-line matrix is to go from prerequisite skills to higher-order skills and to present the

Objective	a	b	c	d	e	f	g	h	i	j	k	l	m	n	Total
F. Demonstrate inheritance of sex-linked trait, using a Punnet square	1										4	5	6,7	9	
E. Demonstrate sex-linked cross on Punnet square	1				2				4	5-7					
D. Demonstrate cross on Pummet square	1				2	4									
C. Identify a sex-linked trait in a chromosome diagram	1	3		2,4	5-7										
B. State how sex-linked trait is carried on a chromosome	1	3	2	4											
A. State the definition of a sex-linked trait	1	3	2	4											
5. Identify the representation of male and female sex chromosomes		9													
4. Classify recessive and dominant, by definition		9													
3. Classify trait, by definition		9													
2. Classify gene, by definition		9													
1. Classify chromosomes by definition		9													
Instructional activities for each objective in minutes	5 a	7 b	5 c	11 d	10 e	8 plus 10 f	5 g	5 h	5 i	7 j	15 k	5 l	7 m	12 n	~115 Total Minutes

FIGURE 12–3

OBJECTIVES/TIME-LINE SEQUENCE OF INSTRUCTIONAL ACTIVITIES IN MINUTES FOR THE LESSON IN FIGURE 12–2, SHOWING HOW THE EXTERNAL EVENTS OF INSTRUCTION ARE GROUPED WITHIN EACH ACTIVITY
Events of instruction: 1. Gain attention. 2. Inform learner of objective. 3. Stimulate recall. 4. Present stimulus materials. 5. Provide learning guidance. 6. Elicit performance. 7. Provide feedback. 8. Assess performance. 9. Enhance retention and transfer.

events of instruction through the instructional activities in a sequential manner that facilitates information processing.

Figure 12–3 represents an objectives/time-line matrix for the lesson map shown in Figure 12–2. The lesson's objectives are listed on the left side of the matrix in the order in which they are to be taught. The time line across the bottom of the matrix depicts the total desired length of time for the learning activity required to teach each objective. In the example, the total amount of time for the lesson is estimated to be 115 minutes. The cells in the matrix contain the number of the corresponding event of instruction that will occur. Notice that the events of instruction can be grouped together, either across objectives or within objectives.

Detailed Explanation of Figure 12–3

Activity a. The first thing you might do is have the instructor spend approximately five minutes gaining the attention of the learners. They might show a videotape or access various Web sites that provide examples of sex-linked traits (male-pattern baldness, red-green color blindness, hemophilia, Duchenne muscular dystrophy, etc.).

Activity b. Next, the instructor will spend approximately seven minutes reviewing the entry skills 1–5 (in Figure 12–2) from previous lessons to enhance retention and transfer (instructional event 9) and get the students to recall prerequisites for the target objectives (instructional event 3). The instructor might use overhead transparencies or PowerPoint slides to review the concepts of chromosomes and genes (recessive and dominant).

Activity c. This activity will last about five minutes. You'll have the instructor inform the learners of the nature of objectives (instructional event 2) for A and B (in Figure 12–2) by saying something like "In this lesson, you will first learn what a sex-linked trait is and how it is inherited." Notice that these are verbal-information objectives. They are planned to be taught first, not because they are required as prerequisites, but because they provide a supportive context by aiding transfer to the learning of the main intellectual skill objectives C, D, and E (in Figure 12–2).

Activity d. In activity d, lasting 11 minutes, the instructor will present the stimulus (instructional event 4) for information objectives A and B by stating the definition of a sex-linked trait.

Activity e. In activity e, lasting 10 minutes, the instructor will present the objective and stimulus material (instructional events 2 and 4) for objective C, with new pictures or slides showing relevant attributes of a chromosome pair with a sex-linked trait. You might have the instructor show three examples— X_cY, X_cX, X_cX_c— and indicate how each gene is carried on the X chromosome.

Activity f. In activity f (8 minutes), the instructor will elicit performance (instructional event 6) for objective C by handing out a worksheet that asks the student to answer the following questions:

1. Does X_cY represent a sex-linked trait? Why?
2. Does X_cX represent a sex-linked trait? Why?
3. Does XY_c represent a sex-linked trait? Why?

You'll follow that exercise, still in activity f, by having the instructor review the correct answers (instructional event 7) with the students (10 minutes).

Activity g. Next, the instructor will tell the students the objectives for D and E (five minutes) by saying "Now you will learn why these traits are more common in men than in women and how you can determine whether or not the trait will be expressed."

Activity h. Next, the instructor will present the stimulus material for objectives D and E, spending five minutes on each. The instructor will show students how to develop a Punnett square (below) for looking at possible outcomes of crosses:

		Female	
		X_c	X
Male	X	XX_c	XX
	Y	X_cY	XY

Activity i. Next, the instructor will present the present stimulus material for objective E, the Punnett square, filled in to show possible combinations of chromosomes and genes in offspring.

Activity j. Next, the instructor will provide learning guidance, elicit performance, and provide feedback for objective E. The instructor will do this by handing out a worksheet and have the students fill out a Punnett square using different examples.

Activity k. Next, the instructor will spend about 15 minutes presenting stimulus material (instructional event 4) for the rule: "A sex-linked trait is always visible in a male because the Y chromosome does not mask the recessive gene on the X chromosome."

Activity l. The instructor will spend 5 minutes presenting learning guidance for Objective F. He or she might show the Punnett square again and demonstrate that the expression of a trait can be determined by looking at the cells, giving at least two examples from the following:

$X_cX; X_cY$
$XX; X_cY$
$X_cX; XY$

The instructor will also identify the concept *carrier,* showing that the recessive trait becomes expressed in the female only when both X chromosomes carry the recessive trait.

Activity m. The students will spend approximately 7 minutes solving several problems (instructional event 6) by applying the rule for determining expression of a trait. For any cross, ask the students:

1. Would a male exhibit the trait?
2. Would a female exhibit the trait?
3. What is the probability that a male or a female will not exhibit or carry the trait?

The instructor will provide feedback (instructional event 7) to the students on their responses.

Activity n. Finally, the instructor will spend about 12 minutes enhancing retention and transfer (instructional event 9) by giving students word problems pertaining to sex-linked crosses. "If your mother's father was bald, what are your chances of being bald?" and have the instructor discuss the relationship of this lesson to work to be undertaken in subsequent lessons.

Naturally, during the design process, the amount of time assigned to each activity is going to be an estimate, and will depend upon the experience of the subject-matter expert. However, designing the lesson around the objectives and combined events is one way of assuring that the desired events are included.

Sequencing Instructional Activities and Selecting Media

Within the framework of a lesson, a teacher or trainer has a fair amount of latitude with respect to which events to include, which to omit, and which to combine across objectives. However, sequencing considerations related to prerequisite skills suggest that a more efficient strategy would be to present content for the supportive objectives first, followed by content related to target objectives.

As previously mentioned, the instructional treatments or strategies that describe what will take place in each of the activities are written on the lesson-planning sheet at the same time the time-line/objectives matrix is being constructed. At this point, it is time to consider the capabilities of media and delivery methods to provide the instructional events for the lesson. Two consistent principles in our model are (1) the effectiveness of instruction depends upon the ability of the media, delivery methods, and instructional strategies employed to provide the events of instruction, and (2) the selection of the events depends on the type of learning outcome and learner characteristics.

If the treatments/strategies are determined before media and delivery methods are chosen, designers are left with a fairly wide latitude within which they can make those decisions. This has been referred to as an *open-media model* of instructional design (Briggs & Wager, 1981). In contrast, if the media and methods are *preselected*, the strategies will have to take their limitations into consideration. For example, in Figure 12–3, we provided an example of how strategies might be used in a classroom delivery system with a teacher. If this lesson were designed for online delivery, the strategies would look very different. Animation and cartoons might be used to gain attention; graphics, animation, video, and audio voice-over might be used to present the stimulus material; interactive practice exercises with automated feedback and "branching" might be used to elicit and assess performance. If the lesson were to be presented in the form of self-paced instruction with printed text, the strategies would also need to change. As discussed in Chapter 11, media, delivery methods, and strategy decisions are most important when the learners are nonreaders because of the requirements for visual display, practice, and feedback.

ROLES AND ACTIVITIES IN INSTRUCTIONAL DEVELOPMENT

There are many types of media, delivery methods, and instructional strategies available to the designer. To the teacher or trainer who is developing lessons or courses, these items have value only in terms of the learning activities to which they apply. To make the best use of media, methods, and strategies a teacher or trainer needs to understand the instructional events that can be supported by them and note this in their lesson plan. The aim is to produce a lesson plan in which all the needed instructional events occur using appropriate media, methods, and strategies.

When new instructional materials are developed, the instructional designer and the subject-matter expert (SME) often work together to analyze the learning task, decide on an appropriate delivery system, and prepare treatments and high-level strategies for the lessons. During this process, both the designer and the SME review existing materials and assess their appropriateness for use within the new course. Then, like the teacher or trainer, they determine which events, learning activities, and lessons the existing materials pertain to. At this point, the designer must determine how the remaining events or activities can be provided. The designer is concerned with how selected media, delivery methods, and instructional strategies most appropriately support the instructional events. The events of instruction and the conditions of learning, as exemplified in Tables 12.1 and 12.2, provide guidance for lesson design. It is unlikely that the process of choosing or developing learning activities can be specified with such complete accuracy that lesson design can be reduced to a "cookbook recipe." Lesson design is as much an art as it is a science. The events of instruction provide a focus that aids both lesson construction and revision after formative evaluation, based on what we now know about learning.

SUMMARY

This chapter has dealt with lesson planning as the accomplishment of major activities: (1) planning for sequences of lessons within a course, unit, or topic; and (2) design of individual lessons in such a way that effective conditions of learning can be incorporated into the instructional events of each lesson.

Determining the sequences of lessons was discussed separately for each domain of learning outcome. The use of learning hierarchies was shown to be of central importance in the design of sequences of lessons for intellectual skill objectives, whereas other considerations enter into sequencing decisions for other kinds of outcomes.

To make each instructional event in the lesson successful, the conditions of learning relevant to the outcome (represented by the lesson objective) must be incorporated into the lesson. Although intuition, ingenuity, creativity, and experience are all valuable when planning lessons, reference to relevant conditions of learning can sharpen instruction by ensuring the use of various desirable functions.

Four steps in lesson planning were discussed. These included (1) listing the objective(s) of the lesson, (2) listing desired instructional events, (3) choosing media, materials, and activities by which events are to be accomplished, and (4) noting roles for teachers, trainers, and designers. An example of a multiobjective lesson plan for a study of the inheritance of sex-linked traits provided an indication of the time scheduling of instructional events and treatments and strategies for teacher activities.

Up to the point of lesson planning, all stages of instructional design can be similarly done whether a team is designing an entire curriculum or a teacher is designing a single course. However, at the point of lesson design, teachers must consider what they personally will bring to the lesson (and what role they will play), whereas designers of self-paced, self-instructional materials must decide how to provide needed activities in a preplanned lesson. The purpose of both designs is the same—to incorporate effective conditions of learning into the instructional events for all lessons and modules.

REFERENCES

Anderson, R. C. (1984). Some reflections on the acquisition of knowledge. *Educational Researcher, 13,* 5–10.

Ausubel, D. P. (1968). *Educational psychology: A cognitive view.* New York: Holt, Rinehart and Winston

Briggs, L. J., Gustafson, K. L., & Tillman M. H. (Eds.) (1991). *Instructional design: Principles and applications* (2nd ed.). Englewood Cliffs, NJ: Educational Technology Publications.

Briggs, L. J., & Wager, W. W. (1981). *Handbook of procedures for the design of instruction.* Englewood Cliffs, NJ: Educational Technology Publications.

Crovitz, H. E. (1970). *Galton's walk.* New York: Harper & Row.

Frase, L. T. (1970). Boundary conditions for mathemagenic behaviors. *Review of Educational Research, 40,* 337–347.

Gagné, R. M. (1985). *The conditions of learning* (4th ed.). New York: Holt, Rinehart and Winston.

Gagné, R. M., & Merrill, M. D. (1990). Integrative goals for instructional design. *Educational Technology Research and Development, 38*(1), 23–30.

Martin, B. L., & Briggs, L. J. (1986). *The affective and cognitive domains: Integration for instruction and research.* Englewood Cliffs, NJ: Educational Technology Publications.

Pressley, M., Levin, J. R., & Delaney, H. D. (1982). The mnemonic keyword method. *Review of Educational Research, 52,* 61–91.

Reiser, R., & Gagné, R. M. (1983). *Selecting media for instruction.* Englewood Cliffs, NJ: Educational Technology Publications.

Robinson, F. P. (1970). *Effective study* (4th ed.). New York: Harper & Row.

Rothkopf, E. Z. (1970). The concept of mathemagenic behavior. *Review of Educational Research, 40,* 325–336.

ASSESSING STUDENT PERFORMANCE

Instruction is designed to bring about the learning of several kinds of capabilities, as evidenced by improved performance on the part of the student. Five domains of capabilities have been identified and discussed in previous chapters: intellectual skills, cognitive strategies, information, motor skills, and attitudes. Although much learning goes on outside of school during everyday life experiences, schools are responsible for organizing and providing curriculum and instruction toward goals that might not be achieved in a less organized manner. The outcomes of planned instruction consist of student performances that show that they have acquired the various kinds of capabilities. Both the instructional designer and the teacher or trainer need a way to determine how successful the instruction has been for the class in general and students in particular. Assessments can show whether or not the newly designed instruction has met its objectives. In this chapter, we discuss how both these purposes can be served by the development of procedures for assessing student performance.

In this chapter, we use the word *assessment* as a measure of performance, we use the term *evaluation* as an interpretation of assessment, either in terms of grades (A, B, C), or qualities (good, fair, poor). We use the word *test* to mean any procedure used to assess the performance described in an objective. The word *test* covers all forms of written and oral tests as well as procedures for evaluating student products such as essays, musical productions, constructed models, or works of art. We use the term *assessment* rather than *achievement* testing because achievement testing is often associated with norm-referenced measurement, which we discuss later in this chapter. At this point we are using *test* and *assessment* to refer to objective-referenced performance measurement.

TYPES OF EVALUATION

We define *evaluation* as the collection and analysis of data for the purpose of making decisions. There are basically two types of evaluation to which assessments are applied—*criterion-referenced evaluation* and *normative-referenced evaluation*.

The difference is based on the purposes for evaluation and how the standard is set. In criterion-referenced evaluation the standard for performance is set *before* assessment, for example 90 percent = A. That is, the standard for acceptable performance can be given to the student ahead of time, and if all students in a class reach the standard we can say the instruction has been successful. The purpose of criterion-referenced performance is simply to see if the student has achieved the standard, or if not, what level was achieved.

The standard in normative-referenced evaluation is set *after* assessment as a function of the classes' performance. This is generally interpreted as a distribution around the mean or average score on the test. The purpose of normative evaluation is to compare students based on their performance. Grades are determined by where the student's grade falls relative to other students. In a normative evaluation system all students cannot achieve an A because the standard varies to prevent it.

In order to assess student performance on the objectives of a course and the effectiveness of instruction, we feel *objective-referenced tests* employing a *criterion-referenced interpretation,* constitute the most suitable type of assessment, and therefore are the focus of this chapter. However, we discuss the uses of normative-referenced tests, such as the SAT or GRE later in the chapter.

METHODS OF ASSESSMENT

There are many different methods of assessment. Here we look at authentic assessment, and assessment using rubrics.

Authentic Assessment

Authentic assessment attempts to measure performance in real-life contexts (McAlpine, 2000). It looks at the big picture, involves complex interrelationships, and values an interdisciplinary approach. Tombari and Borich (1999) point out that authentic learning and assessment enhances intrinsic academic motivation, as described by Keller (1987, 1999), and in Chapter 6, as students become hooked on real-life problem solving and assessment. This brings its own rewards and motivates students to higher levels of performance. Authentic assessment increases relevance by reflecting the kinds of activities, tasks, and challenges typical of adult life—the performances that writers, engineers, architects, and business people accomplish (McAlpine, 2000).

Learning is reflected in authentic assessment in many ways including: (1) products such as books, plays, maps, and exhibits; (2) cognitive processes such as higher-level thinking, including analysis, synthesis, evaluation, and creativity, as well as skills in acquiring, organizing, and using information; (3) performances, such as conducting experiments and research, presenting findings, or performing in a play; and (4) attitudes and social skills, such as those toward cultural diversity, science, and interviewing individuals and groups (McAlpine, 2000).

How Authentic Assessment Is Related to Instructional Design

Instructional designers attempt to align the objectives, methods, and assessments in planning and developing instruction. Obviously we want the student to see the relevance of what they are learning in terms of how the knowledge or skills can be used. Authentic assessment attempts to make the connection of the assessments to the objectives and higher-level outcomes. If we want students to be critical thinkers and problem solvers then we have to challenge them with those types of assessments. And, furthermore, we have to design learning environments and activities that will help them learn to perform these skills. The Jasper Woodbury Project, from Vanderbilt University (CTVG, 1990), is one example of how problem-solving skills can be taught and assessed. Jasper Woodbury is a set of videos that situate its main character, Jasper, in a number of life-like problem scenarios. The students watch the video and are presented with the challenge that Jasper faces. They are then to solve the problem, usually in groups, and present their solutions to the class. The issue is that many different types of outcomes are being learned in the process of solving Jasper's problem. What exactly is it that should be assessed? The math skills might require one type of assessment, the problem-solving skills another, and the presentation skills another. The assessment of a group's performance in presenting their solution would represent one case of authentic assessment of presentation skills.

Authentic assessment is further characterized by the following attributes (Resnick, 1987; Wiggins, 1989, 1992):

1. There is a close relationship between learning and assessment contexts. In other words, assessment is embedded naturally in learning. This makes assessment more natural for the learner.
2. Authentic assessment is complex and involves many different skills and aspects of knowledge. For example, it may involve searching relevant literature, interviewing, map making, experimenting, and developing a product. The assessments relate to different skills, and as a consequence, authentic assessment often yields multiple solutions.
3. The assessment process may continue over a relatively long time period as teaching and learning proceed. This contrasts with testing situations that are over in 30 minutes or an hour. Wiggins (1989) points out that authentic tests do not rely on unrealistic and arbitrary time constraints nor do they rely on selective questions or tasks. They tend to be more like portfolios—the general task is to assess long-term ability on essential tasks and skills.
4. Authentic assessment is nonalgorithmic, that is, the path of action is not fully specified in advance. As in real-life projects, an overall plan may be determined but surprises often occur and tangents are taken. In some respects, there may be a degree of ambiguity and uncertainty with tasks and the assessment, because everything that bears on the task is not known at outset.
5. Authentic assessment can involve both individuals working alone or in small groups. Wiggins (1989) comments that authentic assessment encourages self-regulatory skills and higher-order thinking. Students monitor their own

development of skills and accept challenges to work on tasks requiring critical evaluation and creativity.

6. With authentic assessment, students are much more autonomous. They are also more involved in planning their own tasks and assessment procedures. In authentic assessment, the focus of control often rests with the student, for example, in the choice of topics to investigate, in the methodology of the investigation, and even in some of the techniques of assessment.

7. Hast (1994) writes that, instead of being passive, test takers in authentic assessment become active participants in assessment activities—activities that are designed to reveal what they can do instead of highlighting their weaknesses. Similarly, Tombari and Borich (1999) stress that authentic instruction and assessment are designed to produce the learner's *best* rather than *typical* performance.

8. Authentic assessment offers real challenges based on real tasks. Wiggins (1989) emphasizes that tasks in authentic assessment are "scaffolded up" and not "dumbed down." He points out that authentic assessment is "effortful" and requires considerable mental work to solve problems that may arise. Students are encouraged to use Bloom's (1968) higher-level thinking skills, such as analysis, synthesis, evaluation, and application. In authentic assessment, students often meet new challenges and problems not found in textbooks. Sometimes it is necessary to adopt new ways of thinking to solve such problems.

9. Wiggins (1989) notes that authentic tests often culminate in the student's own research or product, for which content is to be mastered as a means, not as an end. Authentic tests assess student habits and repertoires of skills. They are not simply restricted to recall and do not reflect lucky or unlucky one-shot responses.

10. Scoring assessment tasks can be complex, in that a wide range of scoring techniques may be required (McAlpine, 2000). For example, it is unlikely that many of the tasks will have a simple right/wrong answer. Sometimes scoring criteria have to be determined before a particular product can be assessed or scales and checklists need to be made. Scoring criteria are often developed in partnership with the student and sometimes scoring authentic tasks can be challenging for teachers. It is helpful if they have some background in educational assessment (McAlpine, 2000).

11. Related to scoring are issues of reliability and validity. It is not possible to construct parallel forms of authentic tests to use for traditional psychometric estimates of reliability based on techniques such as equivalent-form correlations, test-retest comparisons, or split-half methods. Claims for the reliability of authentic assessment rest mainly on "repeated measures" or "repeated performances" over time (McAlpine, 2000). In terms of content validity, authentic assessments sample a wide domain of content that matches the real world. There are also claims of high predictive validity. For example, authentic assessment, if used consistently over time, is said to predict adult performance better than conventional pencil-and-paper tests (McAlpine, 2000).

Assessment Rubrics

In order to assess performance in authentic situations, it helps if the evaluator has a list of criteria against which to compare elements of the performance. One form of checklist is called an *assessment rubric,* a one or two-page document, like the one displayed in Table 13.1, that describes varying levels of quality, from excellent to poor, for criteria related to the performance. It is usually used with a relatively complex assignment, such as a long-term project, an essay, or a research paper. Its purposes are to give students informative feedback about their works in progress and to give detailed evaluations of their final products (Andrade, 2003).

Teachers make judgments about students every day, based on informal and formal appraisals of classroom work, homework assignments, and performance on quizzes and tests. Assessment rubrics listing benchmarks for student achievement assist in this evaluation by providing objective guidelines to measure and evaluate learning. These rubrics also improve learning, because students who understand them before a project is due can take the evaluation criteria into account as they complete their work (Holzberg, 2003).

Although the format of assessment rubrics can vary, all rubrics, like the one in Table 13.1, have two features in common: (1) a list of criteria, or "what counts" in a project or assignment; and (2) gradations of quality, with descriptions of strong, satisfactory, and problematic student work (Andrade, 2003).

Andrade (2003) presents the following reasons why rubrics have become a very popular trend in education:

They are easy to use and to explain. Rubrics make sense to people at a glance; they're concise and digestible. For these reasons, teachers like to use them to assess student work, parents appreciate them when helping their children with homework, and students often request them when given a new assignment.

Rubrics make teachers' expectations very clear. When students are given written expectations—such as in the form of a rubric—they will have a better understanding of the basis for their grades.

Assessment rubrics provide students with more informative feedback about their strengths and areas in need of improvement than do traditional forms of assessment. A well-written assessment rubric—one that describes the kinds of mistakes students tend to make, as well as the ways in which their work shines—gives them valuable information. Students can learn from an assessment rubric in a way that they can't learn from a letter grade.

Assessment rubrics increase inter-rater reliability for grading. When multiple graders are assessing student work it is important that they are all using the same standards. Rubrics help make the criteria clear, and lead to more consistency in ratings across raters.

Assessment rubrics support learning, the development of skills, and under-standing. Studies on the effects of rubrics and self-assessment on learning and metacognition—the act of monitoring and regulating one's own thinking (Goodrich, 1996). Andrade (1999) found that self-assessment supported by a rubric was related to an increase in content learning. Students who had used rubrics tended to mention the traditional criteria, plus a variety of other criteria—often the criteria from their rubrics. The conclusion is that assessment rubrics help students gain a deeper understanding of what they are learning.

TABLE 13.1   RUBRIC FOR ASSESSING A BUSINESS PLAN AND PRESENTATION

Criteria	Unsatisfactory 1–4 points	Satisfactory 5–7 points	Good 8–10 Points
Does the business plan contain a needs assessment expressed as a gap between desired and current state of affairs?	Statement of personal opinion about need without documentation.	Documented need from reputable sources.	Documented need supported by data.
Does the business plan contain a description of the solution for meeting the need?	How solution fits the need is ambiguous from description.	Solution is presented and seems to fit the need.	Multiple solutions that fit the need are discussed, and one selected.
Does the business plan have a rationale for the solution selected?	Rationale doesn't seem plausible.	Rationale is plausible.	Rationale discusses advantages of chosen solution over alternatives.
Does the business plan have an action plan and time line?	Time line seem unrealistic, not matched to budget or needs.	Time line ok, milestones identified, human resources identified.	Action plan is charted showing resource allocation and work schedule.
Does the business plan have a budget?	Budget is based on personal opinions of what it will cost.	Budget estimates are based on general guidelines for similar projects.	Costs are researched and related to the action plan.
Does the business plan estimate the return on investment?	Savings or profits are based on personal opinion.	Savings or profits are related to needs assessment.	Savings or profits are related to needs assessment and calculated over time.
Is the plan submitted on time, and with professional appearance?	Submitted late and/or not proofread for errors.	Submitted on time, with attention to spell and error checking.	Submitted on-time, well organized, and carefully checked.

Grades: 56–70 points = A (however, no criterion can be rated unsatisfactory)
49–55 points = B (however, no criterion can be rated unsatisfactory)
35–49 points = C (however, no criterion can be rated unsatisfactory)
less than 35 = F

PURPOSES OF PERFORMANCE MEASURES

In Chapter 2, we pointed out that student performance measures have as many as five different purposes, when considered in relation to instruction in schools. These are briefly discussed in the following sections.

Student Placement

Placement tests are often used to determine which skills a student already possesses so that he or she can be appropriately placed in an instructional curriculum. The tests show a pattern of each student's areas of mastery and nonmastery in order to identify the starting points for instruction. Placement tests are most appropriate for individualized instruction. But they are also used to exempt students from courses for which they have already acquired the target skills. For example, the purpose of CLEP tests is to assess student achievement in various subject areas and exempt students from college courses that teach the same skills.

Diagnosis of Difficulties

Diagnostic tests are constructed to measure prerequisite skills. These tests are especially helpful for learners who are falling behind. When students fall behind, especially in group instruction, it is likely that they have not mastered earlier skills and it is therefore difficult for them to learn additional skills. Using a diagnostic test, learners can be given remedial instruction on prerequisite skills. In some instances the remedial instruction should employ methods and materials that are different from those originally used in order to avoid a second failure at the same trouble point in the sequence of lessons.

Checking Student Progress

Progress tests or quizzes are often administered after lessons to ensure students have mastered the lesson's objectives. Progress "spot checks" can be performed informally with learners on certain occasions. In individualized instruction, such as computer-based training, progress tests are typically incorporated frequently to let learners know if they are keeping up or falling behind. The results of progress tests also represent dependable information for the teacher to use when planning the next steps in instruction. As previously mentioned, it is important that these tests are aligned with the objectives and learning activities.

These types of tests or quizzes tend to be short and cover only a few objectives at most. However, they serve an important role in motivating students to study, thereby lessening cumulative failure. Spot quizzes can also be used as practice tests over desired objectives. They wouldn't be graded, but rather gone over during the class period to provide feedback to the students to see if they are learning the concepts and skills.

Reports to Parents

The use of performance tests not only assures learners and teachers/trainers that things are on track, but for elementary school, and perhaps middle school, it is also a dependable way to show parents what the children are learning in class, and how they are performing. Patterns of performance over a series of tests might reveal learning difficulties or special talents for a particular student.

Evaluation of the Instruction

Performance testing is an excellent way to evaluate and improve instruction. Well-designed instructional materials undergo *formative evaluation* tryouts and revisions with individuals, small groups, and large groups in field test situations. The total scores carried by each student on performance tests significantly indicate the overall degree of success of the materials. Also important is item analysis that shows which items were passed or failed by a majority of students. Item scores are particularly useful in deciding where the instruction needs to be improved. Techniques for formative evaluation are further discussed in Chapter 16.

Performance tests are also used to conduct *summative evaluations* of instruction. These evaluations are conducted after course revisions have been completed and the revised course has been implemented. Summative evaluation is used both to formally recognize skills acquired by the individual (usually in the form of a grade), and judge the overall effectiveness of the instruction. Procedures for summative evaluation are described in detail by Popham (1975), Dick and Carey (1996), and in Chapter 16.

The principles of preparing performance measures are similar for the construction of lesson tests, for an entire topic, or for a larger unit of study. In the remainder of this chapter we discuss tests in terms of their validity for measuring performance on specific objectives. A specific objective could be that of a course, a unit, a single lesson, or an enabling objective.

PROCEDURES FOR OBJECTIVE-REFERENCED ASSESSMENT

The term *objective-referenced assessment* implies that the way to assess student learning is to build tests or other assessment procedures that *directly* measure the human performances described in the objectives. Such performance measures make it possible to infer that the intended performance capability has been achieved as a result of the instruction. Before beginning instruction, teachers normally pretest the students to determine their entry-level capabilities. Given their pretest scores, students can bypass instruction they don't need. Following instruction, teachers assess student performance by administering a posttest covering the objective(s).

Performance objectives are the keystones to planning performance assessments. We have indicated the critical importance of *verbs* in the statement for correctly describing the objective (Chapter 7). Verbs are equally crucial to planning performance assessments because they indicate what the student will be asked to *do* when they take the test. Remember, *capability* verbs refer to the capability that is *inferred* to be present in the student's repertoire when the student has successfully performed the *action* verb in the objective. The capability verb describes the *intent* of the objective; the action verb *indicates* that the learner has achieved the intent.

Congruence of Objective and Test: Validity

Objective-referenced assessment greatly simplifies the *validity* of performance measurement because it results in a direct measure of the objective. In doing so, it eliminates the need to relate the performance measures to a criterion by means of a correlation coefficient, as must be done when indirect measures are used or when tests have been constructed without reference to explicit performance objectives. The matter of test validity can be addressed by answering this question: "Is the test performance the same as the performance described in the objective?" If the answer is yes, the test is valid.

If the test and the objective are congruent with each other, validity assumes that the statement of the objective is itself valid, in the sense that it truly reflects the purposes of the topic or lesson. The procedures described for defining objectives in Chapter 7 are intended to ensure that this is the case; however, inconsistencies sometimes become apparent when the objectives are transformed into tests.

Some of the performance objectives from Chapter 7 can be used to illustrate how judgments about test validity can be made. To estimate the validity of an objective, compare the verbs that describe the *capability* to be learned to the *actions* the student takes in demonstrating this capability. For example, consider the objective "generate a letter by typing." The word *generate* indicates that the student must compose *his own* letter rather than type a letter that was composed by someone else. Two domains, motor skills and intellectual skills, are required to perform the task. If the objective had been to type a letter from a written longhand letter composed by someone else, only one domain (motor skill) would be required. The verb *generate* implies that a problem-solving capability (composing the letter) is required.

In a second example from Chapter 7, the student must *demonstrate* the use of a rule by supplying the missing factor in an equation. Simply copying the missing factor from a textbook or remembering the value from having seen the problem worked out before would not constitute a valid test for this capability. In designing a test, examples different from those used during teaching or from the instructional materials should be used to minimize the chance that the correct response can be supplied by any means other than the intended intellectual process.

To demonstrate mastery of a *concrete concept,* the learner might identify a concept by circling it on a diagram. This is not the same as copying the name of the concept onto a piece of paper or spelling out its name. It is also different from explaining the concept. These latter performances may be useful but they *do not* reflect the intent of the objective regarding the capability (to identify the concept) or the action (to circle the concept) that signifies the capability has been learned.

Exercises on judging the validity of test items by comparing them with the corresponding performance objectives are given by Dick and Carey (1996).

Designing the Test Situation

The form of performance objectives described in Chapter 7 serves as the basis for test construction. The five components of an objective statement are (1) the situation, or context; (2) the learned capability; (3) the content, or object of the performance; (4) the action, or observable part; and (5) the tools and constraints applied to performance. When complete, the objective provides a description of the situation to be tested.

For certain types of objectives and for older (more sophisticated) learners, objectives can be converted into a test by making a few simple changes. For example, the objective for typing a letter could be stated in terms of how to take a keyboarding test; all that needs to be added are the words "longhand letter" and "word processor and printer." The objective and test directions are "given a word processor, a printer, and a letter received in longhand, you will be able to type the letter within 10 minutes to 100 percent accuracy." The person administering the test would be instructed to ensure a favorable environment and to record and call "time" when 10 minutes are up. To demonstrate the procedure of short division, the only thing the test administrator would need to do is supply an appropriate template of the desired division expression and show the students where to fill in their answers.

The more closely objectives follow the outline in Chapter 7, the fewer decisions that will need to be made in planning the test and the fewer directions that will need to be given to the student. Both objectives and test items need to be presented in simpler terms for young children, either in communicating the purpose of the lesson or testing their performance after instruction is completed.

Some Cautions   A few cautions should be noted regarding using objectives to plan tests, especially if the statements of objectives are incomplete.

1. Avoid substituting verbs that change the meaning of either the *capability* or the *action* described in the objective. When synonyms or more simple explanations are needed to translate the objective into a test, review the restatements carefully to make sure they agree with the intent of the objective. For example, in an effort to clarify the instructions, be careful not to change the student's requirement to *construct* or *develop* an answer by using language that says or implies that the student simply has to choose, select, or recall the answer. For example, if an objective says, "generate three hypotheses about the effects of moving to hydrogen as a source of fuel for automobiles," the student can only do this orally or in writing—not by selecting answers from a multiple-choice test. Ambiguity in "guessing at" the meaning of verbs in poorly stated objectives can be avoided by using the standard verbs from Table 7.1. Pay particular attention when using verbs such

as *summarize, describe, list, analyze,* and *complete,* to make sure they are denoting the particular action expected. Reviewing objectives in these terms sometimes reveals that the objectives themselves need to be changed. In this case, you should change the objective before planning the instruction and before using the statement either as a lesson objective or as the directions for a test.

2. Changing other elements of objectives should be avoided, except when needed to simplify directions for the test. Unless a deliberate change is intended, the situation, the object, and the tools and other constraints, as well as the verbs denoting the capability and the action, should be congruent between the objective and the test. The "worst possible" mismatch between an objective and a test would have a different learning domain specified in each. For example, if the learning objective was, "list the factors that make a politician successful, that is, be voted into office," and the instruction only addressed Thomas Jefferson's views on slavery, there is a mismatch between the objective and the instruction. If the test required students to answer questions about how minority vote affects political gains there is maximum incongruence because the instruction itself was from a third domain. A good exercise might be to ask teachers or designers, on three separate occasions, to produce their *objectives,* their *tests* and their *lesson plans*. It is conceivable that the objectives might be for a certain attitude, while the instruction covers facts, and the test calls for the use of concepts and rules.

3. Tests should not be either easier or more difficult than the objectives. The aim of testing is to accurately represent the objective and not simply to make a test "difficult."

4. Tests should not try to achieve a large range in scores or a normal distribution of scores. The purpose of criterion-referenced performance testing is not to find out that one student scored higher or lower than another. Its purpose is to assess and document student success.

THE CONCEPT OF MASTERY

The idea of *mastery* (Bloom, 1968) requires a change in thinking about instructional design as well as assessment. In conventional instruction, both the teacher and the students expect that only a few students will receive an A in the topic or course. The rest will either do fairly well, as represented by a B or C, or they will fail. A normal curve is formed when test scores are plotted as frequency distributions with a certain percentage of students receiving different grades.

In commenting on this system of assessment, Bloom, Hastings, and Madaus (1971) observe that expectations like this tend to fix the academic goals of teachers and students at inappropriately low levels, thus reducing both teacher and student motivation. The particular educational practice that produces these effects is called "group-paced" instruction; all students must try to learn at the same rate and by the same mode of instruction. When both pace and mode are fixed, the achievement of each student becomes primarily a function of aptitude. If both mode and rate can vary among learners, the chances are that more students will become successful in their learning (Block & Anderson, 1975).

It is easier to vary the *rate* of learning among students than to determine the *mode* of learning that will benefit each student the most. Self-paced, self-instructional courses take care of the rate problem and, to some extent (when alternative materials or instructional methods are available) the problem of learning style as well. The diagnostic features of individualized assessment also help students redirect their efforts properly.

Mastery learning essentially means that if the proper conditions can be provided, perhaps 90–95 percent of students will be able to master most objectives to the degree now only reached by "good students." The mastery learning concept abandons the idea that students merely learn more or less well. Instead, an effort is made to find out why students fail to reach mastery and to remedy the situation. Resolving a learning problem usually requires one of the following measures: (1) allow more time for learning; (2) provide different media, methods, or strategies; or (3) determine the prerequisite knowledge or skills that are missing. Within this context, a teacher's personal knowledge can be added to decide what to do when none of these above measures are working. The general aim of mastery learning is to provide materials and conditions by which most learners can be successful at most tasks, in a program that is reasonable for each individual.

Determining Criteria for Mastery

How do you know when a student has performed satisfactorily or attained mastery on a test? If the student has not performed satisfactorily, how do you convey this result to the student in sufficient detail for the student to know how to remediate? Students must be told where they need to apply their efforts, and in order to give sufficient feedback to them, the teacher needs to know which test items relate to each learning objective.

Remedial instruction for intellectual skills objectives is best accomplished by administering a diagnostic test on the capabilities subordinate to the objective. A teacher or trainer might also orally test students to find out where their failure first began. Lessons in individualized instruction often incorporate diagnostic tests or practice exercises on subordinate capabilities. Diagnostic tests of subordinate competencies are particularly useful for slow learners, to ensure that they have mastered each capability before going on to the next one. Small failures can be detected using this procedure before they accumulate into larger failures of entire lessons, topics, or courses. Use of frequent testing can prevent year-after-year failures or, at least, can alert the school earlier to a need to reappraise the program for particular students.

Defining mastery for a test on an objective also defines the criterion of success for that objective. The first step is to define *how well* the learner must perform on the test to indicate success on that objective. Next, a record is made of *how many* students have reached the criterion (mastery). It is then possible to know if the instruction for that objective has reached its design objective. At the end of an entire course, the percentage of students who reached mastery of all objectives (or any specified percent of the objectives) can be computed. From this data one can determine whether the course design criterion was met. A frequent course design criterion is that 90 percent of the students achieve mastery of 90 percent of the objectives. Sometimes three design criteria are set, with one indicating minimal acceptable success, and the others representing higher degrees of success. Course design criteria can be used to provide *accountability* for the performance of students following instruction.

The administration of tests and the definition of mastery level for each objective provide the means for evaluating the course itself as well as the individual performance of the students. For example, students can be promoted on the basis of tests, and the test results can be used in the *formative evaluation* of the course, showing where revisions are needed (see Chapter 16).

Defining mastery of objectives and using objective-referenced tests is intended primarily for monitoring student progress and discovering how successful the course was; data from the same tests can be used to assign grades when required. Grades, in this case, are often preset as a degree of mastery. For example A = 90 percent, B = 80–89 percent, and so on. However, the meaning of mastery should be carefully considered when setting criterion levels—a pilot who landed a plane 90 percent of the time would not be operating at an acceptable level!

CRITERIA FOR OBJECTIVE-REFERENCED ASSESSMENT

Next we look at how to determine mastery criteria for each kind of learning objective. Procedures for each learning domain are described. More extensive procedures for criterion-referenced testing can be found in Berk (1984).

Intellectual Skill Objectives

Problem Solving   To illustrate the criteria for assessing performance for *problem-solving* objectives, we begin with the objective shown in Table 7.1, "generates, *in writing*, a business plan including an estimate of ROI."

To score a business plan as acceptable, it is necessary to prepare a list of features the plan needs to include. No verbatim scoring key is possible for this kind of objective, and mechanical scoring is also not feasible. Table 13.1 is an example of a rubric that might be used to assess performance on this objective. Even though no grammatical requirements are included in the statement of the objective, the rubric includes a criterion related to grammar and punctuation. If several teachers are teaching the same objective, they might work together to define the assessment criteria and agree upon how many actions and what aspects of the business plan need to be included in the paragraph. They could also agree on the minimum number of rules to be synthesized, and which rules would be mandatory or optional.

The test for a problem-solving objective should not be based on a judgment such as "8 out of 10 questions correct." The criteria are usually both qualitative and quantitative in nature. Scoring will always require judgment, not simply a clerical checking of answers with an answer key. Consequently, the degree of agreement among teachers regarding how to score the test is a relevant factor for determining the reliability of the test.

Rule Learning   The example given in Table 7.1 for rule learning is "demonstrates the addition of positive and negative numbers by solving example problems *in writing* showing all work." To convert this objective into a test, one first needs to expand the objective as follows: "Given verbally stated examples involving physical variables that vary over a range of positive and negative values, demonstrates the addition of these values by writing appropriate mathematical expressions yielding their sum." This more complete statement provides more detail, and in doing so, helps to more adequately formulate the test item. Such an item, for example, might say, "The temperature in town at night was 17 °C, during the day it *increased* by 30 °C. What was the highest daytime temperature? The following night the temperature *dropped* 40 degrees, what was the temperature that night?"

A remaining decision pertaining to performance measurement has to do with the question of how many items to develop. Obviously, the aim is to achieve a genuine measurement of what the student mastered. By convention, 10 or 20 items might be considered the right number of items to test an arithmetic rule. However, Lathrop (1983) has shown that, by using reasonable assumptions of sequential analysis (Wald, 1947), decisions about mastery and nonmastery can be made on the basis of as few as three items. The aim of using multiple test items is primarily to avoid measurement errors that might arise because of one or more undesirable idiosyncratic features of a single item. Additional procedures for determining desirable test length are described in the book edited by Berk (1984) on criterion-referenced test construction.

Defined Concepts   We use the following objective as an example for measuring a *defined concept:* "Given a picture of an observer on the Earth and the sky above, classifies the *zenith* as the point in the sky vertically above the observer." Again, the situation described in this statement may be directly represented in the test item. The test item might first depict (in labeled diagram) the Earth, the sky, and an observer standing on the Earth. It could say: "Show, by an angular diagram, the location of the *zenith*." To answer, the student would draw a vertical line from the observer to the sky, indicating that it made a 90-degree angle with the Earth's surface at the point at which the observer was located, and label the point in the sky to which the line was drawn as the zenith.

An item of this type would not require a student to verbalize the answer, and it might be a good form of measurement for that reason. Alternatively, if you could assume the student has a good verbal capability, the item might be stated as follows: "Classifies *zenith* as the point in the sky vertically (or at a 90-degree angle to the surface) above an observer on the Earth by stating a definition orally." It should be noted that measurement in this case is subject to distortion. Unless one is entirely convinced that the student has mastered the subordinate concepts (Earth, sky, observer, 90 degrees), the student's response might have to be interpreted as a *memorized verbalization*. Nevertheless, verbal statements (preferably in the learner's own words) are often employed as criteria for assessment of defined concepts.

Concrete Concepts   To test a *concrete concept* from an objective such as: "Given five common plants and asked to name the major parts, identifies for each the root, leaf, and stem by pointing to each while naming it," the student might be shown five plants and be asked to point to and name the root, leaf, and stem for each. An objective for a different situation, such as, "Given pictures of five common plants, identifies the root, leaf, and stem of each by placing labels bearing these names opposite the appropriate part," implies a specifically different kind of test item. The first test item assumes that the oral responses *root, leaf,* and *stem* can be made without error, whereas the second example requires the student to be able to read the labels.

Another example of testing a concrete concept is provided by the task of identifying a common geometric shape. The objective might read: "Given a set of common geometric shapes and the oral directions 'show me the circles,' identify the circles by pointing." A test item might have the following figures on a sheet of paper and the student would point to the three circular figures in order to show that he or she knows the concept.

Discrimination   Assessing discrimination requires the presentation of stimuli to which the learner indicates "same" or "different." The example in Table 7.1 is "discriminates, by matching the French sounds of *u* and *ou*." To represent this objective as a test item, the sounds of a number of French syllables or words containing these vowels (as in *rue* and *roux*) would be presented and the student would indicate "same" or "different" for each syllable or word.

An example of visual discrimination would be to select the figure that matches the model:

Response Choices

The directions for this item would be "Circle the figure or figures that match the model." Discrimination tasks are purely perceptual; they do not require the learner to name the stimulus or identify its attributes. What is assessed is simply whether the student perceives a difference or not.

Cognitive Strategies

In contrast to the techniques of assessment for intellectual skills, the indicators of cognitive strategies are somewhat indirect and often require a longer chain of inference. For example, the strategy in Table 7.1 asks the student to recall the names of the states by imagining a map of the United States. The observed performance is listing the states. A student could list the states by using a different cognitive strategy, possibly one that was less efficient, such as listing the states in alphabetical order. The performance by itself does not indicate the adoption and use of a particular strategy. To be certain a student used the strategy where they imagined a map of the United States, the teacher would need to observe the student naming the states by regional locations.

Several different strategies for solving geometric problems involving relations between angles of a complex figure were studied by Greeno (1978; see also, Gagné, 1985, pp. 143–145). Here, too, the strategies could not be revealed simply by the successful solution to the geometric problem. Use of the strategies was indicated through verbal reports by the students, who were asked to "think aloud" while working on the problem.

The notion of mastery learning can not be readily applied to the measurement of cognitive strategies. Whether the strategies control the processes of attending, encoding, retrieving, or problem solving, it is the *quality* of the mental process that is being assessed and not simply its presence or absence. Novel problems often have many solutions, not just one solution. In such instances, cognitive strategies are used to achieve the solution, whatever it may be. Accordingly, assessment becomes a matter of judging how good the solution is, and not making a "pass-fail" decision.

In regard to doctoral student education, for example, standards of originality and inventiveness are applied to the assessment of their dissertation. Besides being thorough and technically sound, a doctoral dissertation should make "an original discovery or contribution" to a field of systematic knowledge. Exact criteria or dimensions for judging this quality are typically not specified. Varying numbers of professionally qualified people usually arrive at a consensus concerning the degree of originality exhibited by a dissertation and its acceptability as a novel contribution to an area of knowledge or art.

Productive Thinking Measuring productive thinking and the cognitive strategies that underlie such thinking was investigated by Johnson and Kidder (1972) in undergraduate psychology classes. Students were asked to invent novel hypotheses, questions, and answers to problem statements that went beyond the information in lectures and textbooks. The problems included: (1) predicting the consequences of an unusual psychological event, (2) writing an imaginative sentence incorporating several newly learned (specified) concepts, (3) stating a novel hypothesis related to a described situation, (4) writing a title for a table containing behavioral data, and (5) drawing conclusions from a table or graph. When combined into tests containing 10 to 15 items, reasonably adequate reliabilities of *originality* scores were obtained. Quality was judged by two raters whose judgments were found to agree highly after a short period of training.

Assessments of originality, such those measured by Johnson and Kidder (1972), are often made of students' answers, compositions, and projects at pre-college levels. Such judgments by teachers often occur incidentally or informally and concern a variety of projects and problems undertaken by students.

The assessment of cognitive strategies or the originality of thought as an *outcome* of learning does not have the same aim nor does it use the same methods as those used to measure creativity as a *trait*. Creativity has been extensively studied (Torrance, 1963; Guilford, 1967; Johnson, 1972), and the findings go far beyond the scope of the present discussion. However, when assessing quality of thought as a learning outcome, the findings suggest that two main characteristics must be sought. First, the problem (or project) that is set for the student must require the use of knowledge, concepts, and rules recently learned by the student rather those acquired many years previously. Second, students must show that they learned relevant prerequisite information and skills before the assessment was undertaken. This condition is necessary to ensure that all students have the same opportunity to be original and their solutions are not handicapped by the absence of necessary knowledge and intellectual skills.

Verbal Information

In this domain, the concept of mastery is related to a predetermined set of facts, generalizations, or ideas, and the student must be able to state them completely and accurately. The fundamental distinction between *objective* measurement and *content-referenced* measurement is that one wants to determine whether certain objectives have been attained by the students rather than just determining whether the content was covered by the instructor.

Objective-referenced assessment for verbal information is achieved by precisely specifying the names, facts, and generalizations to be learned. The tests differentiate the core content of information to be recalled from incidental information that represents learning beyond the required level.

It's a mistake to make objectives in the information domain so exhaustive that there is no time to cover related objectives in other domains. One should deliberately seek out and identify the informational outcomes that are likely to contribute the most to the *attainment of objectives in other domains.*

Typically, assessing learning of verbal information means measuring quantity (Gagné & Beard, 1978), for example, assessing *how much* the student knows about some particular historical event or era or about a natural phenomenon like earthquakes. How much do students know about the varieties of oak trees or about cutting logs into lumber? Answers to quantity questions come from content that is fairly well defined. Content may be precisely defined (in a specific long-prose passage) or it may be loosely defined (from declarative knowledge from lectures, text, and other references available on a particular subject). A variety of methods have been proposed for the analysis of prose texts displaying verbal knowledge (Britton & Black, 1985). Some of these proposals suggest the possibility that the *quality* of knowledge can be assessed as a learning outcome. It is possible that some kinds of memory organization resulting from learning represent "deeper understanding" of verbal information. It is also possible to distinguish main ideas from subordinate ideas by these methods. But the fuller meaning of quality or depth of knowledge remains to be shown by research and theoretical development before measures of this aspect of verbal information can be developed.

Examples of Verbal Information Items   Some typical items for assessment of verbal information are:

1. Describe at least three causes of the American Revolution, as discussed in the textbook.
2. State the chemical name for the following substances: baking soda, blue vitriol, chalk.
3. Write a paragraph summarizing how a president is elected if the electoral college fails to elect.
4. Name any 15 of these 20 animals from these pictures.
5. What is guaranteed by the Fourth Amendment to the U.S. Constitution?

As these examples indicate, objective-referenced tests of verbal information require the exact identification of the information to be learned and retained. If listing names or dates is to be learned, this should be made clear. Alternatively, if the substance of a passage is to be recounted, this should be made apparent to the student. In doing so, learning for mastery is feasible, fair, and reasonable.

Attitudes

As Chapter 5 indicated, attitudes vary in the intensity with which they influence the choice of personal actions. During assessment, it is the *strength* of the attitude you will want to assess, not mastery. Assessing the strength of an attitude toward or against choices of action can be obtained by counting the number of times a person behaves in a certain way in a sample of defined situations. For example, attitude toward using public transportation might be assessed by observing the likelihood of a student's choosing various forms of public (rather than private) transportation. The observed incidents would then be the basis for inferring the degree to which the person *tends* to use or not to use public transportation.

In assessing an attitude such as "concern for others," it is evident that you can't use "pass-fail" criteria. A teacher might establish the objective that all her second-grade pupils will improve their concern for others during the school year. From this, it is possible to set the standard that each child will exhibit concern for others, either in verbal expression or overt actions, more times per month in May, for example, than during the previous October. Anecdotal records can be kept, noting actions where concern for others was displayed, and reports of "improvement" or "no improvement" can be made at the end of the school year. The reports can be quantified in terms of the number of positive actions and proportion of positive-to-total (positive plus negative) actions. Behaviors representing neither kind of action would not be recorded, in recognition of the fact that some of the child's time is spent in study periods where there is little opportunity for them to behave either way toward other people. The teacher could develop a system of placing a minus, check or plus next to the student's name in the roster when they observed a student interaction during free play.

Attitudes are often measured by obtaining self-reports of the likelihood of actions, as opposed to direct observations of the actions. The most serious limitation with self-reports is the possibility of bias resulting from students answering questions to win approval rather than to accurately reflect their attitudes. There appears to be no simple solution to the problem of obtaining truly accurate information from self-reports, although many investigations have been carried out for this purpose (for example, Fishbein, 1967). The best results can be achieved when students are assured that the assessment is not intended as an adversarial process; that is, they won't be judged by their answers. Questionnaires administered to groups should ensure that responses are anonymous.

As previously indicated, attitudes are best conceived and measured as a consistency in *choices of personal action* toward some class of object, persons, or events as described in Chapter 5. A domain of assessment items that defines these choices may be carefully specified along several dimensions (Triandis, 1964). For example, to assess an individual's attitude toward public transportation, you might include items that cover several dimensions of personal choice (comfort, speed, cost, vehicle cleanliness, and so on). This method can be used to provide an acceptable quality of objective-referenced scores for assessing attitudes.

Motor Skills

For many years, the motor skills of schoolchildren were evaluated by comparing their performances with certain approved standards. For example, to grade handwriting, a familiar device in the elementary school room was the Palmer Scale. A sample of the student's writing was compared with ideal samples from a chart containing various degrees of "correct" penmanship, each with a numerical value such as 90, 80, 70, and so on. This was a *criterion-referenced* form of grading, in that the standards were predetermined and teachers could say that 60 was "passing" at the third grade, 70 at the fourth grade, and so on.

The standards for assessing motor skills usually refer to the *precision* of the performance and its *speed*. Because motor skills are known to improve with extended practice, it is unrealistic to expect that mastery can be defined in the sense of "learned" or "not learned." A standard of performance must be used to determine whether mastery has been achieved.

Keyboarding skills provide a good example of assessment for motor skills because a number of different performance standards can be set. For example, a standard of 30 words per minute with five errors may be adopted as a reasonable standard in a beginning keyboarding course, whereas 40 or 50 words per minute with three errors may be expected for a midlevel course and 90 words per minute with three errors might be used in an advanced course.

RELIABILITY OF OBJECTIVE-REFERENCED MEASURES

Developing objective referenced tests requires the selection of performance standards that are appropriate to the objective(s). In addition, the test items need to yield measurements that are *dependable*. This feature is referred to as *reliability*, and it has two primary meanings.

Consistency

First, reliability refers to *consistency* of measurement. A student's performance on one test item for an objective must be consistent with his or her performance on other items covering the same objective. For example, a pupil in the seventh grade may be asked to demonstrate mastery of the arithmetic rule: $3M + 2M = 25; M = ?$ The purpose of assessment is to discover whether the student is able to perform a *class* of arithmetic operations of this type, not just one. Additional items belonging to the same class (for example: $4M + 3M = 22; 5M + 1M = 36$) should be used to ensure dependability of the measurement.

In informal testing situations, like when a teacher asks questions of one student after another, single items may be used to assess performance. However, no measure of consistency is available in such situations. A student may make a successful response on any single item because he or she happens to have memorized the answer. Alternatively, the response may be incorrect if the student was misled by some particular characteristic of the item. The answer to the single item does not indicate the student mastered the objective.

In instances where the performance represented by the objective is well-defined (as in the arithmetic example previously given), the procedure for selecting additional assessment items of the same class is fairly straightforward. The conclusion aimed for is not "How many items are correct?" but rather "Does the number of correct items indicate mastery?" Although two items are obviously better than one, they may yield the puzzling outcome, half right and half wrong. Does this mean that the student attained mastery, or does it mean the student got one item right because he or she somehow managed to memorize the answer? Three items will provide a better means of making a reliable decision about mastery. In this case, two out of three correct answers leads to certain confidence that reliability of measurement has been achieved. More items can be employed, but three seems a reasonable minimum on which to base a reliable assessment of mastery.

When cognitive strategies are the aim of assessment, the assessment item might actually be a rather lengthy problem-solving task. For example, such a task might be to "Write a 300-word theme on a student-selected topic, within one hour." It might require several assessment items to obtain a reliable and valid assessment of the performance, because it is necessary to separate prior learning (of information and intellectual skills) from the quality of original thought. A number of occasions must be provided on which the student can display the quality of the performance. The aim is to make it unlikely that a student could meet the criteria without possessing a genuine capability for original writing.

Temporal Dependability

The second meaning of reliability is dependability of the measurement on temporally separated occasions. You want to be sure that the student's demonstration of mastery on Monday is not different from what it would be on Tuesday or on some other day, assuming that the conditions surrounding the testing are the same. Is the performance an ephemeral thing, or does it have the degree of permanence one expects of a learned capability? Has the performance, good or bad, been determined largely by how the student felt that day, by a temporary illness, or by environmental features (room too hot or cold) of the testing situation?

Reliability of measurement in this second meaning is usually determined by a second test separate from the first by a time interval of days or weeks. This test-retest method, in which reliability is indicated by a high degree of correspondence between scores obtained by a group of students on the two occasions, is often used in the formative evaluation of tests. It is also commonly used in practical assessments to determine if what has been learned has a reasonable degree of stability.

NORM-REFERENCED MEASURES

Tests designed to yield scores that compare a student's performance with that of a group or with a norm established by group scores are called *norm-referenced*. Characteristically, such tests are used to obtain assessments of student achievement over relatively large segments of instructional content, such as topics or a course. They differ from objective-referenced tests in that they typically measure cumulative knowledge of a larger number of objectives rather than a few, clearly identifiable objectives. For example, a norm-referenced test is more likely to have the purpose of assessing relative knowledge of history than it is to measure the attainment of individual skills or knowledge related to specific objectives. They also differ, as previously discussed, because the standard is set *after* the test is given as the average performance of the group.

Because of the characteristic of comprehensive coverage, norm-referenced tests are most useful for *summative* kinds of assessment and evaluation (see Chapter 16). They provide answers to such questions as "How much American history does a student know (compared to others at this grade level)?" "How well is the student able to reason using the operations of arithmetic?" "What proficiency does the student have in using grammatical rules?" Obviously, such assessment is most appropriate when applied to instruction extending over reasonably long periods of time, as in midcourse or end-of-course examinations.

The characteristics of norm-referenced measures imply some obvious limitations compared with objective-referenced tests. Because their items usually represent a measure of cumulative knowledge, often impossible to identify singly, they cannot readily be used for the purpose of diagnostic testing of prerequisite skills. For a similar reason, norm-referenced tests typically do not provide direct and unambiguous measures of what has been learned, when the latter is conceived as one or more defined objectives.

Norm-referenced tests can be used to measure a group's relative attainment of intellectual skills, information, and cognitive strategies. In so doing, they assess student capabilities that are "global" rather than specific to identifiable objectives. For this reason, they are particularly appropriate for assessing outcomes of learning in a set of topics or in a total course. Because the scores are representative of a group (a single class or a larger "referenced" group such as 10-year-old children), the score made by each student may be compared with those of others in the group. Percentile scores are often used for this purpose; the score of a student may be expressed, for example, as "falling in the 63rd percentile."

Teacher/Trainer-Made Tests

Teachers might construct either criterion or normative referenced tests. We recommend that teacher tests be criterion-referenced because the purpose of instruction is to have students reach a predetermined level of knowledge and skill. When instruction has been designed to ensure the attainment of objectives, tests should be derived directly from the definition of the objectives themselves, as indicated in the earlier portion of this chapter. Unless objective-referenced tests are used for this purpose, two important purposes of assessment will be neglected: (1) the assessment of mastery of the specific capabilities learned, and (2) the possibility of diagnostic help for students in overcoming particular learning deficiencies by retrieving missing prerequisite skills and knowledge.

With a norm-referenced test it is possible to compare a student's performance within a referenced group (such as last year's class). Such tests are refined over periods of years, using methods of item analysis to select the most "discriminating" items (see, for example, Hills, 1981; Payne, 1968). This means that items that do not discriminate (those that either many or few students answer correctly) are progressively discarded. Tests refined in this manner tend to increasingly measure problem solving and other cognitive strategies. They may also measure general intelligence, rather than what has been directly learned. Although this may be a legitimate intention when the aim is to assess the total effects of a course of study, it is obvious that norm-referenced tests serve different assessment purposes than do objective-referenced tests.

Predictive Tests

Predictive assessment or predictive validity refers to the extent to which a test can be used to draw inferences regarding achievement. Empirical evidence in support of predictive validity must include a comparison of performance on the validated test against performance on outside criteria (Sadoff, 2003). This is why predictive tests are used to forecast some future "state of affairs" (or in the educational context, future performance) (Darkwa, 2003). For example, the various educational tests used for selection purposes by colleges and universities, such as the Scholastic Aptitude Test (SAT) and the Graduate Record Examination (GRE), are used to predict how students will do in school. Students who score high on the SAT are predicted to do better in college than low-scorers.

Standardized Tests

Norm-referenced tests intended for broad usage among many schools within a school system, a region, or in the nation as a whole may have norms that are *standardized*. This means that the tests have been given to large samples of students in specified age (or grade) groups and the resulting distributions of scores become the standards to which the scores of any given student or class of students may be compared. Sometimes the standard norms are expressed as percentiles, indicating what percentage of the sample attained or fell below particular scores. Such standards are also often expressed as grade-equivalent scores, indicating the scores attained by all children in the group who were in the first grade, the second grade, and so on. Procedures used in the development and validation of standardized tests are described in many books on this subject (for example, Cronbach, 1984; Thorndike & Hagen, 1986; Tyler, 1971).

Standardized tests are norm-referenced. Accordingly, standardized tests typically exhibit the characteristics previously described. They are usually mixed in their measurement of particular objectives because their items have not been directly derived from particular objectives. Their items are selected to produce the largest possible variation in scores among students, and their scores tend to be rather highly correlated with intelligence rather than with particular learning outcomes. With a few exceptions, they fail to provide the identification of missing subordinate capabilities essential to diagnostic aims.

Standardized tests are appropriate for the purpose of summative evaluation of total courses of several years of instruction. When employed for these purposes, standardized tests can provide valuable information about the long-term effects of courses and of larger instructional programs.

SUMMARY

Up to this point, we have been concerned primarily with goals and performance objectives, with the domains of learning they represent, and with the design of lessons that employ instructional events and conditions of learning suitable for the chosen objectives. In this chapter, we turned our attention to the assessment of student performance on objectives. Thus, we proceed from the *what* and the *how* to the *how well* aspect of learning.

While various types of assessment were discussed, including authentic testing and rubrics, the main focus of the chapter was on *objective-referenced tests employing a criterion-referenced interpretation*. Such tests serve several important purposes:

1. They show whether each student has mastered an objective and, hence, may go on to study another objective.
2. They permit early detection and diagnosis of failure to learn, thus helping to identify the remedial study needed.
3. They provide data for making improvements in the instruction itself.

4. They are *fair* evaluations in that they measure performance on the objective that was given to the student as an indication of what he or she was supposed to learn.

Objective-referenced tests are direct rather than indirect measures of performance on objectives. They deal with each objective separately rather than with very large units of instruction, such as an entire year of study. For this reason, they have diagnostic value as well as value for formative evaluation of the course.

The *validity* of objective-referenced tests is found by determining the congruence of the test with the objective. *Reliability* is obtained by measuring the consistency of the performance assessment and its dependability over time. The concept of *mastery* is relevant for objective-referenced tests in the domains of intellectual skills, motor skills, and information. For these types of learning outcomes, mastery levels can be defined in terms of degree of learning as reflected in test performance. In the case of cognitive strategies and attitudes, because assessments are less direct and more difficult to observe, the standards that define mastery are more difficult to determine.

Another type of test is called *norm-referenced*. Such tests do not measure separate, specific objectives of the course. Rather, they measure mixtures or composite sets of objectives, whether these are identified or not. When a norm-referenced test is a standardized test, it has been carefully designed and revised to yield high variability of scores. The interpretation of the scores is made by reference to norms, which represent performance on the test for large groups of learners. Such tests permit comparison of a score of one pupil with that of others; they also permit comparing the average score for a group with the scores of a larger norm group.

REFERENCES

Andrade, H. G. (1999). When assessment is instruction and instruction is assessment: Using rubrics to promote thinking and understanding. In L. Hetland & S. Veenema (Eds.), *The project zero classroom: Views on understanding*. Cambridge, MA: Project Zero.

Andrade, H. G. (2003). Retrieved January 2004 from: http://www.ascd.org/cms/index.cfm?TheViewID=347.

Berk, R. A. (Ed.). (1984). *A guide to criterion-referenced test construction*. Baltimore, MD: Johns Hopkins University Press.

Block, J. H., & Anderson, L. W. (1975). *Mastery learning to classroom instruction*. New York: Macmillan.

Bloom, B. S. (1968). Learning for mastery. *Evaluation Comment, 1*(2), 1–5.

Bloom, B. S., Hastings, J. T., & Madaus, G. F. (1971). *Handbook for formative and summative evaluation of student learning*. New York: McGraw-Hill

Briggs, L. J., & Wager, W. W. (1981). *Handbook of procedures for the design of instruction* (2nd ed.). Englewood Cliffs NJ: Educational Technology Publications.

Britton, B. K., & Black, J.B (1985). *Understanding expository text.* Hillsdale, NJ: Erlbaum.

CTVG Cognition and Technology Group at Vanderbilt (1990). Anchored Instruction and its relationship to situated cognition, *Educational Researcher, 19*(6), pp. 2–10

Cronbach, L. J. (1984). *Essentials of psychological testing* (4th ed.). New York: Harper & Row.

Darkwa, O. (2003). Retrieved summer 2003 from: http://www.uic.edu/classes/socw/socw560/MEASURE/tsld001.htm.

Dick, W., & Carey, L. (1996). The systematic design of instruction (4th ed.). New York: HarperCollins College Publishers.

Fishbein, M. A. (Ed.) (1967). *Attitude theory and measurement.* New York: Wiley.

Gagné, R. M. (1985). *The conditions of learning* (4th ed.). New York: Holt, Rinehart and Winston.

Gagné, R. M., & Beard, J. G. (1978). Assessment of learning outcomes. In R. Glaser (Ed.), *Advances in instructional psychology* (Vol. 1). Hillsdale, NJ: Erlbaum.

Goodrich, H. (1996). Student self-assessment: At the intersection of metacognition and authentic assessment. *Doctoral dissertation,* Harvard University, Cambridge, MA.

Greeno, J. G. (1978). A study of problem solving. In R. Glaser (Ed.), *Advances in instructional psychology* (Vol. 1). Hillsdale, NJ: Erlbaum.

Guilford, J. P. (1967). *The nature of human intelligence.* New York: McGraw-Hill.

Hast, D. (1994) *Authentic assessment: A handbook for educators.* Boston: MA: Addison-Wesley.

Hills, J. R. (1981). *Measurement and evaluation in the classroom.* Columbus, OH: Merrill.

Holzberg, C. (2003). Retrieved from: http://www.techlearning.com/db_area/arehives/WCE/arehives/evalguid.html.

Johnson, D. M. (1972). *A systematic introduction to the psychology of thinking.* New York: Harper & Row.

Johnson, D. M., & Kidder, R. C. (1972). Productive thinking in psychology, classes. *American Psychologist, 27,* 672–674.

Keller, J. M. (1987). Development and use of the ARCS model of motivational design. *Journal of Instructional Development, 10*(3), 2–10.

Keller, J. M. (1999). Motivation in cyber learning environments. *International Journal of Educational Technology, 1*(1), 7–30.

Lathrop, R. L. (1983). The number of performance assessments necessary to determine competence. *Journal of Instructional Development, 6(3),* 26–31.

McAlpine, D. (2000) Assessment and the gifted. *Tall Poppies, 25*(1).

Payne, D. A. (1968). *The specification and measurement of learning outcomes.* Waltham, MA: Blaisdell.

Piirto, J. (1999) *Talented children and adults: Their development and education.* Upper Saddle River, NJ: Prentice-Hall.

Popham, W. J. (1975). *Educational evaluation.* Englewood Cliffs, NJ: Prentice Hall.

Renzulli, J. S. (1977) *The enrichment triad model: A guide for developing defensible programs for the gifted and talented.* Wethersfield, CT: Creative Learning Press.

Resnick, L. (1987) *Education and learning to think.* Washington, DC: National Academy Press.

Sadoff, J. (2003). Retrieved summer 2003 from: http://www.sabes.org/resources/fieldnotes/vol10/f03facts.htm.

Thorndike, R. L., & Hagen, E. (1986). *Measurement and evaluation in psychology and education.* New York: Wiley.

Tombari, M., and Borich, G. (1999) *Authentic assessment in the classroom: Applications and practice.* Columbus, OH: Merrill.

Torrance, E. P. (1963). *Education and the creative potential.* Minneapolis, MN: University of Minnesota Press.

Triandis, H. C. (1964). Exploratory factor analyses of the behavioral component of social attitudes. *Journal of Abnormal and Social Psychology, 68,* 420–430.

Tyler, L. E. (1971). *Tests and measurements* (2nd ed.). Englewood Cliffs, NJ: Prentice Hall.

Wald, A. (1947). *Sequential analysis.* New York: Wiley.

Wiggins, G. (1989, May) A true test: Toward more authentic and equitable assessment. *Phi Delta Kappan, 70*(9), 703–713.

Wiggins, G. (1992, May) Creating tests worth taking. *Educational Leadership.*

GROUP LEARNING ENVIRONMENTS

A great deal of instruction is done with learners assembled in groups of various sizes. The group sizes that are of particular significance to instructional design include: (1) the two-person group, or *dyad,* where *tutoring* is possible; (2) the *small group,* where roughly three to eight members engage in *discussion, interactive recitation,* or *collaborative activity,* and (3) the *large group,* with nine or more members. The most common mode of instruction for large groups is *lecture* with mediated materials such as projected slides and demonstrations. Another instructional technique with large groups is *individual recitation,* commonly used with foreign-language courses. However, technology and a resurging interest in social constructivism has increased interest in group instruction and collaborative learning in large groups, and the establishment of learning communities has changed the way instructional designers think about group instruction. In today's digital world, electronic classrooms are rapidly emerging with the capability to support group learning even for large groups of students beyond the four walls of the building.

Of course there are all kinds of reasons for putting students into groups. Small groups support many instructional methods associated with active learning—involving learners as participants in the process of acquiring, analyzing, and organizing information, and turning it into knowledge. Although the three group sizes have different implications for instructional methods, the distinctions among them are not hard and fast. For example, with a group containing between eight and 15 members, instruction might begin with discussion or with a lecture, followed by division of the class into smaller groups for various kinds of learning activities. When instruction is delivered to a *very large group* (a hundred or more students) logistical matters pertaining to seating arrangements, acoustics, and visual aids and other factors affecting communication with the learner are very important considerations in the design process. Many large lecture halls do not lend themselves easily to group work, but there are strategies where even two students sitting side-by-side can be engaged in a learning activity as a dyad.

CHARACTERISTICS OF GROUP INSTRUCTION

One way to characterize the instructional features of different kinds of groups is to describe the various methods of instruction, such as *lecture, discussion*, and *recitation*, in terms of the events of instruction they can provide for the learner. Each method has different characteristics and various strengths and weaknesses when used with different sizes of groups. There are also variations in what is done by the lecturer, in what happens during a discussion, and in what occurs during recitation. Systematic knowledge of several of these instructional methods is summarized in a volume edited by Gage (1976).

Rather than describing the features of the different methods of instruction, our approach in this chapter is to consider how varieties of instruction can be planned for different group sizes —the dyad (two-person group), the small group, and the large group. Our discussion covers the instructional arrangements (including instructional methods) that are *possible* and are likely to be *most effective* with each type of group.

Patterns of Interaction in Instructional Groups

The size of an instructional group impacts the pattern of interaction among teachers and students. Depending on how they are perceived by students, these patterns may influence the outcomes of learning. Some classroom interaction patterns, similar to those described by Walberg (1976), are depicted in Figure 14–1.

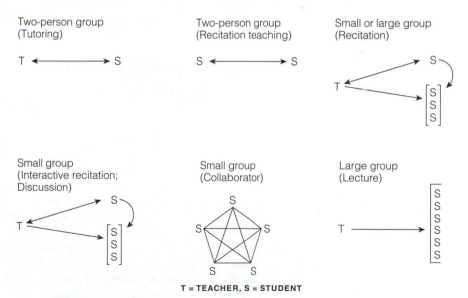

T = TEACHER, S = STUDENT

FIGURE **14–1**

SOME PATTERNS OF CLASSROOM INTERACTION IN GROUPS OF VARIOUS SIZES (ARROWS INDICATE THE DIRECTION OF INTERACTIONS)

As the figure shows, communication between teacher and student flows in both directions during instruction in the dyad. When recitation is the adopted mode, with either a small or a large group, mutual interaction occurs between the teacher and one student at a time, while the other students are recipients of only the teacher's communication. Interactive recitation and discussion occur in a small group when there is interaction among students as well as between teacher and student. In the lecture method of instruction, used typically with a large group, the communication flow is from teacher to students.

Variations in Instructional Events

Any or all of the events of instruction (Chapter 10) will vary with group size, both in their form and in their feasibility. For example, the event of gaining attention can be precisely managed in the dyad, but only loosely controlled for individual learners in a large group. An exception to this occurs in large group instruction when electronic classrooms are used. A description of the advantages of electronic classrooms in terms of the implementation of instructional events is presented later in this chapter.

Learning guidance in the dyad is typically under the control of the instructor (tutor). When feedback consists of providing correct or incorrect answers, it can be controlled in a large group with generally the same precision provided to a single student. However, when the feedback includes information about the *causes* of incorrect responding, it will vary with the individual student. The primary factors subject to variation of different group sizes pertain to the events of instruction. Group size not only determines some of the necessary characteristics of these events but also sets limits upon their effectiveness in supporting learning. It is these features of group instruction that are considered in the following sections.

Diagnosing Entry Capabilities of Students

An important factor regarding instructional effectiveness is the assessment of *entry capabilities* of students (Bloom, 1976). Procedures for assessing entry capabilities are not instructional events themselves, but they do impact certain events. The way a teacher or trainer conducts diagnostic procedures will vary with the size of the group.

Entry capabilities can be assessed at the beginning of a course of study or at the start of a semester or school year. Student capabilities can also be assessed just prior to the beginning of each new topic of a course. Diagnosis of this latter sort is commonly used to uncover weaknesses or gaps in the student's capabilities. More finely tuned diagnostic procedures are often used for beginning reading, mathematics and in foreign language study, and they are likely to be most successful if based upon learning hierarchies. Simple tests or probing questions can be administered to reveal specific gaps in enabling skills. This form of diagnosis is not severely affected by group size, because testing for gaps in enabling skills can usually be done as effectively with large groups as with small.

Designing and executing instruction based on the diagnosis of entry capabilities is, however, greatly affected by the size of the instructional group. The effects of group size on instruction are particularly critical when the concern is with *imme-*

diate prerequisites (diagnosis that is relevant to each lesson). This provides the basic rationale for individualized instruction. Depending on previous efforts to prepare students for a particular lesson, a different pattern of prerequisite capabilities may appear for each student in a group. For example, one might discover 20 different entry-level capabilities within a group of 20 students. Such instructional needs can readily be managed in a tutorial situation; in fact, this feature is often considered the most prominent advantage of the tutoring mode. However, these varying patterns present a considerable challenge to the teacher or trainer of a 20-person group, even in an electronic classroom. Some further implications of this circumstance will be discussed in a later section.

INSTRUCTION IN THE TWO-PERSON GROUP OR DYAD

Instructional groups of two persons consist of one student and one instructor or tutor. Dyads can also be composed only of students, with one assuming the tutoring role. In schools, the tutoring of younger students by older ones is a common practice. Peer tutoring, a form of reciprocal teaching, has also been successfully done in early grades (Gartner, Kohler, & Riessman, 1971; Palincsar, 1986). In many organizations, particularly the military, one-on-one training or mentoring is still highly valued. The alternation of student-tutor roles by pairs of older students or of adults is another form of a dyad. With any of these possible arrangements, it is worthy to note the learning gains are frequently reported for tutors as well as students (Ellson, 1976; Devin-Sheehan, Feldman, & Allen, 1976; Sharan, 1980).

As noted in Chapter 13, systems of individualized instruction are usually designed so that diagnostic tests of student weaknesses (or gaps) are followed by instruction designed to fill these gaps. Teachers or trainers are essentially behaving as tutors when they provide oral instruction and, for this reason, individualized instruction often involves tutoring in the dyad.

Events of Instruction in Tutoring

The group composed of a single student and a single tutor has long been considered an ideal situation for teaching and learning. The primary reason for this is the opportunities the two-person group provides for the *flexible adjustment of instructional events*. For example, a tutor can provide just enough stimulation to gain the attention of the student, or increase the amount if the first attempt fails. The tutor can provide learning guidance in many different ways; if one doesn't work well, another one might. The student's comprehension and storing of a new idea can be assessed immediately, and again after a lapse of time, in order to affirm its learning and to reinforce it.

Some of the main features that exemplify flexible adjustment of instructional events for the dyad are:

1. *Gaining attention:* If a student is participating willingly in a tutoring situation, gaining his or her attention (in the sense of alertness) is readily accomplished.

The tutor can verbally demand the student's attention and watch to see if the student is paying attention. Immediate adjustments can be made if the student's attention begins to wander.

2. *Informing the leaner of the objective:* Flexibility is typically achieved by repeating the objective using different terms or by demonstrating the expected performance. This event can be entirely omitted if the student already knows the objective of the instruction.

3. *Stimulating recall of prerequisite learning:* The flexibility of this event with tutoring is a definite advantage. Once a diagnosis of previously learned prerequisites has been made, the tutor can fill in the gaps (if necessary) and proceed to require recall by the student. By making prerequisite skills accessible in the working memory, the tutor does much to ensure that learning will proceed smoothly.

4. *Presenting the stimulus material:* As with Event 3, there is a great flexibility of choice available to the tutor in this event. Selective perception is readily aided: the tutor can emphasize lesson components by changing their oral delivery, by pointing, by drawing a picture, and in many other ways. For example, if a foreign language is being learned, the tutor can choose the oral expression that best illustrates the grammatical rule to be taught.

5. *Providing learning guidance:* This event is also one in which the flexibility of the dyad provides an important advantage. The phrase "adapting instruction to the needs of the learner" has its clearest meaning in this context. The tutor can employ a variety of means to encourage *semantic encoding* on the part of the learner. Furthermore, the tutor can try different strategies, one after another if necessary, until one is found that works best. Rule applications can be demonstrated; pictures can be used to suggest visual imagery; organized information can be provided as a meaningful context to learn new knowledge.

6. *Eliciting the performance:* In the dyad, learner performance can be elicited with a degree of precision not possible in larger groups. On a moment-to-moment basis, the tutor is usually able to judge (by the learner's behavior) that the necessary internal processing has occurred and that the learner is ready to show what he or she has learned.

7. *Providing feedback:* Feedback can be provided more precisely in the dyad than in other groups. Precision in this case pertains not to the timing of feedback but to the nature of the information given to the learner. The learner can be told, with a high degree of accuracy, what is right or wrong with his or her performance and can be directed to correct errors or inadequacies.

8. *Assessing the performance:* Flexibility in assessment is available to the tutor, in the sense that the performance may be tested at various intervals following learning. Testing can be repeated as many times as necessary for a reliable decision to be made.

9. *Enhancing retention and transfer:* The management of this kind of event can be done with considerable flexibility and precision in the dyad. The tutor can select cues that, according to past experience, work effectively to facilitate retrieval for a particular learner. Just enough varied examples can be chosen

to aid the transfer of learning. Spaced reviews can be conducted to ensure long-term retention for the student, based upon previous experience with that student in the tutoring situation.

The Flow of Instruction in Tutoring

It is evident that the two-person instructional group permits maximum control of instructional events by the tutor. As the manager of instruction, the tutor can decide which events to employ, which to emphasize, and which to let the learner control. By properly timing these events, each act of learning can be optimally efficient. In addition, the flexibility of exactly how to select and arrange each event makes it possible for a tutor to provide instruction that meets the needs of the individual student. In the tutoring mode, instruction can be readily *adapted* to the instructional needs of each student.

In practice, tutoring has taken a variety of forms (Gartner, Kohler, & Riessman, 1971). Tutoring has often been shown to yield favorable results in student achievement, although not always (Cloward, 1967; Ellson, 1976). The evidence shows that the advantages of tutoring do not result from the individual attention provided to the student in the dyad. Rather, tutoring works best when the instruction is highly *systematic* (Ellson, 1976). In other words, tutoring can be a highly effective mode because of the flexibility it provides in achieving *precision* of the instructional events. However, the freedom made possible by the dyad will not produce good results if the instruction itself is poorly designed.

Typically, an episode in tutoring runs somewhat as follows. We assume a task in beginning reading for a six-year-old student, with the objective, "Given an unfamiliar printed two-syllable word, demonstrates phonics rules by sounding the word." The printed word is *plunder*.

First, the tutor gains the child's attention and tells him or her of the objective by saying, "Here is a word you probably haven't seen before in your reading (*plunder*). I want you to show me how you can sound it out." If the pupil sounds out the word immediately, either by correctly using rules or by recognizing the printed word, the tutor says "Good!" and goes on to another printed word. Otherwise, the tutor encourages the child to sound out the first syllable (*plun*) then the second one (*der*), and then both together. Actually, the procedure is one of combining reminders of what the child already knows (recall of prerequisites), such as the sounds of *pl* and *un*, and learning guidance that suggests the strategy called "blending." The tutor may tell the child to place his or her finger over the last part of the word, leaving the letters *p* and *l* exposed, and then ask, "What sound does *pl* make?" If the student answers correctly, positive feedback is given. If the student gives an incorrect response, the child is told what the correct response is and asked to repeat it. The procedure is followed for each sound and for successive combinations of sounds, until the entire word can be sounded correctly. At that point, the child is asked to repeat the word, and some acknowledgement is made of the accomplishment. (In fulfilling a secondary objective, the meaning of the word would probably also be explained to the child.)

The systematic steps in this tutoring situation are: stimulating recall of prerequisites, presenting the stimulus material, providing learning guidance, eliciting and assessing the performance, and providing feedback. Essentially, the same steps would be followed in the tutoring of older students or adults in learning intellectual skills, except that somewhat greater dependence might be placed on encouraging the student to institute these events himself. Tutoring at the university level usually consists entirely of self-instruction—the tutor's activities are largely confined to assessing performance and to suggesting how retention can be enhanced and learning transferred to other situations.

INSTRUCTION IN THE SMALL GROUP

Instructional groups of up to eight students are sometimes found in formally planned education and training courses. The university teacher, or the teacher of adult classes, meets with a small group of students on some occasions. In the elementary and middle grades, the schoolteacher may find it desirable to form small groups from an entire class of students in order to instruct students who have progressed to approximately the same point in their learning of a particular subject.

In corporate training, the federal government, and the military in particular, small group instruction in the form of structured on-the-job training (SOJT) remains a popular method of training. With SOJT, an experienced person, often a manager or supervisor, trains a small group of inexperienced personnel on specific tasks. The technical expertise and seasoning of experienced personnel as they actually perform a task is captured, documented, and organized into instructional products called SOJT guides. The guides are based on learning objectives made up of behaviors, standards, conditions, and performance measures, allowing new workers to be trained to predefined, measurable standards. With SOJT, emphasis is often placed on pre-task preparation, safety, and compliance with published technical directives.

For many years, the Army has implemented SOJT for a soldier's individual training or retraining into a new Military Occupational Specialty (MOS) career field. The Army requires SOJT to be made a part of the unit training program. SOJT is called *cross training* when supervisors train soldiers in other jobs in their career fields. The Army has shown that SOJT also enhances a unit's combat readiness. The Army requires trainers to use SOJT guides to record the progress of soldiers in learning the new skills and requires training managers to set milestones and evaluate progress by checking a soldier's performance against approved standards.

The use of small groups is a common practice in elementary school subjects such as reading and mathematics. For example, in the first grade, a teacher may find that some students have not yet mastered the oral language skills of reading readiness; others may be just beginning to learn to sound the letters and syllables of printed words, while others may be reading entire printed sentences without hesitation. Obviously, these students need to be taught different sets of enabling skills. It would accomplish nothing to present pages of print to students who are still struggling with oral language. Nor will it help students who can read to have to suffer through lessons that require them to make oral descriptions of objects shown in pictures. The practical solution is to divide the class into a number of small groups.

Classes of older students or adults are also sometimes divided into several sets of smaller groups. The groups may meet on separate occasions, as in "quiz sections," or they may meet in separate small groups for a portion of the scheduled class. In either case, the aim is to attain some of the advantages of small-group instruction and to provide some added variation to the instruction possible with large groups.

Events of Instruction in Small Groups

The control of instructional events in a small group (three to eight students) can be compared to the tutorial situation; think of it as "multistudent tutoring." In the small group, the teacher or trainer typically attempts to use tutorial methods, sometimes with single students, sometimes with more than one, and most often by "taking turns." The general result is the management of instructional events in a way that applies to each individual in the group, with some loss of flexibility and precision.

Diagnostic procedures can be used to establish small groups for instruction. As previously noted, this is typical for small groups in elementary reading, language, and mathematics. During an instructional session with a small group, it is also possible for the teacher or trainer to diagnose each student's *immediate prerequisites*. By questioning each student in turn, the teacher or trainer is able to fairly accurately determine if the necessary enabling skills are present in all students. This estimate of students' readiness for the next step in learning is nearly as precise as the assessment in the dyad.

Some of the main features that exemplify flexible adjustment of instructional events for a small group are:

1. *Gaining attention:* In a small group, the teacher or trainer can maintain frequent eye contact with each student, so gaining and maintaining student attention poses no major difficulties.

2. *Informing the learner of the objective:* This event is also readily managed in a small group. The teacher can express the objective of the lesson and ensure that it is understood by each member of the group. Of course, it may take a bit more time to ensure understanding of objectives for eight students than it does for only one (as in the dyad).

3. *Stimulating recall of prerequisite learning:* By questioning several students in turn, the teacher can be fairly certain that necessary enabling skills and relevant items of supportive information are accessible in the working memories of *all* students. Using their best judgment, the teacher may direct questions that require certain students to recall relevant items. The questions have the added effect of reminding other students of material they need to know to learn the new information or task.

4. *Presenting the stimulus material:* Learning materials can be presented in ways that are appropriate to the objective without necessarily being tailored to individual student characteristics. For example, an oral presentation may be given emphasis by voice changes. In pictures or diagrams, particular features

of objects and events may be made prominent. For this instructional event, the degree of flexibility compared with that of the dyad appears to be generally the same.

5. *Providing learning guidance:* Here, the choice is either to communicate to the group or to members of the group in turn. In the first alternative, the teacher is behaving as though in a large-group setting; with the second, the event is managed as in the tutoring mode, involving teacher interaction with one student, then with another, and so on. Obviously, the more students there are in the group, the more time the latter procedure takes. It is not uncommon for the teacher of a small group to alternate between these two approaches, judging one to be more appropriate at one time, one at another. In any case, the function of the event remains the same—providing cues and suggesting strategies that will aid the semantic encoding of material to be learned.

   Quite a different kind of learning guidance is provided by the small group when members of the group are engaged in *discussion*. In such groups, the discussion may be managed and led by the teacher. In other instances, the small groups formed out of large classes may designate students as discussion leaders. The function of learning guidance provided by discussion depends on the nature of the objective. Discussions generally place a fairly high degree of dependence on the self-instructional strategies of individual students. Members of a group discussion use the strategies of deciding what they want to learn and selecting those elements from what they hear or say as part of the discussion.

6. *Eliciting the performance:* It is clear in the case of this event that the only way of eliciting *each* student's performance in a small group is to do it one by one. Because this uses up a good deal of time, it is not always done. Instead, the teacher usually calls on one or two students to show what they have learned and assumes that the learning has been equally effective for those not called upon. As the lesson proceeds, other students take turns being called upon. Obviously, this procedure aims at approximating the dyad, but the precision of the event is considerably reduced. The teacher comes to depend on a probabilistic estimate of learning outcomes rather than a precise determination of them.

7. *Provide direct feedback:* Because this event is tied directly to student performance, it is subject to the same kinds of limitations as the small group. For the student who is called upon, feedback may be precisely provided. For the other students, it is only probable because it depends on which of them has made the same response (perhaps covertly).

8. *Assessing the performance:* Performance assessment may also lose some precision of control, because only one student's performance can be assessed at a time by oral questioning. The other students must wait their turns; this means that a sample of performances will be assessed for each student but not the entire repertoire each is supposed to have learned. Of course, a test covering an entire lesson or topic may later be given to all of the students (a technique equally applicable to large groups).

9. *Enhancing retention and transfer:* For instructional groups in elementary grades, the teacher is able to estimate the desirability of varied examples and additional spaced reviews in providing favorable conditions for retention and learning transfer. Such estimates are made by a kind of averaging of the group's performance and, thus, do not have the precision afforded in the tutoring situation of the dyad. In the case of older students and adults, the major purpose of discussions is to enhance retention and transfer.

Recitation in the Small Group

Suppose that a teacher has assembled a small group of pupils to learn the skill of adding fractions with dissimilar denominators. Because one of the steps in this procedure is "finding the least common multiple of the denominators," it may be assumed that diagnostic tests have indicated that students already possess such prerequisite concepts as *numerator, denominator, factor,* and *multiple,* as well as rules for multiplying and dividing small whole numbers and the rule for adding fractions with identical denominators.

Once the attention of all members of the group is gained, the teacher tells the students the objective of the lesson, using an illustration such as $\frac{2}{5} + \frac{4}{15}$. Calling upon one or two members of the group in turn, the teacher stimulates recall of prerequisite concepts and rules. For example, students may be asked to add $\frac{2}{13} + \frac{5}{13}$, to obtain $\frac{7}{13}$. Having assurance that prerequisite skills are readily accessible, the teacher presents a single example such as $\frac{2}{5} + \frac{3}{7}$ as stimulus material. The next step is to provide suitable learning guidance for the learning of the rule having to do with finding a least common multiple. This may be done by demonstrating the multiplication of denominators ($5 \times 7 = 35$); alternatively, a discovery method may be employed, initiated by such a question as, "How might we make it possible to change these into fractions that could be added?" In this case, one student in the group is called upon to answer while others wait a later turn. A different student may then be called upon for performance, that is, in arriving at the changed expression $\frac{14}{35} + \frac{15}{35}$ and in supplying the sum $\frac{29}{35}$. Feedback, in the form of affirming the correct response or correcting a wrong one, is then provided.

Subsequent instructional events are conducted in such a group by calling on different students, using different examples. Performance is followed by appropriate feedback for the students in the group by taking turns. The immediate performance of each student is assessed in this manner. The varied examples serve the function of enhancing retention and transfer, assuming that students other than the one called upon are learning by answering the questions in their heads.

Instruction in Discussion Groups

Instruction that takes the form of discussion is said to be characterized as "interactive communication" (Gall & Gall, 1976). One student speaks at a time as the group listens. The order in which students initiate or respond to speech is not predetermined. Often, one student is responding to the remarks or questions introduced by another student. The teacher may interpose remarks or questions and sometimes may call upon individual students to speak. Small groups of this sort may be organized with students as discussion leaders. Three kinds of objectives are often considered appropriate for instruction by group discussion: (1) subject-matter mastery, (2) attitude formation, and (3) problem solving (Gall & Gall, 1976). It is not unusual for a class discussion to have more than one of these types of objectives.

The formation and modification of attitudes is usually the major aim of *issue-oriented discussion,* examples of which are found in the "jurisprudential model" and the "social inquiry model" described by Joyce and Weil (1980). The discussion may be initiated by the account of an incident illustrating a social issue (such as freedom of speech or job discrimination). The teacher or group leader may then ask for one or more opinions about the issue. Comments are made about these opinions, either by the discussion leader or by other students. As the discussion proceeds, the leader attempts to achieve progressive sharpening and clarification of the issue by introducing different examples and by encouraging statements by various group members. Often, what is aimed for is a group consensus, as represented by a set of statements to which no major disagreements remain. This attitude-forming situation may be conceived as a particular kind of learning guidance, namely one involving communications from a number of human models. These models are members of the group and its leader. This kind of learning guidance, particularly effective in attitude formation, is followed by performance (choice of action) by the individual students and by feedback in the form of group consensus.

Problem solving is also a commonly adopted goal for discussion groups (Maier, 1963). The kinds of problems that provide the most effective instruction in discussion groups are those with multiple solutions and those that include attitudinal components. Maier (1971) points out that dividing large college classes into small groups can increase the opportunities for student participation and can be used to form discussion groups for problem solving and other related purposes. As a means of motivating, Maier suggests presenting problems or issues that capture student interest and emotional involvement. With this kind of objective, small groups have the chance to practice both communication skills and problem-solving strategies. Obviously, this type of instructional group depends largely upon the students to manage instructional events for themselves. The students must stimulate their own recall and employ their own cognitive strategies of encoding and problem solving. Attitude changes are a secondary, although not necessarily less important, outcome of this type of discussion session.

INSTRUCTION IN THE LARGE GROUP

When instructing large groups, the teacher employs communications that do not differ in function from those employed with dyads or small groups; the teacher initiates and manages the events of instruction that are specifically relevant to the primary objective of the lesson. Because the teacher's cues for timing and emphasis come from several (or many) sources rather than from a single student, there is a marked *reduction in precision* in the management of instructional events. Teachers of large groups can't be sure they have gained the attention of *all* students; they can't always be sure that *all* students have recalled prerequisites or that the semantic encoding they suggest will work well with *all* students. The strategy of instruction in a large group is, therefore, a *probabilistic strategy*. Large group instruction will be effective "on the average" but can't by itself be ensured as effective for each individual learner (Gagné, 1974, pp. 124–131).

Many believe that large-group instruction is the way instruction should be designed in general. The instruction itself (that is, the communications of the teacher) is "good," and it is up to the student to profit from it. Students, in this view, must organize the events of instruction themselves—it is sometimes up to students to infer the objective of instruction, to remind themselves to recall prerequisite skills, to choose a method of encoding, and so on. Large-group lecture is still widely employed in college and university teaching. However, this conception of instruction runs contrary to the notion of *mastery learning* proposed by Bloom (1974, 1976). Bloom's conception relates the quality of instruction to the occurrence of events described as providing *cues, participation, reinforcement*, and *feedback/correctives*. This set of instructional features closely resembles the instructional events we have described. Mastery learning requires the management of events that go beyond "giving of information" by the teacher. Technologies, such as the Internet, and course management software, have the potential to change the format of lectures to lectures with class interaction, either in real time or asynchronously. Discussions can be carried on among students in small groups, asynchronously, in a virtual workspace, they can't even complain about not being able to get together!

Instructional Events in the Large Group

As with a small group, the influence of instructional events in the large group is only *probable*. The teacher will reach individual students with different levels of effectiveness, and the effect is difficult to monitor with certainty. The degree of instructional readiness, the intensity of motivation and alertness, the appropriateness of the semantic encoding, and the accessibility of relevant cognitive strategies vary from individual to individual. For this reason, instruction is relatively imprecise. The lack of effectiveness of instruction for one individual can be overcome by a student's self-instruction. For example, what some students fail to learn from a lecture they may learn by employing their own encoding strategies from their notes from the lecture. Other students may find this kind of encoding ineffective and may look for an alternate method of learning the material.

Some of the main features that exemplify flexible adjustment of instructional events for a large group are:

1. *Gaining attention:* This event, as all teachers know, is very important for the effectiveness of instruction delivered to a group. The use of demonstrations and audiovisual media can help gain the attention of a group.

2. *Informing the learner of the objective:* The objective can readily be stated and demonstrated to a large group. When suitably presented, it will probably be comprehended by all students.

3. *Stimulating recall of prerequisite learning:* As indicated previously, this event is critically important. It is also one of the most difficult events to accomplish with reasonable probability in a large group. Typically, the teacher calls upon one or two students to recall relevant concepts, rules, or information. The necessary retrieval may not be achieved by other students, many of whom are hoping to avoid being called upon. As a result, the management of this event may often be inadequately accomplished. Those students who have not recalled prerequisite skills will probably not learn the relevant objective, and the cumulative effects of this inadequacy can be quite serious. Various means (such as "spot quizzes" for the entire group) are employed to improve the operation of this event. Instructional designers should pay particular attention to this event.

4. *Presenting the stimulus material:* The content to be learned can be presented in a way that emphasizes distinctive features. This means that the presentation can be made optimally effective, on the average. For example, if students need to learn the concept of *energy conservation,* the teacher might line several boxes with different types of insulating materials and place the boxes over light bulbs to show the students the difference in heat retention depending on the type of insulation.

5. *Providing learning guidance:* In a large group, learning guidance can be readily provided to most members of the group. For example, the encoding of a historical event can be suggested by a picture or dramatic episode, which may be generally effective in the group as a whole. However, the particular encoding can't be adapted to each individual as it can in smaller groups.

6. *Eliciting performance:* Control over a learner's performance is difficult in a large group. Whereas a tutor can expect a student to exhibit what he or she learned several times during the course of a single lesson, this isn't possible in a large group. In a typical class, the teacher can call on only one student at a time. Quizzes and tests are often used to elicit performance from the group. To be most effective as instructional events, quizzes should be frequent. However, even daily quizzes can't approximate the frequency with which the tutor can elicit student performances that reflect the capabilities just learned. Group discussions on a topic can be viewed as a form of practice, since the students are retrieving, rehearsing, and encoding the information being studied. Another common form of practice involves group presentations. Since members of a group are engaging in a joint effort, there is intrinsic motivation to learn and perform well.

An interesting phenomenon at Florida State University (2004) is the use of technology to provide practice and immediate feedback through an open source Web-based system called LON-CAPA. LON-CAPA contains drill and practice software, and it works by presenting a wide range of problems to a student. Students are encouraged to use the system, because it also generates their exams from the same set of practice items. Students are even encouraged to work together to help learn to solve the problems. The result has reduced the failure rate among students in the first-year college math course from 48 percent to 19 percent.

7. *Providing feedback:* Because this event is inevitably tied to the occurrence of performances by the students, it is subject to the same limitations as those described for Event 6. Feedback to students in a large group occurs with low frequency and is often a summary of how the group did as a whole. However, this can be expanded by having other students or groups discuss or critique each other's presentations. This greatly leverages the capabilities of the instructor.

8. *Assessing the performance:* Similar comments to Events 6 and 7 may be made concerning this event. Frequent testing with feedback leads to better study habits and better learning. For example, regularly scheduled quizzes following segments of material are considered the most valuable feature of some computer-based courses in college subjects (Anderson et al., 1974). When a computer is used for assessment, this event can be managed with a degree of precision that is impossible for a teacher of a large group.

9. *Enhancing retention and transfer:* Events of this nature can be accomplished by the teacher of a large group, again in a probabilistic sense. That is, a teacher can use varied examples and spaced reviews that have been found to work on average, but be unable to adapt these techniques to differences in individual learners.

The Lecture

The most common mode of instruction for a large group is a lecture. The teacher's oral communication may be accompanied by pictures, diagrams, video, or slides and presented using various media, including a chalkboard. Students listen and often take notes, which they use later for recall or as a means of generating their own semantic encoding.

As McLeish (1976) pointed out, a lecture can accomplish positive instructional purposes. In particular, the lecturer can (1) inspire an audience with his or her own enthusiasm, (2) relate his or her field of study to human purposes (and, thus, to student interests), and (3) relate theory and research to practical problems. The lecture attains these goals with the utmost economy, which certainly accounts for its preservation as an instructional method for over two thousand years of higher education.

McLeish's interpretation implies that a good lecture can attain certain instructional objectives very well because it is able to implement certain instructional events effectively. For example, "Inspiring students with his enthusiasm" implies that the lecturer is functioning as a human model to establish positive attitudes toward the subject of study. Lectures are motivational when they relate a specialized field of study to a more general concern of human living. As for relating research findings to practical problems, a lecture can provide cues that will aid retention and learning transfer.

As pointed out in the previous section, the communications delivered to groups of learners by a lecture can be aimed at optimizing the effectiveness of many of the events of instruction in a probabilistic sense. For example, attention can be gained by dramatic episodes; instructional objectives can be simply and clearly stated; suggested encoding of material to be learned can be provided by summary statements, visually presented tabular arrays, or diagrams; and so on. While many of the events of instruction can be presented within a lecture, they can't be managed with precision. Their momentary effects can't be ensured for all students, and their specific forms can't be adapted to individual differences in students. For example it is difficult to maintain attention—studies of the lecture method have shown that attention wanes after 15 or 20 minutes. It is here that the instructor must re-establish attention by engaging students in another way—perhaps by having them discuss with their neighbor some question over what was just said. There are many kinds of "active learning" techniques (searching for "active learning" using www.google.com on 2/4/04 retrieved over five million Web links) that when used with lecture make them more effective. However, these must be planned into the lecture, and students should be informed of why they are being used and how they aid learning (Penner, 1984).

Viewed from the standpoint of instructional events, perhaps the weakest features of the lecture reside in its lack of control over eliciting performance and providing corrective feedback. The lecturer can ask questions, but only one or two students will have the chance to respond. Usually the lecturer calls for volunteers so students who know the answer raise their hands. Because the students raising their hands likely know the correct answer, the feedback isn't likely to clarify the issue for many students who didn't understand. When a lecture is used as the sole method of instruction, there is heavy dependence upon students to institute these events for themselves. This degree of self-instruction is a common expectation in college and university instruction, as well as in adult education. It is worth noting that quizzes and tests can be used to overcome a lecture's limitations, but only to a small degree, because they are typically both infrequent and aimed at specific learning objectives.

The Recitation Class

Another form of large-group instruction, more frequently used with subjects such as foreign-language learning, is the recitation class. This mode of instruction partially overcomes some of the limitations of the lecture. In a recitation class, the teacher calls upon one student after another to respond to questions. For example, in a foreign-language class, one student at a time may answer questions posed in that language or otherwise engage in a conversation using the foreign language.

The teacher's *questions* in a recitation class may represent several different instructional events at different times during a single lesson. A question may be designed to stimulate recall of a prerequisite capability, bringing it to the forefront of the student's memory. Or, a question may be one that asks a student to perform—to show what he or she has learned. A different kind of question might suggest the student think about something to help guide the learning in the sense of semantic encoding. Still another kind of question might require the student to think of examples of how to apply the newly learned skill or knowledge. This process helps develop cues for recall and learning transfer. For example, having learned the concept of homeostatic control, questions might ask students to describe several examples of practical homeostatic devices.

In recitation classes, some instructional events are often left for the student to manage. This is typically the case when recitation follows a homework assignment. In such instances, events, such as gaining information about the objective, semantic encoding, and the provision of corrective feedback, are managed by the student as they do their homework. These events are relevant to the student's various study activities, such as reading the textbook, practicing new skills through examples, or rehearsing. Good study habits are, in these circumstances, the determiners of effective learning.

The control of instructional events in a large recitation class is decidedly imprecise with regard to its effect on individual students. When questions are asked, for whatever purpose, there is time for only a few students to respond. Should the teacher call upon students who are typically well prepared and in doing so neglect students who may be less able to guide their own learning? Or should the teacher call upon the less able students, and through corrective feedback, bore those who have already learned? Usually in large recitation classes the necessary events of instruction affect only a few students at any one time. Time does not permit everyone to take a turn, and too frequently, students learn to avoid being called upon.

FEATURES OF TUTORING IN LARGE GROUPS

Methods of large-group instruction, including lecture and recitation, may be combined in various ways with small-group, two-person, or individualized instruction. One rather simple scheme is to divide the large group into small groups for part of its meeting time or into classes of smaller groups for meetings subsequent to a large-group lecture or recitation. These arrangements are intended to provide a degree of precision in the control of instructional events.

Mastery Learning

An outstanding system of teaching that directly attempts to introduce precision in the management of instructional events is called *mastery learning* (Bloom, 1974; Block & Anderson, 1975). Generally speaking, this method supplements large-group methods of teaching with *diagnostic progress testing* and *feedback with correction* procedures.

In using this system, the teacher divides a course of study into units of approximately two weeks' length, with each unit having clearly defined objectives. Following the teaching of the unit, students take a test to determine who has mastered the objectives. Students who exhibit mastery are permitted to engage in self-instructional enrichment activities. For example, they could take quizzes where they practice answering additional questions about the topic, or they could be given extra reading assignments covering the topic. Those who do not show mastery, are provided additional sessions of instruction, such as small-group study, individual tutoring, or additional self-study materials. The students are tested again when they believe they have mastered the skill or knowledge. Adding instructional sessions, as required with diagnostic and corrective feedback, makes a distinct contribution to instructional precision. Evidence of the system's effectiveness has been reviewed by Block and Burns (1976).

LARGE-GROUP INSTRUCTION USING DIGITAL TECHNOLOGIES

Advances in digital technologies and the Internet are providing exciting new methods for delivering large-group classroom instruction. Many colleges and universities, as well as government agencies and the military, are designing and developing *electronic classrooms*.

Electronic classrooms generally come in two basic types: lecturer and interactive (George Mason University, 2003). The lecturer classroom consists of an electronically equipped instructor's station or a podium with a monitor and standard student seating. The interactive classroom offers the same instructor's stations, as well as computer stations for each student. Electronic classrooms are usually outfitted to make presentation capabilities and network connectivity available to instructors using laptops or PCs.

Electronic classrooms are designed to accommodate a variety of technology needs. The equipment in the classrooms usually includes computers for students networked to an instructor's electronic podium, projection systems, DVD/CD players, scanners, electronic whiteboards, VCRs, and audio systems. The software on the computers typically includes a standard set of applications and Internet software (Landay, 1999).

Most electronic classrooms have high-speed connections to the Internet or intranet networks to allow fast access to data on a campus or an organization's network and the World Wide Web. For example, instructors can access information on a university Web server, a computer in their office, or from a computer at another university or research center. Instructors can also transfer and execute their own files or programs across the network (Landay, 1999).

Electronic classrooms provide for the use of multimedia presentations using animation, video, and simulation. Video (both analog and digital) can be used for demonstrations and to teach difficult concepts. With interactive electronic classrooms, computer displays in the form of simulations and demonstrations can be projected onto each student's desktop or laptop computer to allow them to interact with the material. Electronic classrooms make it easy for lecturers to bring up and edit materials and view presentations from a file server. With the connection to the Internet, teachers can easily access outside materials to improve their own materials. Additionally, students and teachers can interact with colleagues (locally and remotely) and/or with experts in the field of study. Computers allow teachers to capture informal interactions that occur in the classroom via whiteboard markings made in response to questions and the audio and video records of what was said and shown (Landay, 1999).

Electronic classroom technologies are making it possible for teachers and instructors to have increased control over instructional events in a large group. For example, teachers can access a multimedia presentation on the Internet to gain the attention of the students. The learning objectives can be presented on students' desktop or laptop computers, and the students can then click on a button on the computer screen to indicate they have read the objectives. Students can return to the objectives at any time during the lecture to reinforce what it is they're expected to learn. With electronic classrooms, students tend to pay more attention to lectures because of the dynamic nature of the lecture materials and the interactive elements. Students can print out materials at a later time, and they don't need to take as many notes during the lecture. Teachers can provide a short lecture to the entire group followed by a practice exercise that each student must complete on his or her desktop or laptop computer. Teachers can "watch" each student's progress on the practice exercise and provide individualized informative feedback practically in real time. Many different scenarios can be provided to enhance retention and transfer.

Another electronic solution for allowing group interaction and responding is the infrared responder. These are keypads that are identified with each student that can be used to collect and display responses to multiple-choice questions. The distribution of responses can quickly be displayed as a histogram on LCD projector and the instructor immediately knows if the class has a problem. Later the same system can be used for testing mastery of the skills.

In some instances, electronic classrooms are designed to be reconfigurable to support both the large-group lecture and a collaborative exercise. For example, electronic classrooms at Georgia Tech have been designed with desks and chairs that are on wheels so they can change from lecture style to group "pods" in a matter of seconds (Landay, 1999).

SUMMARY

The nature of instruction delivered to groups is generally determined by the size of the group. To distinguish the various characteristics of instruction, we have considered three different group sizes: (1) dyads, or two-person groups, (2) small groups with three to eight students, and (3) large groups of 15 or more students.

The characteristics of instruction applicable to these three different group sizes depend on the degree of precision with which the instructional events can be managed by the teacher. Generally speaking, the dyad consisting of a tutor and a student, affords the greatest degree of precision for instructional events. As the size of the group increases, control over the management of instructional events grows progressively weaker and learning outcomes come to depend increasingly upon a student's self-instructional strategies.

A particular feature of the instructional situation that is typically more difficult to manage as group size increases is the diagnosis of entering capabilities. Means of assessing what the students know or do not know at the beginning of each lesson are readily available to a tutor but become more difficult with larger groups. This factor is particularly important for *stimulating recall of prerequisites,* because students will obviously be unable to recall something they have not previously learned. Control of this event grows weaker with larger groups, and the result may be a cumulative deficit in student learning.

Precise management of instructional events, from early ones, such as gaining attention, to the late ones, providing for retention and learning transfer, are possible with tutoring in a two-person group. In small groups, control of instructional events is attained largely by multiperson tutoring, where instructional events are initiated for the different members of the group one at a time. In such circumstances, some events become only probable (rather than certain) for some students on some occasions. With the aid of self-instructional strategies, small-group instruction can be very effective. Small groups are frequently formed from larger groups. Examples of small groups formed in this manner are those for instruction in basic skills in the elementary grades and student-led discussion groups in college classes.

Large-group instruction is characterized by weak control of the effects of instructional events by the teacher. The gaining of attention, the cuing of semantic encoding, the eliciting of student performance, and the provision of corrective feedback can all be instituted as events, but their effects on the learning process are only probable. Electronic classrooms are emerging as an excellent tool for blending traditional lectures with individualized or collaborative instruction, and as such have made a positive impact on the learner's own strategies of self-instruction in large-group settings.

Typical methods of instruction in large groups are lecture and the recitation class. A number of techniques have been suggested for overcoming the weaknesses of large-group instructional methods. Frequently, large groups are divided into smaller groups, and sometimes into dyads, in order to bring about some of the advantages of increased control over instructional events. One system for improvement of large-group instruction is mastery learning, in which units of instruction are managed so that diagnosis and corrective feedback follow the learning of each unit until mastery is achieved.

Studies have also shown that aspects of the tutoring situation, such as enhancing the learning of prerequisites, encouraging student participation in learning guidance, and adding elaboration cues for retrieval, can bring about substantial improvements in achievement in large-group situations.

There is no doubt that learning and teaching are enhanced through the use of electronic classrooms. Notes written on an electronic whiteboard during a class can be captured and placed on the Internet allowing students to review them at a later time. Lectures can be captured and reviewed. Students often pay more attention in electronic classrooms because they don't have to take copious notes. Electronic classrooms support group-based learning because teachers can "lecture" to the entire group (when the entire group needs it), and students can work on projects, collaboratively or individually, at other times with teachers acting as "roving tutors."

REFERENCES

Anderson, T. H., Anderson, R. C., Dalgaard, B. R., Wietecha, E. J., Biddle, W. B. Paden, D. W., Smock, H. R., Alessi, S. M., Surber, J. R., & Klemt, L. L. (1974). A computer-based study management system. *Educational Psychologist, 11,* 36–45.

Block, J. H., & Anderson, L. W. (1975). *Mastery learning in classroom instruction.* New York: Macmillan.

Block, J. H., & Burns, R. B. (1976). Mastery learning. In L. S. Shulman (Ed.), *Review of research in education, 4.* Itasca, IL: Peacock.

Bloom, B. S. (1974). An introduction to mastery learning theory. In J. H. Block (Ed.), *Schools, society and mastery learning.* New York: Holt, Rinehart and Winston.

Bloom, B. S. (1976). *Human characteristics and school learning.* New York: McGraw-Hill.

Cloward, R. D. (1967). Studies in tutoring. *Journal of Experimental Education, 36,* 14–25.

Devin-Sheehan, L., Feldman, R. S., & Allen, V. L. (1976). Research on children tutoring children: A critical review. *Review of Educational Research, 46,* 355–385.

Ellson, D. G. (1976). Tutoring. In N. L. Gage (Ed.), *The psychology of teaching methods* (Seventy-fifth Yearbook of the National Society for the Study of Education). Chicago: University of Chicago Press.

Florida State University (2003). Retrieved on 1/2/9/04 from: http://www.lon-capa.org.

Gage, N. L. (Ed.). (1976). *The psychology of teaching methods* (Seventy-fifth Yearbook of the National Society for the Study of Education). Chicago: University of Chicago Press.

Gagné, R. M. (1974). *Essentials of learning for instruction.* New York: Dryden Press/Holt, Rinehart and Winston.

Gall, M. D., & Gall, J. P. (1976). The discussion method. In N. L. Gage (Ed.), *The psychology of teaching methods* (Seventy-fifth Yearbook of the National Society for the Study of Education). Chicago: University of Chicago Press.

Gartner, A., Kohler, M., & Riessman, F. (1971). *Children teach children.* New York: Harper & Row.

George Mason University (2003). Retrieved summer 2003 from http://ec.gmu.edu.

Joyce, B., & Weil, M. (1980). *Models of teaching* (2nd ed.). Englewood Cliffs, NJ: Prentice Hall.

Landay, J. A. (1999). The present and future of electronic classrooms: The Berkeley CS division experience. Berkeley, CA: University of California, Press.

Maier, N. R. F. (1963). *Problem-solving discussions and conferences.* New York: McGraw-Hill.

Maier, N. R. F. (1971). Innovation in education. *American Psychologist, 26,* 722–725.

McLeish, J. (1976). The lecture method. In N. L. Gage (Ed.), *The psychology of teaching methods* (Seventy-fifth Yearbook of the National Society for the Study of Education). Chicago: University of Chicago Press.

Palincsar, A.S. (1986). Reciprocal teaching. In *Teaching reading as thinking*. Oak Brook, IL: North Central Regional Educational Laboratory.

Penner, Jon G. (1984). Why college teachers cannot lecture. IL: Charles Thomas Publishers.

Sharan, S. (1980). Cooperative learning in small groups: Recent methods and effects on achievement, attitudes, and ethnic relations. *Review of Educational Research, 50,* 241–271.

Walberg, H. J. (1976). Psychology of learning environments: Behavioral, structural, or perceptual? In L. S. Shulman (Ed.), *Review of research in education, 4.* Itasca, IL: Peacock.

ONLINE LEARNING

The emergence of the Internet and networking technologies have made it possible to connect learners, separated by time and space, with distributed instructional resources. Distributed instructional resources include such things as training courses, instructional job aids, reference materials, training guides, and lesson plans, as well as teachers, trainers, and other learners. Distributed instructional resources are all of the resources accessible to the learner as he or she seeks to achieve an instructional goal or objective. Online learning refers to teaching and learning that is mediated by a computer connected to the Internet (Golas, 2000). While many terms are used to describe online learning, such as Web-based training, Internet-based training, e-learning, advanced distributed learning, and distance education, they all imply a connection to a computer system at a venue distinct from the learner's personal computer. This venue can be across the world or across campus (Online Pedagogy Report, 1999).

This chapter explores the advantages and challenges to designing online learning and discusses current trends, technological capabilities, development strategies, and issues to be considered when designing online instruction.

THE INTERNET

History

Designed in the early 1960s under the aegis of the U.S. Department of Defense, the Internet was first called ARPANET (Advance Research Project Agency Network). This network was widely used in the 1980s by the military and universities connected through telephone lines. Researchers from the scientific community and the military were able to solve technical problems by sharing and communicating information more readily, because, as a whole, written communication was more effective than oral communication. The system was built in such a way as to enable any network user to access any other computer on the same network.

During the late 1980s and early 1990s, the Internet grew at a rapid pace. Many new networks and hundreds of thousands of new hosts were added. By the mid-1990s, the system had become so large and complex it was impossible to say that a single organization controlled it. By September 2002, the Internet had become an international platform with over 680 million users (Global Reach, 2003). An International Data Corporation (IDC) study (2002) predicts that the volume of Internet traffic generated by end users worldwide will nearly double annually over the next five years. Even so, Internet technologies are still considered to be in their infancy.

Statistics

Data regarding the growth of the online learning market varies, but is generally impressive. According to the Directory of Schools (2002), more than 350,000 students have enrolled in online degree programs, generating $1.75 billion in tuition revenues for institutions in the United States. The data also showed that the distance learning market for fully online degree programs is growing at a rate of 40 percent annually and over the next few years there will be over 2.3 million students taking distance-learning courses in the United States. According to IDC (2002), the higher education distance-learning market is growing at a compound annual growth rate of 33.1 percent.

In industry and the government, online learning-technology and training providers generated over $125 million in annual revenues last year, and these revenues are expected to continue growing at approximately 50 percent per annum, reaching $750 million by 2005 (Gallagher & Newman, 2002). Analysts are predicting that the greatest growth of customized online course development will be in nontechnical training areas such as process, policy, or company product training (Beam, 2002).

Features of Online Learning Technologies

Many instructional design strategies used for stand-alone computer-based training (CBT) since the early 1980s continue to be directly applicable to the design of today's online learning. However, because of the power of networking technologies and digital software tools and techniques, there are many *additional* capabilities that impact instructional design strategies and methods. Though they differ in required bandwidth, user interface, and degree of interactivity, online learning technologies share a common strategy, which is to deliver education and training to audiences at disparate locations (Golas, 2000). Additionally:

- Students can be linked around the world in interactive exercises, instructional materials can be accessed via Web browsers on any platform, and Web browser software and Internet connections are widely available.
- Learning-center portals are increasingly being used to improve business practices through online learning.
- Moving appropriate existing courses to online delivery enables organizations to train more people faster and possibly for lower cost.

- Digital technologies are supporting business leaders' curriculum decisions, as digital content standards and content management tools are shown to improve the bottom line.

Advantages and Benefits

Online education and training provides numerous advantages and benefits over traditional computer-based training.

Convenience

- Web-browser software and Internet connections are now widely available.
- There is no need to bring remote employees to a centralized location for training.
- Students proceed at their own pace and on their own schedules.

Efficiency

- Drop-out rates normally encountered with traditional correspondence courses are significantly reduced.
- Students access relevant content faster.
- Workforce efficiencies are gained through job and company-specific courses.
- Relevant course content is quickly delivered.
- A wide range of courses is available, including formal degrees, certification programs, and continuing education units.
- Worldwide collaboration opportunities are possible.
- There is broad access to group knowledge and support.

Flexibility

- Learning styles and preferences are better accommodated.
- Instruction is matched to students' entry-level skills and knowledge and "branches" or links them to instruction according to their performances in a course.
- Learners can choose instructor-led or self-study courses or a blended approach.

Cost-Effectiveness

- Worldwide distribution is inexpensive.
- Content can be instantly updated.
- Course maintenance costs are greatly reduced because content changed on the server instantly updates all distributed course materials.
- More students are trained for less money.
- Return on investment and corporate learning assets are increased.
- Content can be used in a variety of different learning materials, either "as is" or with minor modifications (Carliner, 1999).

Instructional Effectiveness

- A broad range of learning styles and preferences are addressed, which guide individuals toward learning and mastering critical skills more effectively than delivery systems, such as classrooms, where "one size fits all."
- It is possible to deliver a wide range of media, including video, animation, graphics, and photographs.

- It brings people together for many purposes, such as one-on-one development and coaching, online communities for information and practice, pre- and postclass listservs, and individual instruction with complex simulations and practice exercises.
- It provides automated guidance, assessment, tracking, and information feedback.
- Managers, instructors, and teachers are afforded a better view of employee/student skills/knowledge and training needs.
- It provides training professionals with a better understanding of their target audiences by tracking the Web sites they visit, how long they stay, how they move from site to site, whether they return to a particular site, and so on.
- Statistics derived from practice exercises and tests provide students with a clear understanding of how they compare to others in terms of their perceptions of the course or performance within the course.
- It enables a more democratic learning environment.
- Quantity and complexity of interaction is increased.
- Motivation, often through gaming techniques, is increased.
- Refresher training is easy to implement.
- Multimedia and facilitated feedback support retention and transfer.
- Students are drawn to topics they enjoy.

Supports Knowledge Management (KM) Applications and Technologies
- It provides the ability to capture, organize, and deliver data for complex information systems aimed at maximizing the information, skills, and knowledge that exist within people and organizations.
- KM systems can be developed, updated, and managed in real time, 24 hours a day, seven days a week.

Challenges

While using the Internet to deliver online learning provides broader access to information, and encourages the exchange of ideas, which leads to increased knowledge, it has also generated new pedagogical problems and challenges to instructional designers and developers.

Accessing Information   Slow connection speeds, reception problems, and long download times that are due to limited bandwidths can cause students to become impatient, angry, or even give up. Another common problem is the need to stay online while participating in a course. This can be a serious problem in households where several family members all share a single modem. A strategy that can be used to minimize these problems is a hybrid approach, where high-bandwidth resources (such as digital video/audio) are provided on a CD-ROM or DVD. A CD-ROM or DVD might contain the content of the online version of the course and employ a Web browser for delivery and display of the course content. However, instead of receiving content via the Internet transmitted from a Web server, the CD-ROM links to files on the course from the user's local CD-ROM drive. With the hybrid approach, much of the functionality of the online course is managed by server-side programs. Some of these operations are handled in the stand-alone course with client-side scripting and additional hyperlinking. Client-side scripting is often used to program the user interface for an application, for example, to change a Web page's text dynamically or respond to user actions such as button clicks (Vadlakunta, 2004).This may be complex for some courses because the HTTP protocol and Web browsers are designed to prevent extensive interaction with a client-side computer's file system, and some server-side functions of the online course, such as student data tracking, may not be provided on the stand-alone version.

Another problem related to accessing information during online courses was mentioned previously, and is one that the Army National Guard faces continually—namely, the problem of having only one phone line at home. Other family members, and in particular school-age children, will be competing for access to the Internet. Until the time when modems will be replaced by high-speed fast wireless connections or satellite connections, the hybrid approach is the only solution to this problem (Warren, 2002).

Information Overload and Failure to Accommodate Human Learning Processes   Humans have a limited capacity for the amount of information they can simultaneously process. To translate the content of the job into effective online learning courses, a range of expertise on the design team is required, including instructional psychology, multimedia production, graphics, programming, and interface design. Experienced multimedia developers acknowledge that it takes from 10 to 20 times more labor and skill to produce good courseware for online learning than for traditional classroom materials. (Clark & Mayer, 2002). Too many links or too many threads leading in all directions can quickly confuse and distract learners from the objectives. There is a strong need for online learning designers to develop methods for both retaining and integrating content from longer-duration online learning experiences to support the learner's comprehension and memory of vast amounts of information they've learned over these lengthy periods. Clark and Mayer (2002) believe designers need to think about how they can construct a "content briefcase," where information from course to course is collected and filtered to facilitate memory and comprehension.

Loss of Personal Contact   As noted in Chapter 11, online learning generally reduces personal face-to-face contact between teachers and learners and among learners themselves, and this social aspect of learning is both highly valued and serves an important instructional purpose. Even with advances in synchronous video, significant instructional design efforts are required to enhance social relationships through chat rooms, threaded discussions, virtual meetings, and other collaboration techniques.

Irrelevant, Inappropriate, and Incorrect Content   Also as noted in Chapter 11, while significant progress has been made to incorporate the wealth of information available on the Internet into online curricula, there remains a need to create *valid* educational or instructional content (Golas, 2000). Factual knowledge must be transformed into useful, relevant knowledge. Designers of online curricula must be careful to control what students have access to, because most information published on the Internet is not juried by content experts, as are articles published in most professional journals.

The most effective method of controlling content during collaborative exercises or events is the use of *online moderators*. A survey conducted by Masie (2000) regarding the roles and responsibilities of moderators in online learning revealed that 88 percent of students and 91 percent of managers recommend that a trainer or facilitator be a part of the online learning experience. The survey respondents placed a high value on having a trainer/facilitator read threaded discussions and monitor other collaborative exercises in order to keep irrelevant and incorrect information from being disseminated. Online monitors also check student progress and contact students if necessary, evaluate online project work and provide feedback, build and facilitate an online learning community for the course participants, and are available via e-mail or threaded discussions to respond to content questions. As of this writing, the military commonly does not allow collaborative instructional strategies, such as threaded discussions and chat rooms, to be incorporated into online courses because they often can't provide course monitors at all times to ensure that incorrect information is not being disseminated among the servicemen and women.

Compatibility Issues   If course content is developed in a vacuum and it can't be re-used by other developers, a major benefit of the Internet will not be recognized. With standards such as SCORM (described in Chapter 11), content becomes usable worldwide by people in government, industry, and academia, and through customization it can be used to support a variety of learning objectives for disparate target audiences. In corporate America, online learning formats are expanding in conjunction with strategic business plans. The number of online materials that provide performance support, training, coaching, mentoring, and collaboration is growing rapidly, and developers who produce learning objects that can be repurposed to support a variety of these products or capabilities will see a marked return on investment.

Giving People the Time and Space to Learn   A serious problem with implementation of online courses, particularly in corporate America, is that many employers don't provide their staff with *uninterrupted* time during the workday to complete mandatory online courses. This is less of a problem in the federal government and the military, where "time to train" is specifically provided for during the regular work schedule. Additionally, strategies such as the use of streaming video, where a sequence of moving images is sent in compressed form over the Internet and displayed by the viewer upon arrival (Miller, 2003), should not be underused. If online lectures are scheduled for a *specific* time rather than using streamed video that allows synchronous (anytime) viewing, some members of the online course may not be able to participate.

A study conducted by the MASIE Center (2001) showed that where and when learners are engaged in online learning courses *significantly* affects their level of satisfaction and motivation to complete the courses. Seventy-six percent of the students in the study said that they preferred to take online learning courses during working hours, either at their desk, in a shared workplace, or at an on-site training center. This is attributed to the fact that many of the learners did not want the online training to disrupt their personal lives. The study revealed that employers who provide mandatory training during work hours have a more satisfied workforce. The learners who took the mandatory courses at home, on the road, or at a customer's site were significantly less satisfied with the online learning experience.

Keeping Students Motivated   Unlike the classroom, where the learner is a captive audience and a live instructor can stimulate attention, completion of online learning requires individual discipline and commitment in a world full of competing alternatives for worker time and attention (Clark & Mayer, 2003). When an instructor or teacher notices that students are becoming bored and uninterested, they can instantly modify their approach. Online learning, on the other hand, is immutable during instruction. Frustrated, stymied, or bored, the online learner will "tune out" when the experience lacks precise anticipation of their needs (Clark & Mayer, 2003). The savvy online learning developer must predict the interests, concerns, and stumbling blocks of learners (Clark & Mayer, 2003). Learner motivation and the skills needed for successful self-directed learning are greatly aided by the implementation of engaging courseware strategies, such as online discussions, interactive games, animation and graphics, and stories or real-world scenarios.

Managers and supervisors need to continually ensure that their employees are aware that online learning courses will contribute to their personal development, which in turn will help to create an overall learning culture within their organization that will drive intrinsic motivation (Masie, 2001). Managerial participation in learners' personal development plans will further drive and motivate employees to acquire new skills as well as aid in increasing the awareness and benefits of particular courses. If managers encourage peer acceptance and support, the drive to excel beyond one's peers will serve as an additional, and very compelling, motivator (Masie, 2001).

PLANNING ONLINE LEARNING

Whether planning online learning for academic instruction or technical training, a few of the key operational, administrative, and technological issues that should be considered prior to creating online courses are addressed below. Specific issues related to development of online learning for academic institutions follows.

Internet Access

Prior to developing an online course, the computing environment should be analyzed to determine how users will be accessing the course. This is important for two reasons: (1) connection speed, and (2) availability of access. Students might be accessing the course materials by dialing up from home, by using equipment in a classroom or training lab, or through network connections in their facility. Online course developers need to determine if students will be able to access the course material at any time from any place and if there are issues with accessing or downloading material because of firewalls. Although firewalls are used for security purposes to protect information, they can sometimes hinder online learning. Developers need to work closely with information-technology/management staff to ensure that the online solution will work within the organization's firewall software.

As noted previously, connection speeds will vary depending on whether students are accessing the online materials via network connections or through dial-up modems. This is an important factor to take into account when deciding what types of media to include in the course materials. For example, full-motion video is appropriate only if students have fast network connections.

Equipment and Software

As previously mentioned in Chapter 11, the Internet offers a wide range of methods for delivering content. These methods range from simple text to audio, video, and animation. Although this wealth of media exists for delivery, all learners may not be able to receive the content in all forms due to modem speed and bandwidth. The student's choice of Internet Service Provider (ISP) may play a role in this, as well as the computing platform they are using. It is important to consider the facilities available to students and select content that they will be able to receive and comfortably use.

The choice of content delivery methods should also be periodically analyzed. As more people acquire high-speed Internet access, and new, more capable hardware and software becomes widespread, content delivery should be altered to present a richer learning experience. This may also be necessary for programs targeted at selected audiences, such as corporate programs, that already possess high-speed access and more advanced capabilities.

Design or development strategies for online learning that are not supported by the end user's computer should be avoided by first identifying computer hardware, software, and network requirements for the client (student or end-user) machine. The online learning courses need to work regardless of what students have on their desktop at school, at work, or at home. If course access requires special browser add-ons or ancillary programs, all the receiving workstations or home/office PCs must be properly configured before the course starts. The student's machine should meet a minimum set of hardware specifications, such as the CPU (central processing unit), RAM (random access memory), and disk size. Operating systems and application software requirements such as Web browser and plug-ins, e-mail software, and the word processor must also be determined.

Even in larger corporations, where state-of-the-art equipment may be readily available, networked computers may not be universally equipped with simple multimedia features, such as sound cards or Web-browser plug-ins. Requiring students to conform to using a single browser is sometimes necessary in order to make it easier for users to configure their computers with the appropriate software (for example, plug-ins). It is also important to identify hardware and software requirements for the server machine. Web server specifications include hardware (CPU, RAM, disk size, etc.), operating system, and application software requirements (Web server, mail server, newsgroup server, CGI [Common Gateway Interface] server, etc.). Because hardware and software requirements will change over time for both the client and the server machines, the requirements will need to be updated as technologies evolve.

End-User Capabilities

The computer literacy of the target audience needs to be considered carefully. Developers should not make assumptions about participants' knowledge of basic computer technology and terminology. At a minimum, they need to be able to access the course material and use the tools necessary to work through the course. Some end users may simply not be sufficiently "computer savvy" for online courses. For example, users may not be able to download and install specialized Web browser plug-ins or ancillary software programs needed to access and run the course. At times it may be necessary to direct users to appropriate technical assistance and allow them to ask basic questions and be tutored through set-up processes. Overestimating the computer skills of end users is a common problem that is often overlooked by online course developers.

Electronic learning materials can easily conceal much of the information they contain, and for this reason developers need to be forthcoming about the amount of time it will take learners to complete the courses. This will allow participants to be realistic in their commitments. Both developers and learners need to understand how extremely challenging it is to complete a comprehensive online learning program, hold down a job, raise a family, participate in social activities, and maintain day-to-day activities all at the same time.

Administrative Policies

Organizational policies regarding Web publishing should be known, along with the person(s) responsible for Web maintenance and Web policies. For example, if online training will be delivered to multiple company locations, it is advisable to check with the network administrators at all receiving locations to ensure that the course is compatible across their desktop and network configurations.

Standards and Specifications

Training developers who are developing online courses for industry, the federal government, and the military need to pay close attention to evolving models, such as SCORM, and standards, such as Section 508 of the Rehabilitation Act. (See Chapter 11 for descriptions of SCORM and Section 508.)

Academic/Educational Perspective

From an academic or formal education perspective, offering courses through the Web raises specific issues regarding intellectual property, pedagogical rigor, methods, course management, and instructional compensation. McAlister, Rivera, and Hallam (2001) outlined the following questions that individuals responsible for developing and offering online learning and education at academic institutions need to address.

Will the online curriculum be congruent with the institution's mission and strategy?

An online curriculum requires a significant commitment of institutional resources. Instructional and staff resources are usually a scarce commodity, and their commitment to this type of program may detract from other programs. Prior to committing to an online curriculum, analyses should be conducted to ensure that it will be designed to operate *in concert with* the institution's goals, objectives, existing offerings, core values, and competencies. For example, while one goal might be to increase "reach" and foreign-student enrollment, achieving that goal might dilute the institution's core programs and reputation. Institutions might "cannibalize" existing programs and classes, as participants switch to online instruction, and this can severely damage the institution's reputation.

Do you have administrative support?

Developing an online curriculum shares many similarities with the development of new information systems. An important common attribute is the degree of administrative support necessary to successfully undertake a project. This support is vital to securing adequate resources and to successful nurturing of the project through its early stages. A commitment must be made to fund the technical and human resources to develop and deliver the course content, and this commitment must be strong enough to weather initial setbacks and problems as the program is put in place. Part of this commitment should include the definition of realistic goals and performance measures through which the program's progress can be evaluated.

Are there institutional obstacles to adopting an online curriculum?

Institutionally, adopting an online learning curriculum may represent radical change to the traditional academic model, and not all institutions and faculties will be open to or capable of accepting the new paradigm. Instructors will need to spend a significant amount of time familiarizing themselves with Internet technologies, and they will have to adapt their instructional techniques and materials to take advantage of distance-learning opportunities in order to minimize the impact of a remote teaching environment. Students must be prepared to accept the demands that are imposed on them, such as the need to exert a higher degree of self-discipline and motivation. Online classes also change the nature of the student-instructor interaction. Typically, this type of environment limits the amount of face-to-face and verbal interaction, while increasing the use of written communications. Students must quickly grasp the need to use Web and e-mail resources to achieve the interaction required to meet their needs. Another obstacle is the development of new competitors. Traditionally, higher education institutions faced competition from other similar institutions in close geographical proximity. Recently, publishing companies and other private firms, as well as high-profile higher-education institutions are investing in online educational programs. These developments may make it difficult for smaller institutions to offer competitive online curricula.

How will you handle intellectual property (IP) issues?

In most institutions, class materials are generally considered to be the intellectual property (IP) of the instructor. Course delivery through the Internet opens up a new range of options regarding how class materials are authored and used. For example, someone other than the person that developed the course materials may administer the course. Course materials may be used for many sections of the same course with multiple instructors. There are many unresolved questions about the ownership of IP, and its continued use. Solutions range from ignoring IP issues to proactively addressing this issue by specifically compensating instructors for developing online materials that then become the institution's property. The proactive approach to settling intellectual property issues will avoid future problems and the potential for litigation.

Intellectual property issues also arise when supplementary materials are used as part of a course's pedagogy. Arranging for the use of someone else's intellectual property or copyrighted materials should be part of the initial online curriculum development effort. A mechanism for acquiring and administering intellectual rights to these materials is important, because part of the administration of these materials may require restricting the dissemination of the materials. Putting in place the policies, procedures, and technologies to administer this area is an important part of an online curriculum. An example of this dilemma is the restrictions some publishers place on the use of supplemental materials.

How will instructors be compensated for offering or administering online courses?

Even upon satisfactory settlement of IP issues, there is the issue of compensation for those teaching or administering online courses. In educational institutions, the traditional model for compensating instructors for a set class load may no longer be appropriate. To begin with, a definition of what constitutes a class must be established. In most institutions there are minimum and maximum class-size limits arrived at through pedagogical, economic, and physical facilities constraints. Course delivery through the Internet can radically alter these time-honored definitions and require new and innovative solutions.

Further complicating the compensation issue is the wide range of latitude in determining how classes are conducted. Theoretically, online classes could range in size from very small to extremely large, and it may be possible to conduct a class that completely ignores the traditional academic calendar. Emphasis should be placed on defining these parameters early on, because these issues have a direct impact on course revenue and compensation. Instructor compensation should be defined well before offering Web courses to minimize misunderstandings and future problems.

Do you have clear, well-defined criteria for selecting the classes to be offered online?

Development of an online curriculum is in many ways a learning experience for most institutions. To promote early stakeholder acceptance of online courses, McAlister, Rivera, and Hallam (2003) believe that serious thought should be given to selecting those courses with the greatest potential for success. Courses that appeal to a large audience and have less rigorous pedagogical requirements may be more appropriate initial selections. Before selecting courses for online delivery it is important to evaluate them for their pedagogical requirements as well as the desired degree of student interaction. Course delivery though the Internet imposes some limitations on the pedagogy and student interaction used when offering a course. Classes requiring strong, personal instructor interaction, such as those that teach hands-on skills or complex problem solving, may not be appropriate for online delivery. While all courses are not suitable for online delivery, taking a creative approach to pedagogy can overcome may of the inherent limitations imposed by this medium.

What facilities or capabilities are available to assist in the preparation and delivery of course materials?

Few instructors have the technical expertise necessary to prepare class materials in the appropriate format for online delivery. Furthermore, once the materials are in the right format, there is no guarantee that students will be capable of using them. It is crucial that adequate provisions be made for technical support of both course instructors and students. Among those provisions required, instructional design expertise must be available to help instructors develop and organize their course content.

Preparing materials for online delivery requires facilities for the collection of graphic, video, audio, and text content. Hardware and software development systems may not be readily available and require some investment in adequate facilities. It is unreasonable to expect the development of adequate online course materials without providing adequate support. Because new tools and technologies for online learning design and development are continually being introduced, ongoing updates of the systems and tools and training in their use is critical.

How will student progress be assessed?

Depending on the class being offered and its pedagogy, how student progress is assessed can vary. While student assessment may not be a critical issue for classes not granting academic credit, it is an important one for credit granting institutions. Choices range from online assessment instruments to requiring that students go to learning centers at the institution to take tests. For degree-granting institutions, there is the additional concern of making sure that assessment methods and practices are acceptable to their accrediting bodies. If reliable identification is necessary to maintain course integrity, arrangements must be made to administer assessment instruments through a proctored arrangement. This may require that participants meet periodically at a central location, or that arrangements be made at a reliable institution near the participant's vicinity.

Do the students have the necessary skills for taking courses online?

Not all potential students will have a high degree of technical computer skill and for this reason it is crucial to develop programs that train students in delivery methods as well as provide course content. Some institutions have addressed this by requiring that students enrolling in online courses attend a class where they are taught the necessary skills. Other institutions have made a conscious effort to design their instructional materials so that participants of all skill levels will be able to use them. Either way, it is the institution's responsibility to develop an effective mechanism to help their students develop the technical skills necessary for their participation. It is also necessary to provide students with access to ongoing assistance, either online or over the telephone, as they work their way through the course.

What learning management system (LMS) will you use?

A number of companies have developed LMSs, sometimes called course management systems (CMS), that facilitate the organization and transmission of course materials. Selection of one of these products can greatly simplify the task of delivering and maintaining course materials. Although adoption of one of these platforms is an attractive prospect, it may also impose constraints on delivery of course materials. Specific guidelines for selecting an LMS are presented later in this chapter.

Where will the class materials be maintained?

The question of where course materials are physically maintained is important, to the extent that the organization will have appropriate facilities to store and deliver them. Theoretically, the Internet allows one to maintain course materials anywhere in the world, but for practical purposes, it is important to select a site that can adequately deliver materials to the intended audience. Adequate facilities will ensure that course content is delivered in a timely fashion, and that demand for these materials will not overwhelm the delivery site's capabilities. Most organizations assume they will have the institutional facilities to host an online curriculum, however, those facilities may be inadequate. Depending on the mix of content that is offered in online courses, it may be more economical to use commercial facilities that guarantee an appropriate level of service. Thoughtful consideration should be given to this decision, because course participants may be negatively impacted by poor or unreliable delivery of course materials.

INSTRUCTIONAL DESIGN STRATEGIES

Overview

This section describes high-level instructional design strategies and techniques for online learning, including strategies for individualizing instruction, collaboration, hyperlinking, navigation, and testing. Before delving into these the specific strategies there are several instructional design issues that should be considered for academic or educational online courses as well as training courses of a more technical nature.

Develop a vision.

Whether developing a single online course or an entire curriculum, developing a realistic vision is paramount. A vision statement addresses expectations in terms of the ideal way in which decisions will be made and how the online learning organization will operate. It includes value statements that reflect the desired organizational culture, management style, and client service perspectives (Penrod, 2003). The vision should also define the fundamental purpose of developing an online course or curriculum and the comparative advantages. Goals the organization intends to work toward over a specified period and measurable objectives should also be considered during development of the vision. A "futures scenario" can be used to spell out, in broad terms, where the institution or organization wants to be within the specified planning schedule (Penrod, 2003).

Create a pilot program, sample lesson, or prototype.

As mentioned previously, depending on the learning objectives and outcomes, online learning content can be very dynamic and interactive and incorporate both multimedia, collaboration, and simulation strategies. Because of the highly visual and highly interactive nature of most online learning courses, particularly for technical training, producing a sample lesson or module to demonstrate the media treatment and interactivity before developing the entire course is essential. One lesson or module from the overall course should be developed to demonstrate the "look and feel" of the overall online course design. The selected lesson should establish the support structures for online course delivery to include validation of the registration function, testing of any synchronous or asynchronous video, downloading of media elements, student data collection features, and other LMS features.

There are many advantages to developing a prototype or sample lesson, including establishing a mechanism for collecting feedback from the target audience, subject-matter experts, managers, and customer representatives early in the development process. This is particularly important if it's the customer or user's first venture into online learning, as the sample lesson can be used to assess how they react to the new form of course delivery. Without a doubt, the greatest costs associated with building online courses come during the development phase. If the customer or user has only reviewed paper storyboards with line drawings, they can easily misinterpret what the instructional designer had in mind and approve the design documents. Then, when they see the finished product, they might feel misled and might insist on changes. Again, it's critical to remember that the cost of correction *increases* with the level of product that has been developed. By developing a prototype, the users or customers get to see *very early on* in the development process what the courses will actually look like and how they will function. Mistakes can be caught early, and failures can be tossed away without causing great concern to the design team. By allowing customers and users to provide feedback early in the design cycle, they will feel freer to explore other options for the course(s). By allowing the customers or users to work with the prototype, the effort needed later on to learn about the application will be reduced. Prototypes for online learning should demonstrate everything a user will be able to do or want to do with the system, such as collaborating through threaded discussions and practicing skills via simulation.

Design for the future.

As mentioned in Chapter 11, Internet technologies are changing rapidly and instructional designers need to continually plan for the future. For example, most instructional products today should be Web-enabled, even if the content is not being moved to an intranet or the Internet immediately. The designer needs to build a model that will allow porting it to the Web in the future.

Break instruction into small units.

Units of online learning, particularly for technical training content, should be short so as not to overwhelm the learner. The units should also be modular and able to "stand-alone." The SCORM recommends breaking a design into the smallest objects possible, aiming for 5 to 15 minute units of interaction or engagement so that potential reuse across multiple learning objectives is more feasible.

Use audio.

Audio, such as voice-over narration and sound effects, is often a neglected medium in online courses. Instructional designers should use audio appropriately and build in flexibility to let students control the use of it. Many authors believe that audio will play a key role in most online learning programs in the future, and it will require careful planning to do so appropriately. For example, a lesson with full audio may run perfectly on an office network but only a snippet of compressed audio might be available when the lesson is accessed on the student's home computer. New software tools, like Impatica for PowerPoint, or PowerConverter, compress audio so that it will stream from a standard HTTP server, making it possible for students with dial-up modem connections to receive audio presentations.

Provide a focus and role for the instructor or trainer.

Making the potential user of online instruction a stakeholder in the project is an important component of adoption of innovation (Rogers & Shoemaker, 1971). This is a particularly important issue for courses developed for industry or the federal government. Trainers or instructors should not feel left out or that a project is being launched without them. They will play an important role in facilitating the course, and it's important that they feel a strong sense of personal ownership or involvement in the design. They need to know that they add value to the organization's missions and goals.

Use instructional design principles when designing online instruction.

In today's digital world, many individuals such as teachers, trainers, instructors, and subject-matter experts, find themselves involved in the process of designing online instruction. Significant gains are possible when principles of good instructional design are applied. Support materials for the online learner is even more important than in classroom face-to-face instruction because visual feedback indicating that the students are understanding is not present. The importance of developing learning objectives, relevant and meaningful learning activities, eliciting performance, and providing feedback can't be overstated. In recent years, the skills required of instructional designers for online learning projects have changed significantly. The following section addresses these changes.

New Capabilities for Instructional Designers

Digital technologies are affecting the types of skills instructional designers need today in order to design online courses. More often, instructional designers need to be able to *develop* instruction as well as *design* it. Just the way a writer today needs to learn to use word-processing software on a computer instead of writing out in longhand and expecting a secretary to "type it up," instructional designers need to learn to use modern software programs to create and visualize their designs (Shank, 2003). This approach requires less rework, less time, and achieves better results in the long run (Shank, 2003). The days of developing paper-based storyboards, scripting content, and then handing it to someone else to develop are over. Just as word-processing skills potentially produce faster/better documents, authoring skills potentially produce faster/better instructional materials (Shank, 2003). Development isn't just the next phase after design; it augments and improves the design process. Authoring tools, like word-processing tools, are critical cognitive tools in the process of bringing instructional ideas to fruition (Shank, 2003).

When instructional designers can perform some level of development, they'll know what's possible and optimal, recognize the implications of various design and development decisions, better understand digital technologies, be able to converse with technical staff, be better prepared for managing the development process, know how to build some materials and fix some problems without having to wait on others, and, in general, design better online instruction (Shank, 2003).

To develop online courses, instructional designers need to have

- good writing and editing skills
- respectable word-processing skills
- competence with all phases of the instructional design process
- insight into the difference between developing text for the Internet versus paper-based publications
- an understanding of Internet usability and accessibility issues
- respectable knowledge of applications of learning theory and instructional strategies for online learning
- awareness of graphic design principles and their influence on learning
- the ability to converse with information technology experts
- the ability to build prototypes using some variation of development tools

Lacking these skills and/or not knowing when and how to get help is one of the reasons that many online instructional materials are rather dismal (Shank, 2003). Instructionally dismal sites do not support effective and efficient learning, and they are often produced by individuals with a lot of technical skill but no instructional design skill (Shank, 2003).

As mentioned above, instructional design for online courses requires multiple skills, including some software development skills. For instructional designers who only have stand-alone, computer-based design experience or expertise in delivery systems other than computers, Shank (2003) recommends they start by learning basic HTML. This starting point will help the designer understand how Internet pages and Web sites are put together. Next, Shank (2003) recommends they learn Dreamweaver MX, which is an extremely powerful tool for building Web sites and a better selection than specialty authoring tools designed just for creating online learning. Dreamweaver is the standard in the Web development industry and has tremendous capability to integrate with Macromedia Flash animation, streaming video, and other programs. CourseBuilder, Macromedia's free e-learning quiz and assessment extension that works with Dreamweaver MX, might also be a useful priority for instructional designers to learn. Although the learning curve may be steep for some, Shank (2003) believes instructional designers should also consider learning Flash and some basic JavaScript in order to learn how to read and reuse others' scripts. Finally, instructional designers should consider learning how to use software simulation tools for Internet-based application and software skills. Shank (2003) recommends learning RoboDemo, which outputs as Flash and is easy to learn. While it may seem like a lot to learn and even more to keep up with, the most important skill instructional designers will learn is the ability to keep up with constantly changing requirements and technologies in the digital world (Shank, 2003).

Instructional Design and Development Teams   The military and many federal government agencies and corporations differentiate between *levels* of interactive courseware, where *level I* courses are typically simplistic and passive courses that can be developed by individuals who have rudimentary design and authoring skills; *level II* courses incorporate interactivity, multimedia, use a learning manager system to track student data, and can be developed by a team of individuals with varying skills; and *level III* courses are highly interactive and often use simulation strategies and are typically built by a large team of designers/developers with diverse skills.

The types of staff members that make up a typical level II or III online learning project include

- instructional designers/developers with knowledge of learning theory/instructional strategies
- multimedia designers/developers, including 2D graphic artists, photographers, audio/video engineers, and 3D animators
- software designers/developers (authoring, programming, and database)
- project managers
- system administrators
- information technologists (IT people) and system architecture designers/developers
- networking/infrastructure technologists
- human factors/graphical user interface designers/developers
- subject-matter experts/technical writers

Individualizing Online Instruction

Learning theorists generally agree that no two people learn in exactly the same way, and when it comes to instruction, one size does *not* fit all. Computer technology has, from the beginning, been used interactively to tailor the pace, content, and sequencing of instructional materials to the individual needs of learners. In doing so, substantial improvements in instructional effectiveness are obtainable. Internet technology, with its ability to adapt interactions in real time and on demand, significantly supports individualization beyond that of traditional stand-alone, computer-based training. The Internet also lends itself to student-centered learning, where students take a greater responsibility for learning (Golas, 2000). As noted in Chapter 11, student-centered systems and learning activities encourage the learners to actively create their own learning, and to relate the information to real-world problems (National Research Council, 1997; Siegel & Kirkley, 1997). Cognitive psychology has been persuasive in arguing that the expert learner's rich fabric of meaning, or schema, does not come from acquiring a single strand of knowledge but from weaving together relationships among topics into a complex and synthetic whole (March, 1995). Similarly, constructivism suggests that truly comprehensive understanding of a complex topic comes from learners stitching together the facts, relationships, perspectives, variations, and nonexamples from an array of contextually rich inputs (March, 1995).

An example of the use of Internet technologies to support individualized instruction is the use of "within-site" links. These links to pages created by the site developer, located on the same server as the course, can include interactive activities created using programs such as CGI scripts or JavaScript. Such activities can require the learner to respond to some type of question or exercise provided by the instructor/facilitator, and the learner's response can be sent to an external location, or the program can provide instant feedback to the learner. A learner can be directed to explore a site or group of sites, and to provide some sort of analysis, comparison, and/or synthesis (Dodge, 1997; Ritchie & Hoffman, 1996). Such exploratory activities, in which learners are allowed to make the materials relevant to their own needs, can act to increase motivation (Cornell & Martin, 1997; Duchastel, 1997; Keller & Burkman, 1993). In either case, to encourage the learner to actively process the information it is important to link the exploration of the site to some specific activity (Butler, 1997; Duchastel, 1997; Duchastel & Turcotte, 1996).

Learning Styles

There is significant controversy about the validity of learning styles. While intuitively it seems as though learning styles are identifiable, less is known about how to design instruction to capitalize on various styles. Information about learning styles is presented here to convey the continuing interest researchers have in the topic, and to provide at least one view of how learning styles might affect instruction. Learning styles refers to the way in which an individual prefers to and most efficiently learns new information. Learning styles are generally not related to core intelligence or prior learned capabilities (Miller, 2000), and while there aren't "good" or "bad" learning styles, there are effective and ineffective matches between the way an individual learns and the way instructional materials are presented or a course is taught.

The online environment can be particularly well suited to certain learning styles and personality needs. For example, introverted students might find it easier to communicate via computer-mediated communication than in face-to-face situations. Also, the online environment lends itself to a less hierarchical approach to instruction, which meets the learning needs of people who do not approach new information in a systematic or linear fashion. Online learning environments are used to their highest potential for collaborative learning, which complements many students' learning styles. Independent learners have also found online courses to be well suited to their needs.

Because learners have different learning styles or a combination of styles, online educators should design activities that address their modes of learning in order to provide significant experiences for each class participant. This can best be accomplished by utilizing multiple instructional strategies. Following is a description of the most common learning styles (Miller, 2000). These descriptions reflect the different channels of perception, namely, reading (visual), listening (auditory), seeing (visual), speaking (auditory), and doing (tactile/kinesthetic). The first three (reading, listening, and seeing) represent *passive* types of learning, while the last two (speaking and doing) are *active* types of learning. How much a person tends to remember is a function of both the type of learning they prefer and their level of involvement in the learning. People often learn through a combination of styles.

With online learning, although there is a significant amount of passive learning through reading text, listening to audio clips, and looking at video, graphics, or animation, the active speaking and doing modes can also be accommodated through e-mail, chat rooms, threaded discussions, synchronous video, and interactive simulation exercises.

Visual/Verbal Learning Style   Visual/verbal learners learn best when information is presented visually and in a written language format (Miller, 2000). Visual/verbal learners benefit from instructors or teachers who use the blackboard or overhead projector to list the essential points of a lecture, or who provide an outline for lectures. They benefit significantly from information obtained from textbooks and class notes, and tend to like to study alone and in quiet. The online environment can be particularly appropriate for visual/verbal learners when most of the instructional content is presented in written form. Visual/verbal learners

- see information "in their mind's eye" when trying to remember information
- use "color coding" with highlighter pens when studying new information in textbooks or notes
- write out sentences and phrases that summarize key information obtained from textbooks and lectures
- develop flashcards of vocabulary words and concepts that need to be memorized and use highlighter pens to emphasize key points on the cards

Listed below are several online learning strategies for individuals with predominantly visual/verbal learning styles.

- Limit the amount of information per frame or page so the learner can make and remember a mental "picture" of the information.
- Provide a means by which the learner can type out explanations for information presented in diagrams or illustrations, sentences, or key phrases when learning technical information, and how to perform each step when a problem involves learning a sequence of steps.
- Provide a mechanism for copying key information from notes and textbooks into an online course notebook and suggest the learner print out information for visual review.
- Before an exam, remind the student to make visual reminders of information that must be memorized. Suggest that they make Post-it Notes containing key words and concepts and place them in highly visible places such as on a mirror, notebook, closet door, and so on. (Miller, 2000).

Visual/Nonverbal Learning Style   Visual/nonverbal learners learn best when information is presented visually in a picture or diagram format. These learners benefit from instructors or instructional materials that use visual media such as film, video, animation, maps, and charts. The online environment is well suited for this type of learner because graphical representations of information can help them remember concepts and ideas (Miller, 2000). Graphical information can be presented using charts, tables, graphs, and other images. Visual/verbal learners tend to

- like to work quietly and independently
- often visualize a picture of what they are learning in their mind when trying to remember something
- tend to be artistic and enjoy activities involving visual art and design

Consider the following online learning strategies for individuals with predominantly visual/nonverbal learning styles:

- Translate words and ideas into symbols, pictures, diagrams, and drawings as much as possible.
- Summarize information that needs to be memorized and use symbols and pictures to facilitate recall.
- Mark up online text by highlighting key words.
- Limit the amount of information on frames or pages so the learner can make a mental "picture" of the information.
- Develop charts to organize technical information.
- When a problem involves a sequence of steps, draw a flowchart with each box containing the appropriate bit of information in sequence.
- Create tables, charts, and diagrams with graphics to illustrate key concepts and help the student understand and retain course material.
- Use spreadsheet and database software to further organize material that needs to be learned.

Tactile/Kinesthetic Learning Style The tactical/kinesthetic learner learns best when physically engaged in a "hands-on" activity. They benefit from lab settings where they can manipulate materials to learn new information. They are happiest when they can be physically active in the learning environment. They benefit from demonstrations, "hands-on" learning experiences, and fieldwork. Online environments can provide learning opportunities for tactile/kinesthetic learners through simulations with three-dimensional graphics that replicate physical demonstrations. Lab sessions can be conducted either at predetermined locations or at home and then discussed online. Also, outside fieldwork can be incorporated into the coursework, with ample online discussion both preceding and following the experience. Online learners are often self-directed, and when they are working in their chosen fields they can immediately apply the new knowledge or skills directly to the job. For this reason, many online learners say they learn more in online classes than traditional settings and have better retention. Finally, the online environment is well-suited for presentation and discussion of either group or individual projects and activities (Miller, 2000).

Consider the following online learning strategies for individuals with predominantly tactile/kinesthetic learning styles:

- Use the computer to reinforce learning through the sense of touch.
- Incorporate word-processing software and exercises where the student must copy essential information from the course.

- Develop interactive exercises using graphics, tables, and spreadsheets to further help the student organize material that must be learned.
- Help students stay focused as they proceed through the course by telling them to jot down key words and draw pictures or make charts to help them remember the information they've read or heard.
- After a certain period of time online, prompt the student to stand up and walk around and use written notes or flashcards to read information learned out loud.
- Think of ways to make the learning tangible (i.e., something the students can put their hands on), for example, incorporate an exercise in which the student is required to actually make a model that illustrates a key concept.
- Integrate lab exercises or field exercises with the online course to engage learners and allow them to gain first-hand experience of the subject matter.
- When learning a sequence of steps, incorporate a tool that will let the student design online flashcards for each step and arrange them on the computer screen to represent the correct sequence.
- Provide a tool that will allow students to put words, symbols, or pictures on their flashcards—anything that will help them remember the information.
- Use contrasting colors to emphasize important points.
- Limit the amount of information per frame to aid recall.

Auditory/Verbal Learning Style   Auditory/verbal learners learn best when information is presented in an oral language format. They benefit from listening to lectures and participating in group discussions. They also benefit from audio recordings, voice-over narration, and sound effects. To recall information, they often "hear" the way the information was told to them, or they repeat the information out loud. They learn best when interacting with others in a listening/speaking exchange. Online learning environments can complement the auditory/verbal learner style through collaboration and group activities. Although information is typically presented visually, either through text or graphically, streaming audio and computer conferencing can be incorporated into an online course to address the auditory/verbal learning style.

Consider the following online learning strategies for individuals with predominantly auditory/verbal learning styles:

- Maximize the use of audio, including voice-over narration and sound effects.
- Incorporate synchronous and /or asynchronous collaborative exercises or strategies to allow the learner to participate in group learning.
- Provide an online mentor or instructor on an ongoing basis to review key information and help students prepare for exams.
- Suggest that the student talk out loud to aid recall.
- Incorporate speech recognition technology into the online course to allow the student to verbalize information, tape it online, and play it back.
- When learning technical information, have students talk their way through new information by stating the problem in their own words and reason through solutions by talking out loud to themselves or with a study partner.

- When learning a sequence of steps, have the student type them out in sentence form and read them out loud.
- Create musical jingles or use mnemonics to aid memorization.
- Incorporate verbal analogies and storytelling into the course to demonstrate key points.

Collaboration

Collaborative learning approaches engage students in active learning and give them access to the shared knowledge, experience, and insights of other members of a learning team (Golas, 2000). This is particularly important for higher-order, critical thinking skills that must move beyond the passive memorization of facts to a more "constructivist" engagement in which students comprehend, assess, and apply information in ways that lead to new insights and understanding. Interaction among students is a critical variable in learning, especially in formal education contexts. Collaboration is especially important in online learning (Klemm, 1998) where distance learners tend to be isolated, without the usual social support systems found in on-campus or classroom-based instruction.

Distance learners need to be more motivated in order to cope with the constraints and limitations of physical isolation that occur via distance education technologies. For this reason it is crucial to complement delivery of instruction by distance education technologies with electronic means so that students can support and communicate with each other. To achieve learning outcomes, learners need to construct their knowledge by acting on it, reformulating it, making their own personal interpretation of it, sharing it with others, and building on these ideas and concepts through the reactions and responses of their peers (Harasim, 1990). Online education, with its computer-mediated communications systems, offers a potentially rich social learning environment, which can support and facilitate active learning collaboration (Brown, 1997). Optimally, students need a learning environment that lets them work together on problems and produce, as a group, some kind of cohesive deliverable product, which might be in the form of a group plan, research project, report, or case study, for example (Klemm, 1998). Learning management systems and hosted training solutions provide the infrastructure to support collaborative learning environments.

Collaboration Examples   *Synchronous* collaboration options include live, face-to-face interaction or live distance learning options, such as audio, video, and Web conferencing. *Asynchronous* collaboration includes options as simple as a printed newsletter, an e-mail listserv, or as sophisticated as a dedicated community-of-practice Web site. Communities of practice are groups of people who share similar goals and interests. In pursuit of these goals and interests, they employ common practices, work with the same tools, and express themselves in a common language. Through such common activity, they come to hold similar beliefs and value systems (Collaborative Visualization Project, 2004). Online collaborative Web sites are often used in university settings, while corporate training organizations are just starting to include collaboration in their offerings (Bedinger, 2002). Online discussion has been shown to provide a number of advantages over face-to-face discussion. For example, the asynchronous nature of online discussion allows learners to respond at a time that best suits them. It allows students time to reflect on or further research the topic before responding. Hiltz (1986) found that "time for reflection" was an important factor in learning effectiveness. Online discussion also provides a more egalitarian learning environment (Brown, 1997). The physical anonymity of the contributors is a great equalizer. More reclusive learners no longer need to struggle for a "turn to speak"; they can make a contribution to the discussion whenever they like with the surety that it will be "heard" by all class members (Brown, 1997). Faculty in many disciplines have found that online discussion forums can lead to fuller participation in class discussion by all students.

Collaboration and Blended Learning   In the same way that the power of a systems approach to training has become prevalent, the value of including collaborative learning solutions within a blended learning scenario is now widely recognized. Collaborative elements might include activities within instructor-led training or lab exercises. Collaboration can also be facilitated during on-the-job activities. Field support might be provided through an online moderated-discussion Web site supporting threaded discussions or chat. Live follow-up events using a virtual classroom can also include collaborative elements. Collaboration needs a context and a platform in order to flourish, and blended learning is well-positioned to provide both (Golas, 2000). As the pendulum of learning reaches equilibrium in blended learning, markets for collaboration and related tools and systems will increase. Such tools will need to be aligned with the platforms that support blended learning to ensure that collaboration will be a part of the blended learning equation. Blended learning coupled with collaboration is a key combination for maximizing training investments, and for enhancing individual and group performance (Bedinger, 2002).

Online Monitoring   According to the MASIE Center (2001), 88 percent of learners and 91 percent of managers recommend that the trainer or facilitator be an active part of the online training program. Survey respondents placed a high value on having the trainer monitor progress and contact the learner, evaluate online project work, build and facilitate an online community for the course participants, and be available via e-mail or threaded discussion to respond to content questions. It's clear that combining self-paced learning with facilitator support keeps the learner from feeling isolated, which assists in the successful completion of the self-paced modules.

Hyperlinking

Including hyperlinks to related content within a course is an instructional strategy that is unique to online learning. Links can direct students to relevant content, other viewpoints, and be a rich resource for instructional material. A course that includes numerous appropriate links can provide a mini-encyclopedia on a particular topic (Rajamanickam & Nichani, 2003). In general, if another Web site or page covers one of the objectives or subtopics in the course, linking to it with a brief summary is efficient. This implies a new composition strategy that starts with a survey of available resources and follows with selection of the hypermedia design (Golas, 2000).

Oliver, Herrington, and Omari (1996) describe a continuum in which different levels and degrees of hyperlinking are recommended. At one end of the continuum, the links are minimal and simply act to connect nodes in a specified sequence. This form of hyperlinking closely resembles conventional text and is referred to as *linear*. In its use, the learner is encouraged, and often compelled, to follow an instructional sequence planned by the instructor/facilitator. Further along the continuum, the links tend to form a hierarchical structure, giving learners more freedom in the choice of a path through the materials. At the extreme, hyperlinking provides a totally unstructured learning environment with multiple links between associated "nodes," or fragments of information. In this environment, learners are free to move between associated nodes using referential links, and very little structure is imposed.

The selection of hyperlinking design for online learning depends on *what* is being trained (the nature of the intended learning outcomes) and *who* is being trained (the intended target audience). Jonassen, Mayes, and McAleese (1993) provide a useful guide for selecting the form of hyperlinking most suited to the nature of intended learning outcomes by suggesting instructional strategies for knowledge acquisition aims. For example, when the materials seek to develop a student's initial knowledge by providing facts, procedures, and rules, linear linking is an appropriate strategy. However, for higher levels of knowledge and more sophisticated learners, such as understanding complex concepts and principles, less structured hierarchical and referential linking is more appropriate. In these instances, students are guided by such factors as their prior knowledge and readiness to assimilate new material. When building on an existing knowledge base, learners can benefit from the freedom to browse and explore, to inquire and seek responses to their own questions rather than following a predetermined path of instruction (Oliver et al., 1996).

It should be noted that research with hypertext systems has shown that including too much learner control can sometimes decrease learning effectiveness (Large, 1996; Niemiec, Sikorski, & Walberg, 1996). To reduce the likelihood of the student getting "lost in cyberspace," it is recommended that a clear and systematic organization scheme be created for the learning site (DeBra, 1996). The information should be presented in a modular fashion within a well-structured hierarchy, and the main points should be obvious to the learner (Shotsberger, 1996). Some sort of advanced organizer might be included in the site design so that the learner can get an overview of how the site is organized (Burbules & Callister, 1996; Cornell & Martins, 1997; Cotrell & Eisenberg, 1997; Dodge, 1997; Everhart, 1997).

Hall (1999) recommends the following guidelines for hyperlinking based on various Web design research studies: (1) Links should be included on a page only if they serve a clear purpose (DeBra, 1996). In one experiment, a negative correlation was found between the number of links on a page and learners' comprehension of the information contained in a site (User Interface Engineering, 1998); (2) links should be clearly labeled (DeBra, 1996; Jones & Farquhar, 1997; User Interface Engineering, 1998); and (3) the overall layout of links on a page should have some organization/structural meaning (Jones & Farquhar, 1997; Nielson, 1997). This not only lets the learners make a more informed decision as to whether or not they should click on the link, but it also gives the learners clearer information about the overall organization of the site. Links on one page to other places within the same page have been found to confuse learners and consequently should be avoided (Jones & Farquhar, 1997).

Orientation

Orientation is the means by which users are able to identify their current position in a course, how they achieved that position, and how they can to return to a previous position. The organizational structure should provide a clear route back to the starting point (Goldberg, 1997). For this reason, a site should never take a user to a page that is a dead end where they can't do anything except close their browser (Shotsberger, 1996).

Because electronic learning materials can easily conceal much of the information they contain, it is important in the design process to provide the learner with a means to orient and move freely within the information space. Oliver et al. (1996) recommend three strategies to aid orientation within learning material: placement cues, hierarchies and indices, and semantic nets.

Placement Cues   In linear sequences, bars or graphs are commonly used to indicate the distance and placement of the learner in the instructional sequence. These bars are created as graphic elements and are interspersed within the text to provide visual cues.

Hierarchies and Indices   These structures provide access to the information nodes within a system, together with an overall structure that is reinforced as nodes are selected and viewed. The use of frames and targetable windows provides a means for materials to continually display these structures as content is selected and accessed. The term frames refers to the simultaneous loading of two or more Web pages at the same time within the same screen. One page or frame often acts as a "control frame," and the other is the "target frame," or "targetable window," where the results of actions taken in the control frame are displayed.

Semantic Nets   Learning can be enhanced when connections and associations between related information are recognized and made specific. The use of image maps as tools by which information nodes can be accessed and selected provides a linking structure, reinforcing associations and connections between the contained information as well as supporting learner orientation (Oliver et al., 1996).

Navigation

Interface design is an important aspect of online course design. When learners are compelled to think about how an interface works, their attention may be split, and the actual learning event requires additional mental effort (Chandler & Sweller, 1991).

A number of guidelines are recommended to minimize the amount of mental and cognitive activity associated with controlling the interface. Brooks and Brooks (1993) suggest a need for simplicity and consistency in design. When screens change, the only thing that should change is the information to which the learner is being directed. Having a consistent set of navigation buttons on each page and organizing the pages into consistent files will give users a sense of where they are in the site. Students often find it confusing if an icon means different things or a navigation button changes positions (Brooks & Brooks, 1993). The preferred number of navigational buttons or icons on a screen is five, plus or minus two.

The use of site maps and hierarchical trees, where content is "layered" (with the home page as the first layer and other pages forming subsidiary layers), is also recommended to facilitate navigation. Students should always know where they are in the site and when they are leaving it. Headings and other essential information should be repeated on each page. Cascading style sheets can be used to provide a consistent look to all of the pages within the site. Cascading style sheets allow a developer to control the rendering (e.g., fonts, colors, leading, margins, typefaces, and other style aspects of a Web document) without compromising the document's structure. For example, the look of a site can be defined in one file, and changing that file will change the appearance of the whole site.

Testing

Seamless Evaluation Young (1993) suggests that online assessment should no longer be viewed as an "add-on" to an instructional design or simply as separate stages in a linear process of pretest, instruction, posttest. Instead, assessment should become an integrated, ongoing, and seamless part of the online learning environment. The enhanced interactive capability of the Internet provides the means for assessment of student learning to extend beyond conventional essays and examinations. McLellan (1993) points out that more reliable assessments can take the form of evaluation measures, such as portfolios, summary statistics of learners' paths through instructional materials, diagnoses, reflection, and self-assessments.

Security and Data Privacy Regardless of the testing strategy, online course designers often ask how it is possible to properly evaluate students they cannot see, hear, or interact with in person. Security issues are at the heart of this question, and there are a number of models to consider. In some online courses, students go to a laboratory or classroom for testing under proctored conditions because the testing requires strictly controlled conditions or a high degree of security. In other instances, testing is accomplished directly using the interactive capabilities of the Internet. Testing on the Internet can be done "live" in real time, or students can take a test off-line and then submit it. A subject in which the learning materials are delivered online does not necessarily need to be assessed online. A student's progress could be monitored by mailing or faxing tests or other assessment instruments to the student.

Security issues include restricting access to a site, allowing no unauthorized access to test banks or answer banks, randomizing test questions, randomizing the order in which answers are presented in multiple-choice questions, reducing the likelihood of tests being taken by someone other than the enrolled student, restricting the availability of the test by date and time, and authenticating the student who is taking the test. Online testing and evaluation programs should provide test security functionality. For example, the program should automatically provide security for development of the question database and student identification checking. Students should be required to enter their personal identification number (PIN) upon starting the test, and they should not be able to discover the correct answer in the HTML code. Each student's name and score should be protected through the use of passwords.

Feedback   Feedback should be provided to the student for any performance activity. In online learning, pages can be linked to appropriate or inappropriate responses by the learner. The pages can either reinforce the correct response or, if an incorrect response is chosen, explain the rationale and guide the user to a more appropriate answer or other remediation. Using CGI scripts, information which students place into online forms, radio buttons (a set of circles beside a list), check boxes, or other types of tests can be compared to preset answers in a database or text file. Feedback can provide individual students with a deeper explanation of their choices, and active links can guide them to additional information. CGI scripts can also be written to capture variables from students, hold them in database fields, and access these fields at a later date. For example, test data can be automated for objective tests or saved in files for instructor/facilitator critique when more open-ended questions are used. CGI scripting allows feedback to become more intelligent, that is, based on individualization, and allows users to leave off and return to instructional content as their scheduling needs require.

Intelligent agents, or knowledge robots, are designed to perform the duties of online facilitators for routine tasks, such as checking computer code, responding to simple questions, reminding learners to complete assignments, exercises, or other learning tasks. An empirical study evaluating the effectiveness of intelligent agents in online instruction (Thaiupathump, Bourne, & Campbell, 1999) showed that they improved learner retention and dramatically increased the completion rate for the majority of learners.

Data Tracking   It is essential that online testing and evaluation provide tracking capabilities. Tracking can include both remembering where a student traveled within a lesson as well as recording a student's performance on test questions and answers. In addition to computation of student grades, the grades should be provided to the student and the privacy of other students' grades should be strictly protected.

LEARNING MANAGEMENT SYSTEMS

The LMS is a critical component of online learning, as its function is to manage the overall distributed learning process. There are a number of commercially available off-the-shelf (COTS) LMS products, and determining the LMS that best matches a business plan or specific training requirements can be a complicated and time-consuming process. Most of the COTS products can handle basic system capabilities, including Internet and registration security, system scalability (the function of a system to maintain consistently acceptable levels of performance while users and processes are added), connectivity to enterprise resource management systems, administration over the Web, and support for third-party content authoring and reporting tools. However, they vary widely when it comes to core features such as collaboration, course and student scheduling, and learning standards.

Education versus Training

To understand the capabilities of the various LMS products, it is useful to distinguish between online *education* (academic institutions) and online *training* (corporate and organizational). Learning objectives for online educational courses tend to cover what students *need to know* (i.e., "knowledges") about a subject, while objectives for online technical training courses tend to cover what students *need to be able to do* (i.e., "skills").

Online Education   LMSs implemented at colleges and universities, including organizations that provide professional military education such as the Air Command and Staff College and Navy/Army War Colleges, need to be able to automate administrative services as well as enable pieces of the learning process. Administrative applications for higher education institutions tend to be large, multimillion-dollar systems that manage student registration, record keeping, financial aid, scheduling, grants management, library systems, and other administrative functions. Because of size, complexity, and reliability, these applications are known as "enterprise" applications.

However, since the learning process also needs to be supported at these institutions, there are a variety of applications that enable professors to post course information, house educational resources, enable synchronous and asynchronous discussion, and provide limited assessment services. Unlike enterprise applications, the applications that support the learning process are generally not as large or complex, and many of them are not scalable or as reliable as enterprise applications.

Online Training The automation of administrative services is often less important for training applications, where the focus shifts to applications that enable and manage the learning process. For example, several commercially available LMSs have built-in software features that are adept at tracking a student's progress to a predetermined learning path. In addition, some LMS products have a built-in feature that compares a student's entry-level knowledge with the training needed to satisfy course requirements.

Selecting an LMS PC Week Labs (Bethoney, 1999) recommends that online developers clearly understand their specific organizational needs and then grill LMS vendors on the ability of their products to meet those needs. The following key criteria were used to evaluate seven LMSs during the PC Week LMS Shoot Out in October 1999.

1. *Installation:* What are the requirements for course installation for both the client and the server maintainer? What instructional features and interface design within the LMS make it easy to access and use?
2. *Registration:* What features are required to make it easy for students to register? Is self-registration authentication a requirement? Will an entire class need to be registered at a single time? How does the LMS handle course auditing and course payment?
3. *Capability:* Is there a requirement for the LMS to be able to verify the trainee's compliance with system requirements? Does the LMS support bookmarking, which allows the user to log off and go right back to where they left off in a course, student profiling, individual and group learning paths, student notification of registration, course prequalification, student progress tracking and evaluation, online testing, online help, and online course catalog, library, and bookstore?
4. *Administration:* Are the administration tools easy to use? How does the product support course, instructor, student, and resource scheduling requirements? Does it support scheduling conflict resolution, profile management, student record management, and course budget tracking?
5. *Collaboration:* Does the LMS support asynchronous online communication via threaded discussions and online text-based chat? Does the LMS support synchronous communication?
6. *Reporting:* What kinds (quality and quantity) of reports does the LMS support? How easy is it to generate reports? Can third-party reporting tools be used seamlessly?
7. *Security:* How does the LMS support security requirements for administration, course and registration accounts, and firewall access?
8. *Scalability:* How many courses and students can the LMS support? Can multiple servers be added easily?
9. *Connectivity:* What bandwidth is supported? What databases are supported? What kinds of data can be imported and exported? Will the LMS support a distributed network architecture?

10. *Content support:* Can the LMS support third-party content authoring, course launching products, and alternate content formats, and if so, which ones?
11. *Tailoring instruction to student:* Does the LMS have the capability to tailor instruction to the user?
12. *Standards and specifications:* Does the LMS comply with academic, industrial, or federal standards?

SUMMARY

As the growth of new information in the digital age accelerates, the rewards of effective education and training are becoming increasingly lucrative (Beam, 2000). This applies to an individual's personal career as well as to businesses that are seeking competitive advantages because they must increasingly keep current to stay competitive. Against this backdrop, the Internet is revolutionizing education and training, along with so many other aspects of our lives (Beam, 2000). Online learning makes businesses more efficient by reducing the time and cost of training, and more effective by expanding the knowledge base of employees. Experts agree that online training can create a 50 percent time saving and a 40–60 percent cost saving compared to regular classroom training. However, the most significant advantage is neither the cost nor the speed, but rather the convenience provided by online learning. Online learning allows students to access a digital cache of information (data, voice, video, animation, etc.) as a part of the course.

To combat the isolation of learning online, the most effective online learning programs accommodate the following key issues:

Instructor Access

This is a key ingredient to successful online learning because having an instructor to "push" students to meet course milestones is an essential safeguard to ensuring they keep progressing, especially given all the freedom of online courses. Unlike traditional classroom training, instructor access is not focused around the few minutes after class where students might have to ask questions in front of other students, or another fixed schedule when the instructor is available to meet. With online learning, the students can send a personal e-mail to the instructor or access a list of FAQs (Frequently Asked Questions) that the course automatically provides the students.

Learning by Doing

By providing online tests, simulation exercises, and personal assignments and feedback, "learning by doing" is supported. Online feedback via tests and marked assignments are critical components of the online learning process. Many online learning proponents believe that an online course should last at least a few weeks to allow time for the personal effort and thinking that is associated with learning.

Collaboration

Frequent, responsive online communication between instructors, students, and colleagues is a significant capability of online learning. Many online courses support group meetings and assignments, facilitated by e-mail, private chat rooms, bulletin boards, and threaded discussions. This form of meeting is certainly more convenient than traditional group meetings, especially for people who prefer the anonymity of an e-mail or chat-room exchange to meeting people face-to-face for one-on-one or group work. Add to this the power of a personal network of classmates that could span the globe and you have a powerful learning tool (Beam, 2000).

Worldwide Access

The speed and reach of the Internet and the ability to continuously update content provides superb access to knowledge sources. The research potential of the Internet is also significant. Imagine a class where the day new research occurs, anywhere in the world, it can become a part of a course. The Internet is rapidly opening new doors to course content and the depth of material individuals are personally interested in. It's like having an unlimited-content textbook (Beam, 2000).

Given all this, it is no surprise that the IDC (2002) expects the market for technology-delivered training to pass $11 billion by 2003 in the United States alone. The online education and training revolution will expand a student's potential to learn by providing them with fast access to tremendous information sources.

REFERENCES

Beam, P. (2002). Retrieved summer 2003 from: http://www.online-earning.com/papers/articlerev.html.

Bedinger, D. (2002). The evolving role of collaboration in eLearning. Retrieved summer 2003 from: http://www.collaborate.com/publication/newsletter/publications_newsletter_jan03.html#.

Bethoney, H. (1999). Retrieved summer 2003 from: http://techupdate.zdnet.com.

Brown, A. (1997). Designing for learning: What are the essential features of an effective online course? *Australian Journal of Educational Technology, 13*(2), 115–126.

Brooks, J. G., & Brooks, M. (1993). *In search of understanding: The case for constructivist classrooms*. Alexandria, VA: ASCD.

Burbules, N. C., & Callister, T. A. (1996). Knowledge at the crossroads: Some alternative futures of hypertext learning environments. *Educational Theory, 46*, 23–50.

Butler, B. S. (1997). Using the World Wide Web to support classroom-based education: Conclusions from a multiple-case study. In B. H. Khan (Ed.), *Web-based instruction*. Englewood Cliffs, NJ: Educational Technology Publications.

Carliner, S. (1999). *An overview of on-line learning.* Amherst, Mass.: HRD Press.

Chandler, P., & Sweller, J. (1991). Cognitive load theory and the format of instruction. *Cognition and Instruction, 8*(4), 293–332.

Clark, R. C., & Mayer, R. E. (2002). *e-Learning and the science of instruction: Proven guidelines for consumers and designers of multimedia learning.* New York: John Wiley.

Collaborative Visualization Project (2004). Retrieved January 2004 from: http://www.co-i-l.com/coil/knowledge-garden/cop/definitions.shtml.

Cotrell, J., & Eisenberg, M. B. (1997). Web design for information problem-solving: Maximizing value for users. *Computers in Libraries, 17*(5), 52–57.

Cornell, R., & Martin, B. L. (1997). The role of motivation in Web-based instruction. In B.H. Khan (Ed.), *Web-based instruction*. Englewood Cliffs, NJ: Educational Technology Publications.

DeBra, P. M. (1996). Hypermedia structures and systems. Web Course, Eidenhoven University of Technology. Retrieved May 2000 from: http://wwwis.win.tue.nl/2L670/static.

Directory of Schools (2002). Retrieved summer 2003 from: http://www.directoryofschools.com.

Dodge, B. (1997). Webquests: A technique for Internet-based learning. *Distance Educator, 1*(2), 10–13.

Duchastel, P. (1997). A motivational framework for Web-based instruction. In B. H. Khan (Ed.), *Web-based instruction.* Englewood Cliffs, NJ: Educational Technology Publications.

Duchastel, P., & Turcotte, S. (1996). *On-line learning and teaching in an information-rich context.* Proceedings of the Ineti96 International Conference, Montreal, Canada.

Everhart, N. (1997). Web page evaluation: Views from the field. *Technology Connection, 4*(3), 24–26.

Gallagher, S., & Newman, A. (2002). Distance learning at the tipping point: Critical success factors to growing fully online distance-learning. Retrieved summer 2003 from: http://www.eduventures.com/research/industry_research_resources/distancelearning.cfm.

Global Reach (2003). Retrieved January 2004 from: http://www.glreach.com/globstats.

Golas, K. C. (2000). Guidelines for Designing Online Learning. Proceedings of the Interservice Industry Training and Education Systems Conference, Orlando, FL.

Goldberg, M. W. (1997). CALOS: First results from an experiment in computer-aided learning. Proceedings of the ACM's 28th SIGCSE Technical Symposium on Computer Science Education. San Jose: California. February.

Hall, R. H. (1999). Instructional Web site design principles: A literature review and synthesis. *Virtual University Journal, 2*(1).

Harasim, L. M. (1990). Online education: An environment for collaboration and intellectual amplification. In L. M. Harasim (Ed.), *Online education: Perspectives on a new environment* (pp. 39–64). New York: Praeger.

Hiltz, S. R. (1986, spring). The virtual classroom: Using computer mediated communication for university teaching. *Journal of Communication, 36*(2), 95–104.

International Data Corporation (2002). Retrieved summer 2003 from: http://www.nua.ie/surveys.

Jonassen, D., Mayes, T., & McAleese, R. (1993). A manifesto for a constructivist approach to uses of technology in higher education. In T. Duffy, J. Lowyck, & D. Jonassen (Eds.), *Designing environments for constructivist learning* (pp. 231–247). Berlin Heidelberg: Springer-Verlag.

Jones, M. G., & Farquhar, J. D. (1997). User interface design for Web-based instruction. In B. H. Khan (Ed.), *Web-based instruction.* Englewood Cliffs, NJ: Educational Technology Publications.

Keller, J., & Burkman, E. (1993). Motivation principles. In M. Fleming & W. H. Levie (Eds.), *Instructional message design: Principles from the behavioral and cognitive sciences* (2nd ed., pp. 3–53). Englewood Cliffs, NJ: Educational Technology Publications.

Klemm, W. R. (1998). Eight ways to get students more engaged in online conferences. *T.H.E. Journal, 26*(1), 62–64.

Large, A. (1996). Hypertext instructional programs and learner control: A research review. *Education for Information, 14,* 96–106.

March, T. (1995, August). Working the Web for education. *Computer-Using Educators Newsletter.*

Masie, E. (2000). Roles and expectations for e-trainers. Retrieved summer 2003 from: http://www.masie.com.

MASIE Center (2001). Retrieved summer 2003 from: http://www.masie.com/masie/researchreports/ASTD_Exec_Summ.pdf.

McAlister, M. K., Rivera, J.C., & Hallam, J. C. (2001). Twelve important questions to answer before you offer a web based curriculum. *Online Journal of Distance Learning Administration,* vol. IV, no. II.

McLellan, H. (1993). Evaluation in a situated learning environment. *Educational Technology, 33*(3), 39–45.

Miller, S. (2000). Learning Styles Survey. Retrieved summer 2003 from: http://www.metamath.com/lsweb/fourls.htm.

Miller, R. (2003). Retrieved January 2004 from: http://mchnetlinkplus.ichp.edu/MediaStreaming/Default.htm.

National Research Council (1997). National science education standards. Washington, DC: National Academy Press.

Nielson, J. (1997). Be succinct! (writing for the Web). Retrieved summer 2003 from: http://www.useit.com/alertbox/9703b.html.

Niemiec, R. P., Sikorski, C., & Walberg, H. J. (1996). Learner-control effects: A review of reviews and a meta-analysis. *Journal of Educational Computing Research, 15,* 157–174.

Oliver, R., Herrington, J., & Omari, A. (1996). Creating effective instructional materials for the World Wide Web. Retrieved May 2000 from: http://elmo.scu.edu.au/sponsored/ausweb/ausweb96/educn/oliver/.

Online Pedagogy Report. University of Illinois (1999). Retrieved summer 2003 from: http://www.vpaa.uillinois.edu/tid/report/tid_report.html.

Penrod, J. I. (2003, March/April). Creating a realistic IT vision: The roles and responsibilities of a chief information officer. *The Technology Source*.

Rajamanickam, V., & Nichani, M. (2003). Effective writing for online instruction. Retrieved summer 2003 from: http://www.elearningpost.com.

Ritchie, D. C. & Hoffman, B. (1996). Instruction and the Internet. Retrieved summer 2003 from: http://edweb.sdsu.edu/clrit/learningtree/DCD/WWWinstrdesign/instruction.html.

Rogers, E. M., & Shoemaker, F. F. (1971). Communication of innovations: A cross-cultural approach (2nd ed.). New York: Macmillan.

Rossett, A. (2001). *Beyond the podium: Delivering training and performance*. New York: Jossey-Bass.

Shank, P. (2003). Retrieved summer 2003 from: http://www.macromedia.com/resources/elearning/article/itskills/.

Shotsberger, P. G. (1996). Instructional uses of the World Wide Web: Exemplars and precautions. *Educational Technology, 36*(2), 47–50.

Siegel, M. A., & Kirkley, S. (1997). Moving toward the digital learning environment: The future of Web-based instruction. In B. H. Khan (Ed.), *Web-based instruction*. Englewood Cliffs, NJ: Educational Technology Publications.

Thaiupathump, C., Bourne, J., & Campbell, J. O. (1999). Intelligent agents for online learning. *Journal of Asynchronous Learning Networks, 3*(2), pp. 1–19.

User Interface Engineering (1998). Retrieved from: http://www.uiereports.com.

Vadlakunta, K. (2004). Retrieved January 2004 from: http://www.asp101.com/articles/kanna/clientscript/default.asp.

Warren, A. (2002). Retrieved summer 2003 from: http://www.clt.soton.ac.uk/LTDI/topics/mle.htm.

Young, M. F. (1993). Instructional design for situated learning. *Educational Technology Research and Development, 41*(1), 43–58.

Evaluating Instruction

Designers of instruction want to know if their topics, or courses, or total systems of instruction meet learning needs, whether in schools or in employee education settings. This means that they wish to at least know whether a newly designed course or system works in the sense of achieving its learning objectives, and, more important perhaps, they are interested in finding out whether their products have positive outcomes in regard to subsequent performances and attitudes of the learners and the overall performance of the organization in which they study and work.

The evaluation of instruction and the evaluation of educational systems are related but different problems. Evaluation of instruction focuses on whether or not learners master the learning objectives. It is assumed that if the learners represent the appropriate target audience and they are not mastering the objectives then there are problems with the instruction. Evaluation then provides information to help the instructor make a decision whether or how to revise, reconceive, or even abandon the project if the problems are too severe.

Learning is a complex enterprise because there are many variables other than the quality of instruction that affect it. This is illustrated in the classic work of Carroll (1963), who describes a "school learning model." This model identifies the following variables: learner perseverance, time allowed for learning (opportunity), learner aptitude (subject specific), learner ability to understand (general intelligence), and quality of instruction. Each of these variables affects either the time any particular learner needs to learn any given skill, or the time that the learner will actually spend. Most design models place a great deal of emphasis on improving the quality of instruction through the use of formative evaluation. However, according to the Carroll model, in order to evaluate instruction, one must also consider the motivation of the learner as well as other environmental variables, such as opportunity to spend the time needed.

This focus on a systems perspective is reflected in the movement toward an even broader perspective on human performance development, most commonly called *human performance technology* (HPT), which has occurred in the field of instructional systems design (ISD). Instruction, or training, is but one influence on the development of human performance. As indicated by Carroll (1963), Gilbert (1978), and others, performance is also influenced by motivation and opportunity

(Keller, 1999b). Furthermore, the HPT perspective takes into consideration that there are outcomes beyond the learning objectives that are important indicators of an instructional system's success. Learning objectives are not ends in themselves; they are means to ends. For example, the purposes of instruction include transfer of knowledge to an application setting and improved performance of the overall instructional system, or *suprasystem,* that encompasses the instructional system. For example, achieving mastery in a ninth-grade math class is not considered a terminal achievement; it is preparation for achievement in other courses and ultimately part of the overall goals of a school to prepare people for survival and success in life. The success of the suprasystem, in the case of the school, is measured in part by the cumulative successes of the students within the school. In an employee education environment, the organization that is supporting the instructional system is concerned about transfer of skills from the classroom to the workplace and about the benefits of education and training on the overall performance of the company.

Indications of how well an instructional product or system performs are best obtained from systematically gathered evidence. The means of gathering, analyzing, and interpreting such evidence are collectively called *methods of evaluation,* which is the subject of this final chapter. The placement of this chapter, by the way, should not be taken to indicate that the planning of evaluation for instruction should be undertaken as a final step. Quite the opposite is true. The design of evaluation requires principles of instructional planning that have been described in every chapter of this book.

INSTRUCTIONAL SYSTEMS EVALUATION—FIVE TYPES

Evaluation activities occur throughout the ISD process, including the implementation and maintenance phases. From a comprehensive perspective, instructional systems evaluation can include at least the following five types:

1. *Evaluation of the instructional materials.* Has a newly developed set of instructional materials been shown to effectively and efficiently result in student achievement of the learning objectives?
2. *Quality review of the ISD process.* Has the ISD process been conducted in a satisfactory manner, and are there are ways to improve the process?
3. *Assessment of learner reactions to the instruction.* Do learners perceive the instruction and aspects of the delivery environment to be appealing and effective?
4. *Measurement of learner achievement of the learning objectives.* Do learners in an established course satisfactorily achieve the course's learning objectives?
5. *Estimation of instructional consequences.* Do learners transfer their knowledge and skills to the appropriate environments and contribute to an organization's successful accomplishment of its goals?

These five types, or categories, of evaluation activities represent different purposes and do not constitute a model or sequence. Some of these types can be conduced in parallel, and aspects of the fifth one are planned even before any materials have been developed. However, implementation of the first two types normally occurs during course development and the other three occur afterward.

The types of evaluation that are most familiar to most instructional designers are the first, *evaluation of instructional materials,* and fourth, *measuring achievement.* The reasons for this are that (1) these types are taught in instructional design textbooks, (2) most instructional designers are not involved with instruction after it has been developed and put into full implementation, and (3) even though they might not be involved in implementation, the tests used in the fourth category are usually prepared during development. However, instructional designers are increasingly called upon to plan and conduct, or at least be involved in, all of the five types.

EVALUATION TYPES AND DECISION TYPES

The five types of evaluation covered in this book should not be confused with the concept of *levels of evaluation* which, together with the concepts of *formative* and *summative evaluation,* are highly prevalent concepts in education and training evaluation. The first, *levels of evaluation,* refers to evaluating the outcomes of training and is used most frequently in contexts of employee education. Within this framework, four "levels" are typically listed (Kirkpatrick, 1959):

Level 1—learner reactions
Level 2—learning achievement
Level 3—transfer of learning
Level 4—organizational results

Learner reactions consist of student attitude questionnaires that are administered after a learning event. They can range from simple four-question surveys of how well students enjoyed the learning event and how well it was taught to much longer questionnaires that probe detailed components of the appeal, effectiveness, and efficiency of the instructor, materials, and environment. The second level, *learning achievement,* refers to measurements of how well learners have achieved the instructional objectives. The third level, *transfer of learning,* examines the extent to which learners use their new knowledge on the job. This level becomes complicated because it can be difficult to establish the connection between learning and job performance. For example, employees might not be using their new skills on the job, even though they learned them, because there is no opportunity or support for using the new skills. Conversely, employees could be using target skills on the job even though they did not learn them in training. They might have acquired the skills after returning to their jobs. Thus, it is important when doing this type of evaluation to establish a "chain of evidence" that connects end-of-course performance to on-the-job performance, and accounts for other influences on performance. The fourth level, *organizational results,* considers whether there is a demonstrable improvement in organization performance when the educational program has been successful. This is a test of whether or not the educational program truly addressed real problems in the performance environment. For example, employees might be using their new skills effectively, but if these skills are not related to the real problems that led to the development of the educational program, then the original problem will still exist, unless it has been overcome in other ways.

The concept of levels of training evaluation was introduced by several writers in the 1950s (Hamblin, 1974) and beyond, but the most frequently referenced version of this classification of levels is that of Kirkpatrick (1959). He refers to the four types as "Level 1, 2, 3, and 4," and these labels are typically used as shorthand references within the field of ISD. Other writers have introduced similar models. Hamblin (1974), for example, introduced a five-level model. The first three levels were the same as in previous models, such as Kirkpatrick's (1959), but Hamblin obtained a fifth level by dividing Kirkpatrick's fourth level into two, which he called "organizational results" and "cost benefit." This division was based on the type of data one collects to estimate organizational results—perceptual information in the form of questionnaires to key executives and stakeholders; performance data, such as improvements in productivity or, in the case of a school system, improved performance on standardized measures of achievement; or cost benefit analysis in which one compares the financial benefits to the overall cost of developing and implementing the solution. Hamblin's fourth level includes perceptual and performance data-based estimates of organizational results, while his fifth level includes cost-benefit analysis. This distinction was reintroduced by Phillips (1991). In contrast, Kaufman and Keller (1994) also introduced a fifth level of evaluation. Instead of subdividing an already existing level and calling it a new level, they logically extended the model to its next higher level—*societal outcomes*. This provides a test of whether an organization's goals are in alignment with societal values and expectations or whether an organization's success can ultimately be a failure if it violates societal laws or expectations. It is difficult to ascertain whether a specific educational program can have such a high level of influence, but curriculum decisions should consider future societal needs, and what skills and attitudes should be fostered by the system.

The other two highly prevalent concepts, *formative* and *summative evaluation,* refer to the type of decision to be made. Formative evaluation can consist of feedback to learners in regard to ways in which they can improve their performance, or similarly, feedback to instructional designers as to how they can improve their products. As illustrated in Chapter 2 by the feedback loops in Figure 2–1, formative evaluation provides data for revising and improvement within any given phase of the ISD process. In this context, it is not sufficient to answer questions about whether or not the instructional materials are well received and effective. One must also determine *why* the materials are having the results indicated by the learners and other reviewers. For example, a learner might indicate that a passage of instruction is boring, but the challenge for the evaluator is to find out why the passage is boring so that the instructional designer knows what to improve. A passage could be boring for many reasons, such as highly abstract language, absence of relevant examples, or simply because of its placement at the end of a series of passages that have not had any breaks with interactive learning tactics.

Summative evaluation supports judgments about the achievements of learners and the effectiveness of instruction. Summative judgments about learners consist of determining whether they have achieved at a satisfactory level with respect to an established criterion. In other words, these are "pass, remediate, or fail" kinds of decisions. Summative decisions about instruction consists of decisions about whether or not to continue offering a course based on the degree to which learners are actually accomplishing the learning objectives and whether the course is serving the goals for which it was established. If the learners are not achieving the objectives, and if there are too many problems within the course to make it feasible to revise it, then the summative judgment might be to cancel the project. Similarly, if an organization's job performance requirements or goals have changed such that the course is judged to be no longer relevant, then the course will be cancelled. On the positive side, summative evaluations of a successful course can provide valuable support for the ISD effort.

There are relationships between the evaluation types and decision types. Some instructional designers consider that formative evaluation pertains to Level 1, learner reactions, and to Level 2, learning outcomes, while summative evaluations apply more to Level 3, transfer, and to Level 4, organizational results. This is true to a degree, but each type of evaluation can be done for either type of decision even though one combination might be more frequent than another. For example, IBM offers courses to its customers, and its instructors are expected to achieve at or above a given criterion level on the student reaction questionnaires. If not, they are given additional training or reassigned. At Florida State University, the provost reviews student reaction evaluations, and professors whose ratings are below a criterion are expected to attend a teaching improvement workshop and take other actions necessary to improve their ratings. Thus, Level 1 evaluation is used for summative purposes in both of these contexts. Similarly, Level 3 evaluation of job application of newly acquired skills can provide formative feedback on how to improve future offerings of a course. Table 16.1 illustrates the combinations that occur more and less frequently.

TABLE 16.1   RELATIONSHIPS BETWEEN EVALUATION LEVEL AND DECISION TYPE

Evaluation Level	Decision Type	
	Formative	Summative
Level 1	X[1]	X
Level 2	X	X
Level 3	x[2]	X
Level 4	x	X

[1]Uppercase X indicates a frequent relationship

[2]Lowercase x indicates a less frequent relationship

While instructional designers are concerned with all four levels of evaluation, they are mostly working with Levels 3 and 4 when considering curriculum, and Levels 1 and 2 when designing materials. This book has concentrated mostly on Levels 1 and 2, but the importance of Levels 3 and 4 cannot be overstated. In fact, entire books are written about Level 3 and Level 4 evaluation (Jackson, 1989; Robinson & Robinson, 1990), and typically a specialist will be primarily responsible for them. In the following descriptions of each type of evaluation, comments will be included about the nature of formative and summative decisions that can occur with each type.

EVALUATION OF INSTRUCTIONAL MATERIALS AND ACTIVITIES

Evidence of an instructional program's effectiveness is sought for use in making decisions about how to revise the program while it is being developed. In other words, the evidence collected and interpreted during design and development is used to form the instructional program itself. If one discovers by means of an evaluation effort that a lesson is not feasible or that the newly designed topic fails short of meeting its objectives, this information is used to revise the lesson or to replace portions of the topic to overcome the defects that have been revealed. Traditionally in ISD, there are four types of evaluation activity that occur in regard to evaluating instructional materials and activities: (1) expert review, (2) development tryout, (3) pilot test, and (4) field trial. These evaluation activities are usually formative in nature. That is, the primary goal of each activity is to identify ways in which the materials are "on target" and ways in which they can be improved. However, there are occasions when summative decisions are made in regard to whether or not to continue with an instructional development project if problems occur with obtaining adequate expert reviews, or if there are major problems in producing a good quality set of instructional materials.

Expert Review

One of the first activities in instructional materials evaluation is an expert review in which a subject-matter expert (SME) makes a determination about the accuracy and completeness of the content. Content for a lesson or course can be produced in one of three ways. The first is for the instructional designer to research the topic, compile information from reference materials, other textbooks, or technical manuals, and then write a draft of the content. The second is for an SME who is assigned to the project to be given the responsibility for writing content in accordance with the instructional objectives. A third approach is for the SME and instructional designer to work collaboratively in the gathering of content information and writing the first draft. When the instructional designer is solely responsible for producing the content, it is important to have the resulting material reviewed by one or more SMEs. However, even when an SME is involved in creating the content, it is good to have the resulting material reviewed by more than one SME. This is because of differences that can occur among SMEs as to the appropriateness of a given body of content and how to present it. Sometimes the differences are purely stylistic, which means that the SMEs disagree as to sequence, relative emphasis, appropriateness of metaphors, and so forth. In other cases, the differences will be substantive. There might be errors or omissions resulting from one SME that will be noticed by another. In both cases, having multiple experts review the content will improve its accuracy and style of presentation.

Expert reviews are typically conducted as soon as possible after a draft of the instructional materials, or at least the content portion, is complete. The SMEs are then asked to read the instructional materials for content accuracy. They do not play the role of a student during this review. If numerous problems are discovered, then the materials will be revised before proceeding to the next materials evaluation activity. However, expert review does not provide good data on the effectiveness of the instruction with learners. It is conducted to ensure the accuracy, completeness, and relevance of the content prior to testing its instructional effectiveness with learners.

A related activity that can occur under this category is the *stakeholder review*. Stakeholders can be one or more managers who are responsible for approving the project and its funding, and they might also be SMEs. The stakeholder, or a group of stakeholders under the guidance of the instructional designer and sometimes in conjunction with the SMEs, will read through the materials to determine whether the content is acceptable and the overall instructional strategies are acceptable. This is sometimes called a *walk through*.

Developmental Tryout

The second instructional materials evaluation activity is the developmental tryout, which is called "one-on-one evaluation" by Dick and Carey (1996). A prototype of the instructional materials is tried one-on-one (one evaluator sitting with one learner at a time). Dick and Carey suggest using three learners from the target audience, one with high aptitude, one with medium aptitude, and one with low aptitude, as identified by the teacher. Each type of learner will provide different kinds of information that can be used when considering revisions. During the developmental tryout, if the content of the instruction is presented via computer screen, for example, the evaluator sits with the student while he or she works through the lesson or module. It might be possible for an instructional designer to monitor two or three learners, but the critical factor is that each participant is working through the materials individually, regardless of whether the prototype is self-directed learning or a set of materials for an instructor-led course. It is also possible for the designer to talk to the participant during the review process, but it is normally better not to interrupt the participant. If the participant is confused and asks a specific question, then the designer should provide the necessary guidance. One variation on this approach is to have the participant "talk through" the thoughts he or she has while going through the material. This extemporaneous information can be a valuable source of helpful insights.

During the developmental tryout, the instructional designer makes notes about the participants' expressions, difficulties, or comments. After the participant has finished, the instructional designer then interviews the participant and asks about such things as clarity of the content and instructions for learning activities, clarity of test questions and directions, and appropriateness of expected learning outcomes. This activity provides a considerable amount of information about the clarity of expression, structure, and logistic problems the learners may have with the lessons. On the basis of such information, systematic revisions of the instructional content can be made.

An alternative to revising the instruction is to determine whether changes should be made in the learner analysis. It might be preferable to add an additional prerequisite skill than to revise the lesson. For example, the designer of a math lesson sees that a tryout student is having trouble with a math problem-solving lesson involving a linear equation. It appears that the student lacks the prerequisite skills for this lesson. Further testing with another tryout student shows the same problem. The designer must consider whether to remediate the math skills needed in the present lesson, or redesign the previous lesson so the needed entry skills are acquired.

Pilot Test

The third level is a pilot test, called "small group tryout" by Dick & Carey (1996), in which the materials are given to a small group of students who are representative of the target population. The pilot test is conducted under "laboratory" conditions in that the instructional designer and an evaluator might be involved in making more observations and administering evaluation instruments that would not be part of a normal delivery setting. Typically, such pilot testing begins with a pretest of the skills and knowledge to be taught during instruction. The instruction is then presented, followed by the administration of a posttest. Additionally, an attitude questionnaire seeks to assess student attitudes toward various aspects of the instructional event. Students may also be asked to discuss the instruction, the pretest, and the posttest.

Information obtained from small-group testing begins to answer questions about the occurrence of learning and its amount, based on comparison of pretest and posttest scores. Other results may provide indications about the clarity of presentations and questions, which will be used to guide revision.

Field Trial

The final materials evaluation activity is a field trial in which the instruction, revised on the basis of the developmental tryouts and pilot tests, is given to a whole class under conditions that are more like a normal delivery environment. In this setting, the activities of the instructional designer and evaluator are as unobtrusive as possible, even though they are still conducting a variety of validation activities.

The instructional program is tried out with an appropriate sample of the population intended as its audience. With this larger group, a pretest and a posttest (revised on the basis of pilot testing) are given, framing the presentation of the instruction itself. Attitude surveys are administered to learners and to participating instructors. Observations are made during this trial regarding the adequacy of the presentation of materials and their directions. In addition, information is collected on the quality and adequacy of instructors' performances in using the materials.

The field trial is designed to be a critical test of the instruction, its feasibility of use, and its effectiveness. Student and instructor behavior and attitudes yield valuable information that can make possible a near-final revision and improvement of the lessons and modules. Regarding effectiveness, the test scores and gains in achievement of students in this representative group, under near-typical conditions of use, is, of course, of crucial interest and importance.

Interpretation of the Evidence

These various kinds of evidence, collected by means of observational records, questionnaires, and tests, are employed throughout the stages of instructional materials evaluation to draw conclusions as to whether a lesson should be kept as is, how it should be revised or reformulated (which constitutes formative evaluation feedback), or if it should be discarded (which is a summative judgment). In making these decisions, one considers issues of feasibility and effectiveness.

The question of feasibility may be decided, for example, by considering reports of the difficulties experienced by instructors or students in the conduct of the lesson. The question of effectiveness is a somewhat more complex judgment. It may depend, in part, on the reports of an observer that the materials could not be used in the manner intended or that the instructor did not carry out the intended procedures. It may also depend, in part, on student attitudes incidentally established by the lesson, as revealed by answers to questionnaires by both instructors and students. And, of course, it may depend to a most important degree upon the extent to which the performance of students, as revealed by tests, is successful.

Validation

In practice, the two most frequently used instructional materials evaluation activities are expert review and pilot testing. Because it can be expensive to conduct both pilot tests and field tests, organizations usually conduct a hybrid of the two. The course will be offered to an actual group of learners as in a field test but with greater-than-normal attention to reviewing content, methods, and results as in a pilot test. Surprisingly, developmental tryouts are not conducted as often as one would expect, given their benefits. An important principle in this regard is to conduct developmental tryouts with anyone who can take the time to participate. Even if the tryout audience is somewhat dissimilar to the target audience, you can still learn a great deal about the clarity and feasibility of the materials.

Also, keep in mind that a key principle in this context is that the overall objective of instructional materials evaluation is *validation*. The purpose is to determine that the instruction will result in successful achievement of the instructional objectives, providing that the learners have the appropriate prerequisite knowledge and skills and are motivated by a "need to know" the content, and providing that the instruction is delivered effectively as designed.

EVALUATING THE ISD PROCESS

The ISD process that one employs can have areas of strength and also areas in which it would benefit from improvements. From the perspective of total quality management, the principle of ISD implementation and evaluation is that a formal review of one's process is likely to lead to continuous improvement in the effectiveness and efficiency of the process. The ISD process typically contains evaluative feedback loops with regard to formative evaluation feedback, as described in the preceding section. It is not so common to include formal process review activities. This has been done in some corporate ISD models, such as IBM's SATE (Systematic Approach to Education) model and Citibank's ISD Process Model, to mention two. It has also been incorporated in at least one textbook (Rothwell & Kazanas, 1998) in which the authors include a section on judging quality at the end of each chapter that describes one of the phases of the ISD process.

Effective process evaluation will require the instructional designer to prepare review criteria for each phase that are specific to the situation. Evaluative questions can refer to how well the process itself was implemented and to the qualities of the products resulting from the process. Table 16.2 provides examples of questions that were included in a process review of the needs analysis phase of an

---

TABLE 16.2   **SAMPLE QUESTIONS FROM A NEEDS ANALYSIS PROCESS EVALUATION**[1]

Needs Analysis Process Questions

- Was there a clear rationale for conducting the needs assessment?
- Were the important elements of a needs assessment plan included: (that is, as many of the following elements as were appropriate: objectives, target audience, sampling procedure, data collection strategy and tactics, instruments, protocols, data analysis methods, and descriptions of how decisions would be made based on the data)?
- Was everyone included who should have been (stakeholders, gate keepers, etc.)?
- Was the needs assessment practical and cost effective to implement?

Needs Analysis Outcomes Questions

- Are the stated goals, or problems related to gaps in current or anticipated results; that is, are the goals based on either gaps in current performance or on anticipated problems that will result from new systems or procedures?
- Are the goals based on desired outcomes that are congruent with organizational vision and goals?
- Are the reasons for the current or anticipated problems identified; that is, what are the "drivers" (incentives, policies, etc.) that are responsible for the current or anticipated problems?
- Are obstacles identified that now keep or might keep the organization from solving this problem and realizing its vision?
- Are the facilitating factors identified that will help the organization accomplish the desired outcomes?
- Are the desired outcomes described in observable and measurable results?
- Do key managers, employees, "gatekeepers," and other stakeholders agree with the description of the problem and desired changes?

---

[1]Adapted from Keller, J. M. (2000). *Quality Review Guidelines for: Needs Assessment, Design, and Development.* Tallahassee, FL: John Keller Associates. Reprinted by permission of the author.

instructional development project sponsored by the Air Certification Service of the Federal Aviation Administration (Keller, 2000). There are two categories of questions. The first refers to the needs analysis process itself and the second to the outcomes of this process. The response options were "very good," "satisfactory," and "needs improvement," together with a "comments" space.

This type of evaluation is often done informally by means of members of a project team, or when an instructional designer decides to produce a "new and improved" version of a model. However, the best results will be obtained by a formal systematic process of review, data collection, and discussion of improvements to be implemented.

ASSESSING LEARNER REACTIONS

Questions about learner attitudes might be collected while course materials are being developed, but the most widespread use of learner reaction questionnaires is when courses are being fully implemented. However, assessing learner reactions to a course is a controversial issue. These evaluations are commonly accepted in employee education settings, even though they might be ridiculed as "smile sheets" and never used for any actual formative or summative decisions. They are frequently required by colleges and universities and may be included in a professor's annual report, but are heavily criticized by professors as to their reliability and validity. They typically are not used in schools at the K–12 levels and would be considered by most teachers to be nothing more that an indicator of popularity.

Why do instructors reject the opinions of students as being valid indicators of their performance when these very same instructors accept consumer judgments of quality in most other aspects of life? What are the actual benefits of this type of evaluation?

There are many benefits to learner reaction questionnaires for both formative and summative purposes, and despite the criticisms they are widely used in support of both kinds of decisions. Generally speaking, there are three ways in which learner reactions questionnaires are used. The first is for problem sensing. These questionnaires tend to be very short, perhaps no more than four questions about the instructor and content. They do not provide sufficient information for formative feedback into specific course revisions, but they do indicate when there are problems that should be investigated more thoroughly.

A second usage is for formative feedback. These questionnaires are longer with specific questions that give insights into which parts of a course might benefit from revisions. Examples of such questions are, "Did the instructor describe the objectives for each lesson?" "Did the content of the lesson match the objectives?" and "Did the instructor show enthusiasm for the subject?" Categories of questions usually include course design (objectives, content, learning activities, tests, relevance to one's work), delivery techniques, and environmental factors. In order to be used as formative feedback, the evaluation must come early enough to make corrections if necessary. At Florida State University's Center for Instructional

Development Services, interim evaluations are administered during the fourth or fifth week of classes, at the instructor's request, to identify possible teaching problems. This gives the instructor time to take student concerns into consideration and make appropriate course revisions.

The third usage of the questionnaires is for summative decisions about the acceptability of a course or instructor. The questionnaire might be based on either of the two preceding types of questionnaires, or be a variation of them, but it usually includes additional questions about whether one believed the course to have been worth the time and cost, relevant to the job, and worth recommending to someone else. With regard to instructors, companies frequently use learner reaction questionnaire results as part of the performance review of trainers and to an increasing degree, teachers and professors are also being assessed by means of this measure.

With respect to validity, research, as opposed to personal opinion, has shown that students do tend to be somewhat objective critics of the courses they take. Murray (1983) used trained observers in the classrooms of 54 college teachers. Each of six to eight observers visited three separate one-hour classes and took notes. Thus, each instructor was observed for a total of 18 to 24 hours during the semester. He found, when compiling the observers' notes, that there were differences between the higher and lower rated instructors on several dimensions of teaching. He also found a positive correlation between the observers' results and the student evaluations. But, there are widely varying results in the research, and it is probably best to combine student evaluations with other indicators when making comprehensive judgments about teaching effectiveness as opposed to establishing a lower limit of acceptability (Kulik, 2001). However, there is strong evidence that the Level 1 student evaluation process can be designed and implemented in a manner that provides valid and useful results (Centra, 1993).

MEASURING LEARNER ACHIEVEMENT

During the ISD process, tests are prepared (see Chapter 13) and used to determine whether the instructional materials are effective in terms of preparing learners to achieve the learning objectives. When learners do not succeed on a particular objective, an effort is made to determine why and to modify that portion of the course to make it more effective. Thus, the primary use of tests in this context is for formative evaluation and the goal is validation of instructional materials.

After a course is developed, tests are used primarily to measure learner accomplishment. They become more of a summative than a formative tool. One of the reasons for this is that after a course is implemented there is seldom as much control over who is admitted to the course as there is in the development phases. Learners might be in a course because of convenience of scheduling, because they couldn't get into the courses they really wanted, or because their manager or advisor assigned them to take it, and not because they have the appropriate prerequisites or a "need to know" the content.

As a summative tool in the evaluation of learner accomplishment, tests can be used in two ways. One is to make judgments about learner achievement and the second is to assess the overall success of a course. Learner achievement is usually determined on a normative or criterion-referenced basis. As previously discussed in Chapter 13 formative evaluation means that a learner's success is relative to the achievement of other learners. This is the basis of grading "on the curve" in which only a certain percentage of students will receive an A, another percentage a B, and so forth. The same actual level of achievement, such as a score of 85 on a test, could result in an A if the other learners in a given class mostly score lower than 85, or could result in a B if a given class has a larger number of high achievers. In a criterion-referenced grading system, criteria are defined for each grade level and there is no specific proportion of learners who are allowed to receive a particular grade; if they earn it, they get it.

The other way tests are used is to determine whether a course is satisfactorily achieving its goals. If the class average is too low, then additional evaluation will be conducted to see if parts of the course are outdated or not being taught properly, or if too many unqualified students are being admitted. If there is evidence of deficiencies in the existing course, then formative evaluation will have to be conducted to identify what changes to make. If too many inappropriate students are being admitted, then a decision will have to be made as to whether to be more stringent about enrollments or to modify the course to more closely match the incoming audience.

EVALUATION OF INSTRUCTIONAL PROGRAMS

The fifth type of evaluation as represented in this book looks at both the instructional system and other system influences on the outcomes of training. Evaluation methods may be applied to lessons or courses and also to entire programs, or systems, of instruction. A program may consist of several courses and other learning experiences, such as on-the-job training that can be viewed as contributing to a common purpose and may have duration of months or years. It also occurs in a setting in which the initial learning and the subsequent use of what one has learned is influenced by noninstructional factors, such as time, opportunity, and motivation as described by Carroll (1963), Gilbert (1978), and others. Consequently, comprehensive evaluation must consider the influence of these additional factors in order to isolate and estimate the effectiveness of an instructional system.

Thus, besides the development of tests or other types of measures, the enterprise of evaluation requires careful, scientifically based methods that serve to ensure that the evidence obtained is truly convincing. Examples of well-known models for designing these approaches are those of Scriven (1967), Stufflebeam (1974), Popham (1975), Robinson and Robinson (1990), and Philips (1991). The approaches of Scriven, Stufflebeam, and Popham fall under the general heading of *program evaluation* and have been applied most commonly in school system environments, but they also have been used in employee education settings. The approaches of Robinson and Robinson and Philips focus primarily on employee education settings where there tend to be more direct relationships on learning, performance, and cost benefits.

The focus in this book is on principles that guide such evaluations, particularly in school learning environments. This kind of overview can help guide one through the maze of approaches and models that have been published on the topics of program evaluation, educational evaluation, and training evaluation. Because of the volume and complexity of this material, in this chapter we can deal only with the logic of evaluation studies, beginning with the types of evaluation already introduced and concluding with this comprehensive look at how to identify and control a variety of factors in instructional systems evaluation so that valid conclusions can be drawn about instructional outcomes.

The Variables of Evaluation Studies

The intention of studies to evaluate an instructional program is to draw conclusions about the effects of the instruction on learning outcomes on the knowledge, skills, and attitudes the instruction has been designed to establish or improve. But those capabilities are affected by other factors in the educational setting, not only by the instruction itself. It is therefore necessary to *control or otherwise account for these other variables* to draw valid conclusions about instructional effectiveness. Considered as a whole, the educational situation into which instruction is introduced contains the classes of variables described in the following paragraphs.

Outcome Variables We begin to list the variables of the educational evaluation situation with outcome variables, the dependent or measured variables that are the primary focus of interest. The primary outcome measures are based on the knowledge, skills, and attitudes that are the immediate goals of instruction. However, outcomes can also include the secondary consequences of instruction, such as transfer of skills to a job or a subsequent course. The classes of variables that influence educational outcomes, and their various sources, are shown in Figure 16–1.

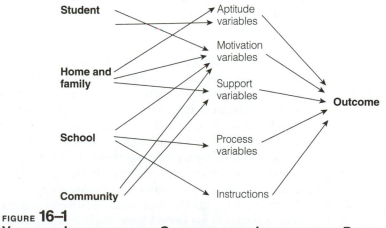

FIGURE 16–1

VARIABLES INFLUENCING THE OUTCOMES OF AN INSTRUCTIONAL PROGRAM

Process Variables   What factors in the learning and performance environment might influence the outcomes of the instructional system? Outcomes may be influenced by the operations in the delivery environment carried out to put the instruction into effect. For example, the instruction as designed may call for a particular type and frequency of teacher questioning, a particular sequence of intellectual skills, some to be mastered before others are undertaken, or a particular sort of feedback to be incorporated in each lesson (see Chapter 9). The evaluator must determine whether these things were systematically and consistently done.

One cannot simply assume that process variables of the sort specified by the designed instruction or intended by the designer will inevitably occur in the way they are expected to. Even though the designer might provide training for the instructors and guidelines for the proper delivery of the instruction, things can and do go wrong. Instructors get their own ideas about how and what to teach, technology does not always work properly, and administrators might not provide the appropriate environment for learning. For example, managers in the workplace might respond positively to the development of self-directed learning packages that their employees can study on the job when they are not busy, thus avoiding the expense of sending them to a training session and having to cover for them. But, as instructional designers who have worked in this setting know, in practice these same managers might not find the time to allow an employee to just "sit around" reading or working on the Web. As a consequence, it is essential that assessments of process variables be made, and this is particularly so when the newly designed instructional entity is being tried out for the first time.

Typically, process variables are assessed by means of systematic observations in the classroom or other delivery setting. This is the function of the observer, not the teacher, in the conduct of the evaluation. The observer may employ a checklist, observation schedule, or interview guide as an aid in obtaining and recording observations.

Support Variables   Still another class of variables, occurring partly in instructional environment and partly in other settings that are supposed to support the learning process, such as the student's home and community, has to be considered as potentially influential in the outcomes of an instructional program. These include such factors as the presence of adequate materials (in the classroom and the school library), the availability of a quiet place for study, the "climate" of the classroom in reference to its encouragement of good achievement, the actions of parents or supervisors in reinforcing favorable attitudes toward homework and other learning activities, and many others. The number of different variables in this class is quite large, and not enough is known about them to make possible a confident differentiation among them with regard to their relative importance.

The general nature of support variables is to be seen in their effects on the opportunities for learning. Materials in the classroom, for example, may present greater or fewer opportunities for learning, depending on their quality and availability; learners might be influenced negatively by peers; noise, excessive heat, and other stressors in the environment might inhibit concentration; and so on. In contrast to process variables, support variables do not directly influence the process of learning in the same way. Instead, they tend to determine the more general environmental conditions of those times during which process variables may exert their effects. For example, the designed instruction may call for a period of independent study on the part of the student. In operation, the teacher may make suitable time provisions for this independent study, thus ensuring that the process variable has been accounted for. But what will be the difference in the outcome for (1) a student who has a relatively quiet place in which to pursue learning uninterrupted and for (2) a student who must perform independent study in an open corner of a noisy classroom? This contrast describes a difference in a support variable, which the evaluator must observe and take into consideration in estimating the outcomes of instruction.

Support variables require various means of assessment. What parents do in encouraging the completion of homework may be assessed by means of a questionnaire. The availability of materials relevant to a topic or course may be assessed by counting books, pamphlets, and other reference sources. The climate of a classroom may be found by the use of a systematic schedule of observations. Other measures of this class, such as number of students or the pupil-to-teacher ratio, may be readily available at the outset of the study. For any of a number of support variables, it is likely to be necessary to select or develop the technique of assessment best suited to the particular situation.

Aptitude Variables   Of all the variables likely to determine the outcomes of learning, the most influential is probably the student's aptitude for learning. Such aptitude is usually measured by means of an intelligence test or a test of scholastic aptitude. This kind of intelligence, sometimes called *crystallized intelligence* (Cattell, 1963; Corno & Snow, 1986), is found to be highly correlated with achievement in school subjects. Whatever may be accomplished by improved methods of instruction, by arrangements of process variables, and by ensuring the best possible support for learning, this entire set of favorable circumstances cannot influence learning outcomes as much as can students' aptitude for learning.

Aptitude for learning is undoubtedly determined in part by genetic inheritance as well as by environmental influences occurring before and after birth, such as nutrition, prior learning, and opportunity to learn. Clearly, aptitude is a variable that has its own multiple determinants. As a factor in an evaluation study, however, aptitude is usually an input variable (Astin & Panos, 1971). In this role, aptitude is not subject to alteration by the evaluation; it can only be measured, not manipulated. It has been well-documented for many years (for example, Bloom, 1976) that aptitude for learning, as measured by intelligence tests, may account for as much as 50 percent of the variations in learning outcomes in areas of achievement pertaining to verbal information, intellectual skills, and cognitive strategies.

Because of the actual and potential effect of aptitude for learning on learning outcomes, an evaluator must attempt to control for this influence when designing a study to determine the effectiveness of instruction on learning outcomes. In evaluation studies in which it is important to control for this influence, learner aptitude would be treated as an input variable. If a given level and type of aptitude was defined as a prerequisite, the evaluator would have to verify that this prerequisite was met. If this variable is not controlled by means of selection, then the evaluator would have to measure or estimate it and include it as a variable in the analysis of results.

Although measures of learning aptitude are often most conveniently identified by scores on intelligence tests, other measures are sometimes employed. A combination of several aptitude tests may be used to yield a combined score to assess learning aptitude. (Actually, most intelligence tests are themselves collections of subtests sampling several different aptitudes.) Another procedure involves the use of measures that are known to correlate with intelligence scores to a fairly high degree. Previous school grades exhibit such high correlations, particularly in subjects such as reading comprehension and mathematics. Aptitude scores are useful in identifying learners for developmental (formative) tryouts. As previously stated, Dick and Carey (1996) suggest trying the instruction with a high, middle, and low aptitude learner. Each will provide different information about the materials.

Motivation Variables Second only to aptitude in overall importance, and sometimes exceeding aptitude in regard to its influence on learning and performance in specific situations, is motivation. This is reflected as the traditional issue of whether the learners *can* learn versus whether they *want* to learn. Certainly there are interactions between the two in that we tend to be more motivated to do the things we are good at, but conversely, we tend to get better at the things we want to do. Factors included under motivation include such things as interest (curiosity, boredom), motives (need to achieve, desire for security), expectancies (self-efficacy, optimism versus pessimism), rewards (extrinsic reinforcement), and cognitive evaluation (intrinsic satisfaction with outcomes).

Furthermore, there are both affective, or emotional, and cognitive aspects of motivation. Emotions such as excitement, fear, pleasure, and arousal can all have an effect on the effort that students will put into a learning experience. Also, cognitive elements such as their beliefs in their abilities to succeed (self-efficacy) and their perceptions of whether they will be tested and rewarded fairly influence students' willingness to try to succeed.

Other components to consider the general concept of learner motivation are social, cultural, and other environmental influences. The enthusiasm of a teacher, the attitudes of one's parents and peers, the degree to which the instructional process and support factors are acceptable to learners based on their cultural background, and the degree to which instructional materials contain enough variety to hold one's interest are all potentially important in determining whether learners are appropriately motivated to learn.

There are many kinds of measures of motivational factors ranging from surveys of specific motivational variables, such as locus of control, to broadly based measures of student attitudes toward learning. It is helpful to use a model, such as the ARCS model (Keller, 1999a), Wlodkowski's time-continuum model (Wlodkowski, 1999), Brophy's catalog of factors influencing the motivation to learn (Brophy, 1998), or models of specific variables such as self-efficacy (Bandura, 1977), curiosity (Berlyne, 1965), or others to identify the specific factors that might be pertinent in a given situation. One might also choose to examine constellations of motivational factors that are represented in factors such as self-regulation (Zimmerman, 1989) and self-motivation (McCombs, 1984). The bottom line is that it is doubtful that one can fully understand the effectiveness of an instructional program without having adequate knowledge of the motivational characteristics of the learners.

INTERPRETING EVALUATIVE EVIDENCE

We have pointed out that measures of the outcomes of an instructional program—that is, measures of learned intellectual skills, cognitive strategies, information attitudes, and motor skills—are influenced by a number of variables in the educational and application situations besides the program itself. Process variables in the operation of the instructional program may directly affect learning and, thus, also affect its outcomes. Support variables in the school or in the home determine the opportunities for learning and thus influence the outcomes of learning that are observed. The learning aptitude of students strongly influences the outcomes measured in an evaluation study. And a learner's motivations to learn and work are critical elements.

If the effectiveness of the designed instruction is to be evaluated, certain controls must be instituted over process, support, and aptitude variables to ensure that the "net effect" of the instruction is revealed. Procedures for accomplishing this control are described in this section. Again, it may be necessary to point out that only the basic logic of these procedures can be accounted for here. However, such logic is of critical importance in the design of evaluation studies.

Controlling for Aptitude Effects

The assessment of instructional outcomes in terms of whether the learning objectives have been achieved needs to take account of the effects of aptitude variables. In the context of this question, it is mainly desirable to state what the level of intelligence is of the students being instructed. This may be done most simply by giving the average score and some measure of dispersion of the distribution of scores (such as the standard deviation) on a standard test of intelligence However, correlated measures such as socioeconomic status (SES) are frequently used for this purpose. Suppose, for example, that students in one school achieve, on the average, 117 of 130 objectives for a designed course, but in a different school in the same district the students' average achievement is 98 of the 130 objectives. Why, one would wonder, was there approximately 90 percent success of the instruction in one setting but only 75 percent in the other one? If aptitude data were collected and showed that the average IQ in the first school was 115 but in the second school it was 102, the aptitude could be considered as a reason for the differences in achievement. If only one of these schools had been used in the evaluation, the evaluator would likely draw a highly inaccurate conclusion about the effectiveness of the instruction. The aims of evaluation may best be accomplished by trying out the instructional entity in several different settings, each having a somewhat different range of student learning aptitude. The variety of settings could be different schools, different classrooms, or different workgroups. In each situation, the evaluator would want to select samples that represent differences in ability that are characteristic of the target learner group.

When the evaluator is doing a comparison study to determine if one instructional program is superior to another, one must go beyond simply reporting the nature and amount of the aptitude variable. In this case, the concern is to show whether any difference exists between the new instructional program and the comparison one. Simply stated, making a comparison requires demonstrating that the two groups of students were equivalent to begin with. Equivalence of students in aptitude is most likely to occur when successive classes of students in the same school, coming from the same neighborhood, are employed as comparison groups. This is the case when a newly designed course is introduced in a classroom or school and is to be compared with a different course given the previous year.

Other methods for establishing equivalence of initial aptitudes can be employed. Sometimes, it is possible to assign students randomly to different classrooms within a single school, half of whom receive the newly designed instruction and half of whom do not. When such a design is used, definite administrative arrangements must be made to ensure randomness—it cannot be assumed. Another procedure is to select a set of schools that are "matched," insofar as possible, in the aptitudes of their students and to try out the new instruction in half of these, making a comparison with the outcomes obtained in those schools not receiving the new instruction. All of these methods contain certain complexities of design that necessitate careful management if valid comparisons are to be made.

Whatever particular procedure is employed, it should be clear that any valid comparison of the effectiveness of instruction in two or more groups of students requires that equivalence of initial aptitudes be established. No study evaluating learning outcomes can provide valid evidence of instructional effectiveness without having a way of controlling this important variable.

Controlling for the Effects of Support Variables

For many purposes of evaluation, support variables may be treated as input variables and may be controlled in ways similar to those used for learning aptitude. Thus, when interest is centered upon the attainment of objectives, measures of support variables can be reported along with outcome measures so that they can be considered in interpreting the outcomes. Here again, a useful procedure is to try out the instruction in a variety of school or workplace settings displaying differing types or levels of support with respect to materials, resources, teaching style, and management or leadership style.

Similarly, comparisons of the effectiveness of one instructional program to another require the demonstration of equivalence among the classes, schools, or workgroups whose learning outcomes are being compared. Suppose that outcome measures are obtained from two different aptitude-equivalent groups of students in a school, one of which has been trying out a newly designed course in English composition, while the other continues with a different course. Assume that, despite differences in the instruction, the objectives of the two courses are largely the same and that assessment of outcomes is based on these common objectives. One class is found to show significantly better performance, on the average, than does the other. Before the evidence that the new instruction is "better" can be truly convincing, it must be shown that no differences exist in support variables. For example, there might be differences in resources such as the library, the kinds of materials available, and technology to support Internet inquiry. Another possibility is the climate of the two classrooms—one may be more encouraging to achievement than the other. If two different teachers are involved, one may be disliked, the other liked. Also, there might be characteristic differences in student attitudes—more students in one class may seek new opportunities for learning than do students in the other. Because variables of this sort have a high probability of affecting outcomes, it is essential that equivalence of groups with respect to these variables be demonstrated or taken into account by statistical means.

Controlling for the Effects of Process Variables

The assessment and control of process variables is of particular concern in seeking evidence bearing on the attainment of stated objectives. An episode of instruction may work either better or worse depending upon how the operations it specifies are implemented. Suppose, for example, that a new course in elementary science presumes that students will work in a largely independent manner when it comes to performing the activities in their exercise booklets, because one of the objectives of the instruction is for learners to develop independent problem-solving skills. Some teachers might implement this program exactly as designed, but others might offer varying degrees of help for a variety of reasons ranging from impatience to simply wanting to be helpful, especially to those students who seek assistance. This process variable differs markedly in these instances, and equally marked differences may show up in measures of outcome. If the evaluation is of the formative type, the designer may interpret such evidence as showing the need for additional teacher training for implementing this instructional program or training event. If summative evaluation is being conducted, then the results from the different groups of students must be treated separately to disclose the effects of the process variable.

In comparison studies process variables are equally important. As in the case of aptitude or support variables, they must be controlled in one way or another in order for valid evidence of the effectiveness of instruction to be obtained. Equivalence of groups in terms of process variables must be shown either by exercising direct control over them, using a randomizing approach, or by statistical means. It may be noted that process variables are more amenable to direct control than are either support or aptitude variables. If a school or class is conducted in a noisy environment (a support variable), the means of changing the noise level may not be readily at hand. If, however, a formative evaluation study shows that some teachers have failed to use the operations specified by the new instructional program (a process variable), instruction of these teachers can be undertaken so that the next trial starts off with a desirable set of process variables.

Unanticipated outcomes might result from process variables and accordingly require similar control procedures. A set of positive attitudes on the part of students of a newly designed program could result from the human modeling of a particular teacher and thus contrast with less favorable attitudes in another group of students who have otherwise had the same instruction. It is necessary in this case, also, to demonstrate equivalence of process variables before drawing conclusions about effects of the instructional entity.

Controlling for the Effects of Motivational Variables

Motivational variables are input variables, but they can vary as the instruction progresses, so they may also be regarded as a special category of process variables. A convenient way of controlling for motivational influences is provided by the ARCS model (Keller, 1999a). As described in Chapter 6, the ARCS model contains both a theory-based synthesis of motivational factors and a design process for systematically influencing students' motivation to learn. The analysis step in the design process helps one chart learner motivation. The four categories of attention, confidence, relevance, and satisfaction allow one to identify specific areas of motivation to assess in terms of students' motivation to learn and motivation to perform. A greater level of precision can be achieved by assessing the characteristics represented by the subcategories (Keller, 1999a) and specific variables. For example, instead of looking at the general factor of confidence, the evaluator might want to measure self-efficacy (Bandura, 1977) or determine whether any of the learners will be detrimentally affected by feelings of helplessness (Seligman, 1975). The level of precision to use depends upon the degree to which one expects to encounter specific motivational influences and the evaluative questions that are posed.

When preparing for an evaluation of the outcomes of instruction, it is important for the evaluator to assess motivational conditions prior to and during instruction and to also assess the degree to which motivational factors influence outcomes at the performance and organizational results levels. The former situation is typically referred to as "motivation to learn" (Brophy, 1998) and the second as "motivation to work" (Keller, 1999b). Even though the emphasis in instructional systems evaluation is on instruction, the outcomes of instruction with respect to transfer of knowledge and evidence of skill application in a subsequent work setting, either on the job or in a higher-level course, can depend on the degree to which one is motivated to use one's new knowledge and skills.

Measurement of motivation is challenging. It can be based on observations of readiness to learn (do the learners come to class and bring their materials?), persistence, attrition, and other indicators of effort. Methods can include observation scales, performance data, and self-report measures. One of the challenges in measuring motivation to learn is the potential for an interference effect because of the novelty or demand characteristics in the learning environment. If learners know they are being observed, or if they are being exposed to an innovative learning strategy, they are likely to be motivated by the novelty of the situation and not by a motivation to learn. This is consistent with the Hawthorne studies (Roethlisberger & Dickson, 1939) that illustrated this phenomenon in a work environment. The evaluator must develop measurements that make it possible to distinguish between these influences. One of the techniques for doing so is to ensure that one collects information for a long enough period of time. Novelty effects usually extinguish after a relatively short time.

With respect to learner performance on objectives, premeasures of learner motivation can be used to statistically co-vary motivation level with achievement. Also, if there are learners with distinctively different motivational profiles in a class, then one can determine whether these differences are related to achievement.

In comparative studies, it is clearly important to examine motivational factors that might differentially affect outcomes. For example, if one group of learners is taking the class as an elective and another group is required to take the class, or if one class is for majors and the other is for a general education requirement, there could be strong differences in performance. There are also situations in which one should consider comparative differences within a single class. This is when one has subgroups within a class that have the same kinds of motivational differences, as with learners for whom the course is elective versus those for whom the course is required.

Charting initial motivational attitudes and also monitoring motivational orientations during a class can help one explain unanticipated outcomes. If there is an unexpected change in motivation during a class, one might be able to investigate and discover that excessive homework requirements in a different class caused an unexpectedly high level of stress in the class being evaluated. This could lead to a drop in performance simply because the students decreased their level of effort.

In all of these contexts, it is helpful to distinguish between the motivational characteristics of the learners, the motivational properties of the instructional materials, and the motivational influences of the environment. Normally, it is not possible to assign learners to an instructional program based on their motivational characteristics, but these elements can be measured and used, as described earlier, to estimate their influence on outcomes. Instructional materials can be evaluated ahead of time in terms of their basic motivational features. And elements of the environment can be manipulated or observed to assess their impact on learner motivation and performance.

Controlling Variables by Randomization

The best way to control for unknown influences or uncontrollable variables on learning in an evaluation study is to ensure that their effects occur in a random fashion. This is the case when students can be assigned to control and experimental groups in a truly random manner or when an entire set of classes or schools can be divided into such groups randomly. In the simplest case, if the outcomes of group A (the new instructional entity) are compared with those of group B (the previously employed instructional entity), and students drawn from a given population have been assigned to these groups in equal numbers at random, the comparison of the outcomes may be assumed to be equally influenced by a variable such as aptitude if it is not possible to measure this variable and systematically assign students to the different groups. Similar reasoning applies to the effects of randomizing the assignment of classrooms, teachers, and schools to experimental and control groups in order to equalize process and support variables.

Randomization has the effect of controlling not only the specific variables that have been identified but cannot be systematically controlled, but also other variables that may not have been singled out for measurement because their potential influence is unknown. Although ideal for purposes of control, in practice, randomizing procedures are usually difficult to arrange. Schools do not customarily draw their students randomly from a community or assign them randomly to classes or teachers. Accordingly, the identification and measurement of aptitude, support, process, and motivation variables must usually be undertaken as described in the preceding sections. When random assignment of students, teachers, or classes is possible, evaluation studies achieve a degree of elegance they do not otherwise possess.

EXAMPLES OF EVALUATION STUDIES

The five kinds of variables in evaluation studies—aptitude, support, process, motivation, and outcome—ought to be given careful consideration and measurement in any evaluation study, whether formative decisions, summative decisions, or a combination of both kinds of decisions will be made. It is difficult to find studies that systematically identify and document variables in all of these areas. Following is an example that carefully considered four of the five categories of variables. This study was reported in 1968 (Heflin & Scheier, 1968), but we have expanded it hypothetically to illustrate the motivational factors. It still serves as an excellent example of all five types of variables.

Evaluation of a Program in Reading for Beginners

A varied set of lessons in reading readiness and beginning reading was developed and evaluated over a two-year period by the Educational Development Laboratories of McGraw-Hill, and by the L. W. Singer Company of Random House (Heflin and Scheier, 1968). This system of instruction is called "Listen Look Learn." In brief, the instructional materials include: (1) a set of filmstrips accompanied by sound, designed to develop listening comprehension and oral recounting; (2) an eye-hand coordination workbook dealing with the identification and printing of letters and numerals; (3) a set of filmstrips providing letter-writing tasks, accompanying the workbook; (4) letter charts for kinesthetic letter identification; (5) picture sequence cards, and other cards for "hear and read" practice; and (6) a set of colored filmstrips for the analysis of word sounds and the presentation of words in story contexts.

As reported by Heflin and Scheier (1968), a systematic formative evaluation of this instructional system was undertaken, which at the same time obtained some initial data for summative purposes. Table 16.3 summarizes some of the main points of the study, abstracted from this report. The purpose of the table is to illustrate how the major classes of variables were treated and interpreted; naturally, many details of the study covered in the report cannot be reported in the brief space of such a table.

Classes of first-grade pupils from schools located in 11 states were included in the evaluation study. A group of 40 classes comprising 917 pupils were given instruction provided by the Listen Look Learn system, and a group of 1,000 pupils in 42 classes served as a control group. Control-group classes used the "basal reading" instructional system. Each school district was asked to provide classes for the experimental and control groups that were as equivalent as possible in terms of characteristics of teachers and pupils.

Aptitude Variables

Owing to differences in the availability of aptitude scores in the various schools, no initial measures of aptitude were employed. Instead, information was obtained concerning the socioeconomic status of the pupils' families, as indicated in Table 16.3. When aptitude measures (Metropolitan Readiness, Pintner Primary IQ) were administered during the second year of the study, verification was obtained of a broad range of aptitude as well as equivalence between the experimental and control groups.

For purposes of formative evaluation, it is necessary to know that the classes selected for instruction included a range of student aptitudes that is representative of schools in the country as a whole, because that is the intended usage for the system being evaluated. From the report (Heflin & Scheier, 1968), it would appear that the schools taking part in the study represented a great majority of U.S. elementary schools, although by no means all of them. For example, inner-city schools were apparently not included. Nevertheless, the study offers reasonably good evidence that a broad range of pupil aptitudes was represented. In addition, it is clear from the reported data that the two groups of pupils were reasonably equivalent in aptitude.

Support Variables

The range of SES of pupils' families provides the additional indication that support for learning, insofar as it may be assumed to originate in the home environment, exhibited a suitable range of variation for the study. Other evidences of learning support are inferred from measures of the characteristics of teachers, as indicated in Table 16.3. The inference is that teachers having a typical range of educational backgrounds will conduct themselves in ways that provide a range of differential opportunities for learning. A reasonable degree of equivalence is also demonstrated on these variables between experimental and control groups.

Other measures of support for learning, not systematically obtained in this study, are perhaps of greater relevance to summative evaluation. Such variables as "availability of reading materials," "encouragement of independent reading," and others of this general nature would be examples. In the Listen Look Learn study, incomplete evidence was obtained of the number of books read by individual children: This number was found to vary from 0 to 132 (Heflin & Scheier, 1968, p. 45).

Process Variables

As Table 16.3 indicates, a measure of the feasibility of the various parts of the problem was obtained by asking teachers to judge the appropriateness of the materials for groups of fast, medium, and slow learners. Various features of the individual lessons might have contributed to appropriateness, such as the familiarity of the

TABLE 16.3 VARIABLES MEASURED AND THEIR INTERPRETATION FOR FORMATIVE AND SUMMATIVE EVALUATION IN A STUDY OF A SYSTEM OF INSTRUCTION FOR BEGINNING READING (LISTEN LOOK LEARN)*

Type of Variable	How Measured	Interpretation
Aptitude	Initially, by socioeconomic status (SES), a correlated measure	*Formative*: A variety of classes providing a range of SES from high to low
	During second year, by standardized test scores for IQ and reading readiness	*Summative:* Equivalence of SES, and later of aptitude, shown for experimental and control groups
Support	1. Level of formal education of teachers	*Formative*: Range of these variables typical of most elementary schools
	2. Amount of teacher education in reading methods	*Summative:* Reasonable equivalence of experimental and control groups on these variables
	3. Years of teaching experience	
Process	1. Appropriateness of lessons, as judged by teachers	*Formative:* Judgments of appropriateness used to test feasibility
	2. Success of program components, as judged by teachers	*Formative:* Indirect indications of effectiveness of pupil learning, based on teachers' estimates
	3. Strength and weaknesses of individual lessons, as judged by teachers	
Motivation	Review materials with a motivational checklist	*Formative:* Teachers record areas where materials lack appeal, areas that are interesting, and changes made to improve appeal
	Pre- and posttest results of learner motivational attitudes	*Summative:* Judgments as to overall appeal of instruction to learners
	Teacher observations of positive and negative motivational influences in the learning environment	
Outcome	Metropolitan Primary I	*Summative:* Achievement scores on standardized tests indicate scores on component reading skills significantly higher than those of an equivalent control group
	Achievement word knowledge means: LLL group—25.5 Control group—24.1 Word discrimination means: LLL group—25.9 Control group—24.7 Reading means: LLL group—27.3 Control group—25.2	

*Information and results presented in this tabular format are supported by the findings in V. B. Heflin & E. Scheier, 1968, *The formative period of Listen Look Learn, a multi-media communication skills system,* Huntington, NY: Educational Development Laboratories.

subject of a story or the difficulty of the words employed. Teacher's judgments led to conclusions about feasibility that resulted in elimination or revision of a number of elements of the program.

Teachers' estimates also formed the bases for evidence of the success of the various activities constituting the Listen Look Learn program. Of course, such measures are indirect evidence bearing on process variables, as contrasted with such indicators as how many exercises were attempted by each student, how much time was spent on each, what feedback was provided for correct or incorrect responses, and other factors of this nature. The materials of this program do not make immediately evident what the desired process variables may have been. Consequently, teachers' reports about "how effective the lesson was" were probably as good indicators of these variables as could be obtained in this instance.

Motivation Variables

In the initial reviews of the materials prior to adopting them for implementation in this program, judgments were made about their potential motivational appeal for the target audience. Teachers and other readers, using a motivational characteristics checklist, indicated that there was good variety of media and teaching strategies that would help maintain student interest, and that the content was relevant to the experiences and interests of the audience.

It was not possible to collect preinstructional data about the learners' motivational profiles, but teachers and administrators in the various settings using the materials made judgments about the motivational readiness of the audience. Given the generally perceived importance of developing reading skills and the diversity of social and cultural perspectives in the material, it was judged that learner attitudes would, overall, be sufficiently positive. Student reactions that were collected during and after the implementation of the program were generally positive.

A positive learning environment was established to support the use of the materials. This included posters and charts that could be used to enhance the classrooms. Also, teachers were asked to keep notes about unexpected events that would positively or negatively affect the learners' motivation in regard to these materials.

In these hypothetical examples of how motivation could be estimated and monitored for the purpose of estimating whether learner motivation had an overall negative, neutral, or positive influence on learning performance, it is important to note that a variety of measurements can be used. These include direct observations, survey questionnaires given to the students, and examination of materials using a checklist.

Outcome Variables

Learning outcomes for this program were assessed by means of standardized tests of word knowledge, word discrimination, and reading (portions of the Metropolitan Primary I Achievement Test). As can be seen from Table 16.3, mean scores on these three kinds of activities were higher for the experimental group than for the control group, which had been shown to be reasonably equivalent with respect to the operation of aptitude and support variables. Statistical tests of the difference between the various pairs of means indicated that these differences were significant at an acceptable level of probability.

It should be pointed out that the evidences of learning outcome obtained in this study were considered by its authors as no more than initial indications of the success of the Listen Look Learn program. Further studies were subsequently conducted to evaluate learning outcomes in a summative sense (Brickner & Scheier, 1968, 1970; Kennard & Scheier, 1971). In general, these studies have yielded data and conclusions that show improvements in early reading achievement considerably greater than are produced by other instructional programs they are designed to supplant (usually basal reading approaches).

These results led to the conclusion that the materials were effective at the transfer of learning level because of the ways in which learners were able to use their improved reading skills in settings beyond the specific classroom-based measures of reading improvement. The overall improvements in reading also contributed to positive organizational results in improving the education and performances of students. There were no studies of cost benefits to determine how the costs of the development and delivery of these materials might be related to financial estimates or measures of the benefits. But, based on perceptual and performance improvements, it was concluded that the program was justified based on results.

SUMMARY

Comprehensive evaluations of instructional materials, courses, and curricula usually include at least the following five areas of investigation and feedback:

1. Evaluation of the instructional materials.
2. Quality review of the ISD process.
3. Assessment of learner reactions to the instruction.
4. Measurement of learner achievement of the learning objectives.
5. Estimation of instructional consequences.

In all of these contexts, formative evaluation is undertaken to provide evidence on deficiencies in the appeal, efficiency, or effectiveness of the program so that feedback to support revisions and improvements can be offered. This process seeks evidence from observers, teachers, and students.

Evaluation of instruction can also lead to summative decisions about the feasibility and acceptability of instruction. Measures in any of the above areas can lead to decisions about whether to continue developing or offering a program, or whether to discontinue a given instructor or delivery system when performance is not satisfactory and it is not feasible to undertake formative efforts to bring about improvements. The primary evidence sought is in terms of student performance. Measures are taken of the kinds of student capabilities the program is intended to establish, as described in Chapters 3 through 6. Other kinds of evidence with regard to environmental influences, such as opportunity to perform, teacher or supervisor management style, and so forth, are covered in books that provide comprehensive guidelines for education and training evaluation (for example, Popham, 1975; Phillips, 1991).

Evaluations may be conducted with a single instructional program, or may be undertaken to compare one entire instructional program with another. Both types of studies can be for the purpose of identifying areas for improvement, or to make summative judgments about the worth or value of a given program. However, comparative studies, because of their complexity and expense, will most often be primarily for summative purposes. The results of these studies, as in international comparative education studies, can lead to subsequent investigations of ways to make improvements in one or more of the programs in the original study. In all of these studies, a number of kinds of variables must be taken into account. The outcomes of the program are influenced by variables whose effects must be controlled (or factored out) in order to test the effects of instruction. These include

1. *Aptitude variables:* Reflecting the students' aptitude for learning
2. *Process variables:* Arising from the manner of operation of instruction in the class or school
3. *Support variables:* Conditions in the home, school, workplace, and community that affect opportunities for learning
4. *Motivation variables:* Characteristics of the learners, materials, and environment that influence the degree to which learners will be interested in the instructional program and have the confidence and persistence to succeed

Evaluation studies use various means to control these influencing variables to demonstrate the effects of the newly designed instruction. Sometimes, the operation of these variables can be made equivalent by assigning students, schools, or communities in a randomized way to different groups to be instructed. More frequently, statistical means must be employed to establish the equivalence of the groups to be compared. If two courses or programs of instruction are to be evaluated to determine which is better, evaluation logic requires that control be exercised over these other variables. Ideally, everything should be equivalent except the instructional programs themselves.

REFERENCES

Astin, A. W., & Panos, R. J. (1971). The evaluation of educational programs. In R. L. Thorndike (Ed.), *Educational measurement* (2nd ed.). Washington, DC: American Council on Education.

Bandura, A. (1977). Self-efficacy: Toward a unifying theory of behavioral change. *Psychological Review, 84,* 191–215.

Berlyne, D. E. (1965). Motivational problems raised by exploratory and epistemic behavior. In S. Koch (Ed.), *Psychology: A study of a science* (Vol. 5). New York: McGraw-Hill.

Bloom, B. S. (1976). *Human characteristics and school learning*. New York: McGraw-Hill.

Brickner, A., & Scheier, E. (1968). *Summative evaluation of Listen Look Learn, Cycles RAO, 1967-68*. Huntington, NY: Educational Development Laboratories.

Brickner, A., & Scheier, E. (1970). *Summative evaluation of Listen Look Learn 2nd year students, Cycles R-70, 1968–69*. Huntington, NY: Educational Development Laboratories.

Brophy, J. E. (1998). *Motivating students to learn*. New York: McGraw-Hill.

Carroll, J. B. (1963). A model of school learning. *Teachers College Record, 64,* 723–733.

Cattell, R. B. (1963). Theory of fluid and crystallized intelligence: A critical experiment. *Journal of Educational Psychology, 54,* 1–22.

Centra, J. A. (1993). *Reflective faculty evaluation: Enhancing teaching and determining faculty effectiveness*. San Francisco: Jossey-Bass.

Corno, L., & Snow, R. E. (1986). Adapting teaching to individual differences among learners. In M. C. Wittrock (Ed.), *Handbook of research on teaching* (3rd ed.). New York: Macmillan.

Dick, W., & Carey, L. (1996). *The systematic design of instruction* (4th ed.). New York: HarperCollins College Publishers.

Gilbert, T. F. (1978). *Human competence*. New York: McGraw-Hill.

Hamblin, A. C. (1974). *Evaluation and control of training*. London: McGraw-Hill.

Heflin, V. B., & Scheier, E. (1968). *The formative period of Listen Look Learn, and multi-media communication skills systems*. Huntington, NY: Educational Development Laboratories.

Jackson, T. (1989). *Evaluation: Relating training to business performance*. San Diego: Pfeiffer.

Kaufman, R., & Keller, J. M. (1994). Levels of evaluation: Beyond Kirkpatrick. *Human Resource Development Quarterly, 5,* 371–380.

Keller, J. M. (1999a). Motivation in cyber learning environments. *International Journal of Educational Technology, 1*(1), 7 – 30.

Keller, J. M. (1999b). Motivational Systems. In H. Stolovitch & E. Keeps (Eds.), *Handbook of Human Performance Technology* (2nd ed.). San Francisco: Jossey Bass.

Keller, J. M. (2000). *Quality review guidelines for needs assessment, design, and development: Federal Aviation Administration, Air Certification Service, Washington, DC*. Tallahassee, FL: John Keller Associates.

Kennard, A. D., & Scheier, E. (1971). *An investigation to compare the effect of three different reading programs on first-grade students in Elk Grove Village, Illinois, 1969–1970*. Huntington, NY: Educational Development Laboratories.

Kirkpatrick, D. L. (1959). Techniques for evaluating training programs. *Journal of the American Society of Training Directors, 13,* 3–9, 21–26.

Kulik, J. A. (2001). Student ratings: Validity, utility, and controversy. In M. Theall, P. C. Abrami, & L. A. Mets (Eds.), *The student rating debate: Are they valid? How can we best use them?* San Francisco: Jossey-Bass.

McCombs, B. L. (1984). Processes and skills underlying intrinsic motivation to learn: Toward a definition of motivational skills training intervention. *Educational Psychologist, 19*(4), 199–218.

Murray, H. G. (1983). Low inference classroom teaching behaviors and student ratings of college teaching effectiveness. *Journal of Educational Psychology, 71,* 856–865.

Phillips, J. J. (1991). *Handbook of training evaluation and measurement tools* (2nd ed). Houston: Gulf Publishing.

Popham, W. J. (1975). *Educational evaluation*. Englewood Cliffs, NJ: Prentice-Hall.

Robinson, D. G., & Robinson, J. C. (1990). *Training for impact: How to link training to business needs and measure the results*. San Francisco: Jossey-Bass.

Rothwell, W. J., & Kazanas, H. C. (1998). *Mastering the instructional design process: A systematic approach,* 2nd ed. San Francisco: Jossey-Bass, Inc.

Scriven, M. (1967). The methodology of evaluation. In R. Tyier, R. M. Gagné, & M. Scriven, *Perspectives of curriculum evaluation* (AERA Monograph Series on Curriculum Evaluation, No. 1). Chicago: Rand McNally.

Stufflebeam, D. L. (1974). Alternative approaches to educational evaluation: A self-study guide for educators. In W. J. Popham (Ed.), *Evaluation in education*. Berkeley, CA: McCutchan.

Roethlisberger, F., & Dickson, W. J. (1939). *Management and the worker*. Cambridge, MA: Harvard University Press.

Seligman, M. E. (1975). *Helplessness*. San Francisco: Freeman.

Wlodkowski, R. J. (1999). *Enhancing adult motivation to learn, Revised edition*. San Francisco: Jossey-Bass.

Zimmerman, B. J. (1989). A social cognitive view of self-regulated academic learning. *Journal of Educational Psychology, 81,* 329–339.

Name Index

Abelson, R. P., 117, 118, 130
Adams, J. A., 100, 104
ADL Co-lab, 220, 221, 233
Alessi, S. M., 303, 309
Allen, V. L., 293, 309
Allen, V. S., 217, 236
Anastasi, A., 120, 129
Anderson, J. R., 50, 58, 85, 105, 112, 117, 125, 129, 141, 150, 172, 190, 192, 207
Anderson, L. W., 275, 287, 305, 309
Anderson, R. C., 243, 262, 303, 309
Anderson, T. H., 303, 309
Andrade, H. G., 268, 287
Aronson, D., 228, 233
Asarnow, J., 75, 83
Astin, A. W., 361, 373
Atkinson, R. C., 7, 17, 50, 58, 74, 82
Austin, G. A., 50, 58
Ausubel, D. P., 5, 17, 77, 82, 93, 104, 243, 262

Bagnall, J., 19, 44
Baker, E. L., 48, 59, 135, 150
Bandura, A., 97, 104, 120, 129, 362, 366, 373
Barry, M., 218, 233
Battersby, A., 225, 233
Beam, P., 312, 341, 342
Beard, J. G., 280, 288
Beck, I. L., 153, 171
Bedinger, D., 333, 334, 342
Bell, H. H., 226, 234
Bergman, R., 38, 43
Berk, R. A., 276, 277, 287
Berliner, D. C., 188, 190
Berlyne, D. E., 362, 373
Bethoney, H., 340, 342
Biddle, W. B., 303, 309
Black, J. B., 280, 288

Block, J. H., 275, 287, 305, 306, 309
Bloom, B. S., 20, 25, 44, 48, 53, 58, 60, 61, 82, 94, 104, 149, 150, 160, 170, 267, 274, 287, 292, 301, 305, 309, 361, 374
Borich, G., 265, 267, 288
Bourne, J., 338, 345
Branch, R. M., 38, 41, 43
Branson, R. K., 38, 43
Breitbach, R. A., 226, 234
Bretz, R., 89, 104
Brickner, A., 372, 374
Briggs, L. J., 25, 29, 43, 94, 105, 143, 150, 160, 163, 170, 224, 228, 233, 234, 238, 244, 260, 262
Britton, B. K., 280, 288
Brooks, C. C., 86, 104
Brooks, J. G., 337, 342
Brooks, M., 337, 342
Brooks, R. B., 226, 234
Brophy, J. E., 114, 129, 362, 366, 374
Brown, A. L., 74, 82, 162, 170, 333, 334, 342
Brown, L. T., 72, 83
Brown, J. S., 6, 17, 72, 83
Bruner, J., 20, 43, 50, 58, 74, 82, 116, 131, 140, 150, 188, 190
Brusilovsky, P., 185, 190
Burbules, N. C., 335, 342
Burkman, E., 329, 344
Burns, R. B., 306, 309
Butler, B. S., 329, 342

Callister, T. A., 335, 342
Campbell, J. O., 338, 345
Carey, J., 36, 38, 43
Carey, L., 36, 38, 43, 271, 273, 288, 352, 353, 362, 374
Carliner, S., 313, 343
Carroll, J. B., 2, 17, 219, 233, 346, 358, 374

Subject Index

TO THE OWNER OF THIS BOOK:

I hope that you have found *Principles of Instructional Design*, Fifth Edition, useful. So that this book can be improved in a future edition, would you take the time to complete this sheet and return it? Thank you.

School and address: _____

Department: _____

Instructor's name: _____

1. What I like most about this book is: _____

   _____

   _____

2. What I like least about this book is: _____

   _____

   _____

3. My general reaction to this book is: _____

   _____

   _____

4. The name of the course in which I used this book is: _____

   _____

5. Were all of the chapters of the book assigned for you to read? _____

   If not, which ones weren't? _____

6. In the space below, or on a separate sheet of paper, please write specific suggestions for improving this book and anything else you'd care to share about your experience in using this book.

   _____

   _____

   _____

   _____

DO NOT STAPLE. PLEASE SEAL WITH TAPE.

FOLD HERE

THOMSON

WADSWORTH ™

BUSINESS REPLY MAIL
FIRST-CLASS MAIL   PERMIT NO. 34   BELMONT CA

POSTAGE WILL BE PAID BY ADDRESSEE

Attn: Dan Alpert, Education Editor

Wadsworth/Thomson Learning
10 Davis Drive
Belmont, CA   94002-9801

NO POSTAGE
NECESSARY
IF MAILED
IN THE
UNITED STATES

FOLD HERE

OPTIONAL:

Your name: _____   Date: _____

May we quote you, either in promotion for *Principles of Instructional Design*, Fifth Edition, or in future publishing ventures?

Yes: ☐   No: ☐

Sincerely yours,

Walter W. Wager, Katherine C. Golas, and John M. Keller